Baby Blues® 18 Scrapbook

Two Plus One is Enough

Other Baby Blues® Books from Andrews McMeel Publishing

Guess Who Didn't Take a Nap?
I Thought Labor Ended When the Baby Was Born
We Are Experiencing Parental Difficulties . . . Please Stand By
Night of the Living Dad
I Saw Elvis in My Ultrasound
One More and We're Outnumbered!
Check, Please . . .
threats, bribes & videotape
If I'm a Stay-At-Home Mom, Why Am I Always in the Car?
Lift and Separate
I Shouldn't Have to Scream More Than Once!
Motherhood Is Not for Wimps
Baby Blues®: Unplugged
Dad to the Bone
Never a Dry Moment

Treasuries

The Super-Absorbent Biodegradable Family-Size Baby Blues®
Baby Blues®: Ten Years and Still in Diapers
Butt-Naked Baby Blues®
Wall-to-Wall Baby Blues®

Baby Blues® 18 Scrapbook

Two Plus One is Enough

by Rick Kirkman & Jerry Scott

Andrews McMeel Publishing

Kansas City

Baby Blues® is syndicated internationally by King Features Syndicate, Inc. For information, write King Features Syndicate, Inc., 888 Seventh Avenue, New York, New York 10019.

04 05 06 07 08 BBG 10 9 8 7 6 5 4 3 2 1

ISBN: 0-7407-4140-3

Library of Congress Control Number: 2003113028

Find *Baby Blues*® on the Web at
www.babyblues.com.

————— **ATTENTION: SCHOOLS AND BUSINESSES** —————

Andrews McMeel books are available at quantity discounts with bulk purchase for educational, business, or sales promotional use. For information, please write to: Special Sales Department, Andrews McMeel Publishing, 4520 Main Street, Kansas City, Missouri 64111.

Many thanks to the young artists who illustrated our back cover:
Katelin Biallas, Cory Boggs, and James Davia. Great work!

And two thumbs up to Maddie for the cover photos!

—R.K. & J.S.

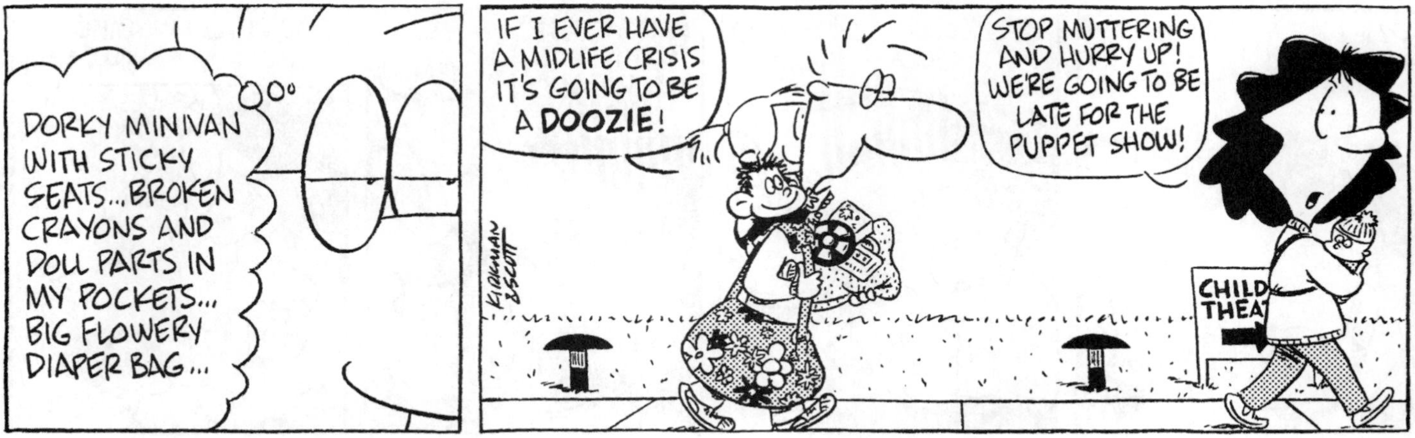
DORKY MINIVAN WITH STICKY SEATS... BROKEN CRAYONS AND DOLL PARTS IN MY POCKETS... BIG FLOWERY DIAPER BAG...
IF I EVER HAVE A MIDLIFE CRISIS IT'S GOING TO BE A **DOOZIE**!
STOP MUTTERING AND HURRY UP! WE'RE GOING TO BE LATE FOR THE PUPPET SHOW!
CHILD
THEA

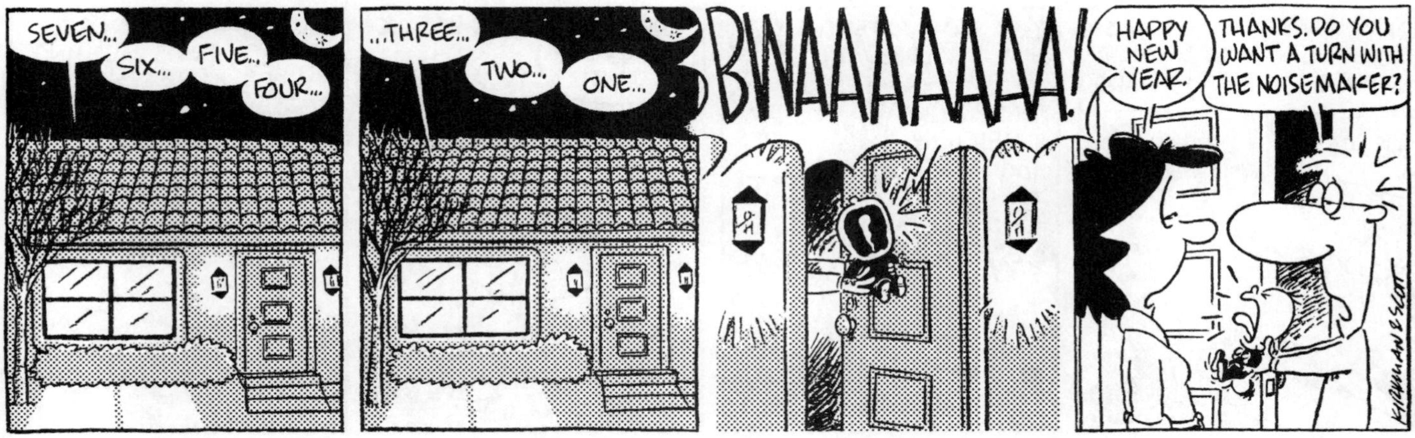
SEVEN...
SIX...
FIVE...
FOUR...
...THREE...
TWO...
ONE...
BWAAAAAAAA!
HAPPY NEW YEAR.
THANKS. DO YOU WANT A TURN WITH THE NOISEMAKER?

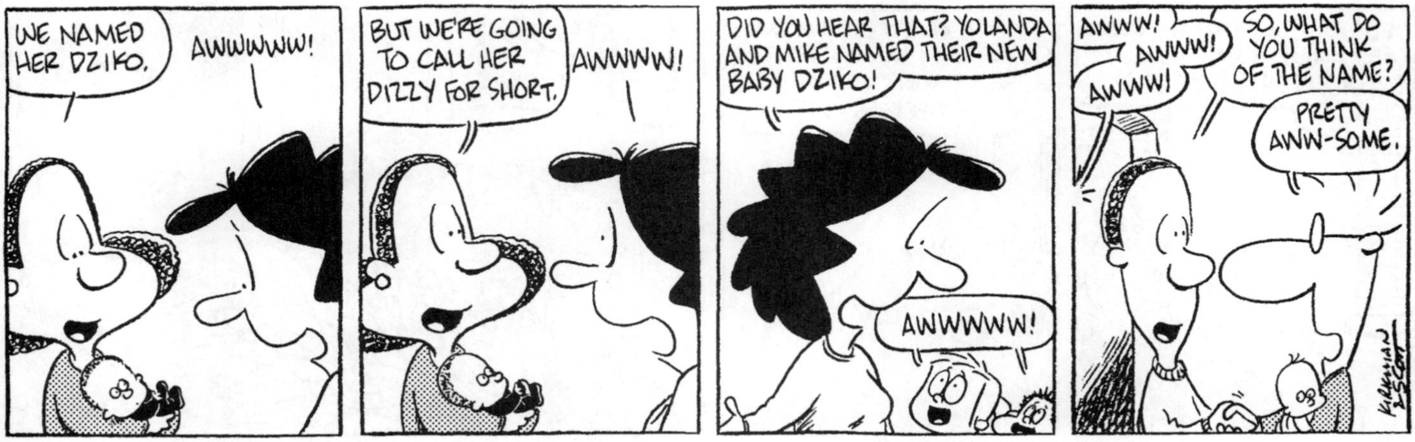
WE NAMED HER DZIKO.
AWWWWW!
BUT WE'RE GOING TO CALL HER DIZZY FOR SHORT.
AWWWW!
DID YOU HEAR THAT? YOLANDA AND MIKE NAMED THEIR NEW BABY DZIKO!
AWWWWW!
AWWW!
AWWW!
AWWW!
SO, WHAT DO YOU THINK OF THE NAME?
PRETTY AWW-SOME.

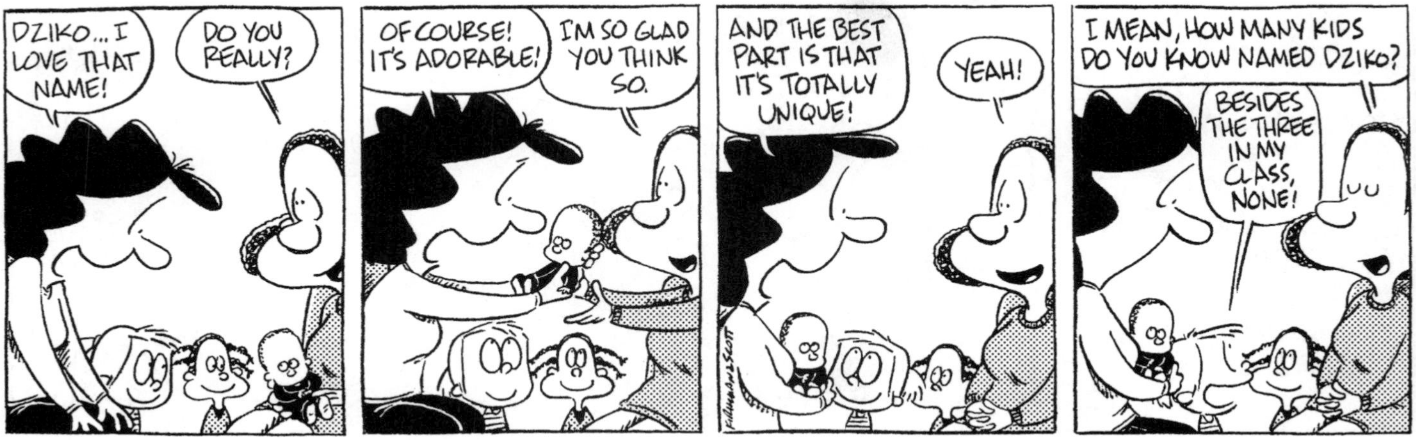
DZIKO... I LOVE THAT NAME!
DO YOU REALLY?
OF COURSE! IT'S ADORABLE!
I'M SO GLAD YOU THINK SO.
AND THE BEST PART IS THAT IT'S TOTALLY UNIQUE!
YEAH!
I MEAN, HOW MANY KIDS DO YOU KNOW NAMED DZIKO?
BESIDES THE THREE IN MY CLASS, NONE!

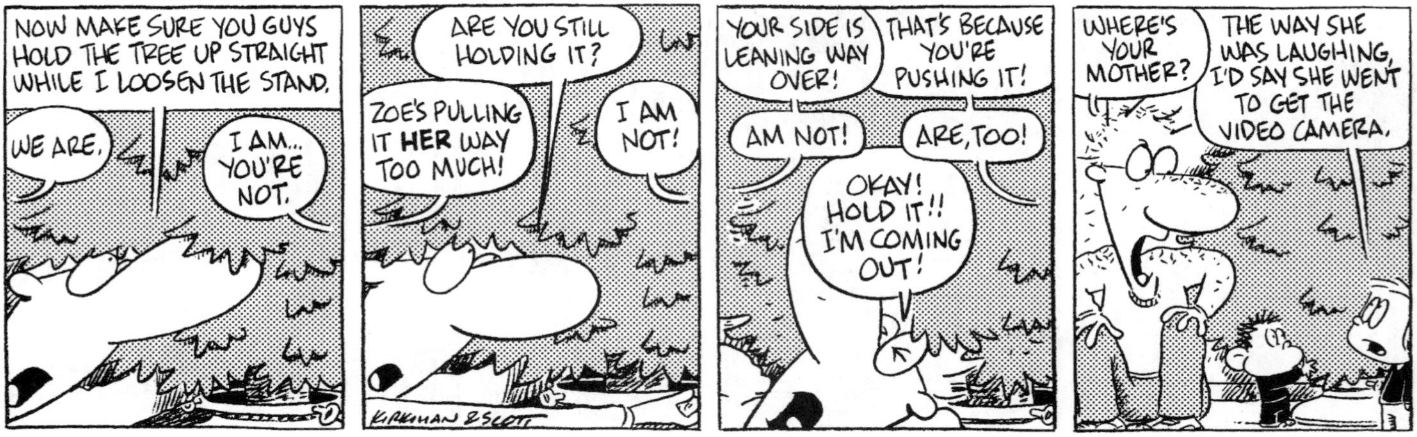
NOW MAKE SURE YOU GUYS HOLD THE TREE UP STRAIGHT WHILE I LOOSEN THE STAND.
WE ARE.
I AM... YOU'RE NOT.
ARE YOU STILL HOLDING IT?
ZOE'S PULLING IT **HER** WAY TOO MUCH!
I AM NOT!
KIRKMAN & SCOTT
YOUR SIDE IS LEANING WAY OVER!
THAT'S BECAUSE YOU'RE PUSHING IT!
AM NOT!
ARE, TOO!
OKAY! HOLD IT!! I'M COMING OUT!
WHERE'S YOUR MOTHER?
THE WAY SHE WAS LAUGHING, I'D SAY SHE WENT TO GET THE VIDEO CAMERA.

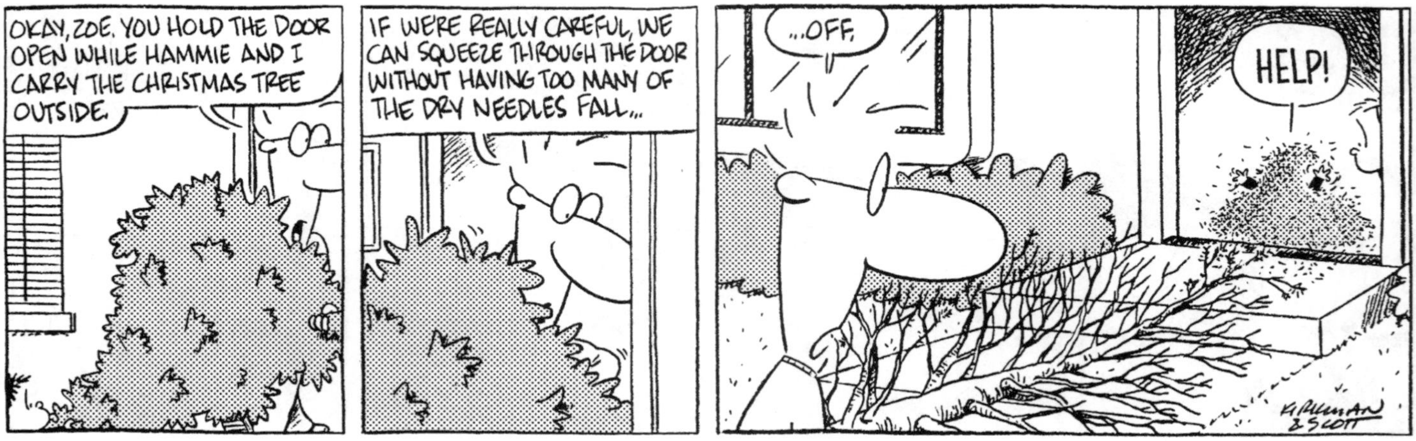
OKAY, ZOE. YOU HOLD THE DOOR OPEN WHILE HAMMIE AND I CARRY THE CHRISTMAS TREE OUTSIDE.
IF WE'RE REALLY CAREFUL, WE CAN SQUEEZE THROUGH THE DOOR WITHOUT HAVING TOO MANY OF THE DRY NEEDLES FALL...
...OFF.
HELP!
KIRKMAN & SCOTT

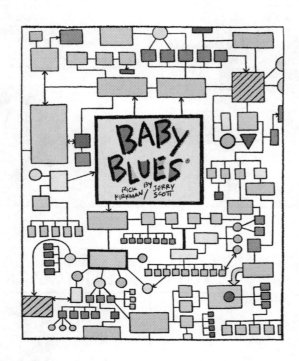

Baby Blues
BY
RICK KIRKMAN / JERRY SCOTT

ZOE, DID YOU GIVE JULIA THAT PAIR OF SOCKS SHE LEFT HERE LAST WEEK?

WELL...

...I GAVE THEM TO KEESHA BECAUSE SHE THOUGHT THEY WERE REALLY LILY'S.

THEN LILY SAID THEY WEREN'T HERS, BUT THEY MIGHT BE RENEÉ'S, SO SHE GAVE THEM TO RENEE.

ONLY THEY WEREN'T RENEÉ'S, SO RENEÉ GAVE THEM TO SOPHIE, WHO GAVE THEM TO TESSA, WHO GAVE THEM TO SAVANNAH, WHO PUT THEM ON ERIN'S DESK, BUT ERIN DIDN'T KNOW WHAT WAS GOING ON, SO SHE PUT THEM IN THE LOST AND FOUND BOX WHERE JULIA FOUND THEM AFTER SCHOOL.

SO THE ANSWER IS "YES"?

ISN'T THAT WHAT I JUST SAID?

WELCOME TO MacPHERSONLAND...

HOME OF THE WORLD'S LONGEST ONE-WORD ANSWERS.

AND YOU WONDER WHY IT TAKES ME SO LONG TO GET ANYTHING DONE AROUND HERE.

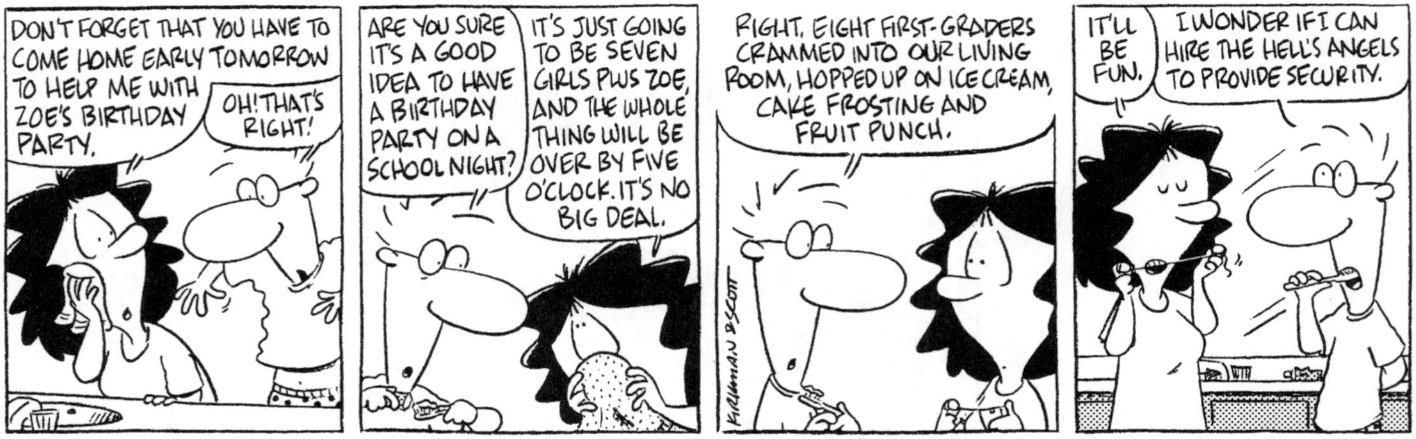
DON'T FORGET THAT YOU HAVE TO COME HOME EARLY TOMORROW TO HELP ME WITH ZOE'S BIRTHDAY PARTY.
OH! THAT'S RIGHT!
ARE YOU SURE IT'S A GOOD IDEA TO HAVE A BIRTHDAY PARTY ON A SCHOOL NIGHT?
IT'S JUST GOING TO BE SEVEN GIRLS PLUS ZOE, AND THE WHOLE THING WILL BE OVER BY FIVE O'CLOCK. IT'S NO BIG DEAL.
RIGHT. EIGHT FIRST-GRADERS CRAMMED INTO OUR LIVING ROOM, HOPPED UP ON ICE CREAM, CAKE FROSTING AND FRUIT PUNCH.
KIRKMAN & SCOTT
IT'LL BE FUN.
I WONDER IF I CAN HIRE THE HELL'S ANGELS TO PROVIDE SECURITY.

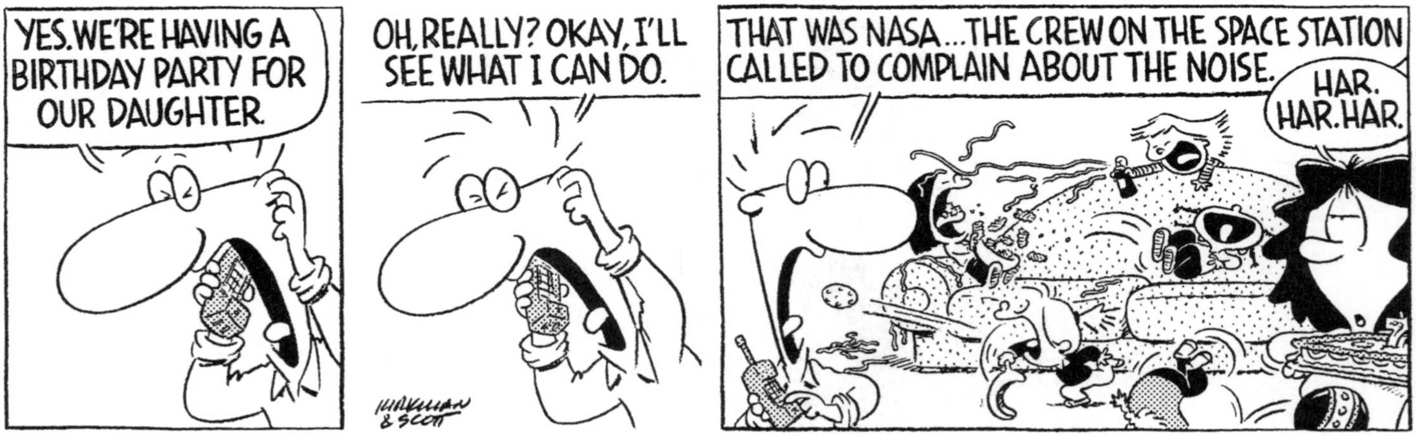
YES. WE'RE HAVING A BIRTHDAY PARTY FOR OUR DAUGHTER.
OH, REALLY? OKAY, I'LL SEE WHAT I CAN DO.
KIRKMAN & SCOTT
THAT WAS NASA... THE CREW ON THE SPACE STATION CALLED TO COMPLAIN ABOUT THE NOISE.
HAR. HAR. HAR.

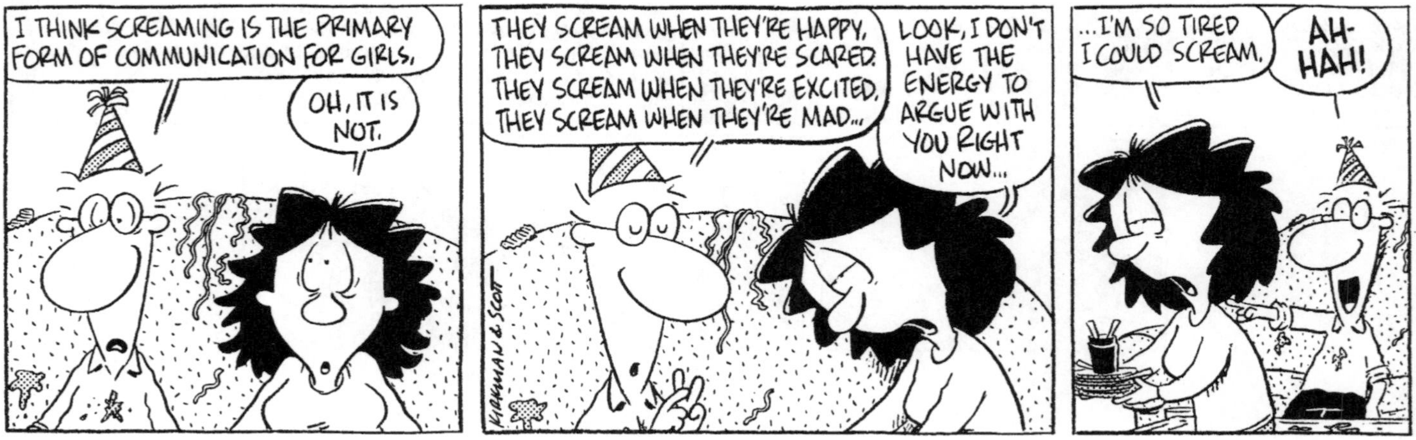
I THINK SCREAMING IS THE PRIMARY FORM OF COMMUNICATION FOR GIRLS.
OH, IT IS NOT.
THEY SCREAM WHEN THEY'RE HAPPY, THEY SCREAM WHEN THEY'RE SCARED. THEY SCREAM WHEN THEY'RE EXCITED, THEY SCREAM WHEN THEY'RE MAD...
LOOK, I DON'T HAVE THE ENERGY TO ARGUE WITH YOU RIGHT NOW...
KIRKMAN & SCOTT
...I'M SO TIRED I COULD SCREAM.
AH-HAH!

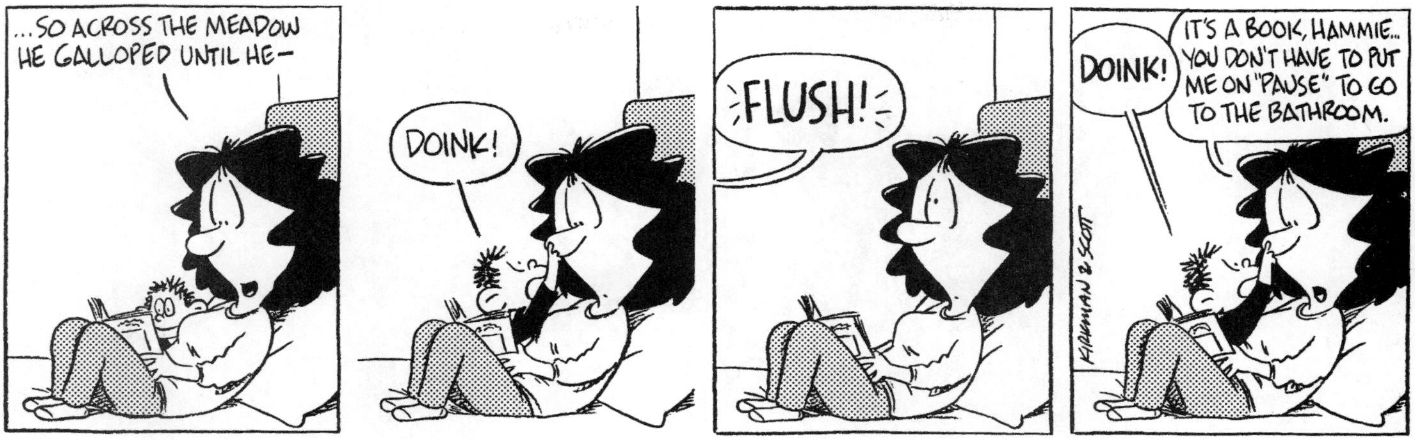
...SO ACROSS THE MEADOW HE GALLOPED UNTIL HE—
DOINK!
FLUSH!
DOINK!
IT'S A BOOK, HAMMIE... YOU DON'T HAVE TO PUT ME ON "PAUSE" TO GO TO THE BATHROOM.

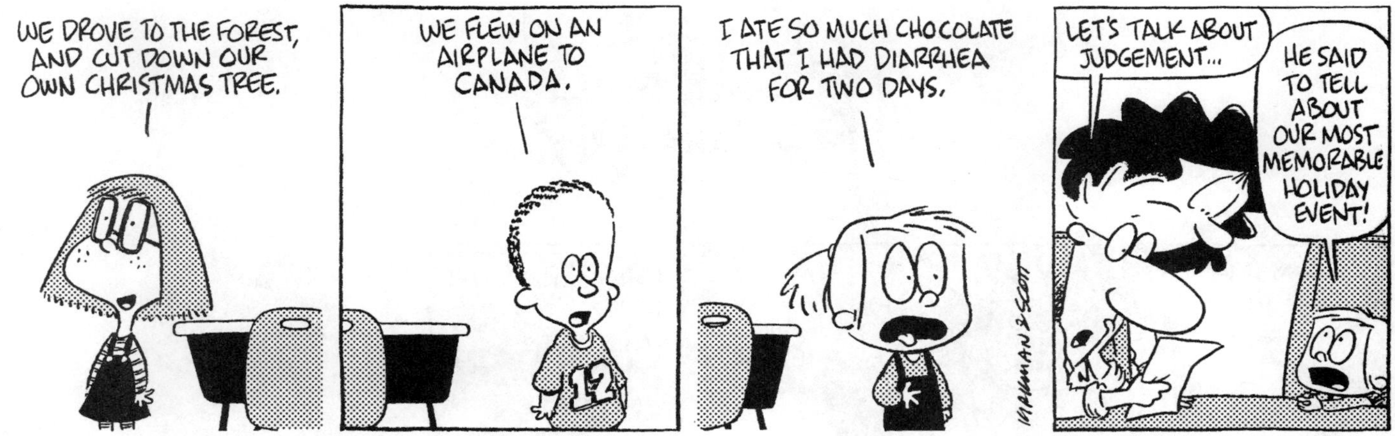
WE DROVE TO THE FOREST, AND CUT DOWN OUR OWN CHRISTMAS TREE.
WE FLEW ON AN AIRPLANE TO CANADA.
I ATE SO MUCH CHOCOLATE THAT I HAD DIARRHEA FOR TWO DAYS.
LET'S TALK ABOUT JUDGEMENT...
HE SAID TO TELL ABOUT OUR MOST MEMORABLE HOLIDAY EVENT!

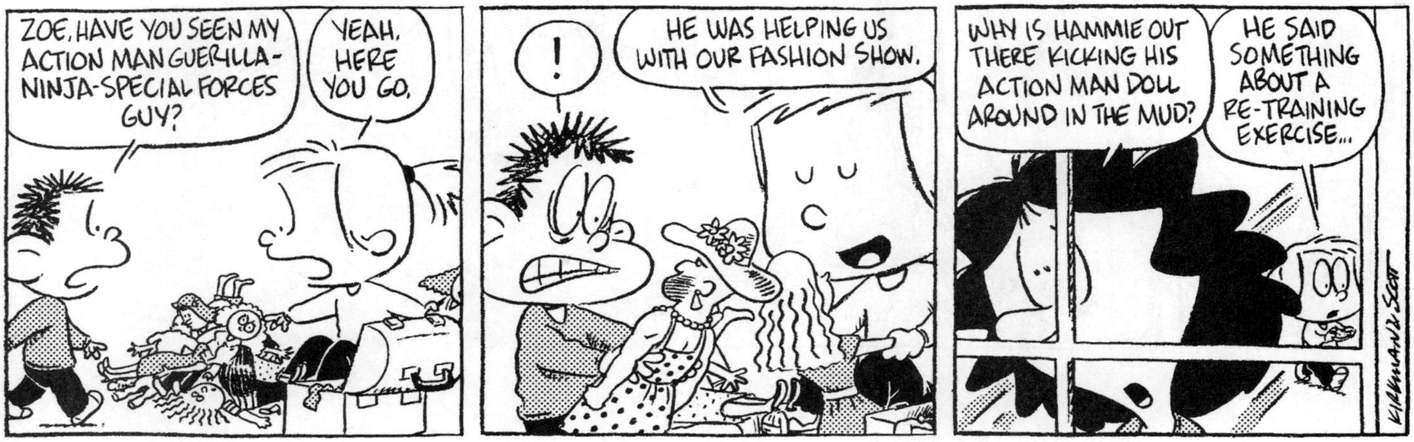
ZOE, HAVE YOU SEEN MY ACTION MAN GUERILLA-NINJA-SPECIAL FORCES GUY?
YEAH. HERE YOU GO.
!
HE WAS HELPING US WITH OUR FASHION SHOW.
WHY IS HAMMIE OUT THERE KICKING HIS ACTION MAN DOLL AROUND IN THE MUD?
HE SAID SOMETHING ABOUT A RE-TRAINING EXERCISE...

BABY BLUES®

by Rick Kirkman / Jerry Scott

OKAY, HERE COMES THE ROPE!
GOT IT!
READY?
SEND IT OVER!
HOW'S THAT?
PRETTY GOOD. LET'S GO!
HOW LONG DO YOU THINK WE'LL BE GONE?
ABOUT AN HOUR.
WE'VE GOTTA LEARN TO TRAVEL LIGHTER.
THAT, OR JUST PUT SOME WHEELS ON THE HOUSE.
KIRKMAN & SCOTT

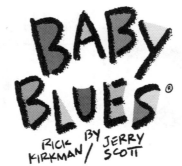

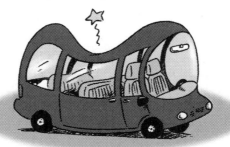

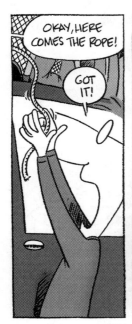

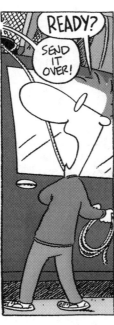

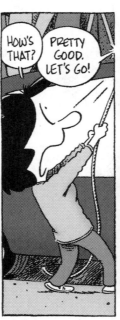

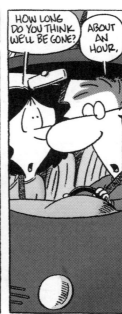

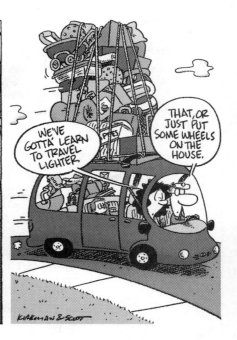

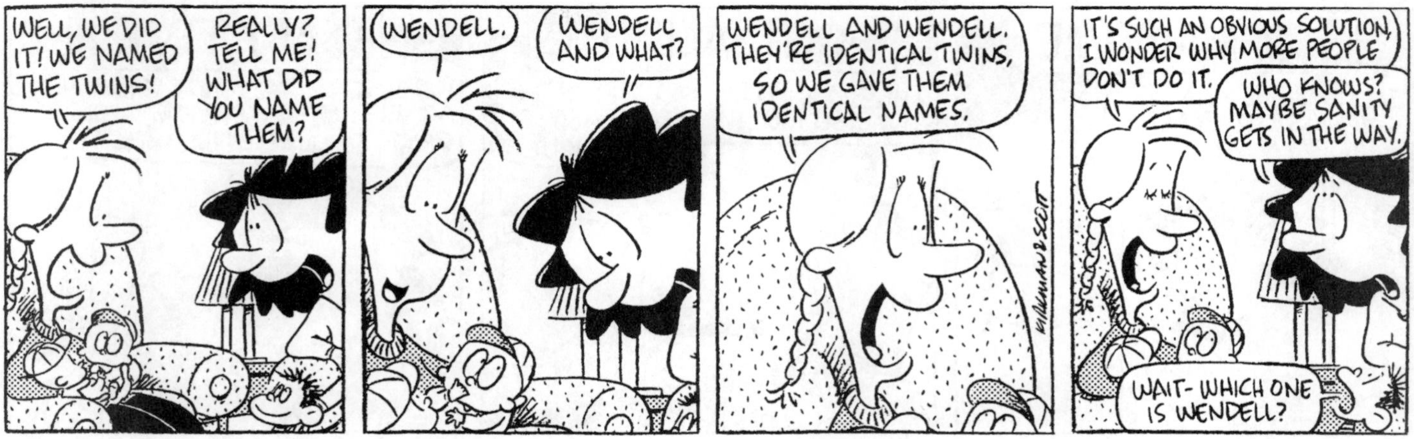
WELL, WE DID IT! WE NAMED THE TWINS!
REALLY? TELL ME! WHAT DID YOU NAME THEM?
WENDELL.
WENDELL AND WHAT?
WENDELL AND WENDELL. THEY'RE IDENTICAL TWINS, SO WE GAVE THEM IDENTICAL NAMES.
IT'S SUCH AN OBVIOUS SOLUTION, I WONDER WHY MORE PEOPLE DON'T DO IT.
WHO KNOWS? MAYBE SANITY GETS IN THE WAY.
WAIT- WHICH ONE IS WENDELL?

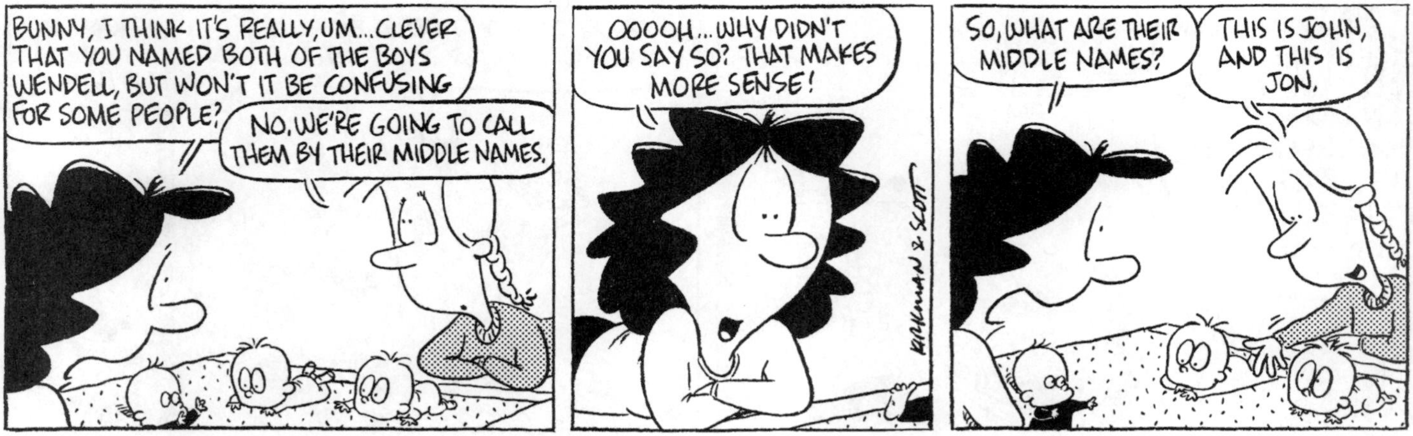
BUNNY, I THINK IT'S REALLY, UM... CLEVER THAT YOU NAMED BOTH OF THE BOYS WENDELL, BUT WON'T IT BE CONFUSING FOR SOME PEOPLE?
NO, WE'RE GOING TO CALL THEM BY THEIR MIDDLE NAMES.
OOOOH... WHY DIDN'T YOU SAY SO? THAT MAKES MORE SENSE!
SO, WHAT ARE THEIR MIDDLE NAMES?
THIS IS JOHN, AND THIS IS JON.

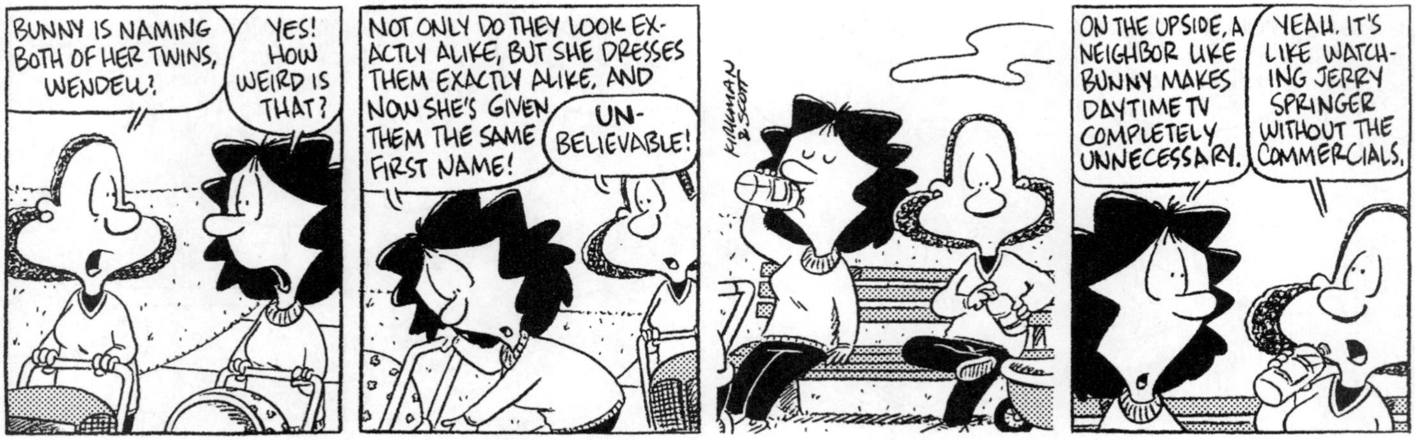
BUNNY IS NAMING BOTH OF HER TWINS, WENDELL?
YES! HOW WEIRD IS THAT?
NOT ONLY DO THEY LOOK EXACTLY ALIKE, BUT SHE DRESSES THEM EXACTLY ALIKE, AND NOW SHE'S GIVEN THEM THE SAME FIRST NAME!
UN-BELIEVABLE!
ON THE UPSIDE, A NEIGHBOR LIKE BUNNY MAKES DAYTIME TV COMPLETELY UNNECESSARY.
YEAH. IT'S LIKE WATCHING JERRY SPRINGER WITHOUT THE COMMERCIALS.

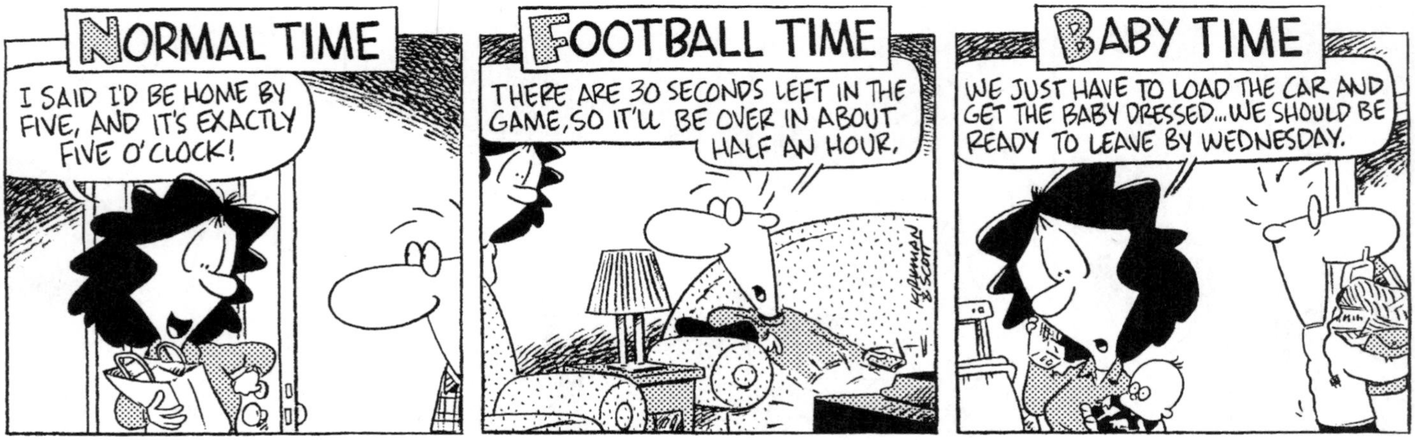
NORMAL TIME
I SAID I'D BE HOME BY FIVE, AND IT'S EXACTLY FIVE O'CLOCK!
FOOTBALL TIME
THERE ARE 30 SECONDS LEFT IN THE GAME, SO IT'LL BE OVER IN ABOUT HALF AN HOUR.
KIRKMAN & SCOTT
BABY TIME
WE JUST HAVE TO LOAD THE CAR AND GET THE BABY DRESSED... WE SHOULD BE READY TO LEAVE BY WEDNESDAY.

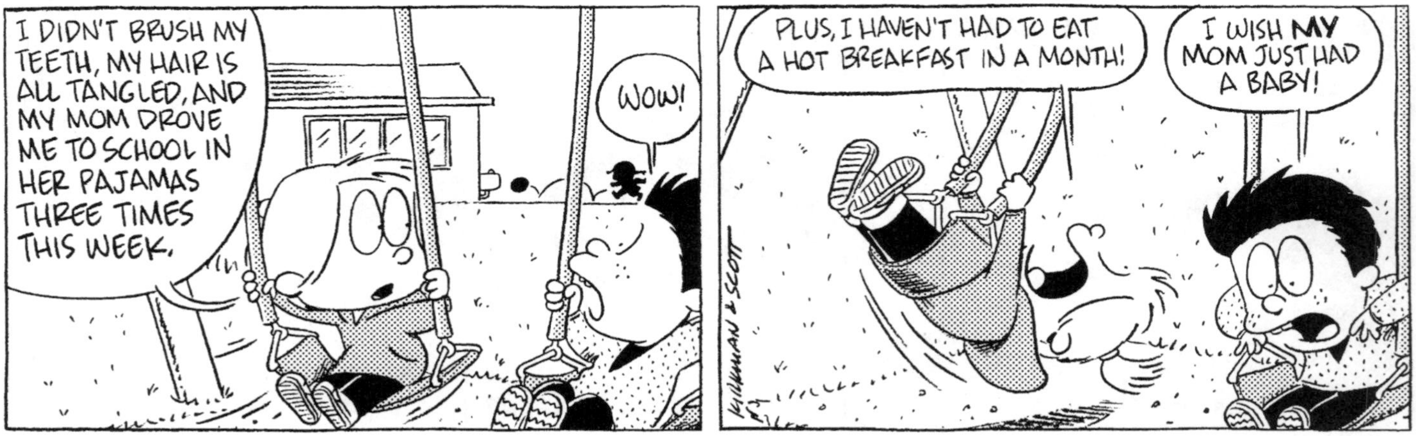
I DIDN'T BRUSH MY TEETH, MY HAIR IS ALL TANGLED, AND MY MOM DROVE ME TO SCHOOL IN HER PAJAMAS THREE TIMES THIS WEEK.
WOW!
KIRKMAN & SCOTT
PLUS, I HAVEN'T HAD TO EAT A HOT BREAKFAST IN A MONTH!
I WISH MY MOM JUST HAD A BABY!

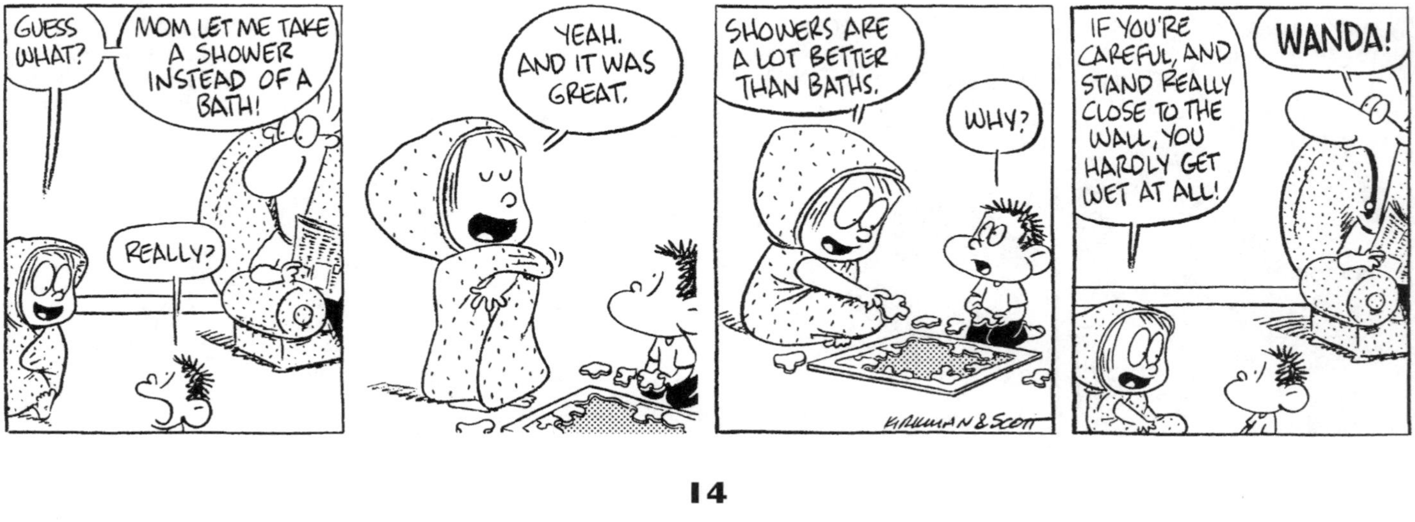
GUESS WHAT?
MOM LET ME TAKE A SHOWER INSTEAD OF A BATH!
REALLY?
YEAH. AND IT WAS GREAT.
SHOWERS ARE A LOT BETTER THAN BATHS.
WHY?
KIRKMAN & SCOTT
IF YOU'RE CAREFUL, AND STAND REALLY CLOSE TO THE WALL, YOU HARDLY GET WET AT ALL!
WANDA!

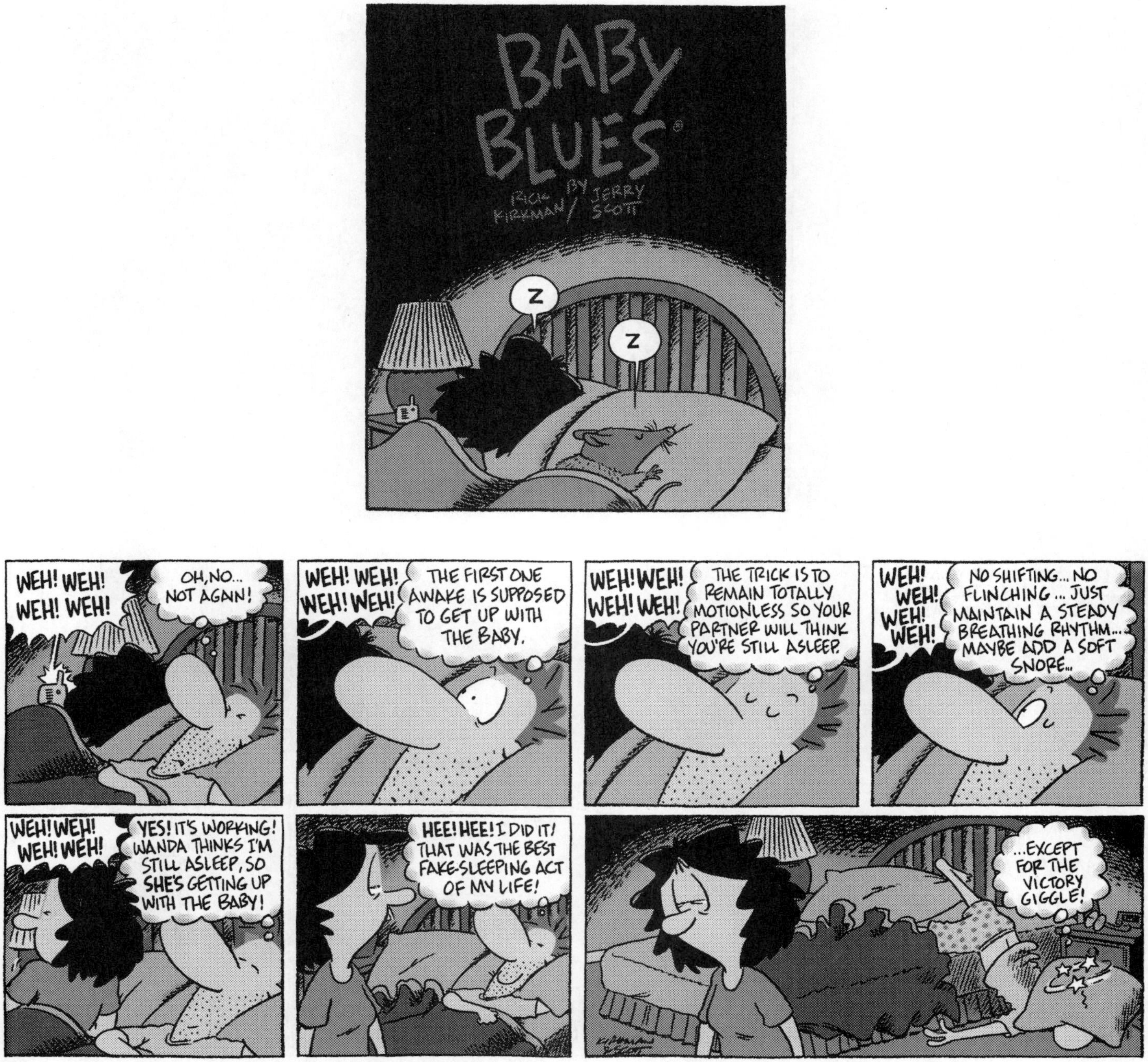
BABY BLUES®
BY RICK KIRKMAN/ JERRY SCOTT
Z
Z
WEH! WEH! WEH! WEH!
OH, NO... NOT AGAIN!
WEH! WEH! WEH! WEH!
THE FIRST ONE AWAKE IS SUPPOSED TO GET UP WITH THE BABY.
WEH! WEH! WEH! WEH!
THE TRICK IS TO REMAIN TOTALLY MOTIONLESS SO YOUR PARTNER WILL THINK YOU'RE STILL ASLEEP.
WEH! WEH! WEH! WEH!
NO SHIFTING... NO FLINCHING... JUST MAINTAIN A STEADY BREATHING RHYTHM... MAYBE ADD A SOFT SNORE...
WEH! WEH! WEH! WEH!
YES! IT'S WORKING! WANDA THINKS I'M STILL ASLEEP, SO SHE'S GETTING UP WITH THE BABY!
HEE! HEE! I DID IT! THAT WAS THE BEST FAKE-SLEEPING ACT OF MY LIFE!
...EXCEPT FOR THE VICTORY GIGGLE!

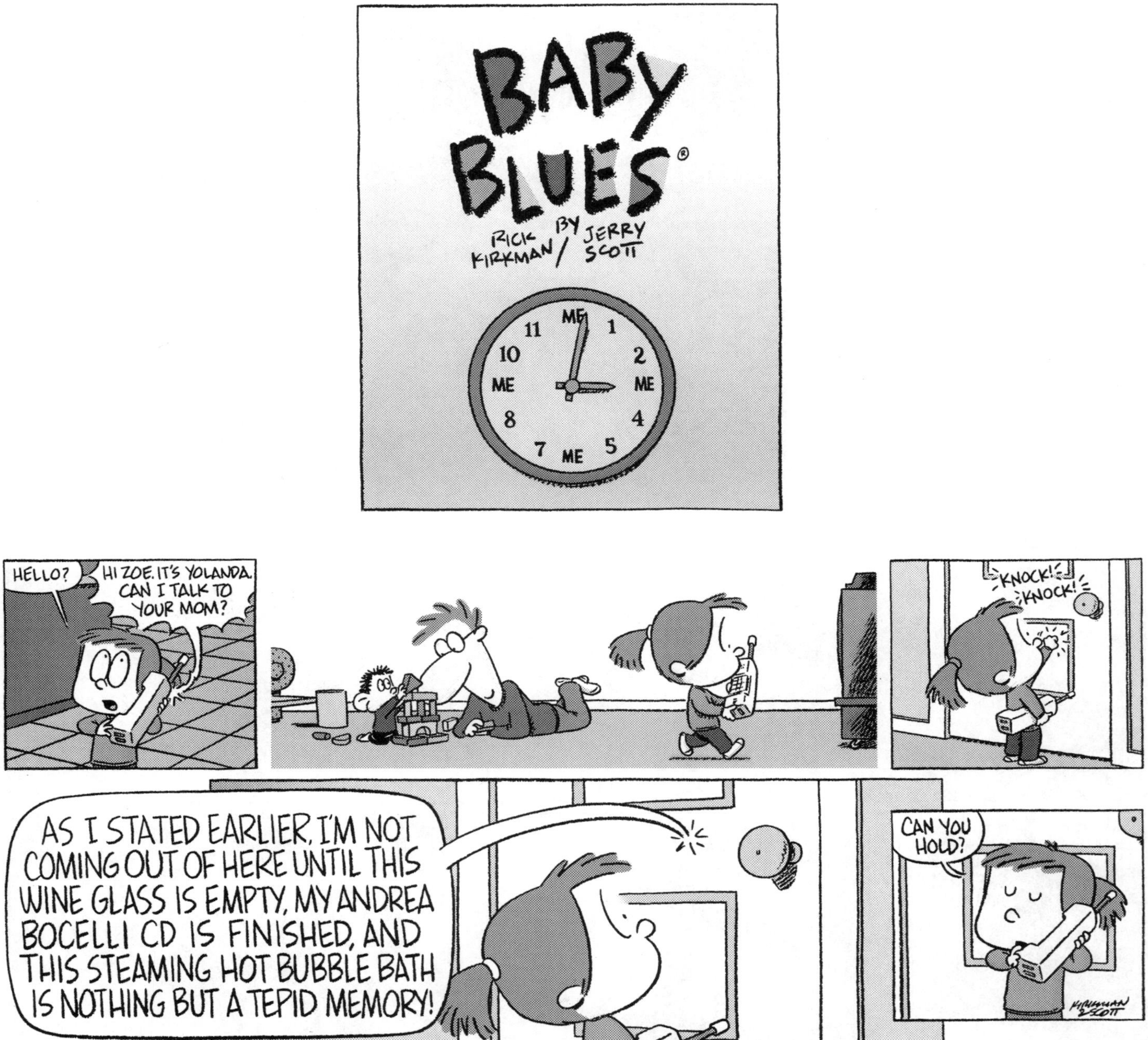
BABY BLUES®
BY RICK KIRKMAN / JERRY SCOTT
HELLO?
HI ZOE. IT'S YOLANDA. CAN I TALK TO YOUR MOM?
KNOCK! KNOCK!
AS I STATED EARLIER, I'M NOT COMING OUT OF HERE UNTIL THIS WINE GLASS IS EMPTY, MY ANDREA BOCELLI CD IS FINISHED, AND THIS STEAMING HOT BUBBLE BATH IS NOTHING BUT A TEPID MEMORY!
CAN YOU HOLD?

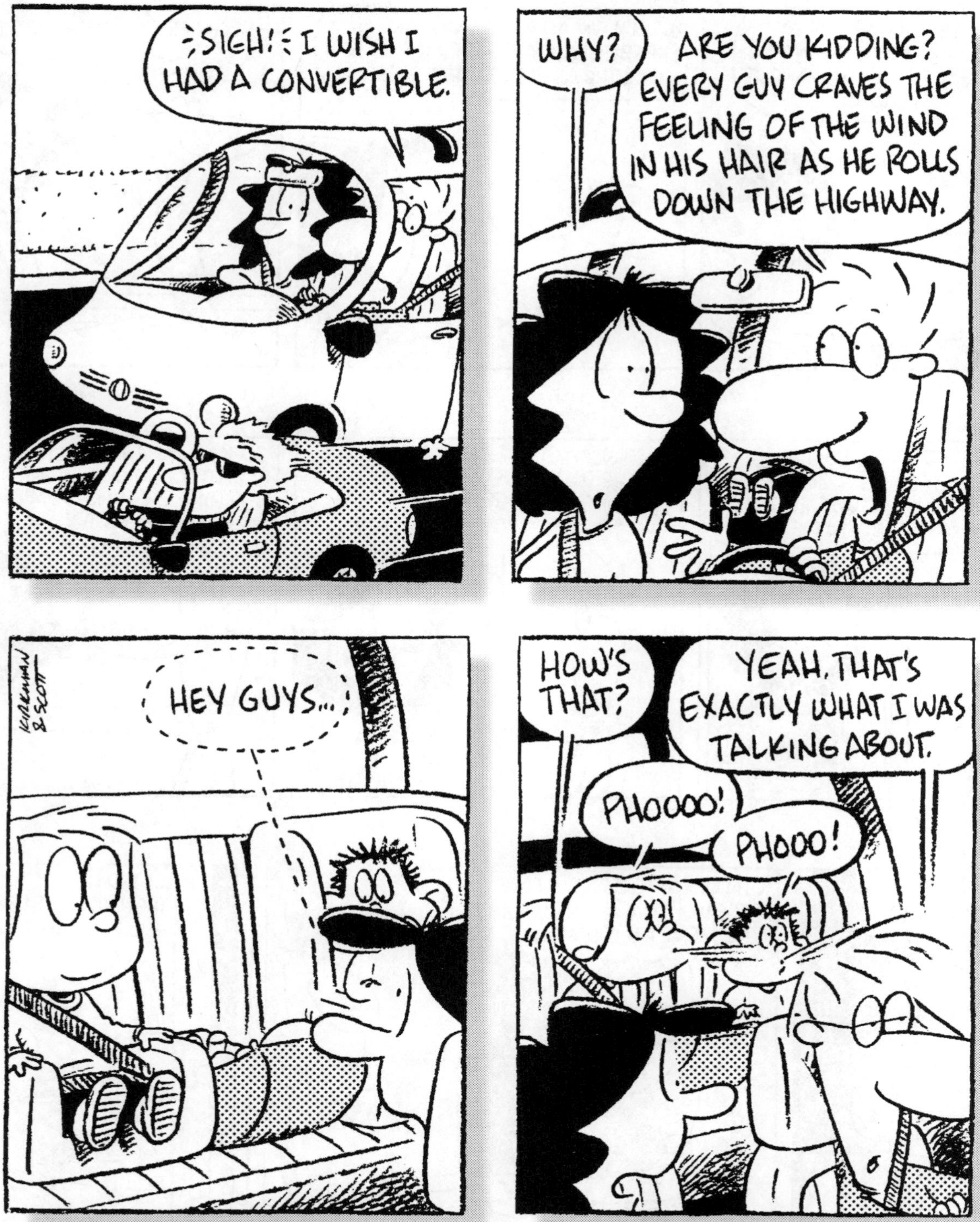

SIGH! I WISH I HAD A CONVERTIBLE.
WHY?
ARE YOU KIDDING? EVERY GUY CRAVES THE FEELING OF THE WIND IN HIS HAIR AS HE ROLLS DOWN THE HIGHWAY.
KIRKMAN & SCOTT
HEY GUYS...
HOW'S THAT?
YEAH, THAT'S EXACTLY WHAT I WAS TALKING ABOUT.
PHOOOO!
PHOOO!

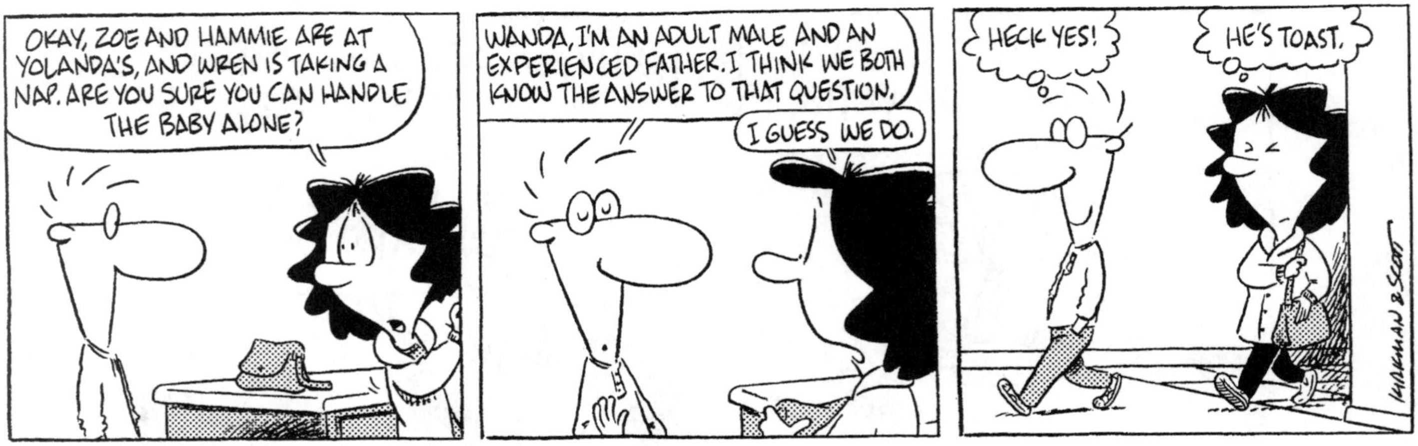
OKAY, ZOE AND HAMMIE ARE AT YOLANDA'S, AND WREN IS TAKING A NAP. ARE YOU SURE YOU CAN HANDLE THE BABY ALONE?
WANDA, I'M AN ADULT MALE AND AN EXPERIENCED FATHER. I THINK WE BOTH KNOW THE ANSWER TO THAT QUESTION.
I GUESS WE DO.
HECK YES!
HE'S TOAST.
KIRKMAN & SCOTT

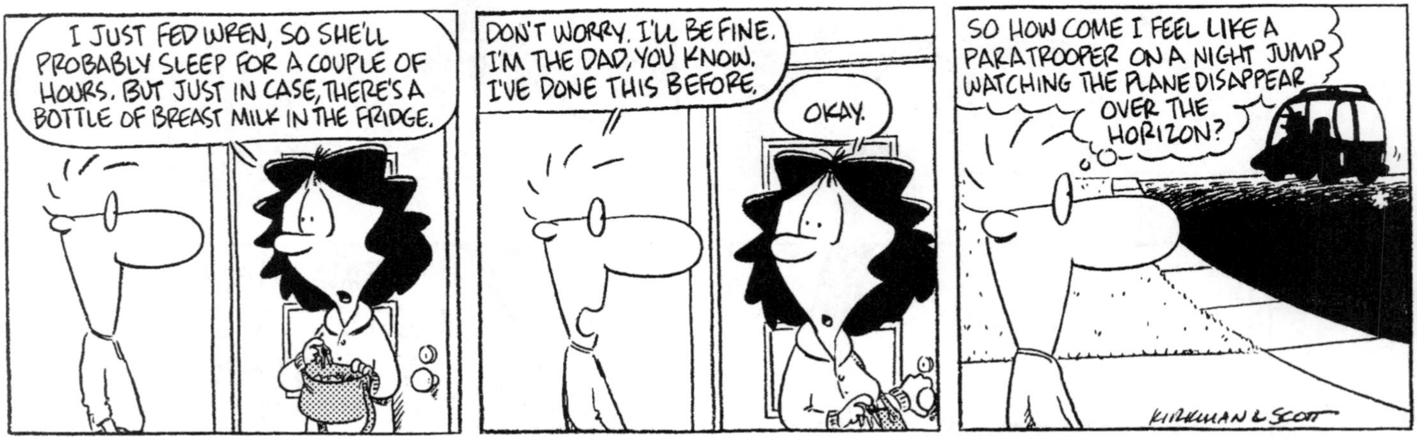
I JUST FED WREN, SO SHE'LL PROBABLY SLEEP FOR A COUPLE OF HOURS. BUT JUST IN CASE, THERE'S A BOTTLE OF BREAST MILK IN THE FRIDGE.
DON'T WORRY. I'LL BE FINE. I'M THE DAD, YOU KNOW. I'VE DONE THIS BEFORE.
OKAY.
SO HOW COME I FEEL LIKE A PARATROOPER ON A NIGHT JUMP WATCHING THE PLANE DISAPPEAR OVER THE HORIZON?
KIRKMAN & SCOTT

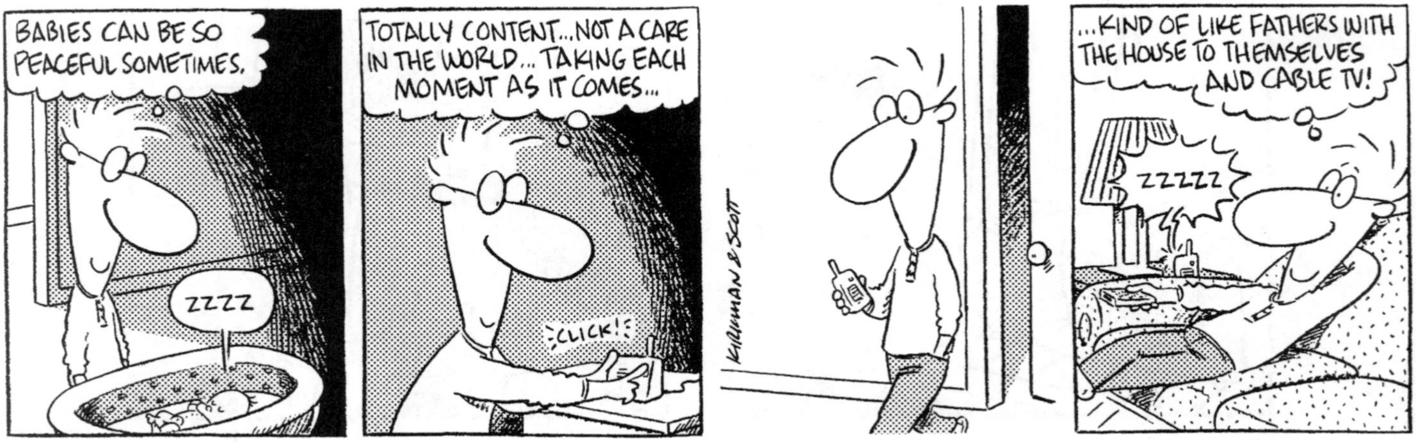
BABIES CAN BE SO PEACEFUL SOMETIMES.
ZZZZ
TOTALLY CONTENT... NOT A CARE IN THE WORLD... TAKING EACH MOMENT AS IT COMES...
CLICK!
KIRKMAN & SCOTT
...KIND OF LIKE FATHERS WITH THE HOUSE TO THEMSELVES AND CABLE TV!
ZZZZZ

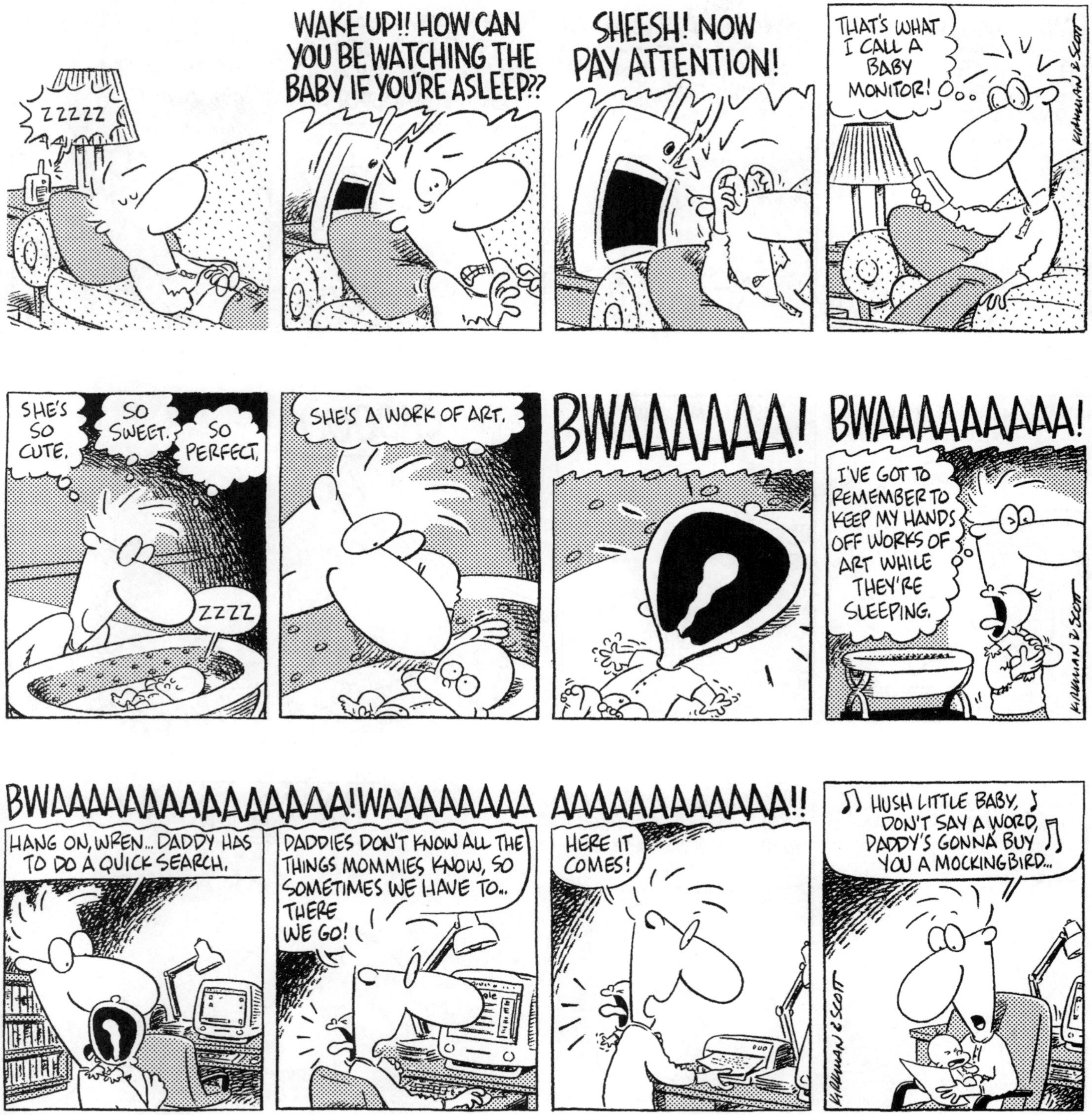
ZZZZZ
WAKE UP!! HOW CAN YOU BE WATCHING THE BABY IF YOU'RE ASLEEP??
SHEESH! NOW PAY ATTENTION!
THAT'S WHAT I CALL A BABY MONITOR!
KIRKMAN & SCOTT
SHE'S SO CUTE.
SO SWEET.
SO PERFECT.
ZZZZ
SHE'S A WORK OF ART.
BWAAAAAA!
BWAAAAAAAAA!
I'VE GOT TO REMEMBER TO KEEP MY HANDS OFF WORKS OF ART WHILE THEY'RE SLEEPING.
KIRKMAN & SCOTT
BWAAAAAAAAAAAAAAAA! WAAAAAAAA AAAAAAAAAAAA!!
HANG ON, WREN... DADDY HAS TO DO A QUICK SEARCH.
DADDIES DON'T KNOW ALL THE THINGS MOMMIES KNOW, SO SOMETIMES WE HAVE TO...
THERE WE GO!
HERE IT COMES!
♫ HUSH LITTLE BABY, ♪ DON'T SAY A WORD, DADDY'S GONNA BUY ♫ YOU A MOCKINGBIRD...
KIRKMAN & SCOTT

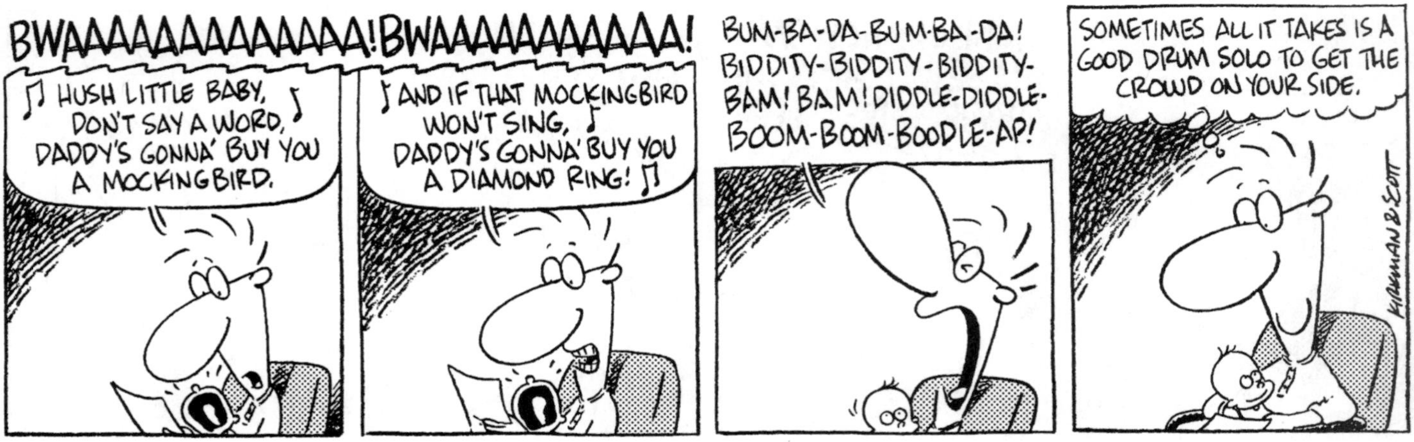
BWAAAAAAAAAAAAA! BWAAAAAAAAAAAA!
♫ HUSH LITTLE BABY, DON'T SAY A WORD, ♪ DADDY'S GONNA' BUY YOU A MOCKINGBIRD.
♪ AND IF THAT MOCKINGBIRD WON'T SING, ♪ DADDY'S GONNA' BUY YOU A DIAMOND RING! ♫
BUM-BA-DA-BUM-BA-DA! BIDDITY-BIDDITY-BIDDITY-BAM! BAM! DIDDLE-DIDDLE-BOOM-BOOM-BOODLE-AP!
SOMETIMES ALL IT TAKES IS A GOOD DRUM SOLO TO GET THE CROWD ON YOUR SIDE.
KIRKMAN & SCOTT

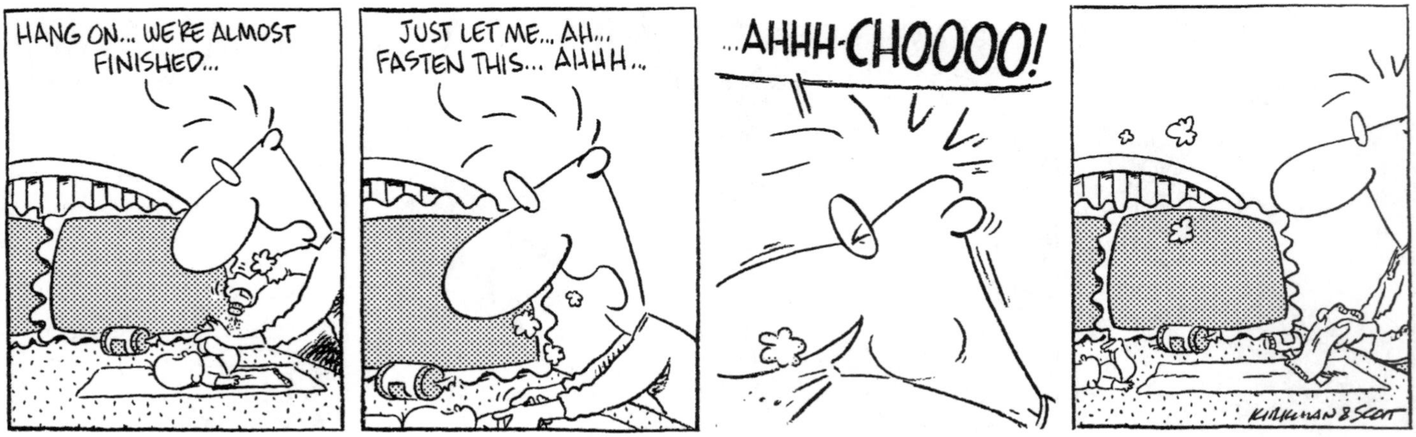
HANG ON... WE'RE ALMOST FINISHED...
JUST LET ME... AH... FASTEN THIS... AHHH...
...AHHH-CHOOOO!
KIRKMAN & SCOTT

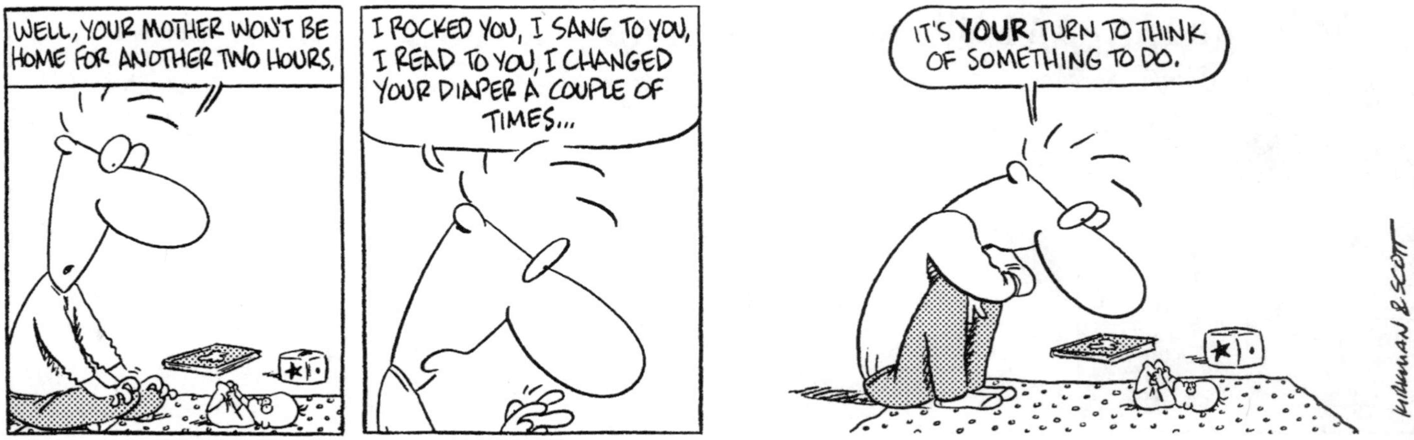
WELL, YOUR MOTHER WON'T BE HOME FOR ANOTHER TWO HOURS.
I ROCKED YOU, I SANG TO YOU, I READ TO YOU, I CHANGED YOUR DIAPER A COUPLE OF TIMES...
IT'S **YOUR** TURN TO THINK OF SOMETHING TO DO.
KIRKMAN & SCOTT

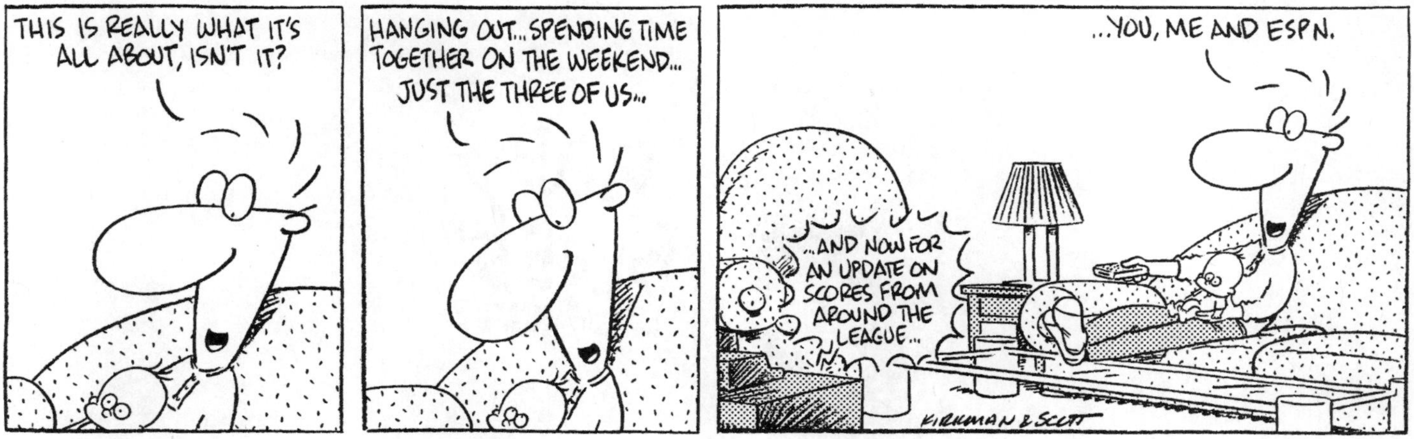
THIS IS REALLY WHAT IT'S ALL ABOUT, ISN'T IT?
HANGING OUT... SPENDING TIME TOGETHER ON THE WEEKEND... JUST THE THREE OF US...
...YOU, ME AND ESPN.
...AND NOW FOR AN UPDATE ON SCORES FROM AROUND THE LEAGUE...
KIRKMAN & SCOTT

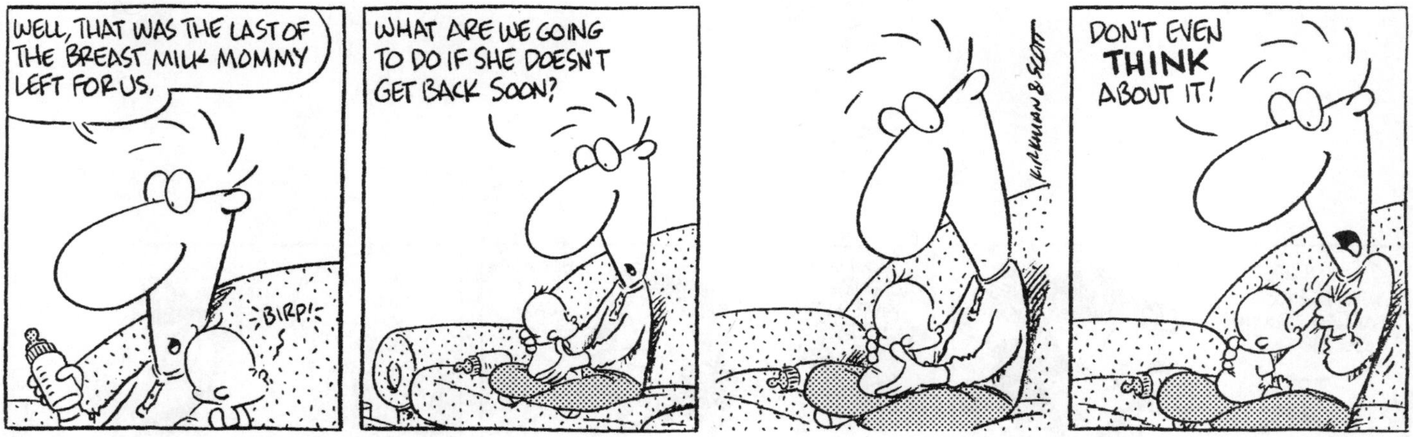
WELL, THAT WAS THE LAST OF THE BREAST MILK MOMMY LEFT FOR US.
BIRP!
WHAT ARE WE GOING TO DO IF SHE DOESN'T GET BACK SOON?
KIRKMAN & SCOTT
DON'T EVEN THINK ABOUT IT!

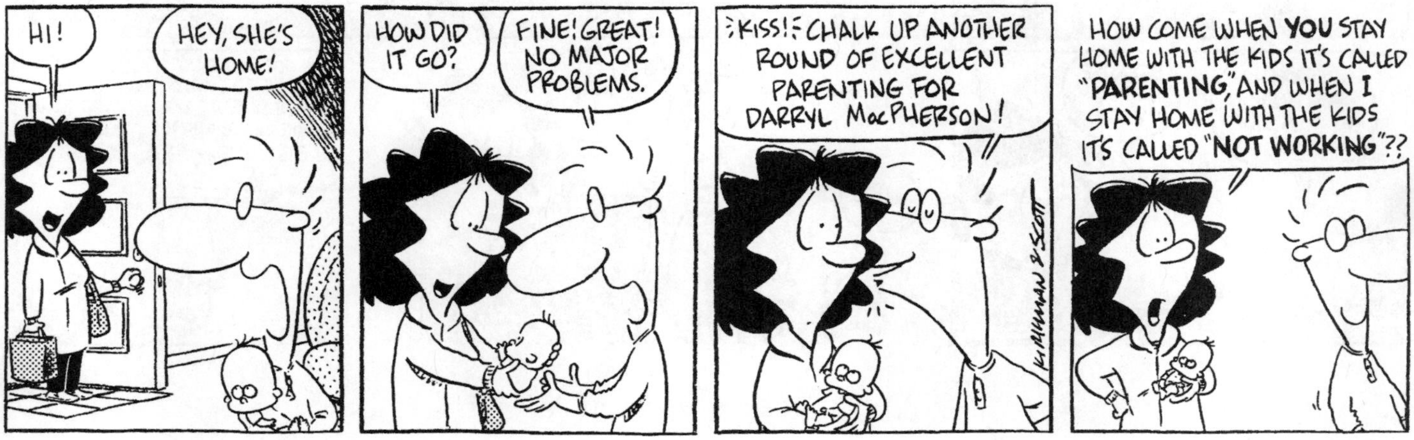
HI!
HEY, SHE'S HOME!
HOW DID IT GO?
FINE! GREAT! NO MAJOR PROBLEMS.
KISS!
CHALK UP ANOTHER ROUND OF EXCELLENT PARENTING FOR DARRYL MacPHERSON!
KIRKMAN & SCOTT
HOW COME WHEN YOU STAY HOME WITH THE KIDS IT'S CALLED "PARENTING," AND WHEN I STAY HOME WITH THE KIDS IT'S CALLED "NOT WORKING"??

BABY BLUES®
BY RICK KIRKMAN / JERRY SCOTT

WHY DOES WREN GET TO BE CARRIED AROUND ALL THE TIME?
BECAUSE SHE'S A BABY.
HOW COME WREN GETS TO RIDE IN THE LAUNDRY BASKET, AND I DON'T?
BECAUSE SHE'S A BABY.
WHY DOES WREN GET TO SIT ON THE TABLE?
BECAUSE SHE'S A BABY.
WHY DOESN'T WREN HAVE TO EAT THIS STUFF, TOO?
BECAUSE SHE'S A BABY.
WHY—
OKAY, ZOE. THAT'S IT. LET'S GO.
KIRKMAN & SCOTT
IT'S NOT FAIR THAT I HAVE TO SIT IN THIS HARD TIME-OUT CHAIR WHILE WREN GETS ROCKED TO SLEEP!
YEAH. YOU'RE BEING A MUCH BIGGER BABY THAN SHE IS TONIGHT.

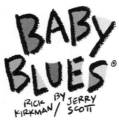

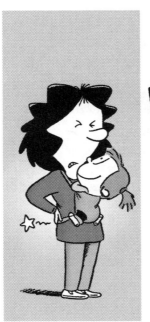

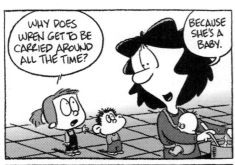

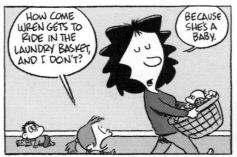

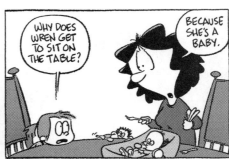

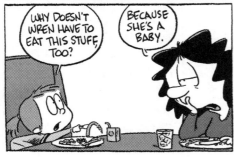

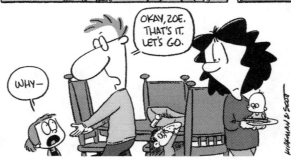

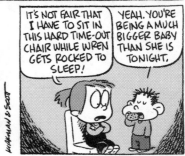

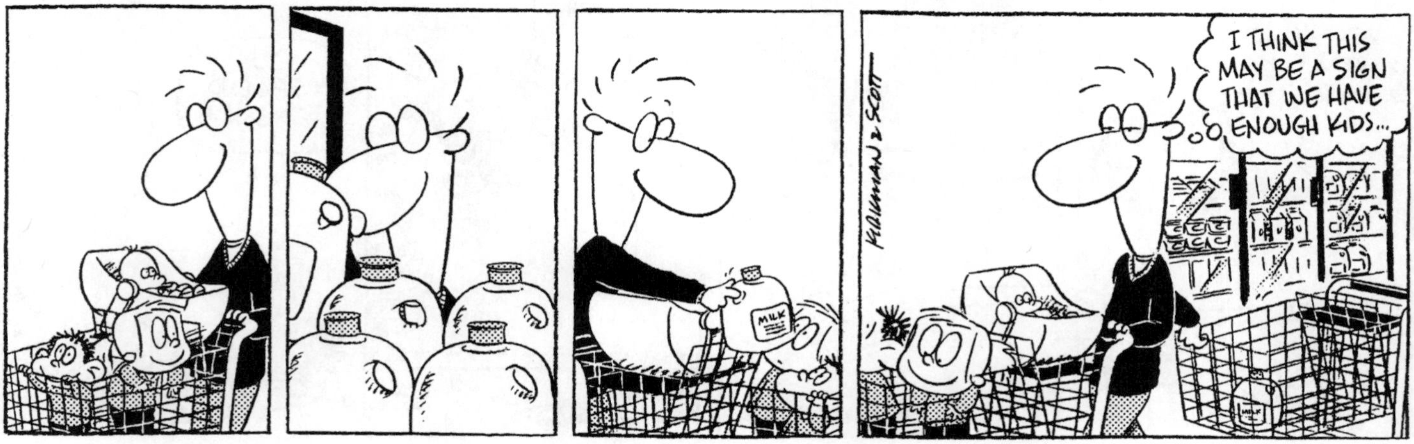
MILK
I THINK THIS MAY BE A SIGN THAT WE HAVE ENOUGH KIDS...

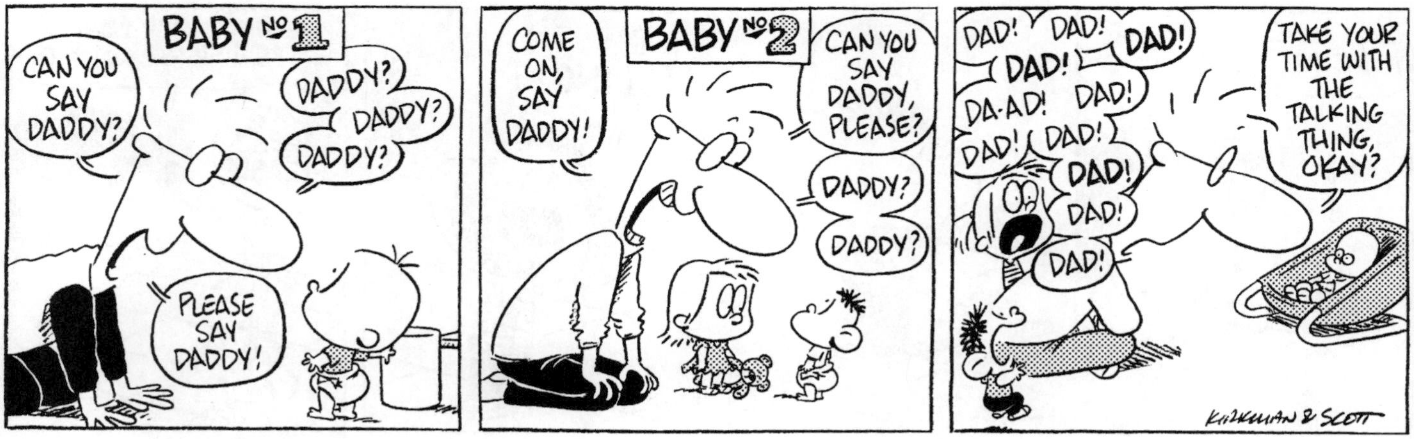
BABY № 1
CAN YOU SAY DADDY?
DADDY?
DADDY?
DADDY?
PLEASE SAY DADDY!
BABY № 2
COME ON, SAY DADDY!
CAN YOU SAY DADDY, PLEASE?
DADDY?
DADDY?
DAD!
DAD!
DAD!
DAD!
DA-AD!
DAD!
DAD!
DAD!
DAD!
DAD!
DAD!
TAKE YOUR TIME WITH THE TALKING THING, OKAY?
KIRKMAN & SCOTT

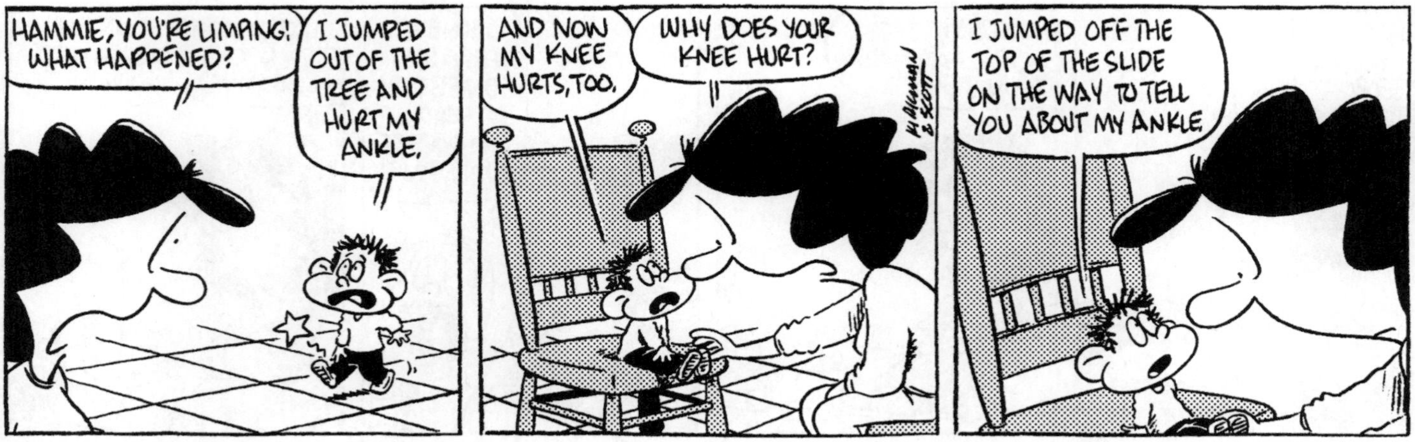
HAMMIE, YOU'RE LIMPING! WHAT HAPPENED?
I JUMPED OUT OF THE TREE AND HURT MY ANKLE.
AND NOW MY KNEE HURTS, TOO.
WHY DOES YOUR KNEE HURT?
I JUMPED OFF THE TOP OF THE SLIDE ON THE WAY TO TELL YOU ABOUT MY ANKLE.

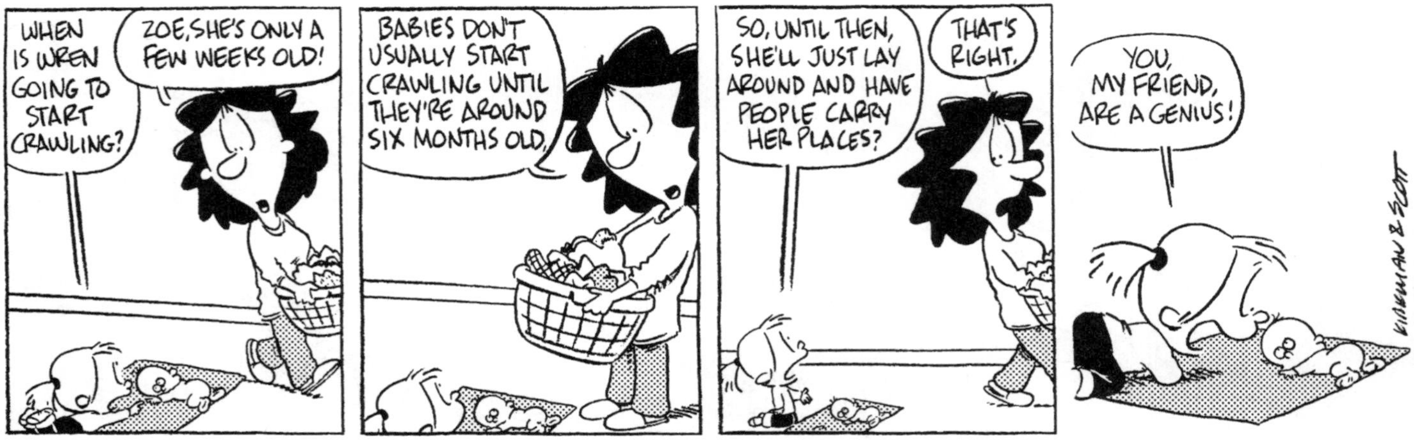
WHEN IS WREN GOING TO START CRAWLING?
ZOE, SHE'S ONLY A FEW WEEKS OLD!
BABIES DON'T USUALLY START CRAWLING UNTIL THEY'RE AROUND SIX MONTHS OLD.
SO, UNTIL THEN, SHE'LL JUST LAY AROUND AND HAVE PEOPLE CARRY HER PLACES?
THAT'S RIGHT.
YOU, MY FRIEND, ARE A GENIUS!
KIRKMAN & SCOTT

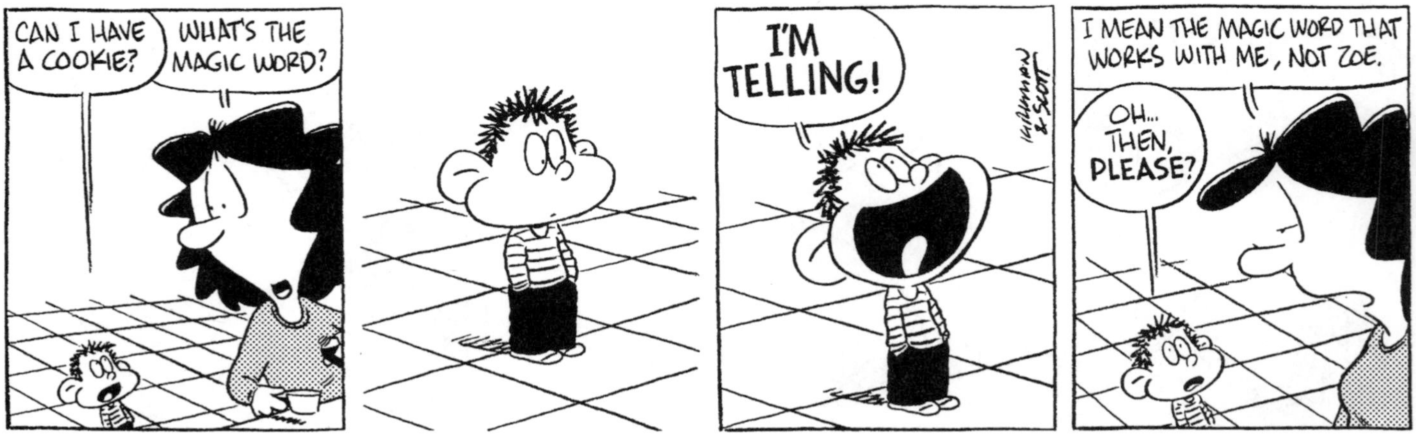
CAN I HAVE A COOKIE?
WHAT'S THE MAGIC WORD?
I'M TELLING!
KIRKMAN & SCOTT
I MEAN THE MAGIC WORD THAT WORKS WITH ME, NOT ZOE.
OH... THEN, PLEASE?

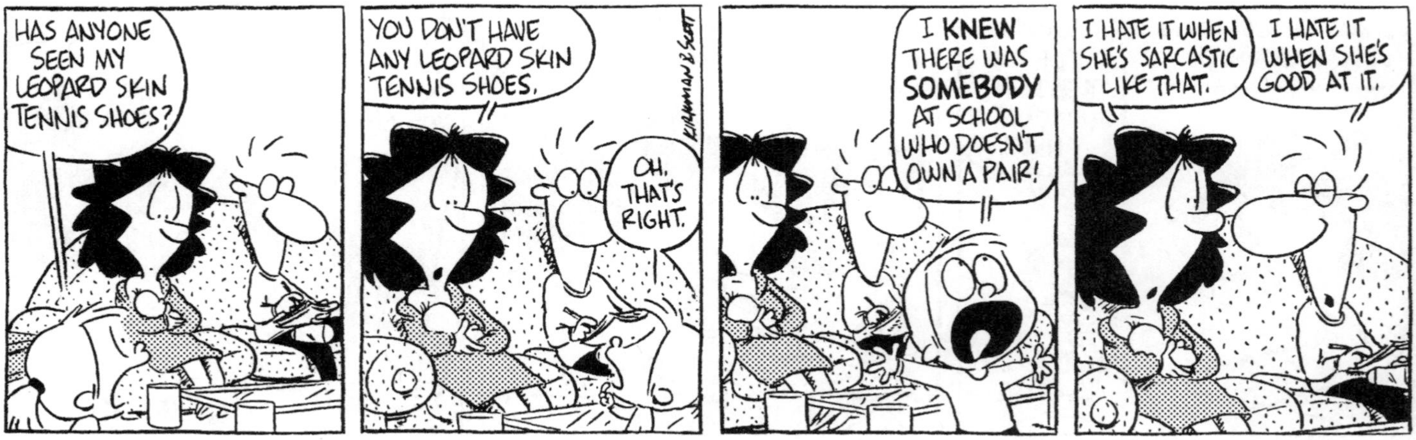
HAS ANYONE SEEN MY LEOPARD SKIN TENNIS SHOES?
YOU DON'T HAVE ANY LEOPARD SKIN TENNIS SHOES.
OH. THAT'S RIGHT.
KIRKMAN & SCOTT
I KNEW THERE WAS SOMEBODY AT SCHOOL WHO DOESN'T OWN A PAIR!
I HATE IT WHEN SHE'S SARCASTIC LIKE THAT.
I HATE IT WHEN SHE'S GOOD AT IT.

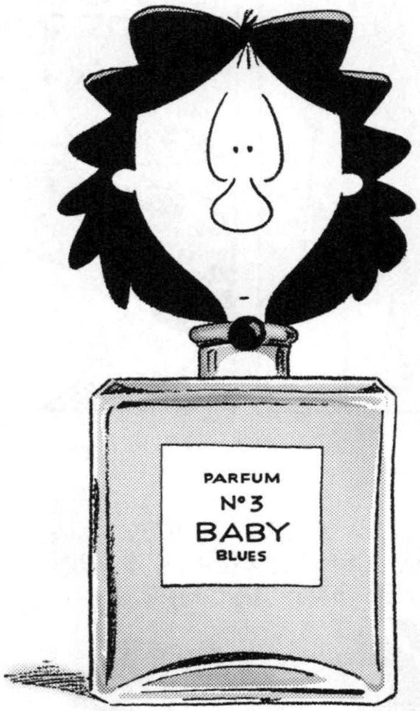
PARFUM
N°3
BABY
BLUES

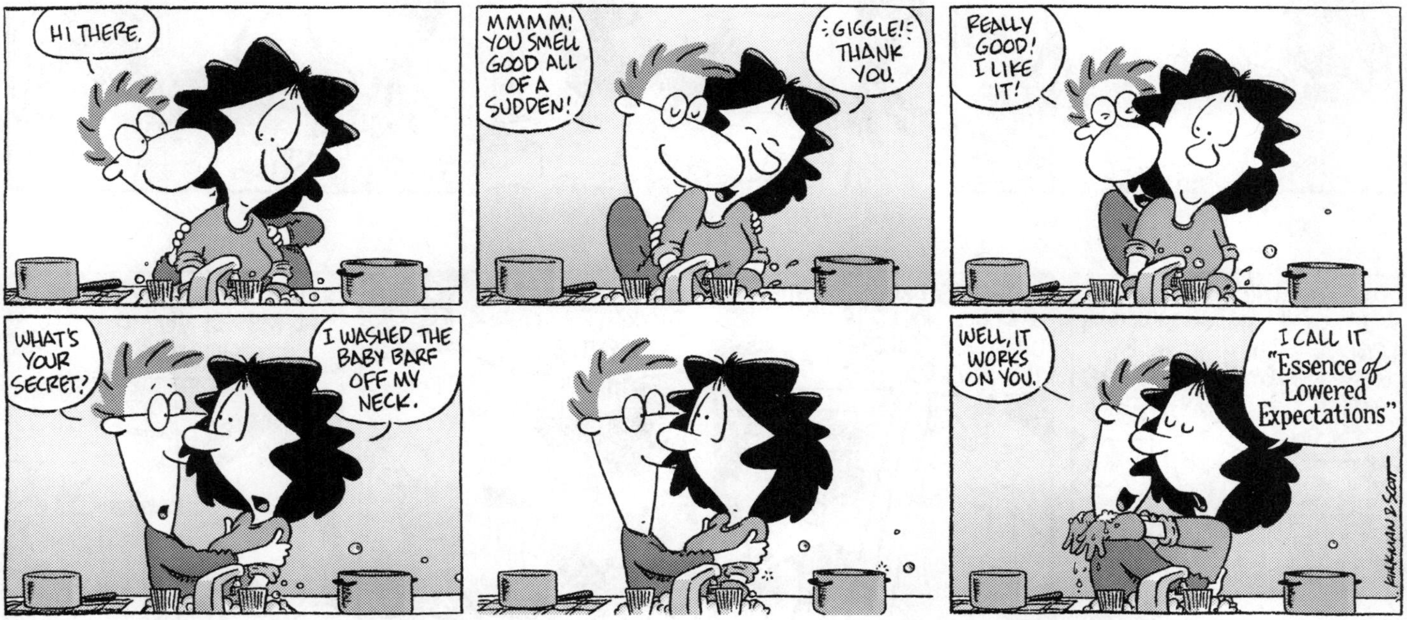
HI THERE.
MMMM! YOU SMELL GOOD ALL OF A SUDDEN!
GIGGLE! THANK YOU.
REALLY GOOD! I LIKE IT!
WHAT'S YOUR SECRET?
I WASHED THE BABY BARF OFF MY NECK.
WELL, IT WORKS ON YOU.
I CALL IT "Essence of Lowered Expectations"
KIRKMAN & SCOTT

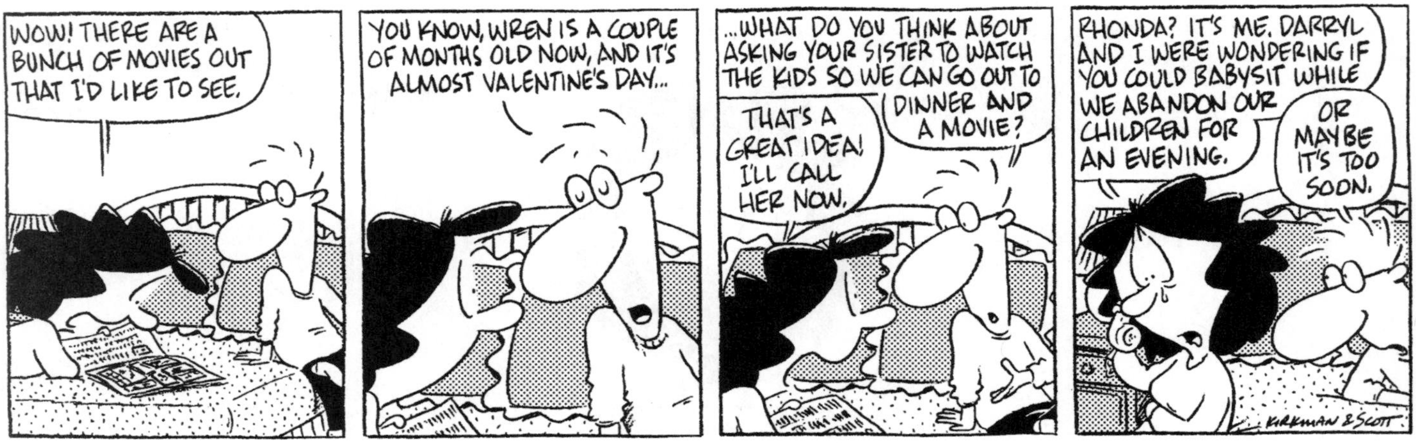
WOW! THERE ARE A BUNCH OF MOVIES OUT THAT I'D LIKE TO SEE.
YOU KNOW, WREN IS A COUPLE OF MONTHS OLD NOW, AND IT'S ALMOST VALENTINE'S DAY...
...WHAT DO YOU THINK ABOUT ASKING YOUR SISTER TO WATCH THE KIDS SO WE CAN GO OUT TO DINNER AND A MOVIE?
THAT'S A GREAT IDEA! I'LL CALL HER NOW.
RHONDA? IT'S ME. DARRYL AND I WERE WONDERING IF YOU COULD BABYSIT WHILE WE ABANDON OUR CHILDREN FOR AN EVENING.
OR MAYBE IT'S TOO SOON.
KIRKMAN & SCOTT

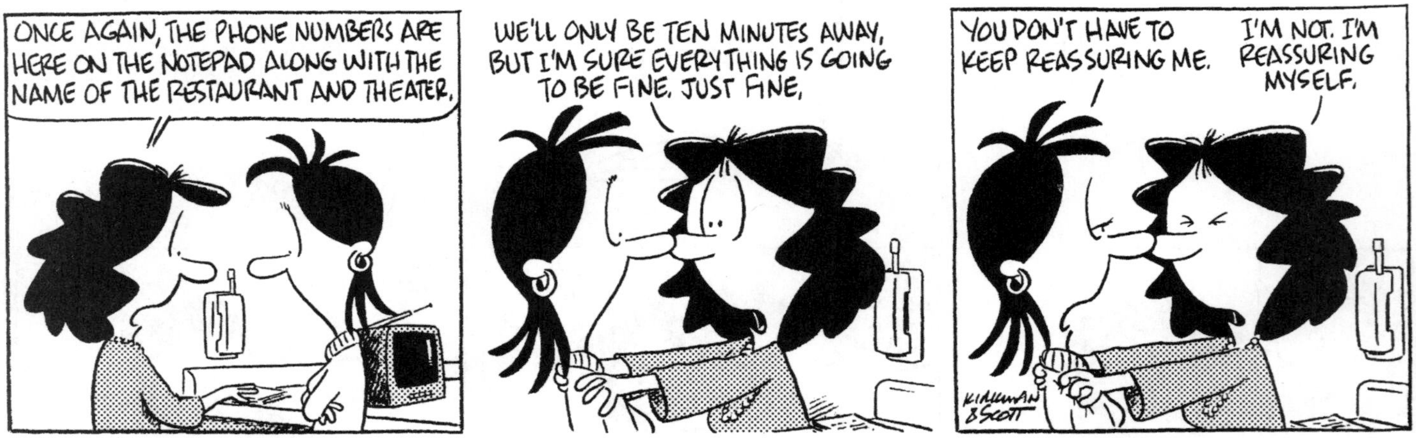
ONCE AGAIN, THE PHONE NUMBERS ARE HERE ON THE NOTEPAD ALONG WITH THE NAME OF THE RESTAURANT AND THEATER.
WE'LL ONLY BE TEN MINUTES AWAY, BUT I'M SURE EVERYTHING IS GOING TO BE FINE. JUST FINE.
YOU DON'T HAVE TO KEEP REASSURING ME.
I'M NOT. I'M REASSURING MYSELF.
KIRKMAN & SCOTT

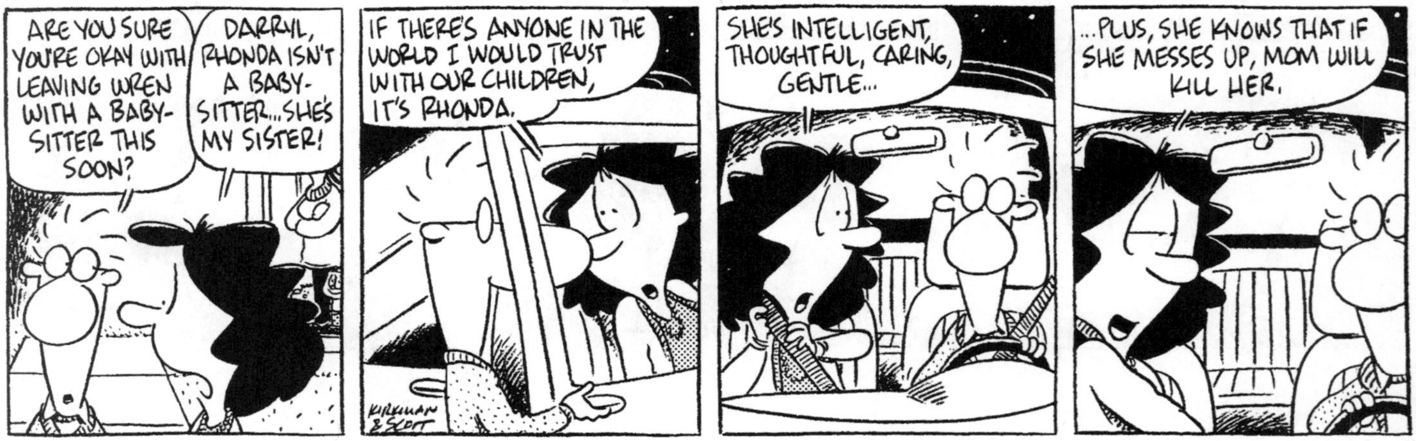
ARE YOU SURE YOU'RE OKAY WITH LEAVING WREN WITH A BABY-SITTER THIS SOON?
DARRYL, RHONDA ISN'T A BABY-SITTER...SHE'S MY SISTER!
IF THERE'S ANYONE IN THE WORLD I WOULD TRUST WITH OUR CHILDREN, IT'S RHONDA.
KIRKMAN & SCOTT
SHE'S INTELLIGENT, THOUGHTFUL, CARING, GENTLE...
...PLUS, SHE KNOWS THAT IF SHE MESSES UP, MOM WILL KILL HER.

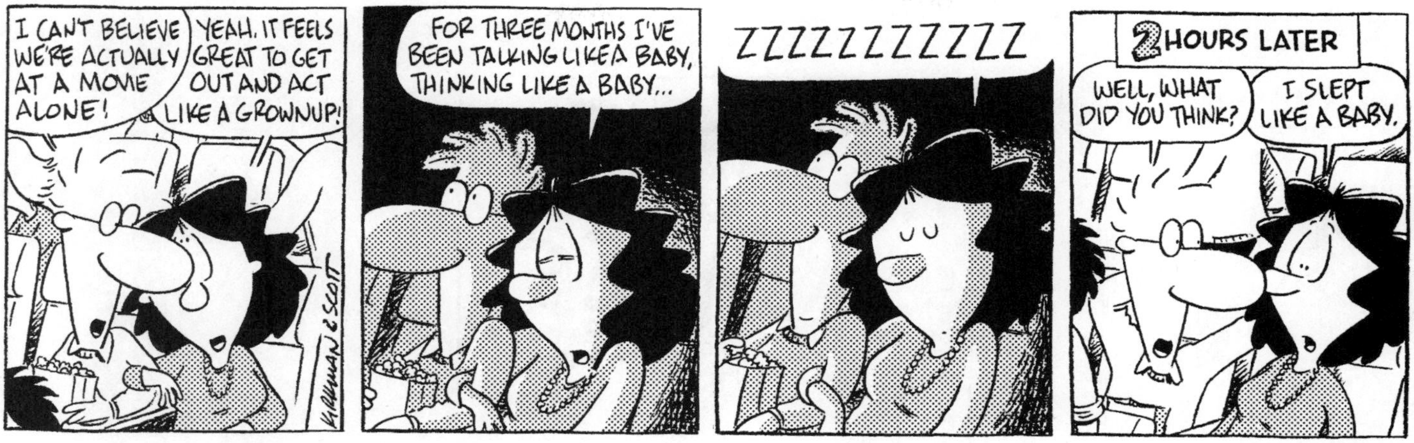
I CAN'T BELIEVE WE'RE ACTUALLY AT A MOVIE ALONE!
YEAH, IT FEELS GREAT TO GET OUT AND ACT LIKE A GROWNUP!
KIRKMAN & SCOTT
FOR THREE MONTHS I'VE BEEN TALKING LIKE A BABY, THINKING LIKE A BABY...
ZZZZZZZZZZZ
2 HOURS LATER
WELL, WHAT DID YOU THINK?
I SLEPT LIKE A BABY.

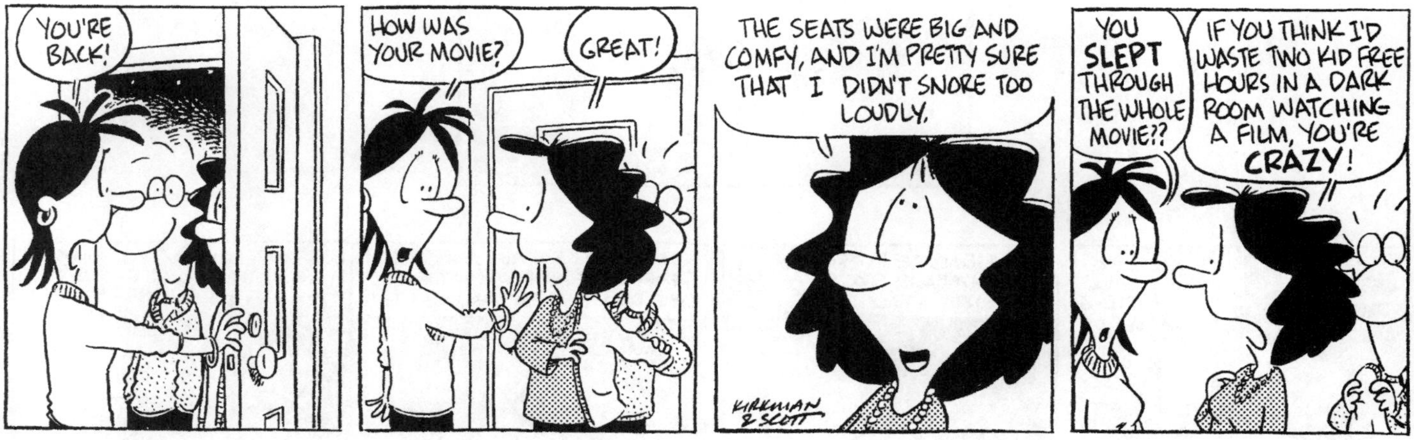
YOU'RE BACK!
HOW WAS YOUR MOVIE?
GREAT!
THE SEATS WERE BIG AND COMFY, AND I'M PRETTY SURE THAT I DIDN'T SNORE TOO LOUDLY.
KIRKMAN & SCOTT
YOU SLEPT THROUGH THE WHOLE MOVIE??
IF YOU THINK I'D WASTE TWO KID FREE HOURS IN A DARK ROOM WATCHING A FILM, YOU'RE CRAZY!

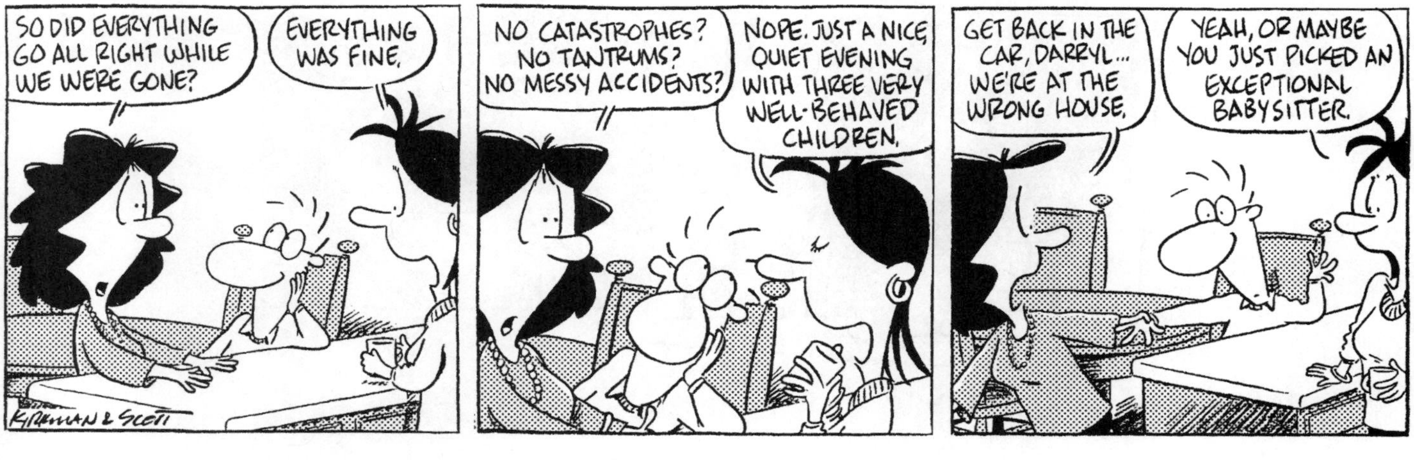
SO DID EVERYTHING GO ALL RIGHT WHILE WE WERE GONE?
EVERYTHING WAS FINE.
KIRKMAN & SCOTT
NO CATASTROPHES? NO TANTRUMS? NO MESSY ACCIDENTS?
NOPE. JUST A NICE, QUIET EVENING WITH THREE VERY WELL-BEHAVED CHILDREN.
GET BACK IN THE CAR, DARRYL... WE'RE AT THE WRONG HOUSE.
YEAH, OR MAYBE YOU JUST PICKED AN EXCEPTIONAL BABYSITTER.

BABY BLUES®
RICK KIRKMAN / BY / JERRY SCOTT
THIS SIDE UP

IN YOU GO, SWEETHEART.
YOU'RE STILL PUTTING HER ON HER BACK, RIGHT?
Z
OF COURSE. ALL THE EXPERTS AGREE THAT BABIES SHOULD SLEEP ON THEIR BACKS.
I KNOW.
BUT WHEN WE WERE KIDS, IT WAS JUST THE OPPOSITE. EVERYBODY PUT THEIR BABIES DOWN ON THEIR TUMMIES TO SLEEP.
Z
EVERYBODY EXCEPT MY FOLKS, THAT IS.
MY MOM SAYS THEY KNEW I SHOULD SLEEP ON MY BACK FROM THE DAY I WAS BORN.
Z
I GUESS THEY WERE JUST AHEAD OF THEIR TIME.
YEAH. THAT WAS PROBABLY IT.
Z

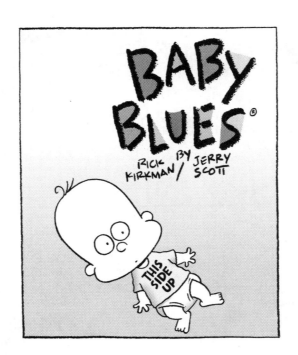

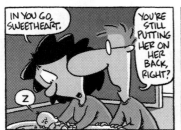

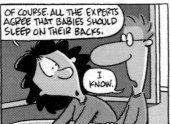

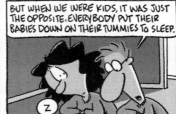

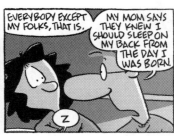

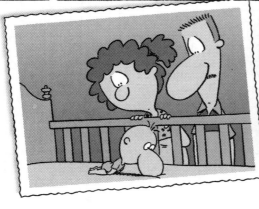

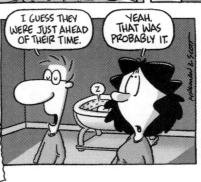

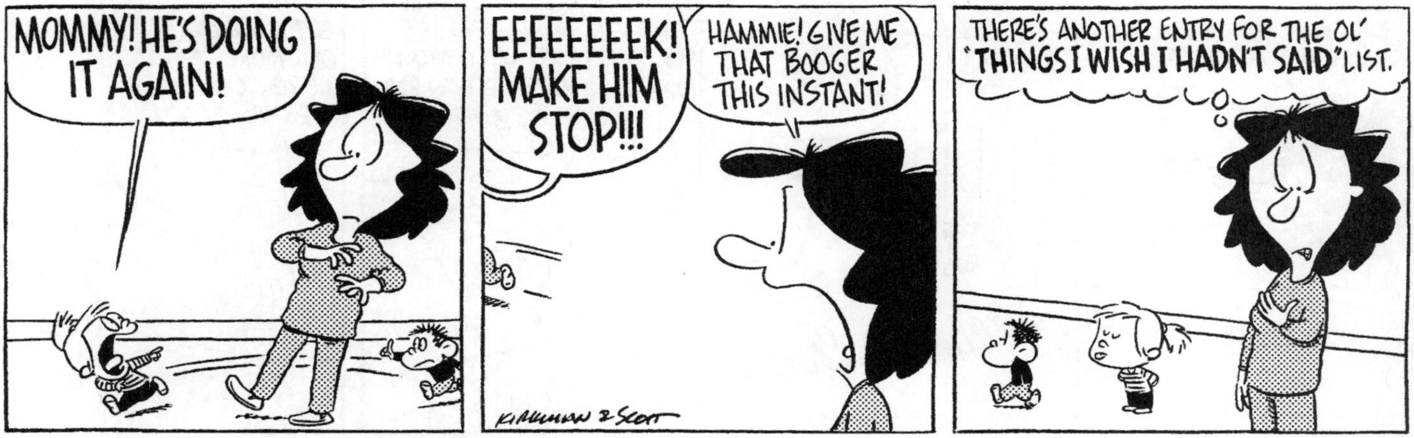
MOMMY! HE'S DOING IT AGAIN!
EEEEEEEEK! MAKE HIM STOP!!!
HAMMIE! GIVE ME THAT BOOGER THIS INSTANT!
KIRKMAN & SCOTT
THERE'S ANOTHER ENTRY FOR THE OL' "THINGS I WISH I HADN'T SAID" LIST.

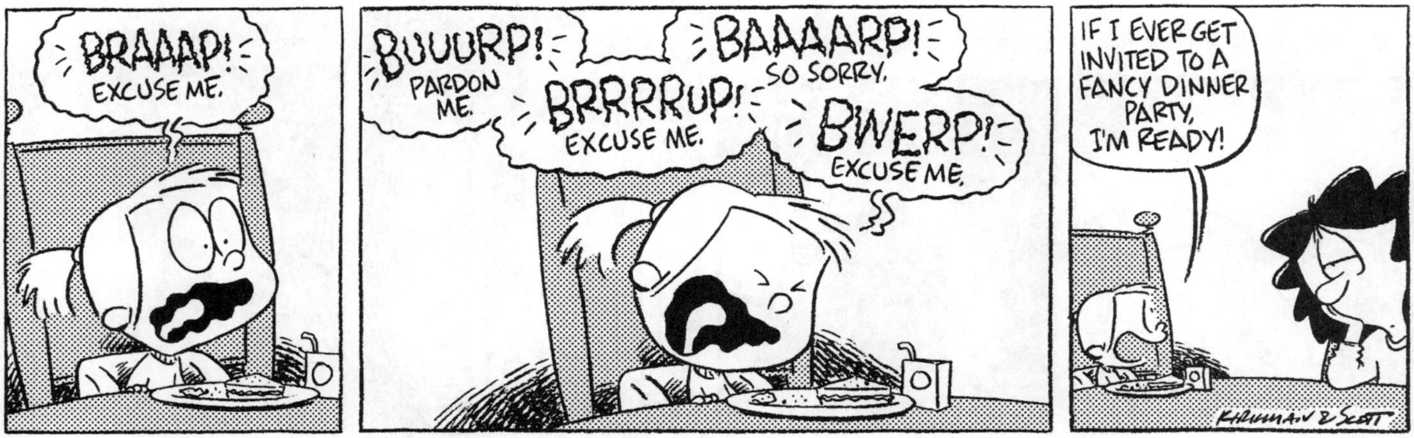
BRAAAP! EXCUSE ME.
BUUURP! PARDON ME.
BAAAAARP! SO SORRY.
BRRRRRUP! EXCUSE ME.
BWERP! EXCUSE ME.
IF I EVER GET INVITED TO A FANCY DINNER PARTY, I'M READY!
KIRKMAN & SCOTT

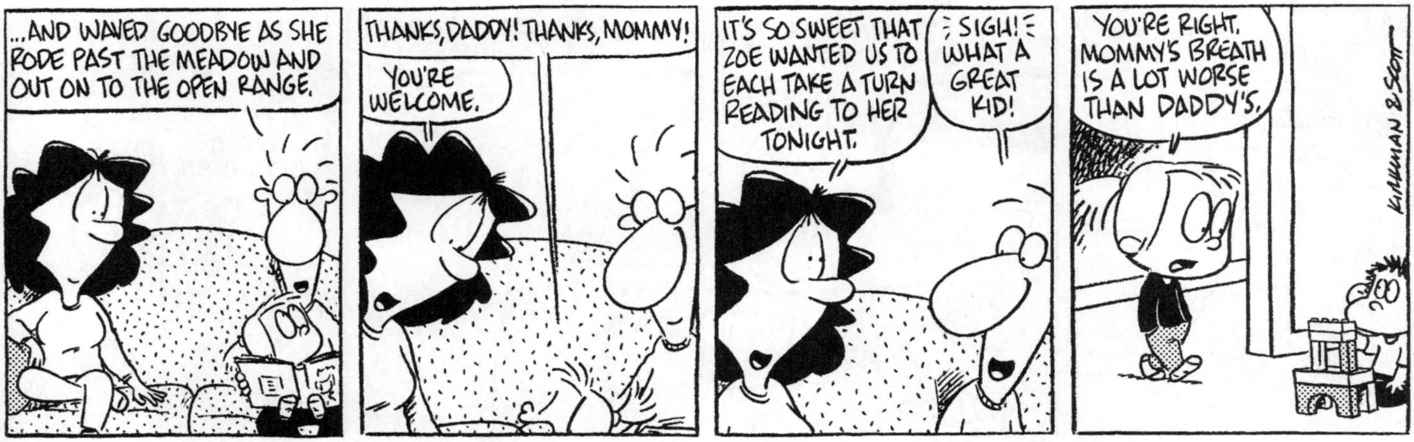
...AND WAVED GOODBYE AS SHE RODE PAST THE MEADOW AND OUT ON TO THE OPEN RANGE.
THANKS, DADDY! THANKS, MOMMY!
YOU'RE WELCOME.
IT'S SO SWEET THAT ZOE WANTED US TO EACH TAKE A TURN READING TO HER TONIGHT.
SIGH! WHAT A GREAT KID!
YOU'RE RIGHT. MOMMY'S BREATH IS A LOT WORSE THAN DADDY'S.
KIRKMAN & SCOTT

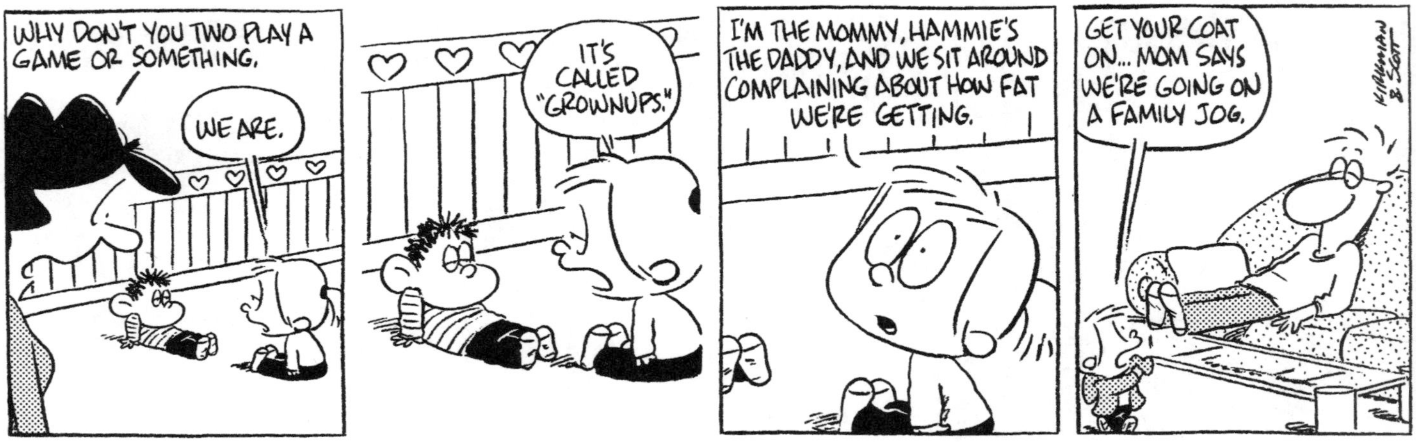
WHY DON'T YOU TWO PLAY A GAME OR SOMETHING.
WE ARE.
IT'S CALLED "GROWNUPS."
I'M THE MOMMY, HAMMIE'S THE DADDY, AND WE SIT AROUND COMPLAINING ABOUT HOW FAT WE'RE GETTING.
GET YOUR COAT ON... MOM SAYS WE'RE GOING ON A FAMILY JOG.
KIRKMAN & SCOTT

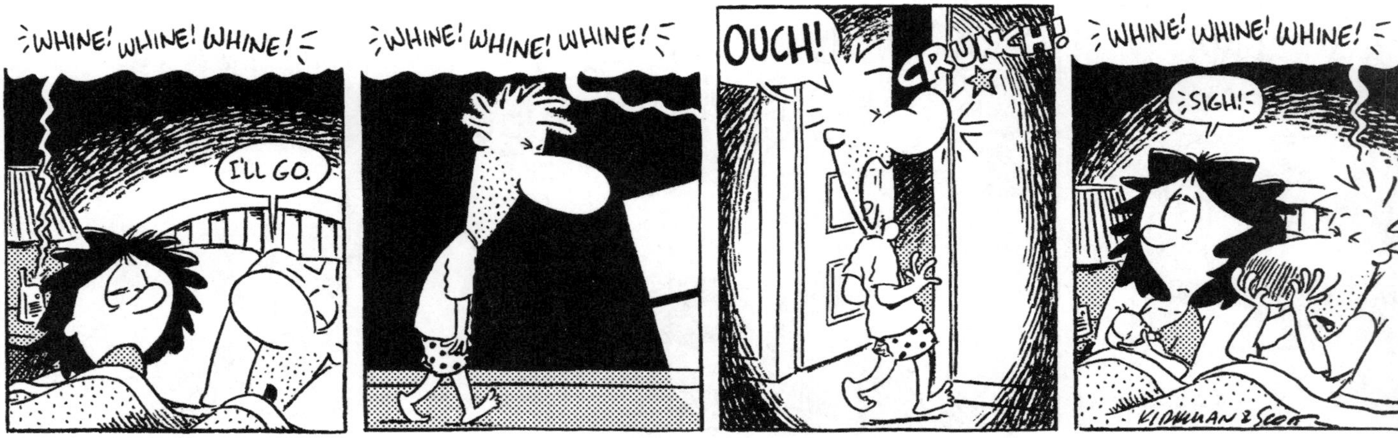
WHINE! WHINE! WHINE!
I'LL GO.
WHINE! WHINE! WHINE!
OUCH!
CRUNCH!
WHINE! WHINE! WHINE!
SIGH!
KIRKMAN & SCOTT

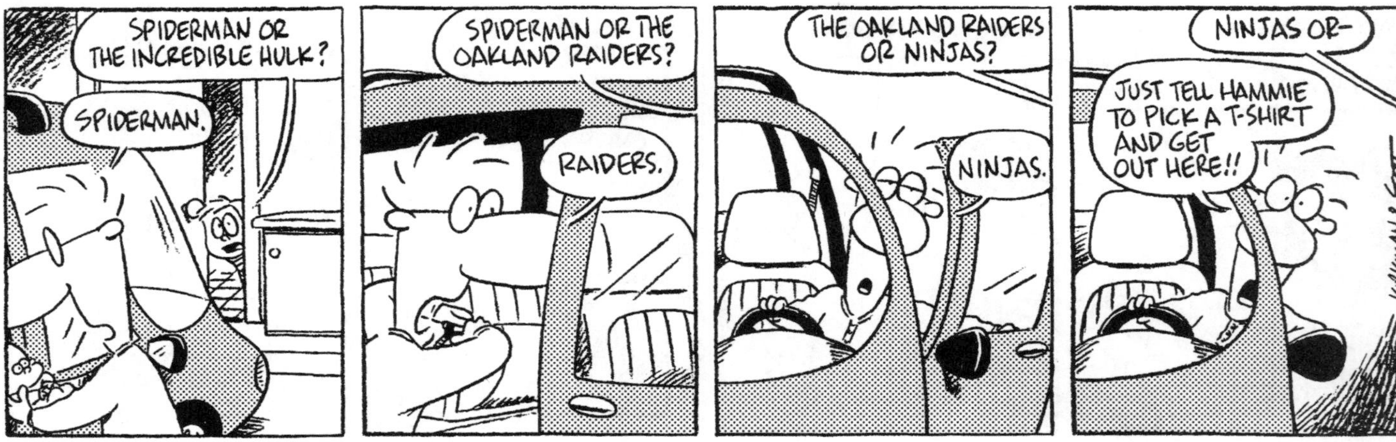
SPIDERMAN OR THE INCREDIBLE HULK?
SPIDERMAN.
SPIDERMAN OR THE OAKLAND RAIDERS?
RAIDERS.
THE OAKLAND RAIDERS OR NINJAS?
NINJAS.
NINJAS OR-
JUST TELL HAMMIE TO PICK A T-SHIRT AND GET OUT HERE!!
KIRKMAN & SCOTT

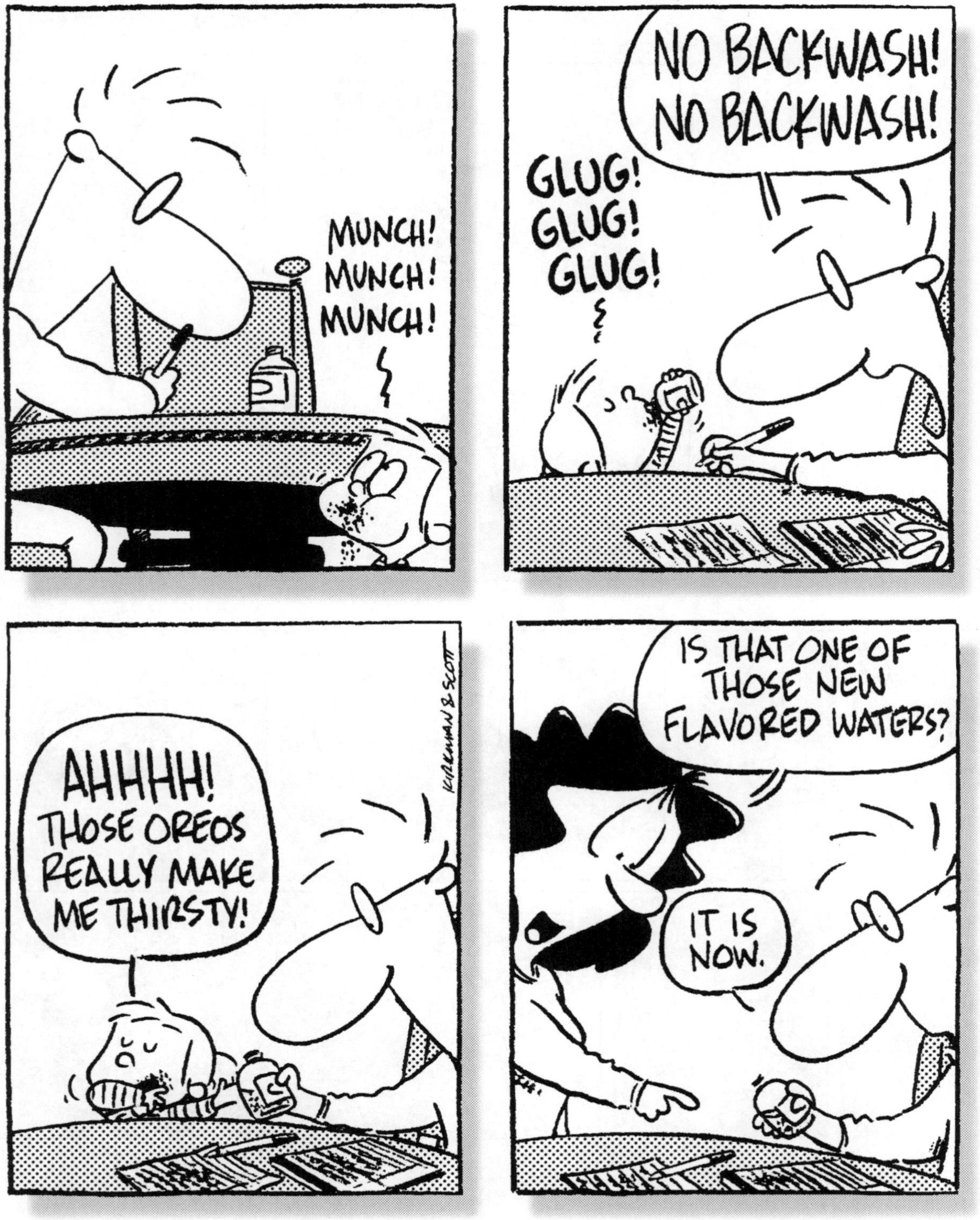
MUNCH! MUNCH! MUNCH!
NO BACKWASH! NO BACKWASH!
GLUG! GLUG! GLUG!
KIRKMAN & SCOTT
AHHHH! THOSE OREOS REALLY MAKE ME THIRSTY!
IS THAT ONE OF THOSE NEW FLAVORED WATERS?
IT IS NOW.

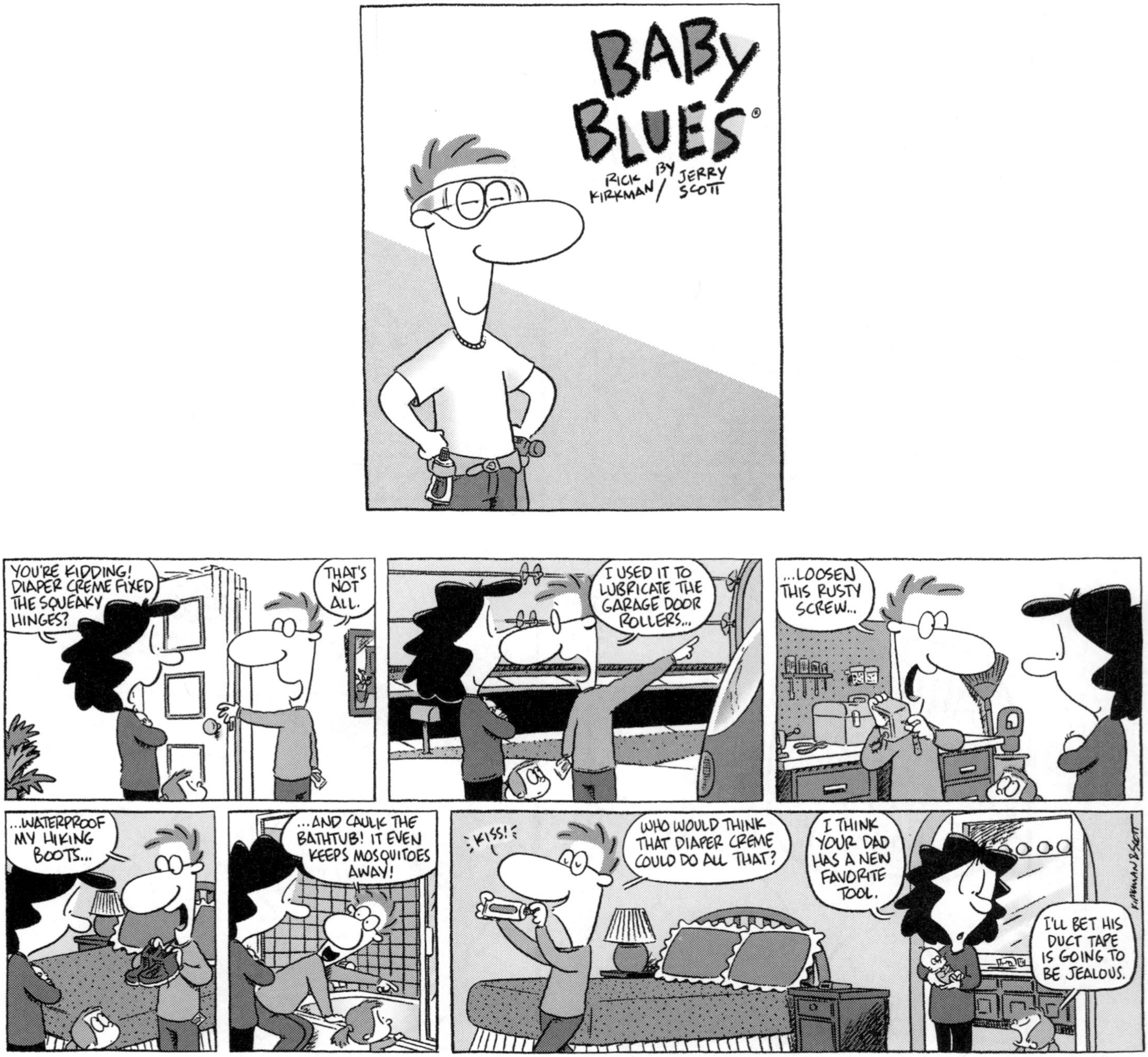
BABY BLUES®
BY RICK KIRKMAN / JERRY SCOTT
YOU'RE KIDDING! DIAPER CREME FIXED THE SQUEAKY HINGES?
THAT'S NOT ALL.
I USED IT TO LUBRICATE THE GARAGE DOOR ROLLERS...
...LOOSEN THIS RUSTY SCREW...
...WATERPROOF MY HIKING BOOTS...
...AND CAULK THE BATHTUB! IT EVEN KEEPS MOSQUITOES AWAY!
KISS!
WHO WOULD THINK THAT DIAPER CREME COULD DO ALL THAT?
I THINK YOUR DAD HAS A NEW FAVORITE TOOL.
I'LL BET HIS DUCT TAPE IS GOING TO BE JEALOUS.
KIRKMAN & SCOTT

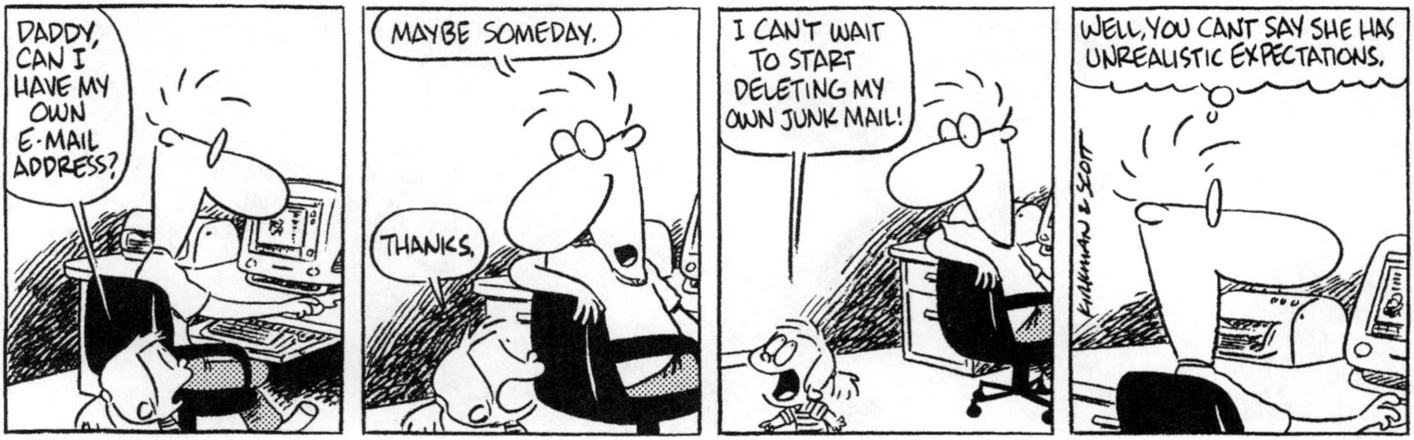
DADDY, CAN I HAVE MY OWN E-MAIL ADDRESS?
MAYBE SOMEDAY.
THANKS.
I CAN'T WAIT TO START DELETING MY OWN JUNK MAIL!
WELL, YOU CAN'T SAY SHE HAS UNREALISTIC EXPECTATIONS.
KIRKMAN & SCOTT

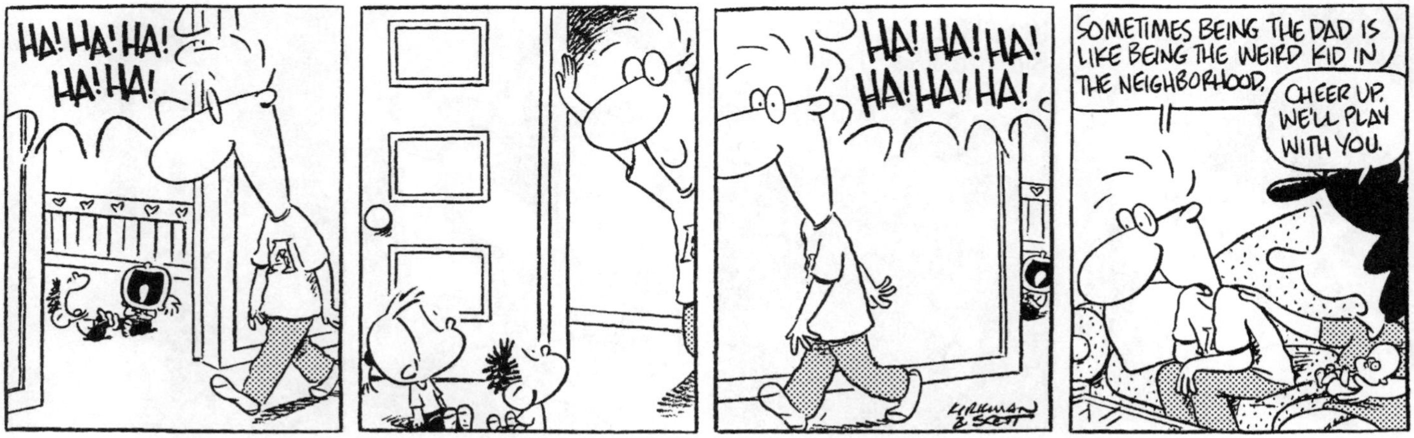
HA! HA! HA! HA! HA!
HA! HA! HA! HA! HA! HA!
KIRKMAN & SCOTT
SOMETIMES BEING THE DAD IS LIKE BEING THE WEIRD KID IN THE NEIGHBORHOOD.
CHEER UP. WE'LL PLAY WITH YOU.

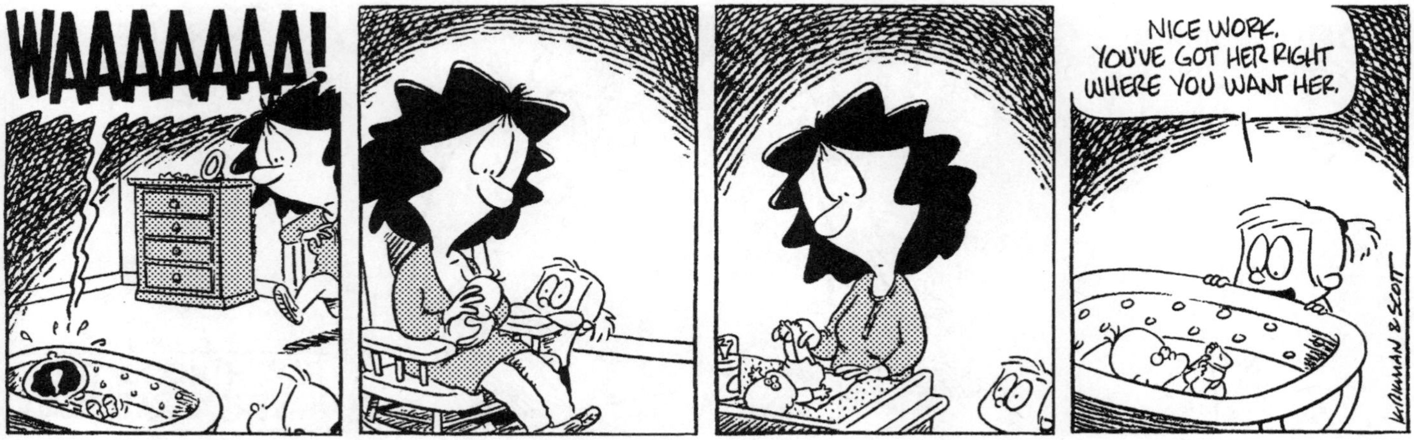
WAAAAAAA!
NICE WORK. YOU'VE GOT HER RIGHT WHERE YOU WANT HER.
KIRKMAN & SCOTT

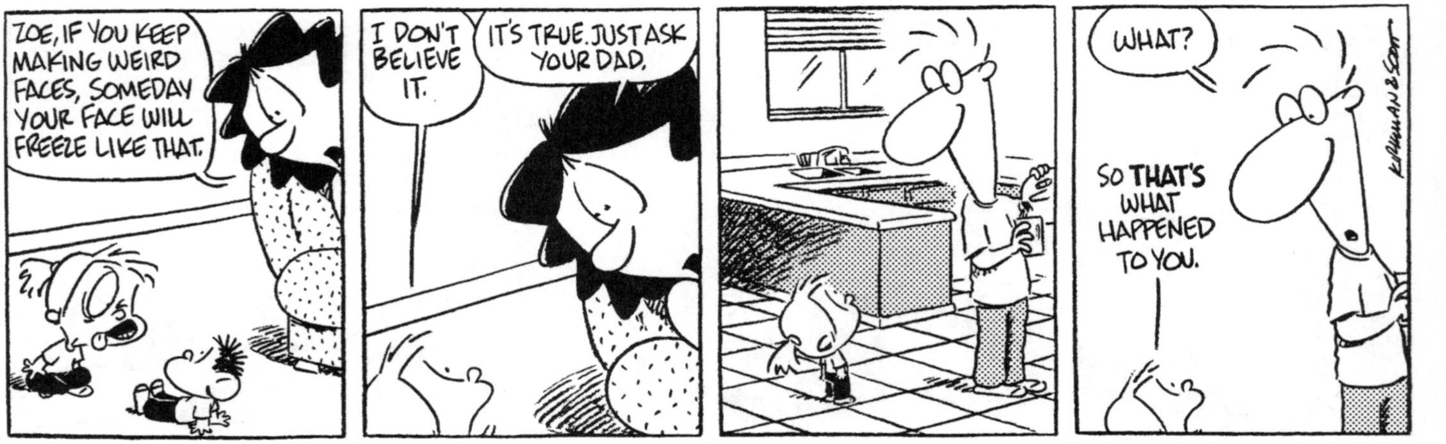
ZOE, IF YOU KEEP MAKING WEIRD FACES, SOMEDAY YOUR FACE WILL FREEZE LIKE THAT.
I DON'T BELIEVE IT.
IT'S TRUE. JUST ASK YOUR DAD.
WHAT?
SO **THAT'S** WHAT HAPPENED TO YOU.
KIRKMAN & SCOTT

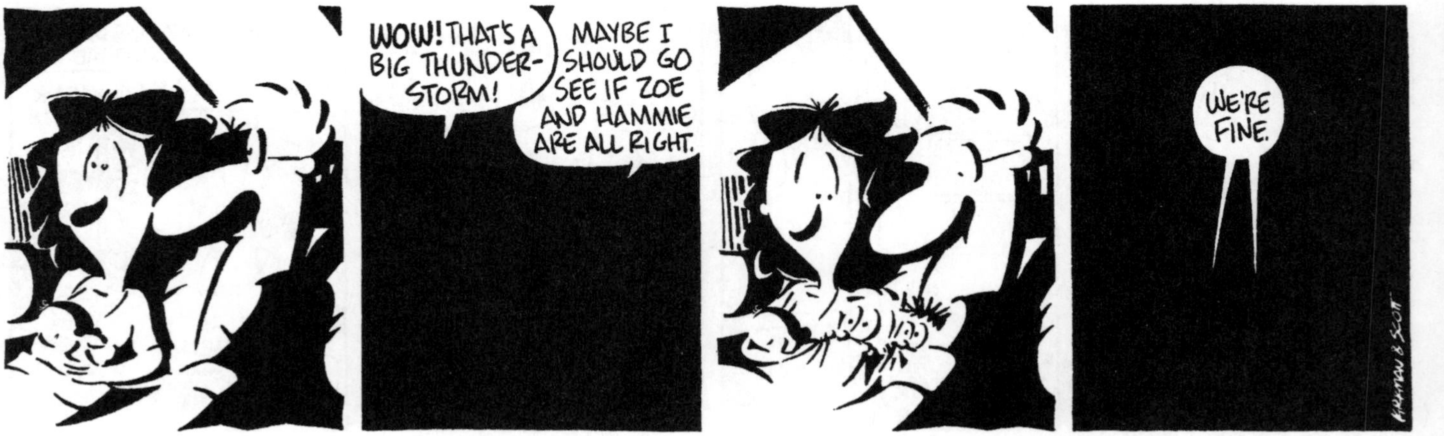
WOW! THAT'S A BIG THUNDERSTORM!
MAYBE I SHOULD GO SEE IF ZOE AND HAMMIE ARE ALL RIGHT.
WE'RE FINE.
KIRKMAN & SCOTT

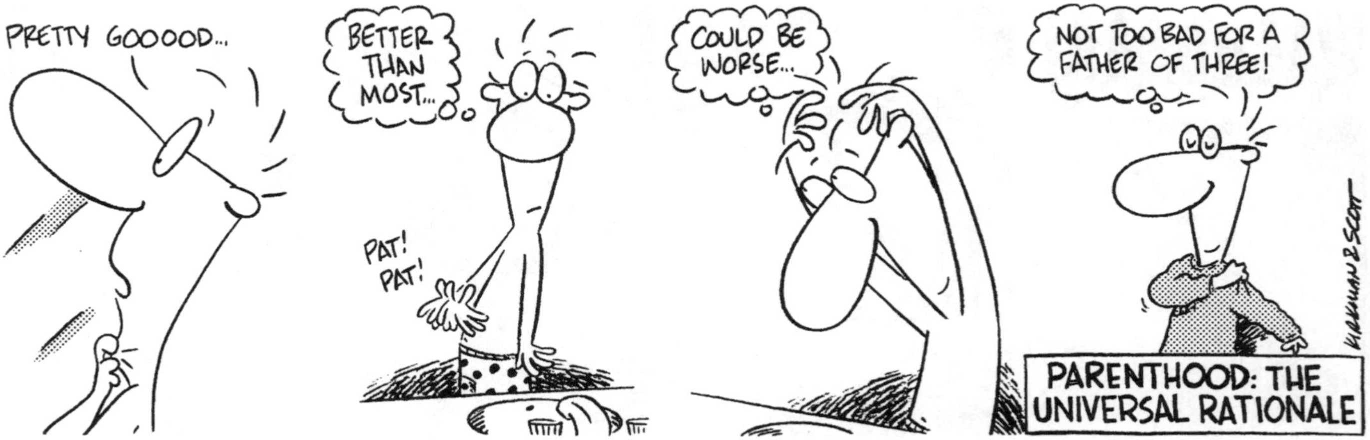
PRETTY GOOOOD...
BETTER THAN MOST...
PAT! PAT!
COULD BE WORSE...
NOT TOO BAD FOR A FATHER OF THREE!
KIRKMAN & SCOTT
PARENTHOOD: THE UNIVERSAL RATIONALE

BABY BLUES®
BY
RICK KIRKMAN / JERRY SCOTT

ARE YOU JEALOUS OF BABY WREN?
I DON'T THINK SO. ARE YOU?
HECK, NO! SHE'S MY BABY SISTER!
MINE, TOO!
I MEAN, SO WHAT IF SHE GETS ALL THE ATTENTION THESE DAYS?
YEAH! SO WHAT?
WHO CARES IF SHE'S THE ONLY THING ANYBODY EVER TALKS ABOUT ANYMORE?
NOT ME!
ME EITHER! BECAUSE WE'RE HER FAMILY, AND FAMILIES NEED TO STICK TOGETHER!
RIGHT!
BESIDES, I STILL HAVE YOU TO PUSH AROUND.
YEAH!
KIRKMAN & SCOTT
WAIT...

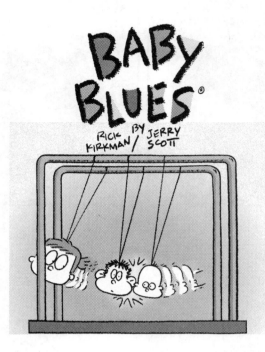

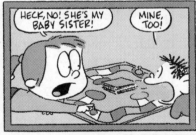

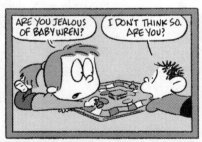

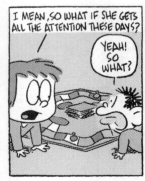

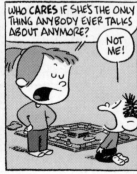

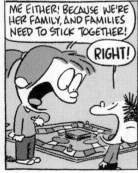

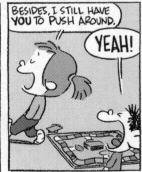

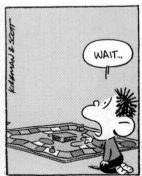

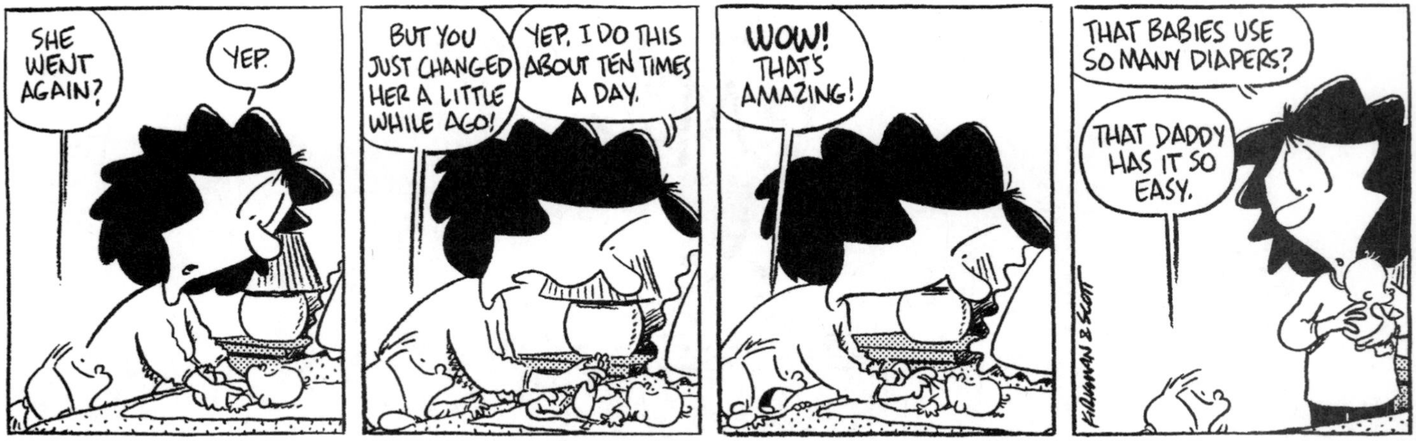
SHE WENT AGAIN?
YEP.
BUT YOU JUST CHANGED HER A LITTLE WHILE AGO!
YEP. I DO THIS ABOUT TEN TIMES A DAY.
WOW! THAT'S AMAZING!
THAT BABIES USE SO MANY DIAPERS?
THAT DADDY HAS IT SO EASY.

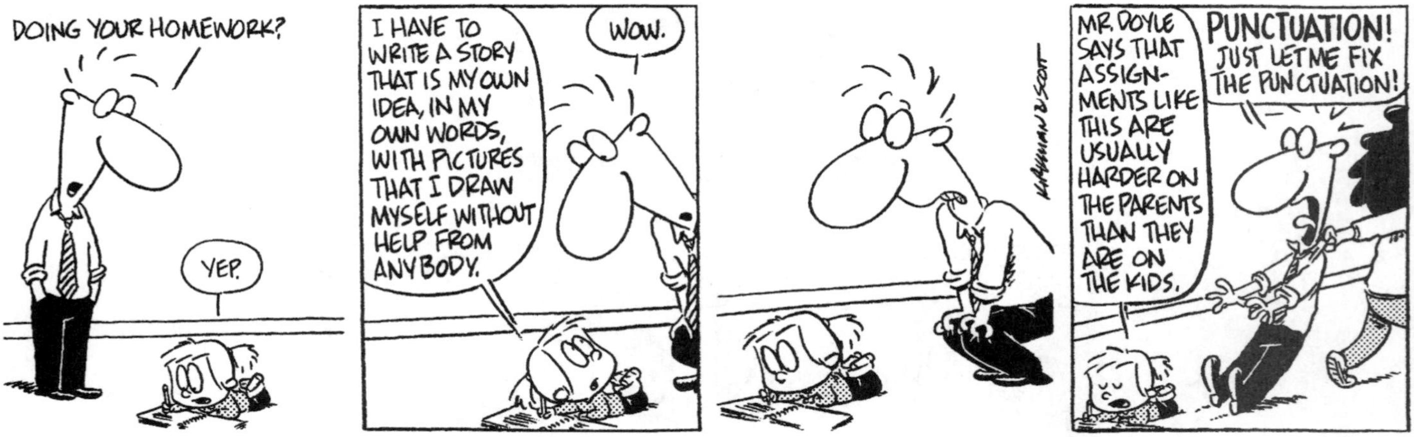
DOING YOUR HOMEWORK?
YEP.
I HAVE TO WRITE A STORY THAT IS MY OWN IDEA, IN MY OWN WORDS, WITH PICTURES THAT I DRAW MYSELF WITHOUT HELP FROM ANYBODY.
WOW.
MR. DOYLE SAYS THAT ASSIGNMENTS LIKE THIS ARE USUALLY HARDER ON THE PARENTS THAN THEY ARE ON THE KIDS.
PUNCTUATION! JUST LET ME FIX THE PUNCTUATION!

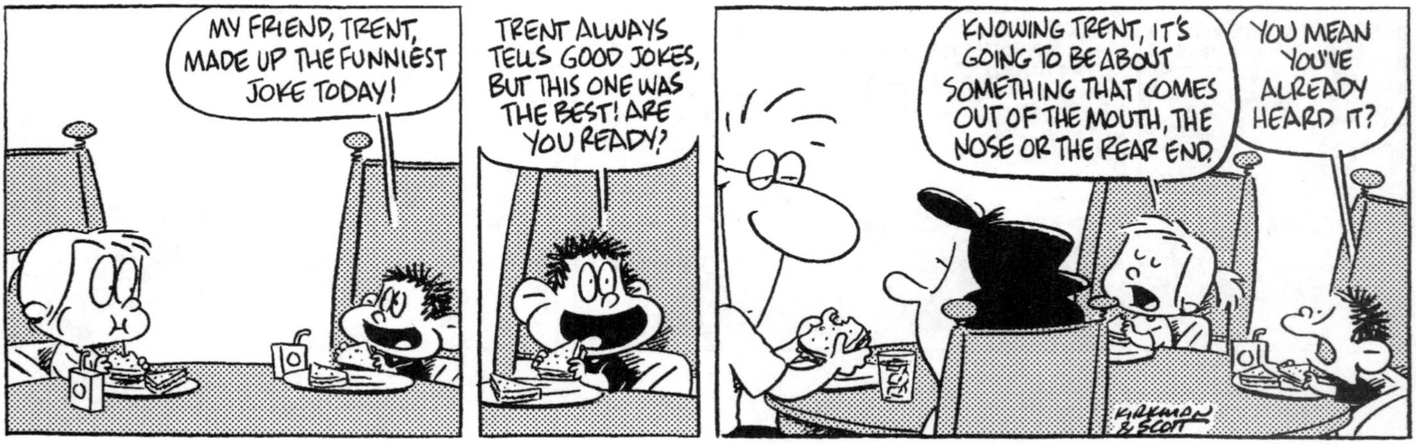
MY FRIEND, TRENT, MADE UP THE FUNNIEST JOKE TODAY!
TRENT ALWAYS TELLS GOOD JOKES, BUT THIS ONE WAS THE BEST! ARE YOU READY?
KNOWING TRENT, IT'S GOING TO BE ABOUT SOMETHING THAT COMES OUT OF THE MOUTH, THE NOSE OR THE REAR END.
YOU MEAN YOU'VE ALREADY HEARD IT?

A Baby Blues Restaurant
MacPherson's
Over One BILLION Toys

DADDY! CAN WE STOP HERE?
PLEASE? WE'RE STARVING! PLEASE? PLEASE? PLEASE?
SIGH
OKAY! OKAY! I GUESS IT IS ALMOST LUNCHTIME.
YAY!
HAVE A NICE DAY.
HEY! COME ON! WAIT 'TIL WE GET TO THE TABLE!
GIMME MINE! NO!
MINE FIRST!
RIP! TEAR! RIP! TEAR!
I GUESS I OUGHT TO START FEEDING YOU GUYS MORE OFTEN!
OKAY. LET'S GO.
I THOUGHT YOU SAID YOU GUYS WERE STARVING!
TOY-STARVING... NOT FOOD-STARVING.
CAN WE GO TO THE PLAYGROUND NOW?

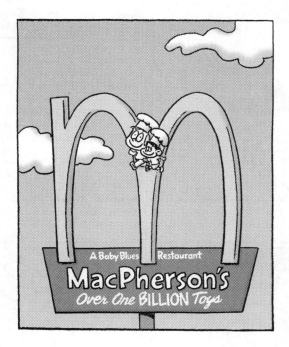

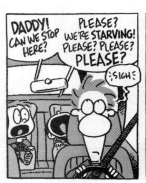

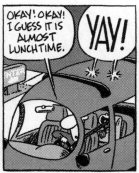

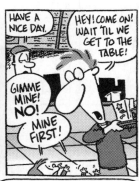

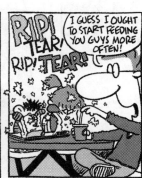

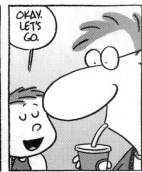

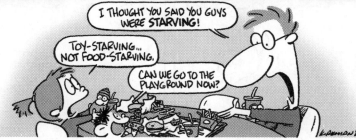

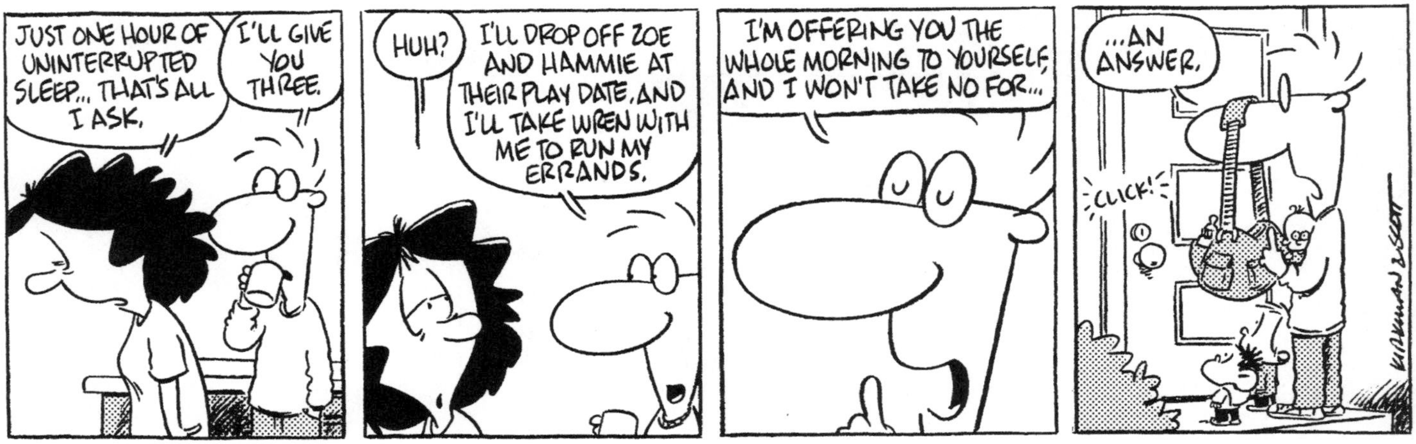
JUST ONE HOUR OF UNINTERRUPTED SLEEP... THAT'S ALL I ASK.
I'LL GIVE YOU THREE.
HUH?
I'LL DROP OFF ZOE AND HAMMIE AT THEIR PLAY DATE, AND I'LL TAKE WREN WITH ME TO RUN MY ERRANDS.
I'M OFFERING YOU THE WHOLE MORNING TO YOURSELF, AND I WON'T TAKE NO FOR...
CLICK!
...AN ANSWER.
KIRKMAN & SCOTT

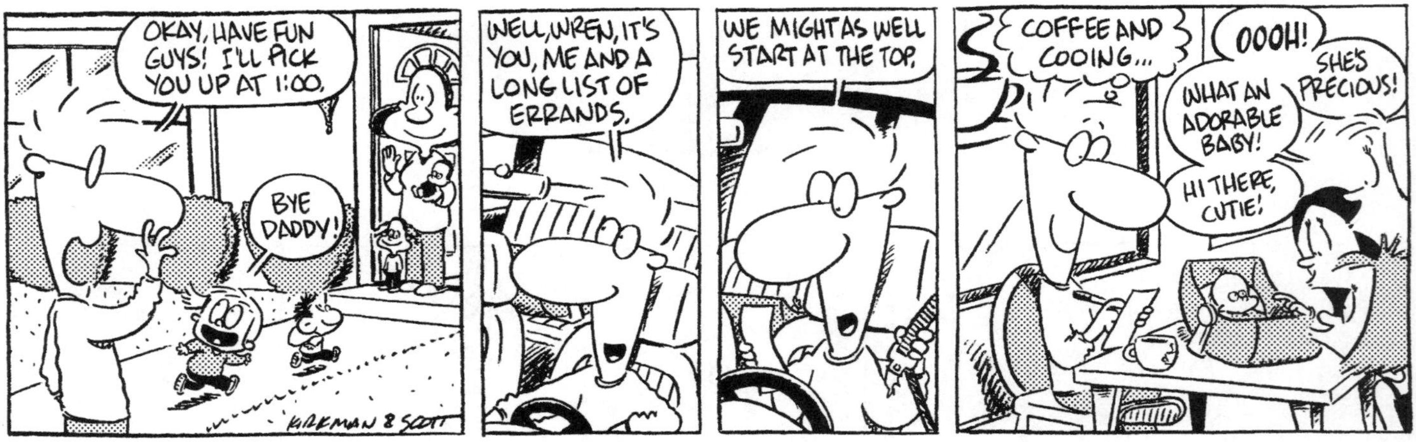
OKAY, HAVE FUN GUYS! I'LL PICK YOU UP AT 1:00.
BYE DADDY!
KIRKMAN & SCOTT
WELL, WREN, IT'S YOU, ME AND A LONG LIST OF ERRANDS.
WE MIGHT AS WELL START AT THE TOP.
COFFEE AND COOING...
OOOH!
SHE'S PRECIOUS!
WHAT AN ADORABLE BABY!
HI THERE, CUTIE!

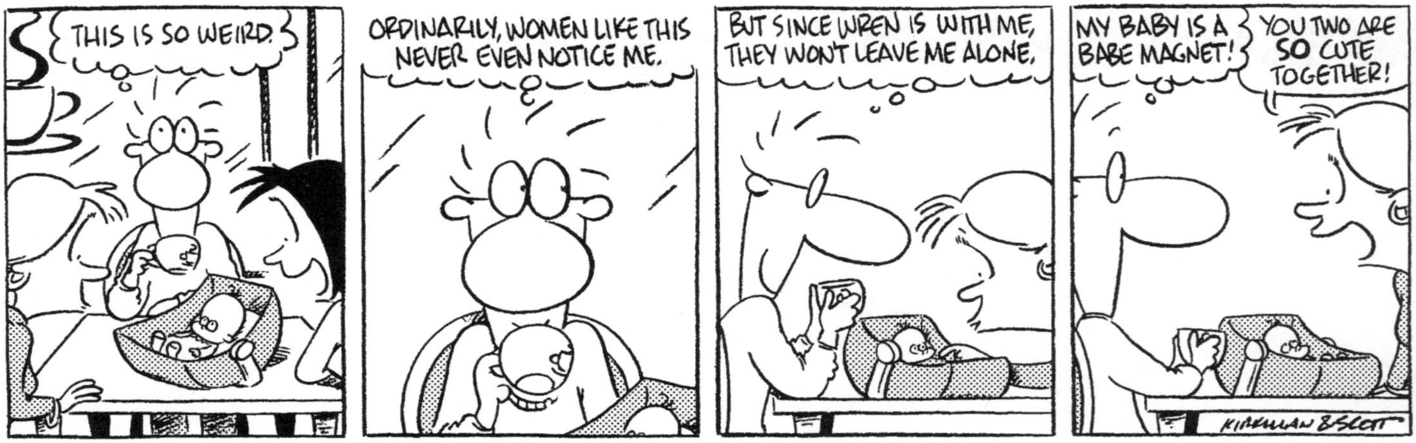
THIS IS SO WEIRD.
ORDINARILY, WOMEN LIKE THIS NEVER EVEN NOTICE ME.
BUT SINCE WREN IS WITH ME, THEY WON'T LEAVE ME ALONE.
MY BABY IS A BABE MAGNET!
YOU TWO ARE SO CUTE TOGETHER!
KIRKMAN & SCOTT

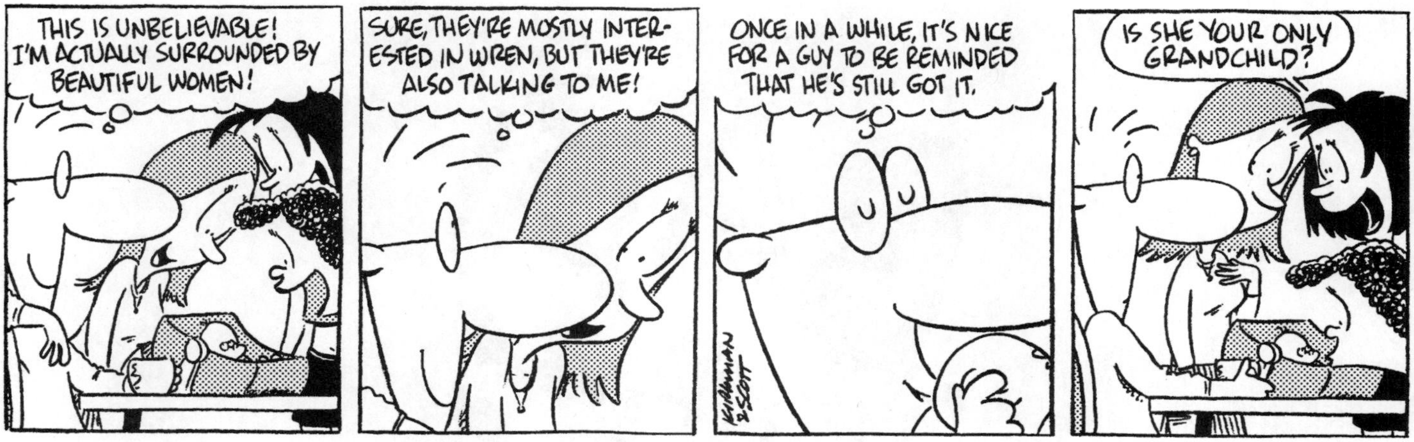
THIS IS UNBELIEVABLE! I'M ACTUALLY SURROUNDED BY BEAUTIFUL WOMEN!
SURE, THEY'RE MOSTLY INTER-ESTED IN WREN, BUT THEY'RE ALSO TALKING TO ME!
ONCE IN A WHILE, IT'S NICE FOR A GUY TO BE REMINDED THAT HE'S STILL GOT IT.
IS SHE YOUR ONLY GRANDCHILD?

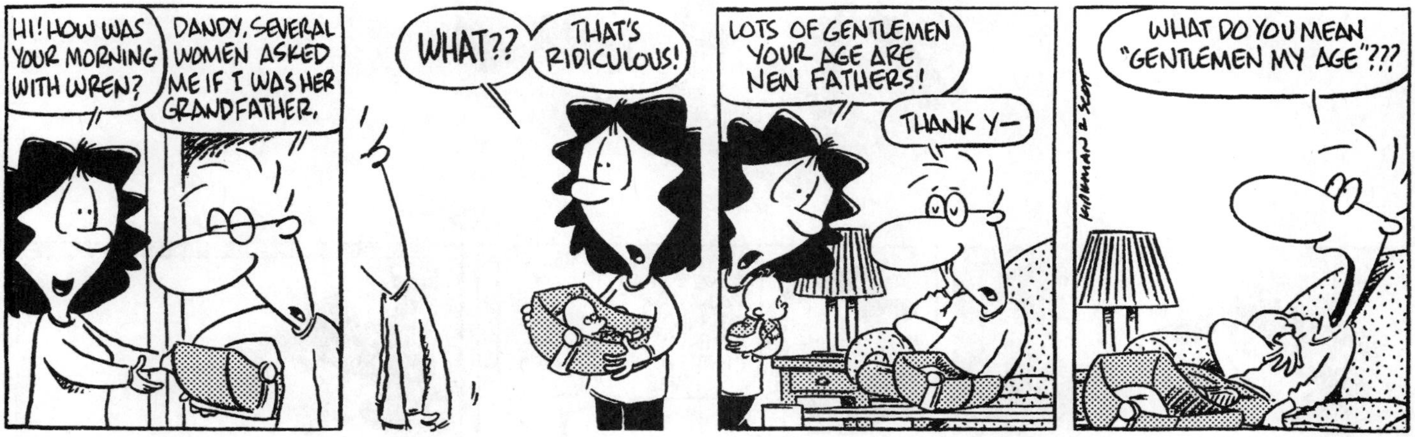
HI! HOW WAS YOUR MORNING WITH WREN?
DANDY. SEVERAL WOMEN ASKED ME IF I WAS HER GRANDFATHER.
WHAT??
THAT'S RIDICULOUS!
LOTS OF GENTLEMEN YOUR AGE ARE NEW FATHERS!
THANK Y—
WHAT DO YOU MEAN "GENTLEMEN MY AGE"???

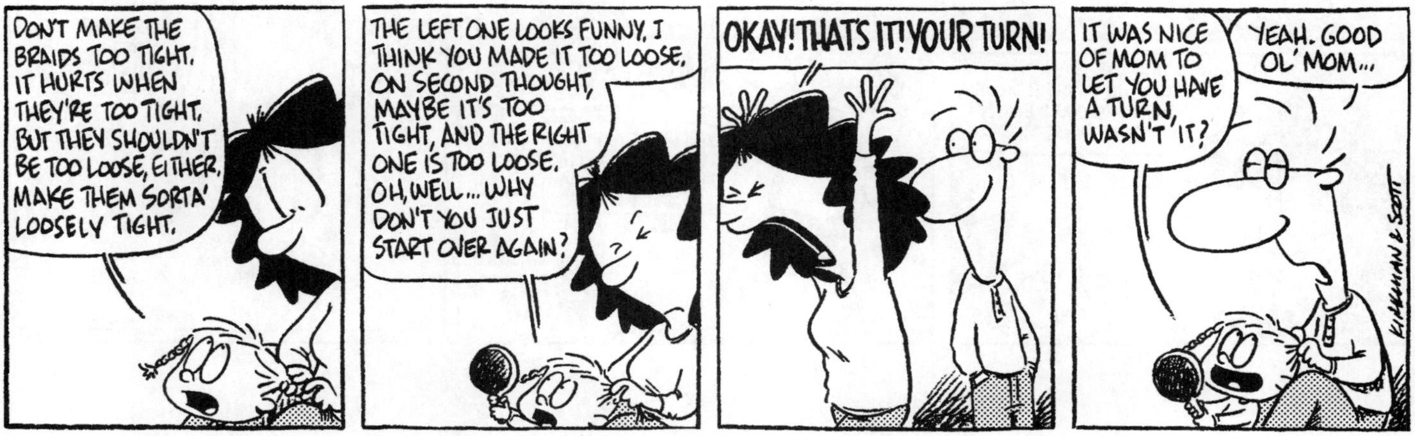
DON'T MAKE THE BRAIDS TOO TIGHT. IT HURTS WHEN THEY'RE TOO TIGHT. BUT THEY SHOULDN'T BE TOO LOOSE, EITHER. MAKE THEM SORTA' LOOSELY TIGHT.
THE LEFT ONE LOOKS FUNNY. I THINK YOU MADE IT TOO LOOSE. ON SECOND THOUGHT, MAYBE IT'S TOO TIGHT, AND THE RIGHT ONE IS TOO LOOSE. OH, WELL... WHY DON'T YOU JUST START OVER AGAIN?
OKAY! THAT'S IT! YOUR TURN!
IT WAS NICE OF MOM TO LET YOU HAVE A TURN, WASN'T IT?
YEAH. GOOD OL' MOM...

BABY BLUES
BY RICK KIRKMAN / JERRY SCOTT

LOOK AT THIS, GUYS...
ONE OF THESE DAYS, WREN IS GOING TO START CRAWLING AROUND, AND IT'S GOING TO BE VERY IMPORTANT THAT WE KEEP TINY TOYS LIKE THIS OFF THE FLOOR AND OUT OF HER REACH.
WHY?
BECAUSE BABIES PUT EVERYTHING IN THEIR MOUTHS, AND SHE COULD EASILY CHOKE ON THINGS LIKE THIS.
WAAAAAAAAAAAAA!
WHY DON'T YOU SEE IF YOU CAN FIND ANY MORE DANGEROUS TOYS WHILE I GET THE BABY.
YOU MEANT JUST THIS ROOM, AND NOT THE WHOLE HOUSE, RIGHT?
KIRKMAN & SCOTT

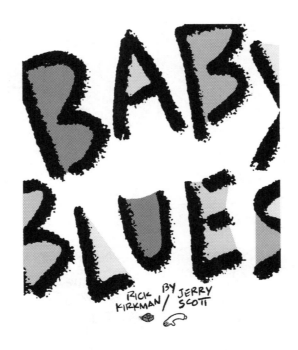

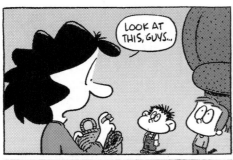

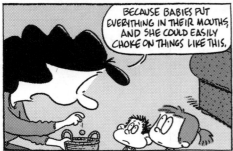

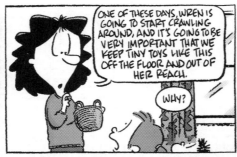

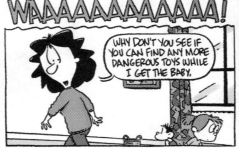

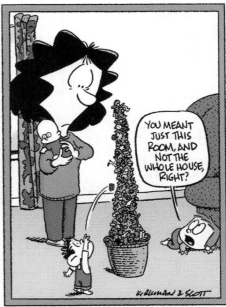

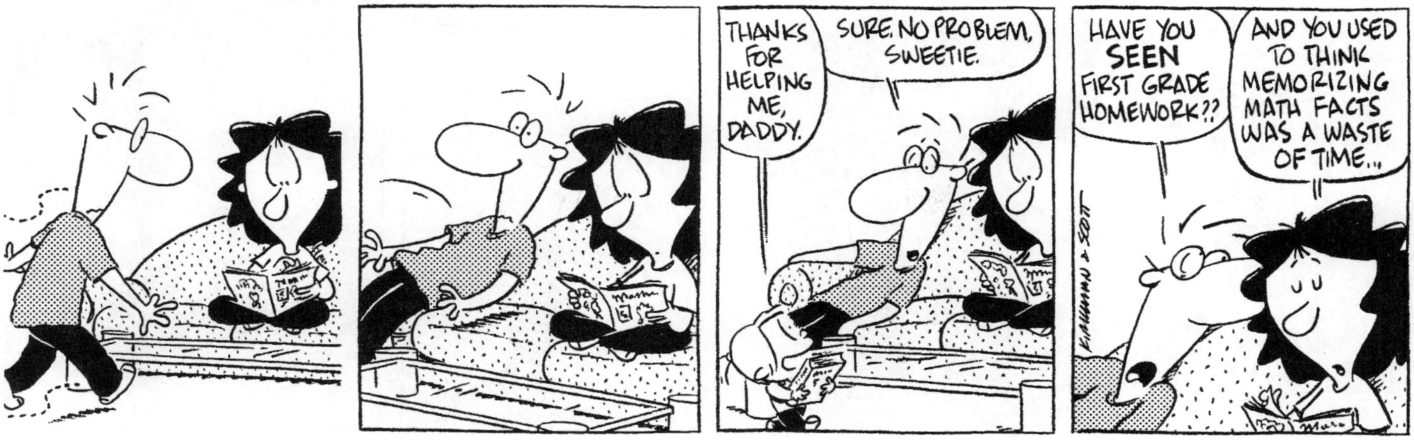
THANKS FOR HELPING ME, DADDY.
SURE. NO PROBLEM, SWEETIE.
HAVE YOU SEEN FIRST GRADE HOMEWORK??
AND YOU USED TO THINK MEMORIZING MATH FACTS WAS A WASTE OF TIME...
KIRKMAN & SCOTT

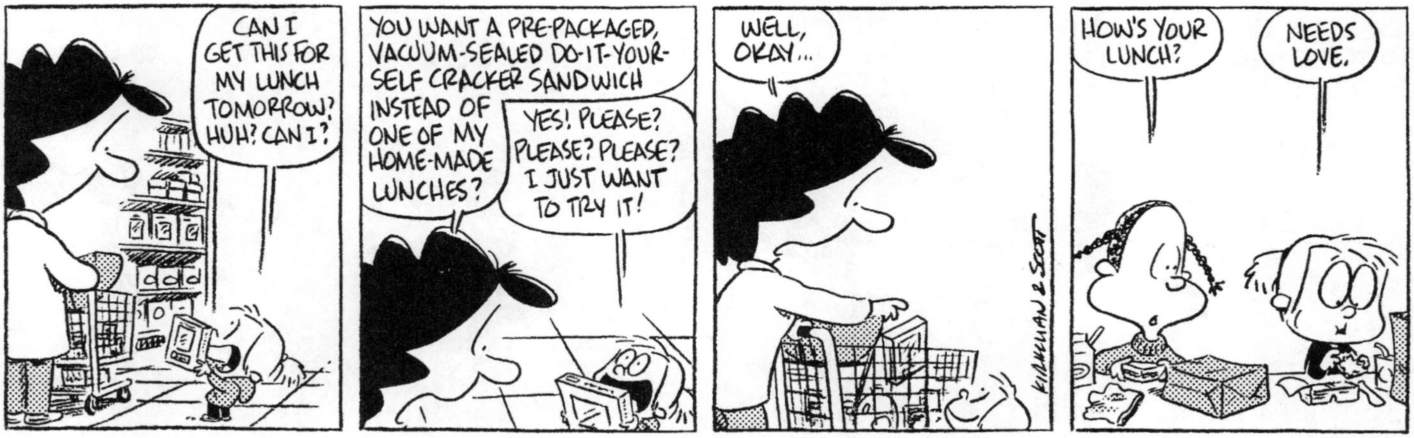
CAN I GET THIS FOR MY LUNCH TOMORROW? HUH? CAN I?
YOU WANT A PRE-PACKAGED, VACUUM-SEALED DO-IT-YOURSELF CRACKER SANDWICH INSTEAD OF ONE OF MY HOME-MADE LUNCHES?
YES! PLEASE? PLEASE? PLEASE? I JUST WANT TO TRY IT!
WELL, OKAY...
KIRKMAN & SCOTT
HOW'S YOUR LUNCH?
NEEDS LOVE.

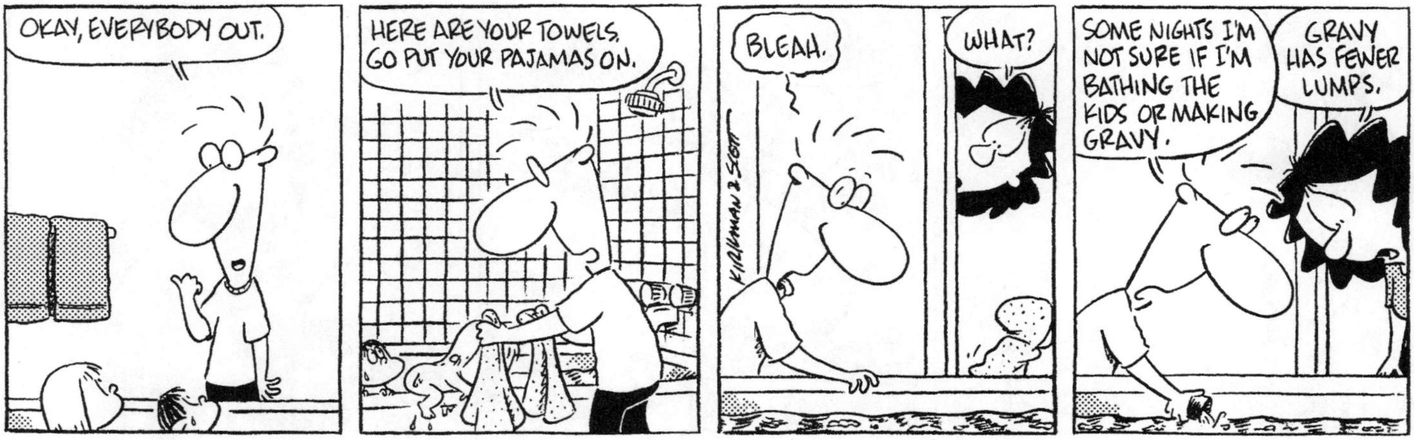
OKAY, EVERYBODY OUT.
HERE ARE YOUR TOWELS. GO PUT YOUR PAJAMAS ON.
KIRKMAN & SCOTT
BLEAH.
WHAT?
SOME NIGHTS I'M NOT SURE IF I'M BATHING THE KIDS OR MAKING GRAVY.
GRAVY HAS FEWER LUMPS.

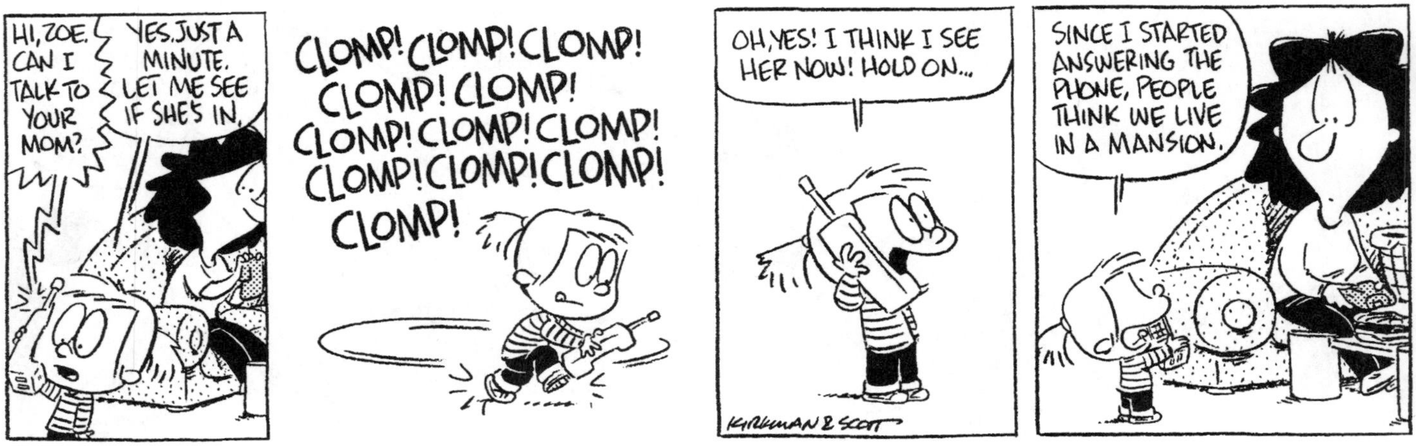
HI, ZOE. CAN I TALK TO YOUR MOM?
YES. JUST A MINUTE. LET ME SEE IF SHE'S IN.
CLOMP! CLOMP! CLOMP! CLOMP! CLOMP! CLOMP! CLOMP! CLOMP! CLOMP! CLOMP! CLOMP! CLOMP!
OH, YES! I THINK I SEE HER NOW! HOLD ON...
KIRKMAN & SCOTT
SINCE I STARTED ANSWERING THE PHONE, PEOPLE THINK WE LIVE IN A MANSION.

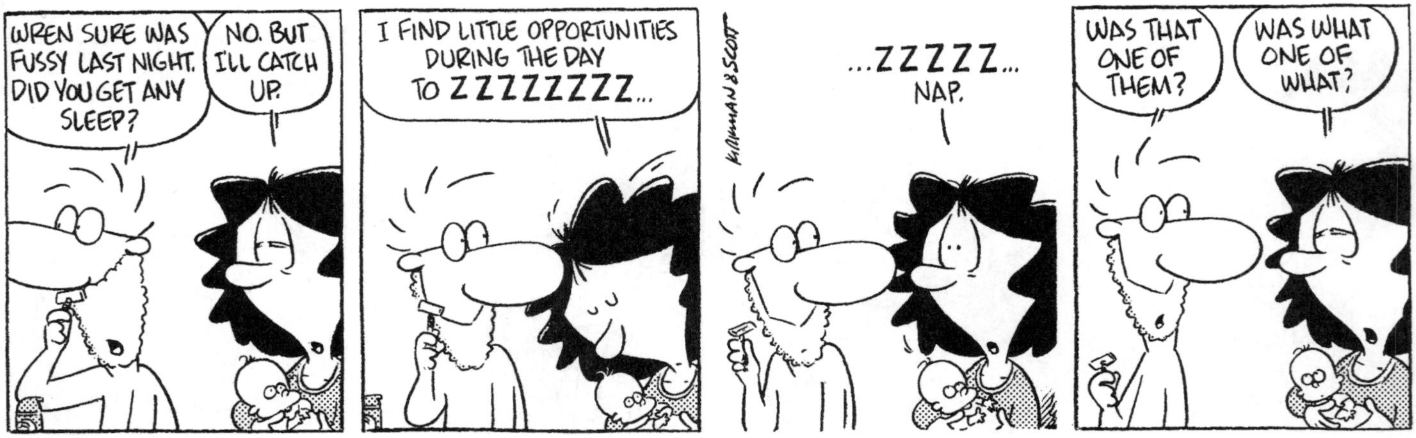
WREN SURE WAS FUSSY LAST NIGHT. DID YOU GET ANY SLEEP?
NO. BUT I'LL CATCH UP.
I FIND LITTLE OPPORTUNITIES DURING THE DAY TO ZZZZZZZZ...
KIRKMAN & SCOTT
...ZZZZZ... NAP.
WAS THAT ONE OF THEM?
WAS WHAT ONE OF WHAT?

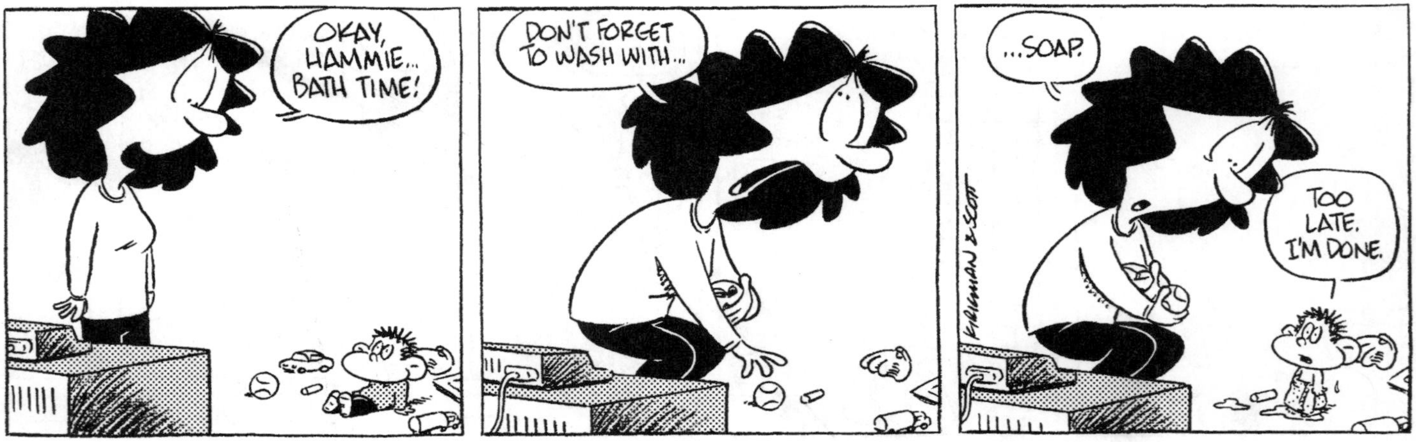
OKAY, HAMMIE... BATH TIME!
DON'T FORGET TO WASH WITH...
KIRKMAN & SCOTT
...SOAP.
TOO LATE. I'M DONE.

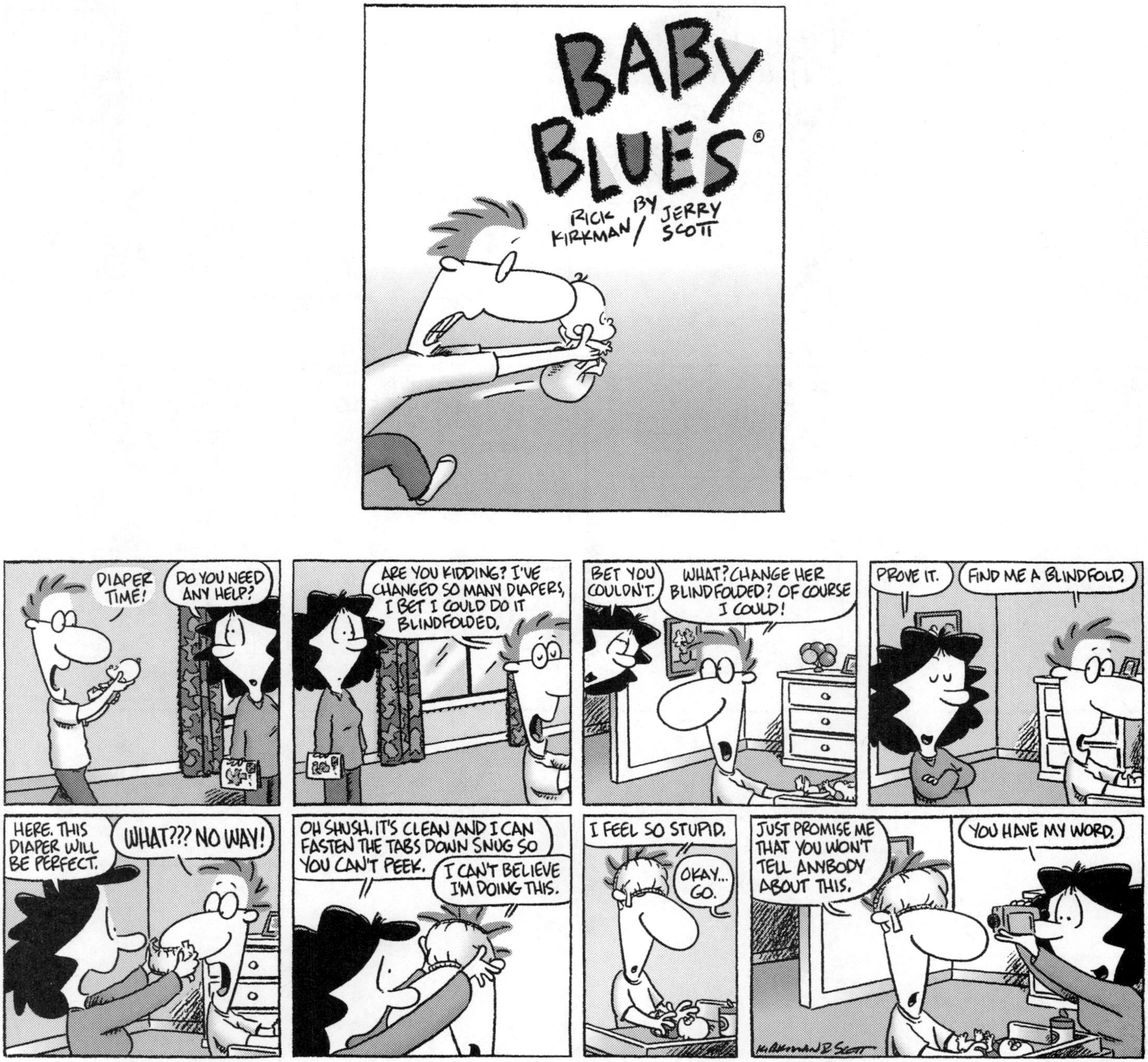
BABY BLUES®
BY RICK KIRKMAN / JERRY SCOTT
DIAPER TIME!
DO YOU NEED ANY HELP?
ARE YOU KIDDING? I'VE CHANGED SO MANY DIAPERS, I BET I COULD DO IT BLINDFOLDED.
BET YOU COULDN'T.
WHAT? CHANGE HER BLINDFOLDED? OF COURSE I COULD!
PROVE IT.
FIND ME A BLINDFOLD.
HERE. THIS DIAPER WILL BE PERFECT.
WHAT??? NO WAY!
OH SHUSH. IT'S CLEAN AND I CAN FASTEN THE TABS DOWN SNUG SO YOU CAN'T PEEK.
I CAN'T BELIEVE I'M DOING THIS.
I FEEL SO STUPID.
OKAY... GO.
JUST PROMISE ME THAT YOU WON'T TELL ANYBODY ABOUT THIS.
YOU HAVE MY WORD.

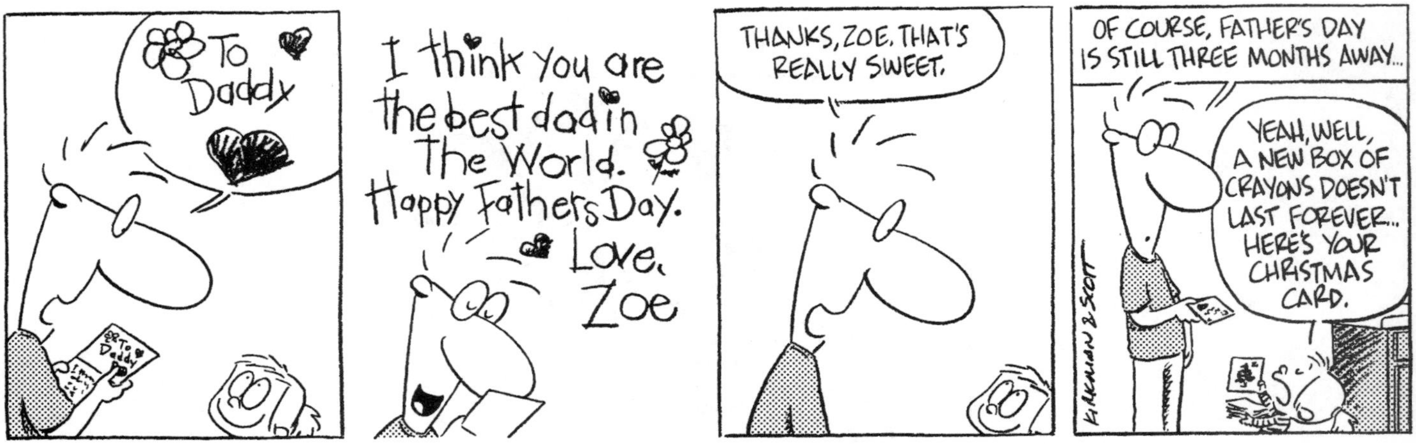
To Daddy
I think you are the best dad in The World. Happy Fathers Day. Love, Zoe
THANKS, ZOE. THAT'S REALLY SWEET.
OF COURSE, FATHER'S DAY IS STILL THREE MONTHS AWAY...
YEAH, WELL, A NEW BOX OF CRAYONS DOESN'T LAST FOREVER... HERE'S YOUR CHRISTMAS CARD.
KIRKMAN & SCOTT

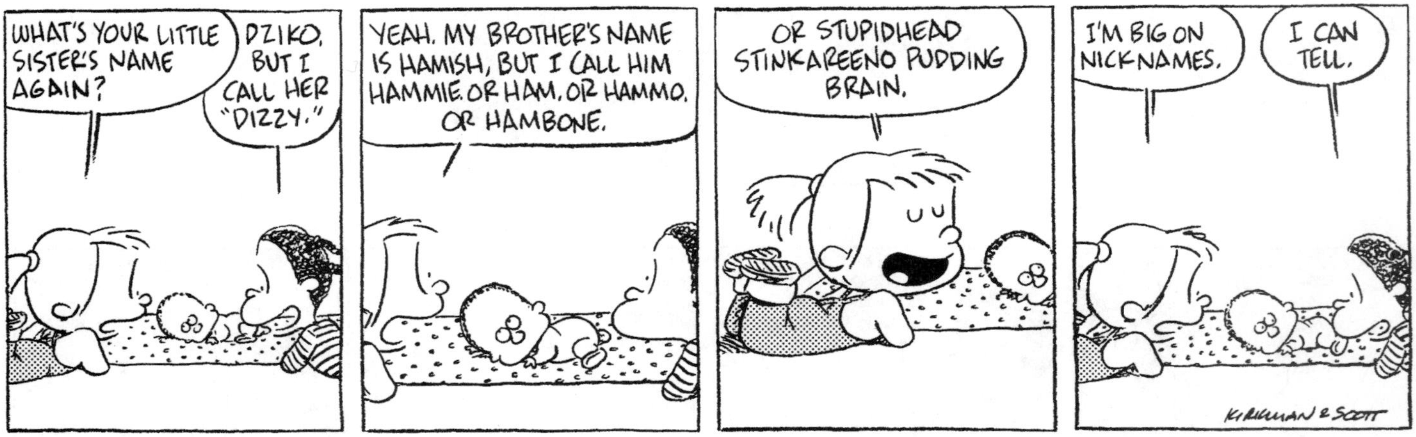
WHAT'S YOUR LITTLE SISTER'S NAME AGAIN?
DZIKO, BUT I CALL HER "DIZZY."
YEAH. MY BROTHER'S NAME IS HAMISH, BUT I CALL HIM HAMMIE. OR HAM. OR HAMMO. OR HAMBONE.
OR STUPIDHEAD STINKAREENO PUDDING BRAIN.
I'M BIG ON NICKNAMES.
I CAN TELL.
KIRKMAN & SCOTT

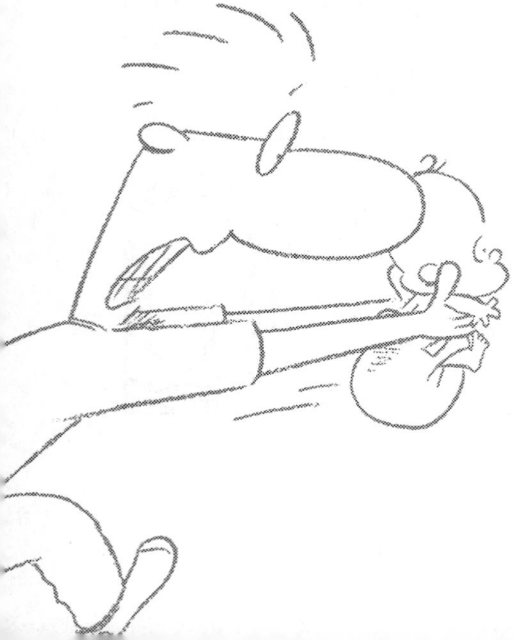

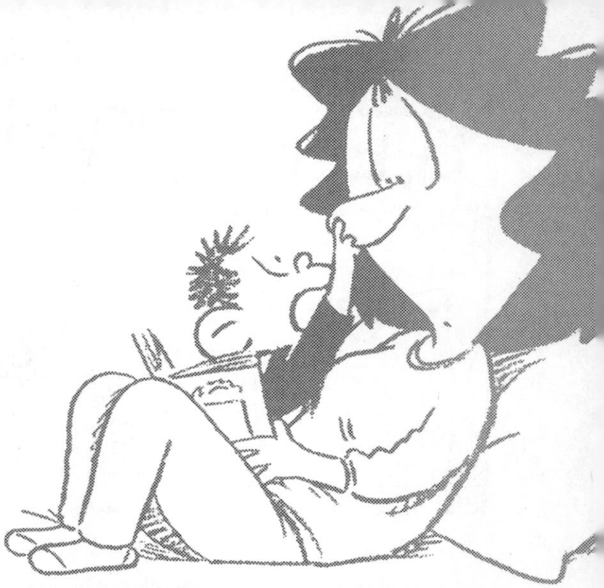

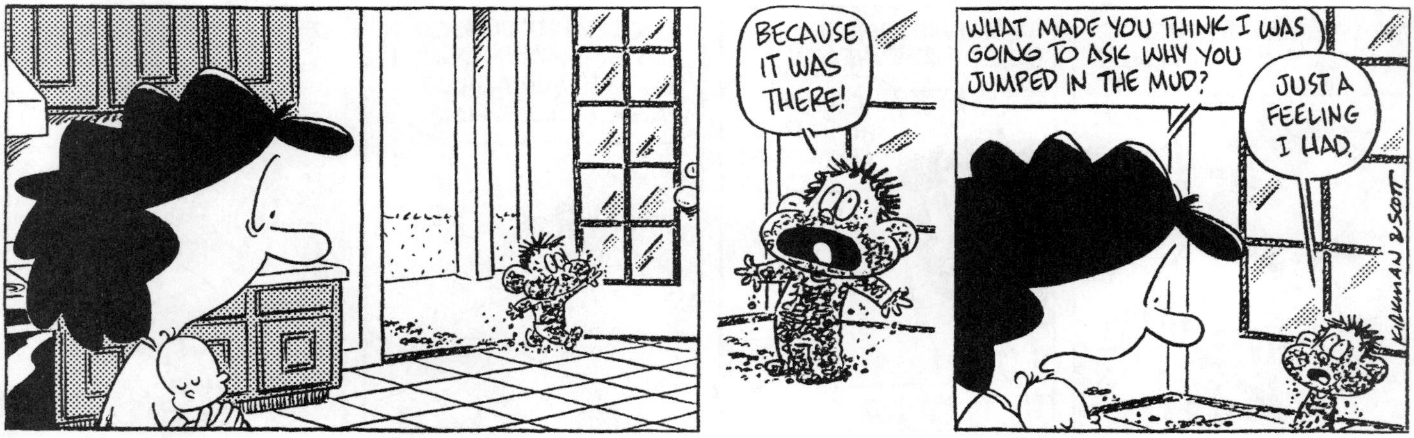
BECAUSE IT WAS THERE!
WHAT MADE YOU THINK I WAS GOING TO ASK WHY YOU JUMPED IN THE MUD?
JUST A FEELING I HAD.
KIRKMAN & SCOTT

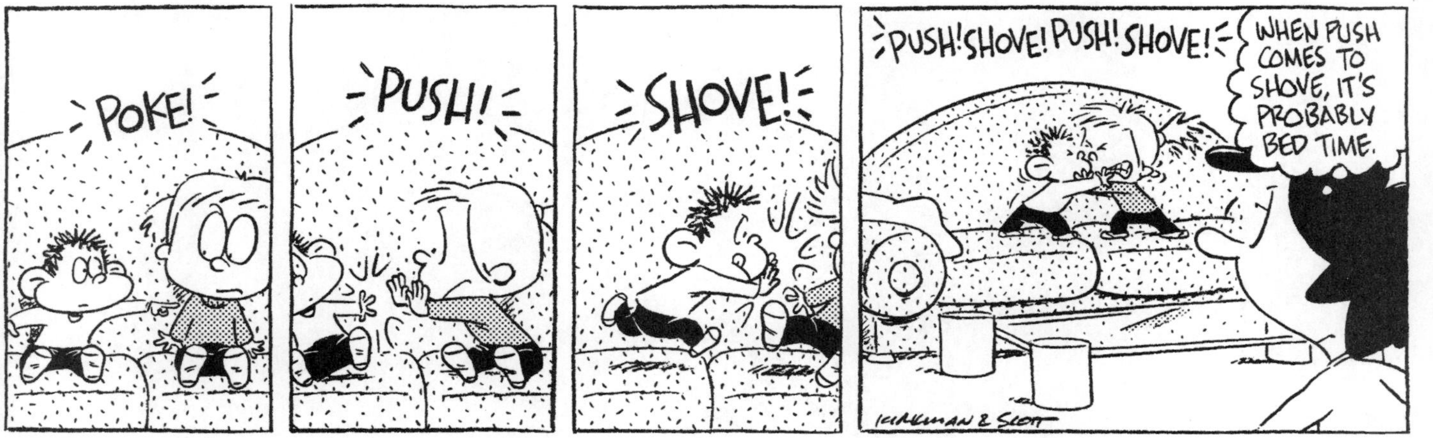
POKE!
PUSH!
SHOVE!
PUSH! SHOVE! PUSH! SHOVE!
WHEN PUSH COMES TO SHOVE, IT'S PROBABLY BED TIME.
KIRKMAN & SCOTT

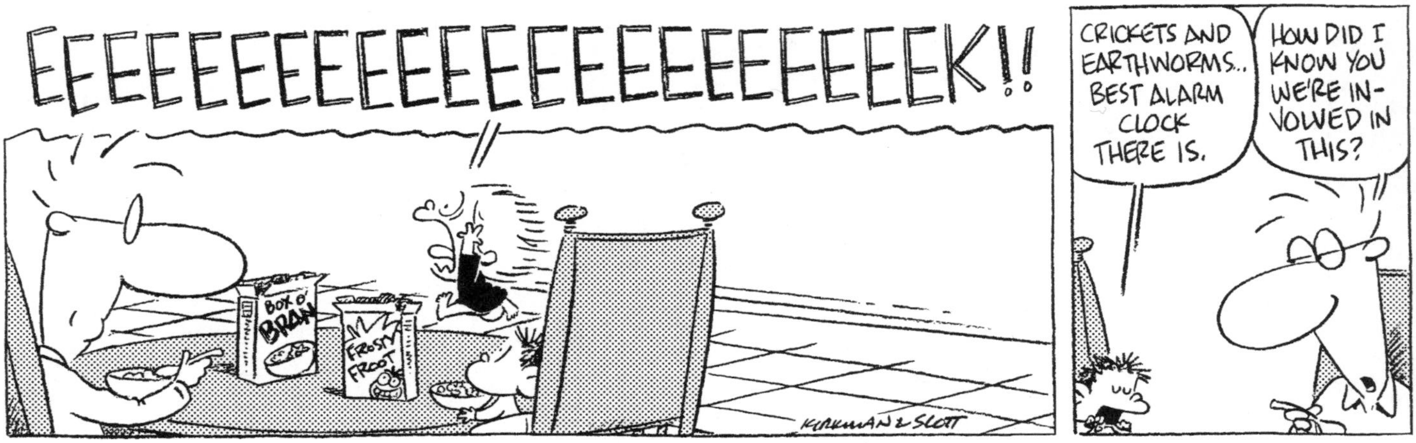
EEEEEEEEEEEEEEEEEEEEEEEEEEK!!
BOX O' BRAN
FROSTY FROOT
KIRKMAN & SCOTT
CRICKETS AND EARTHWORMS... BEST ALARM CLOCK THERE IS.
HOW DID I KNOW YOU WE'RE INVOLVED IN THIS?

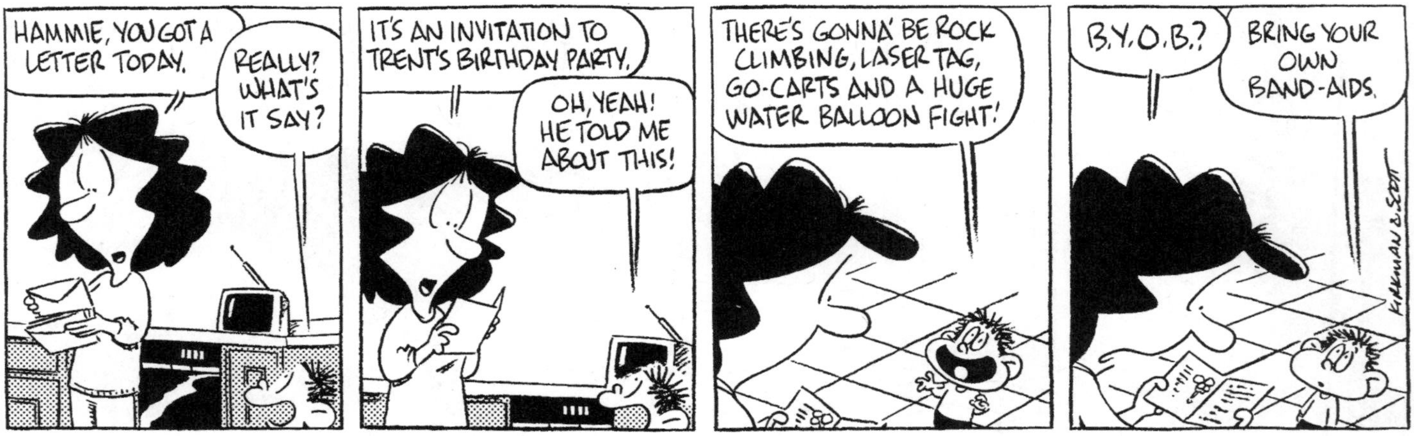
HAMMIE, YOU GOT A LETTER TODAY.
REALLY? WHAT'S IT SAY?
IT'S AN INVITATION TO TRENT'S BIRTHDAY PARTY.
OH, YEAH! HE TOLD ME ABOUT THIS!
THERE'S GONNA' BE ROCK CLIMBING, LASER TAG, GO-CARTS AND A HUGE WATER BALLOON FIGHT!
B.Y.O.B.?
BRING YOUR OWN BAND-AIDS.
KIRKMAN & SCOTT

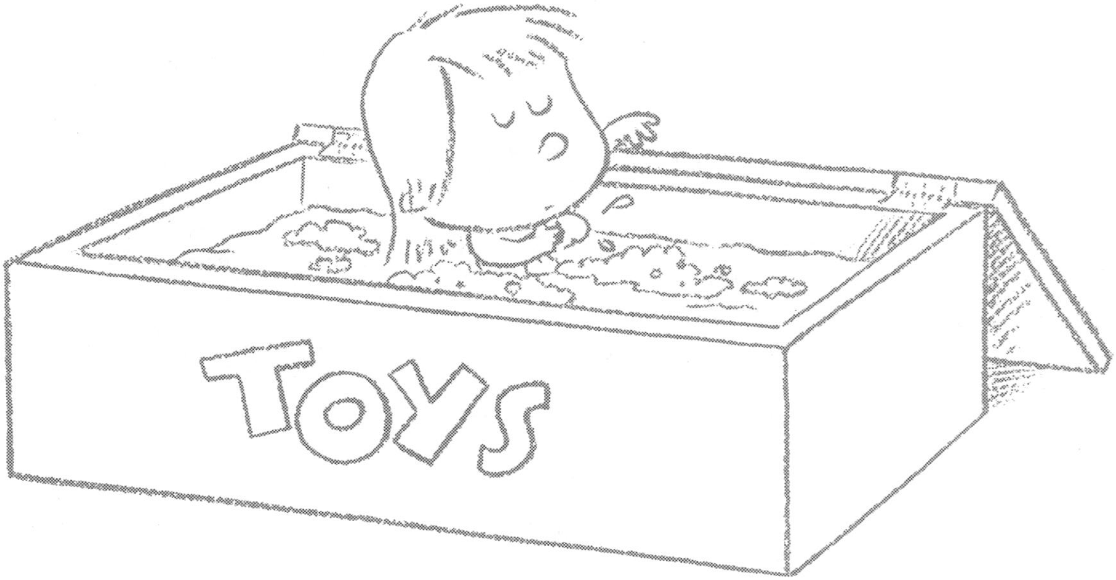
TOYS

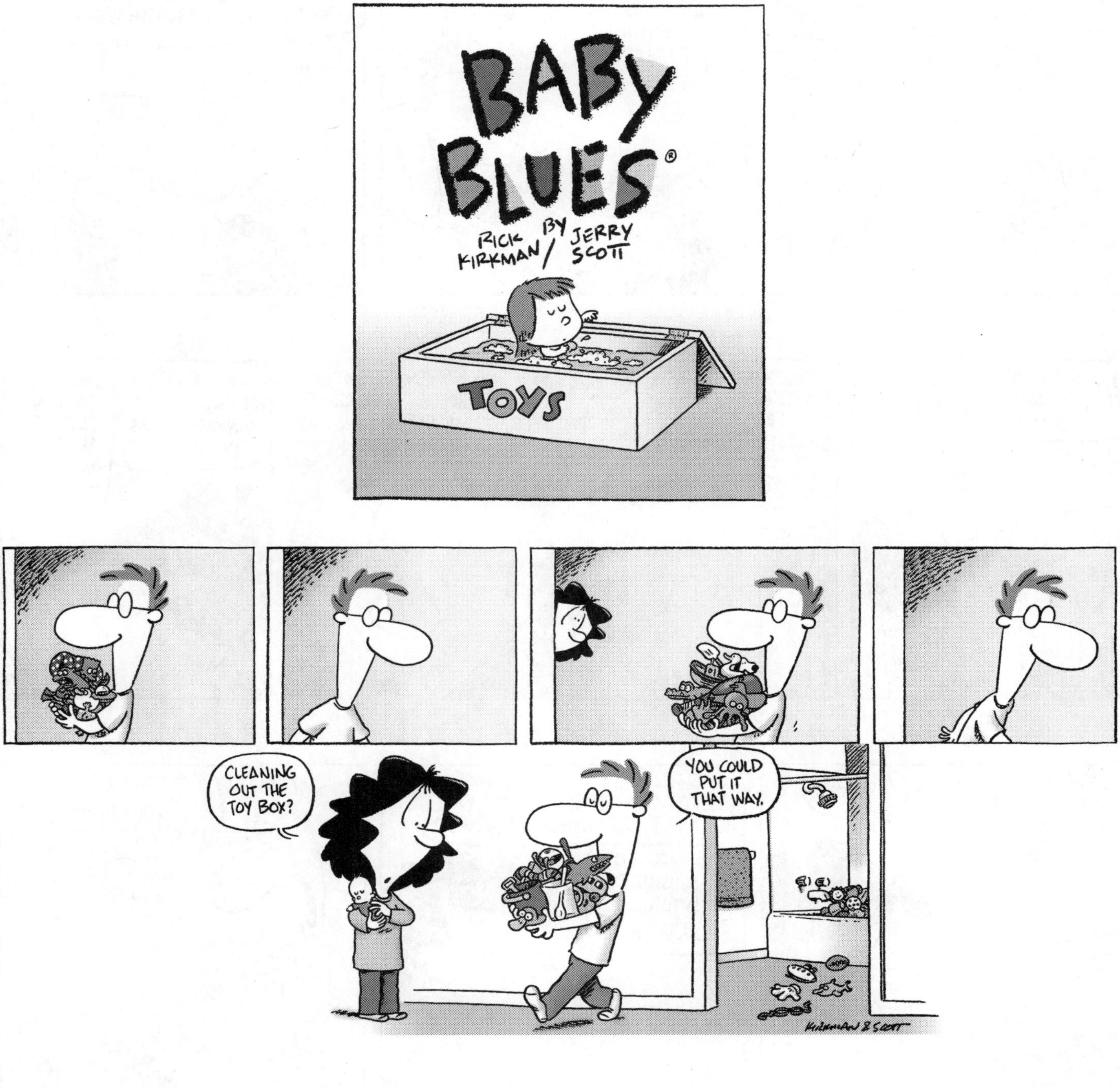
BABY BLUES®
BY RICK KIRKMAN / JERRY SCOTT
TOYS
CLEANING OUT THE TOY BOX?
YOU COULD PUT IT THAT WAY.
KIRKMAN & SCOTT

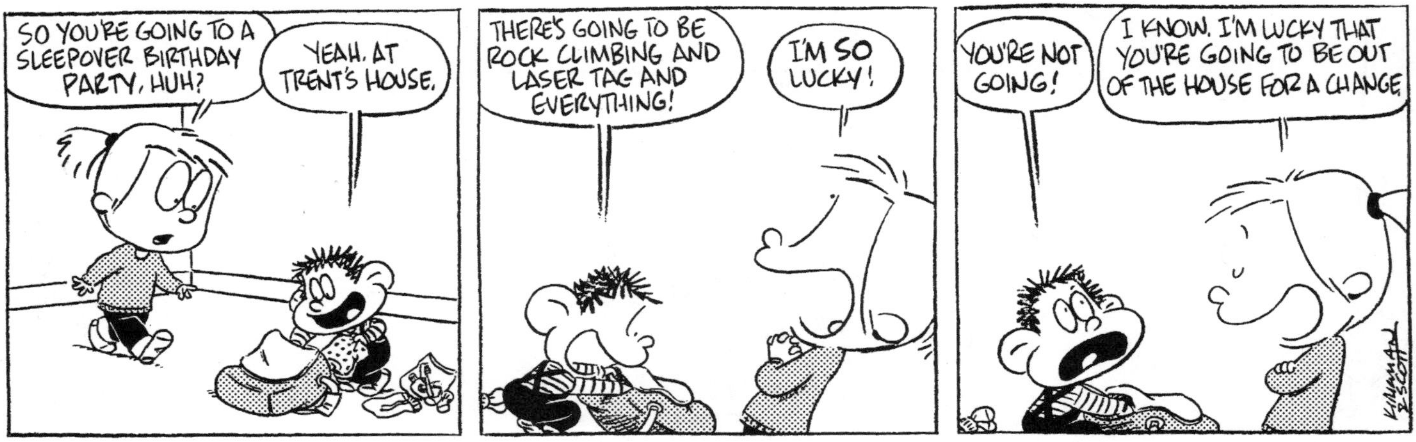
SO YOU'RE GOING TO A SLEEPOVER BIRTHDAY PARTY, HUH?
YEAH. AT TRENT'S HOUSE.
THERE'S GOING TO BE ROCK CLIMBING AND LASER TAG AND EVERYTHING!
I'M SO LUCKY!
YOU'RE NOT GOING!
I KNOW. I'M LUCKY THAT YOU'RE GOING TO BE OUT OF THE HOUSE FOR A CHANGE.

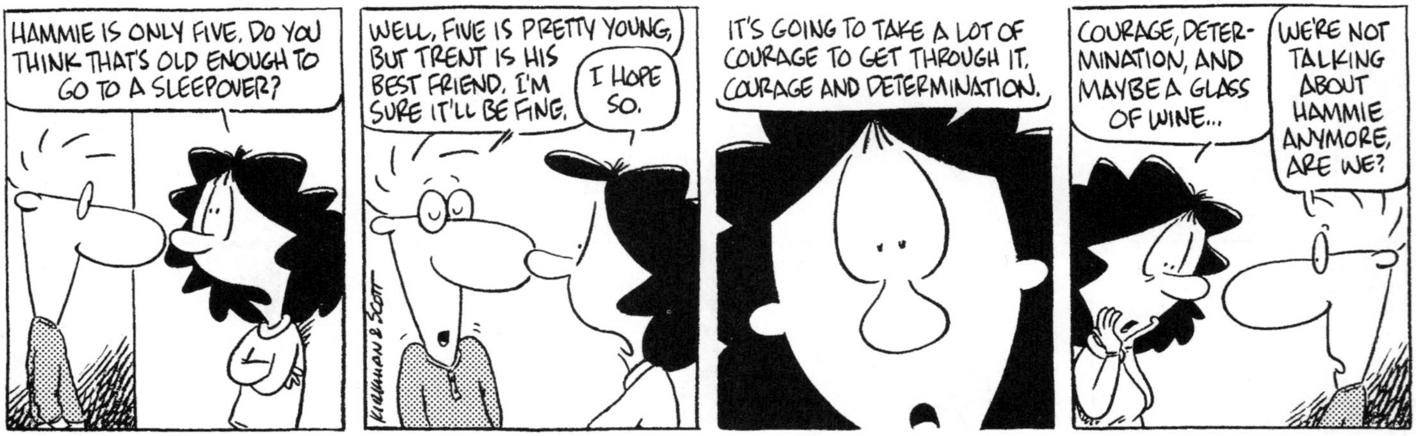
HAMMIE IS ONLY FIVE. DO YOU THINK THAT'S OLD ENOUGH TO GO TO A SLEEPOVER?
WELL, FIVE IS PRETTY YOUNG, BUT TRENT IS HIS BEST FRIEND. I'M SURE IT'LL BE FINE.
I HOPE SO.
IT'S GOING TO TAKE A LOT OF COURAGE TO GET THROUGH IT. COURAGE AND DETERMINATION.
COURAGE, DETERMINATION, AND MAYBE A GLASS OF WINE...
WE'RE NOT TALKING ABOUT HAMMIE ANYMORE, ARE WE?

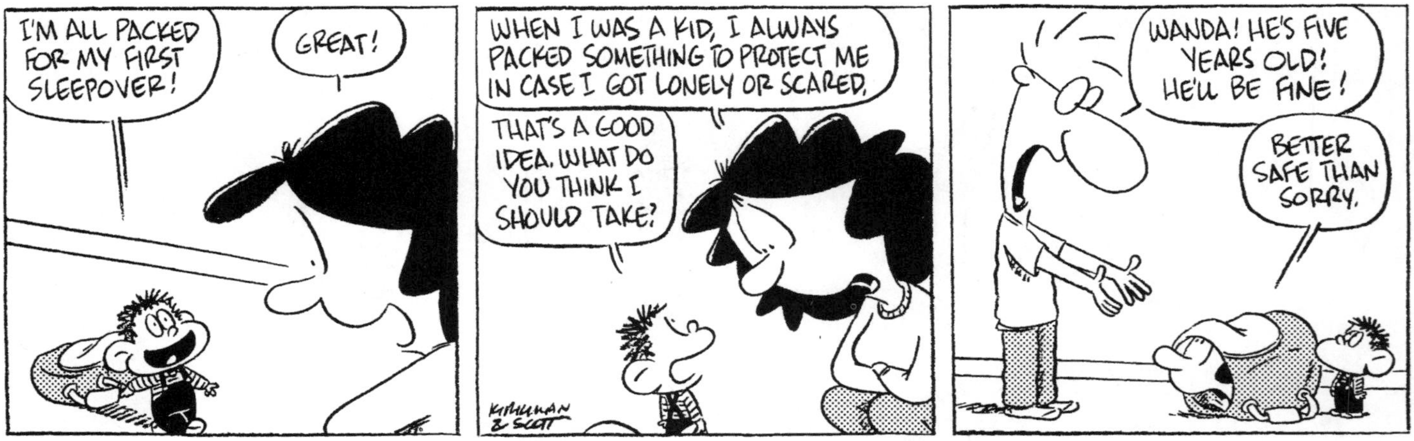
I'M ALL PACKED FOR MY FIRST SLEEPOVER!
GREAT!
WHEN I WAS A KID, I ALWAYS PACKED SOMETHING TO PROTECT ME IN CASE I GOT LONELY OR SCARED.
THAT'S A GOOD IDEA. WHAT DO YOU THINK I SHOULD TAKE?
WANDA! HE'S FIVE YEARS OLD! HE'LL BE FINE!
BETTER SAFE THAN SORRY.

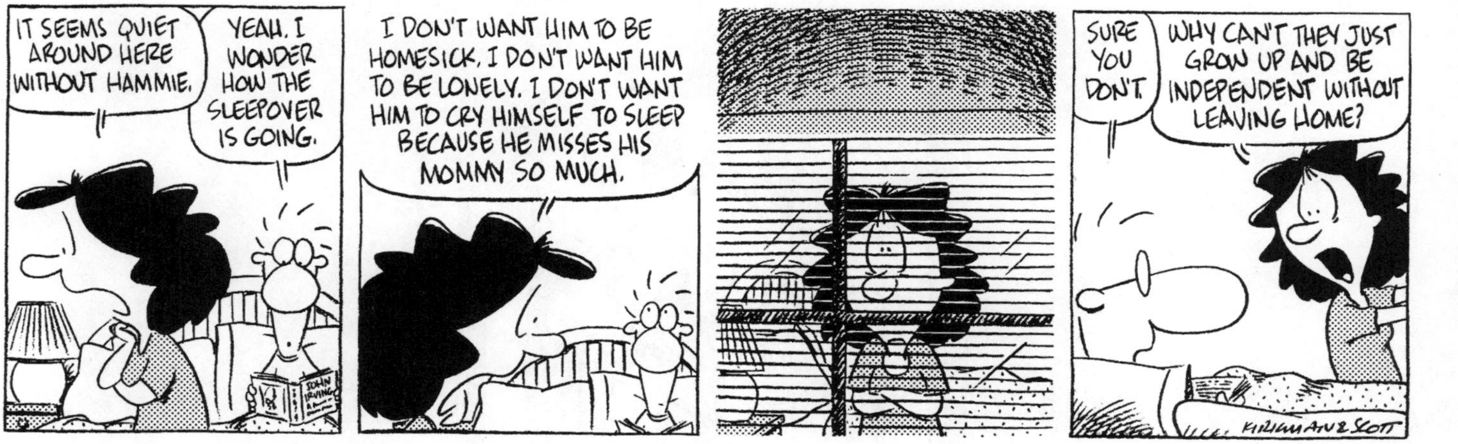
IT SEEMS QUIET AROUND HERE WITHOUT HAMMIE.
YEAH. I WONDER HOW THE SLEEPOVER IS GOING.
JOHN IRVING
I DON'T WANT HIM TO BE HOMESICK. I DON'T WANT HIM TO BE LONELY. I DON'T WANT HIM TO CRY HIMSELF TO SLEEP BECAUSE HE MISSES HIS MOMMY SO MUCH.
SURE YOU DON'T.
WHY CAN'T THEY JUST GROW UP AND BE INDEPENDENT WITHOUT LEAVING HOME?
KIRKMAN & SCOTT

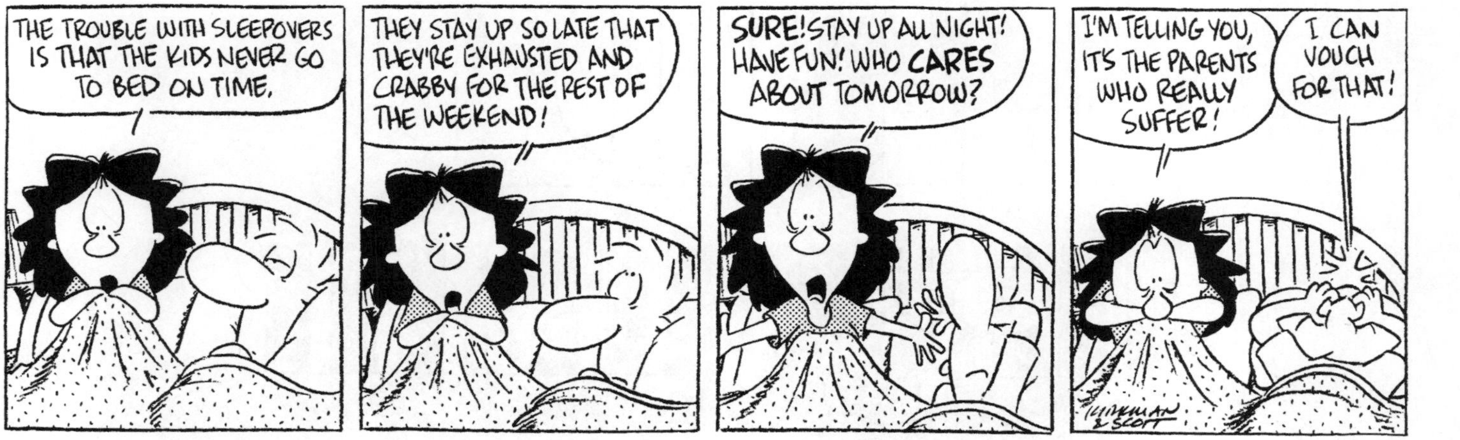
THE TROUBLE WITH SLEEPOVERS IS THAT THE KIDS NEVER GO TO BED ON TIME.
THEY STAY UP SO LATE THAT THEY'RE EXHAUSTED AND CRABBY FOR THE REST OF THE WEEKEND!
SURE! STAY UP ALL NIGHT! HAVE FUN! WHO CARES ABOUT TOMORROW?
I'M TELLING YOU, IT'S THE PARENTS WHO REALLY SUFFER!
I CAN VOUCH FOR THAT!
KIRKMAN & SCOTT

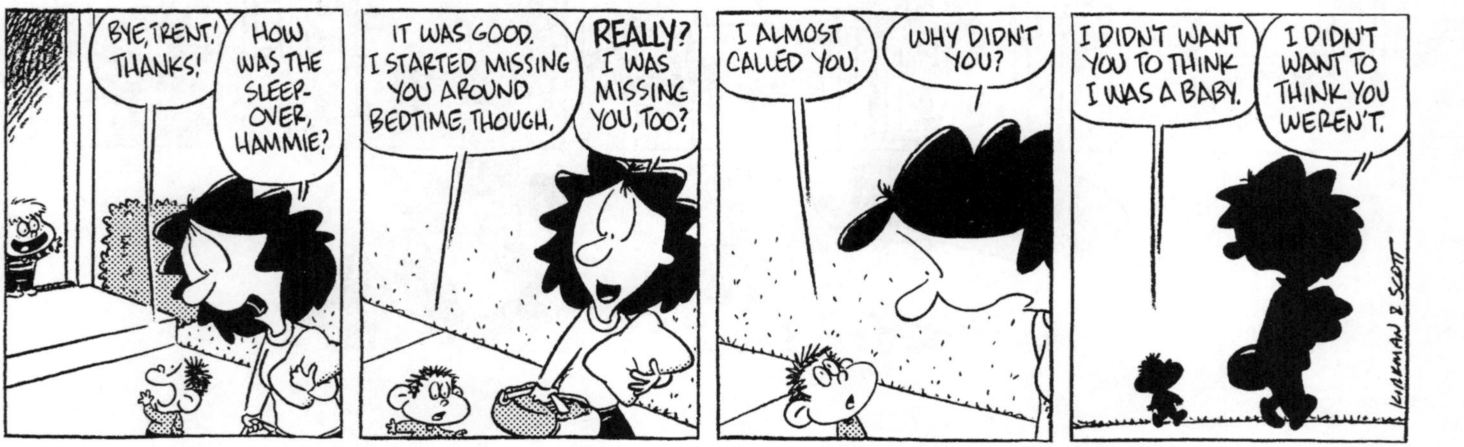
BYE, TRENT! THANKS!
HOW WAS THE SLEEP-OVER, HAMMIE?
IT WAS GOOD. I STARTED MISSING YOU AROUND BEDTIME, THOUGH.
REALLY? I WAS MISSING YOU, TOO?
I ALMOST CALLED YOU.
WHY DIDN'T YOU?
I DIDN'T WANT YOU TO THINK I WAS A BABY.
I DIDN'T WANT TO THINK YOU WEREN'T.
KIRKMAN & SCOTT

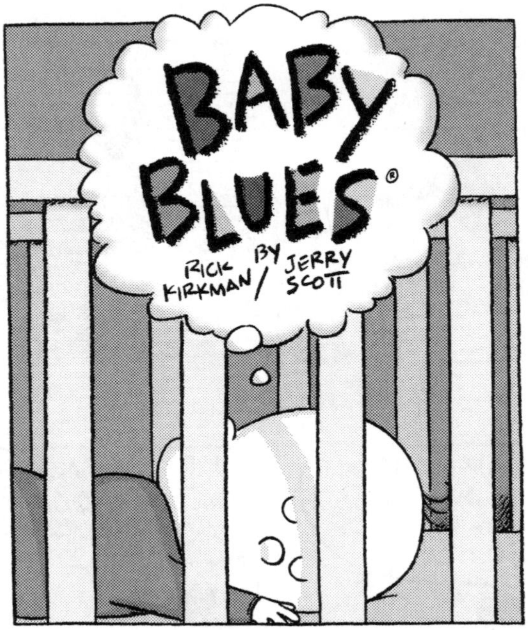
BABY BLUES®
BY RICK KIRKMAN / JERRY SCOTT

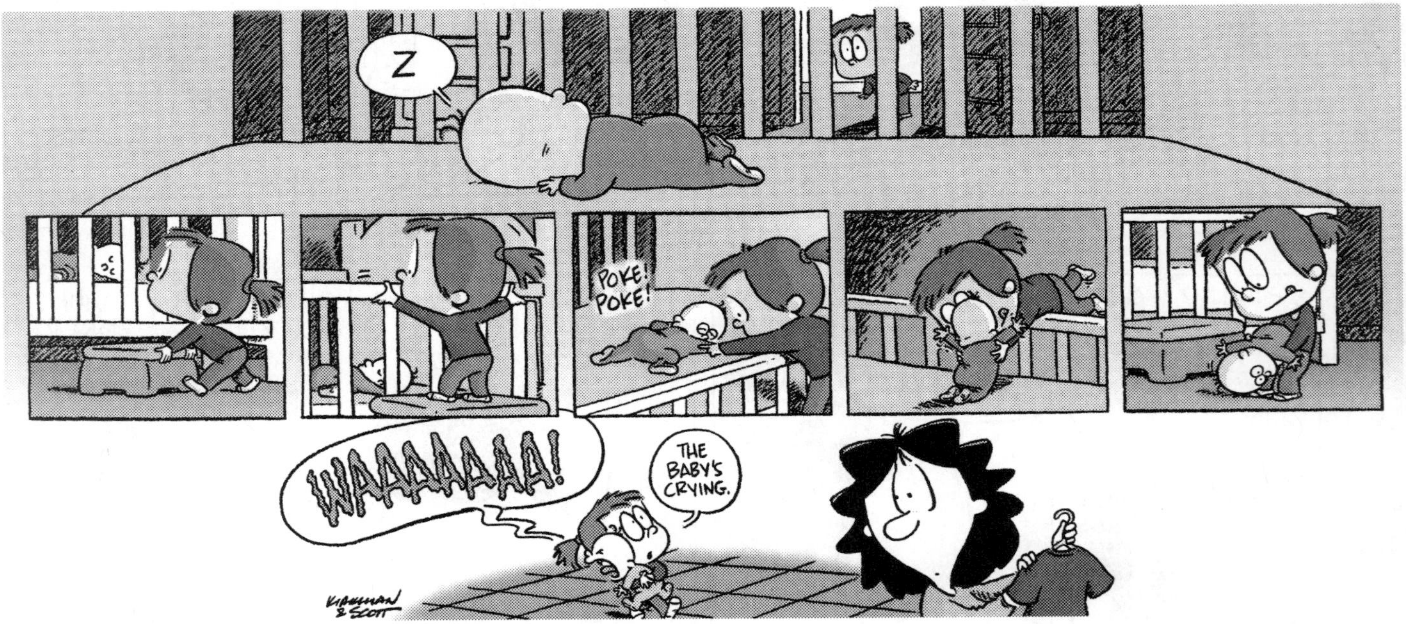
Z
POKE! POKE!
WAAAAAAA!
THE BABY'S CRYING.
KIRKMAN & SCOTT

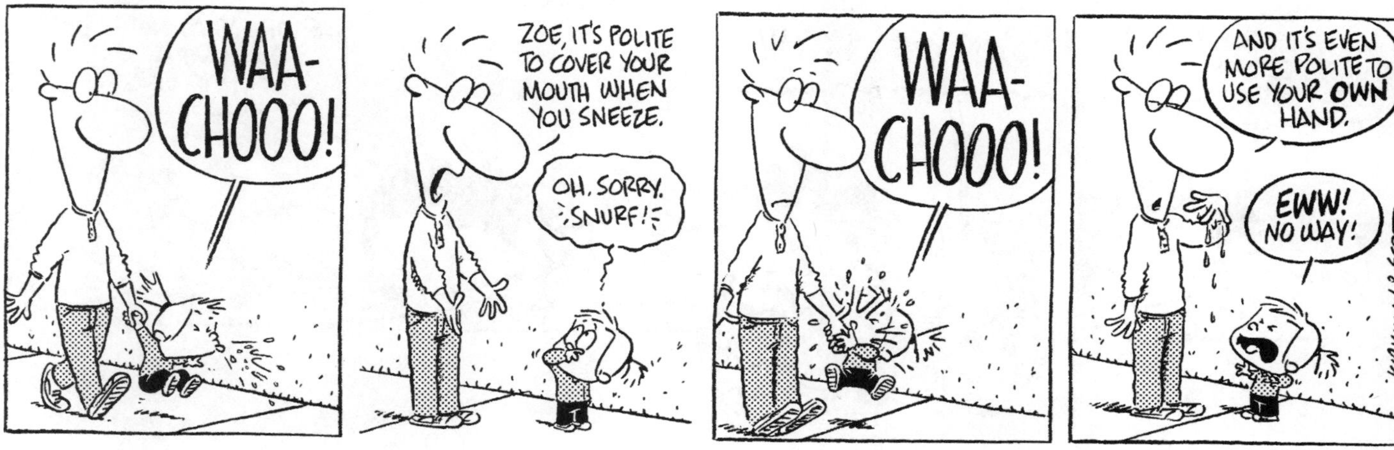
WAA-CHOOO!
ZOE, IT'S POLITE TO COVER YOUR MOUTH WHEN YOU SNEEZE.
OH. SORRY. SNURF!
WAA-CHOOO!
AND IT'S EVEN MORE POLITE TO USE YOUR OWN HAND.
EWW! NO WAY!
KIRKMAN & SCOTT

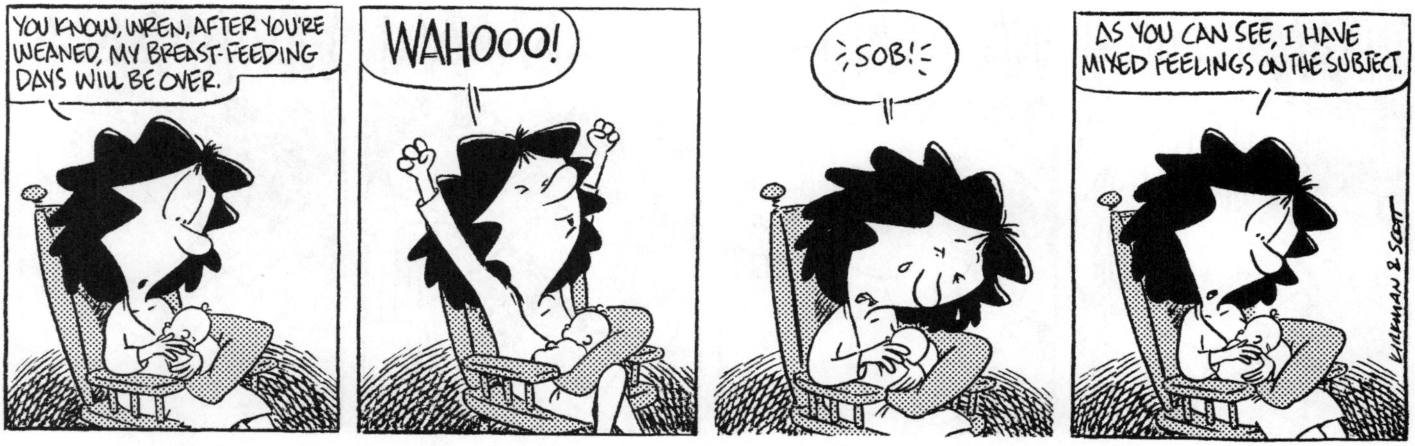
YOU KNOW, WREN, AFTER YOU'RE WEANED, MY BREAST-FEEDING DAYS WILL BE OVER.
WAHOOO!
SOB!
AS YOU CAN SEE, I HAVE MIXED FEELINGS ON THE SUBJECT.
KIRKMAN & SCOTT

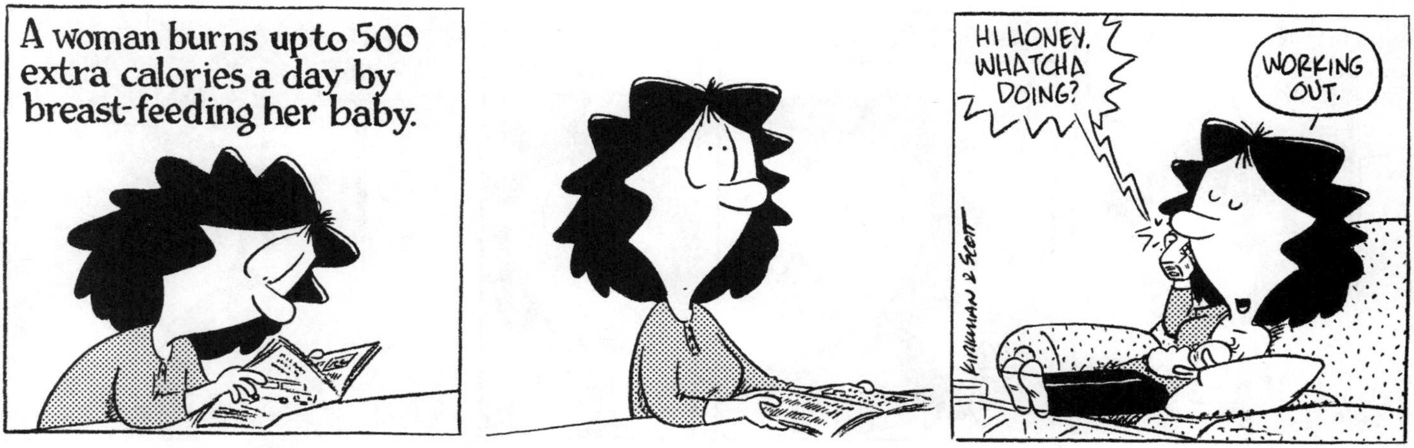
A woman burns up to 500 extra calories a day by breast-feeding her baby.
HI HONEY. WHATCHA DOING?
WORKING OUT.
KIRKMAN & SCOTT

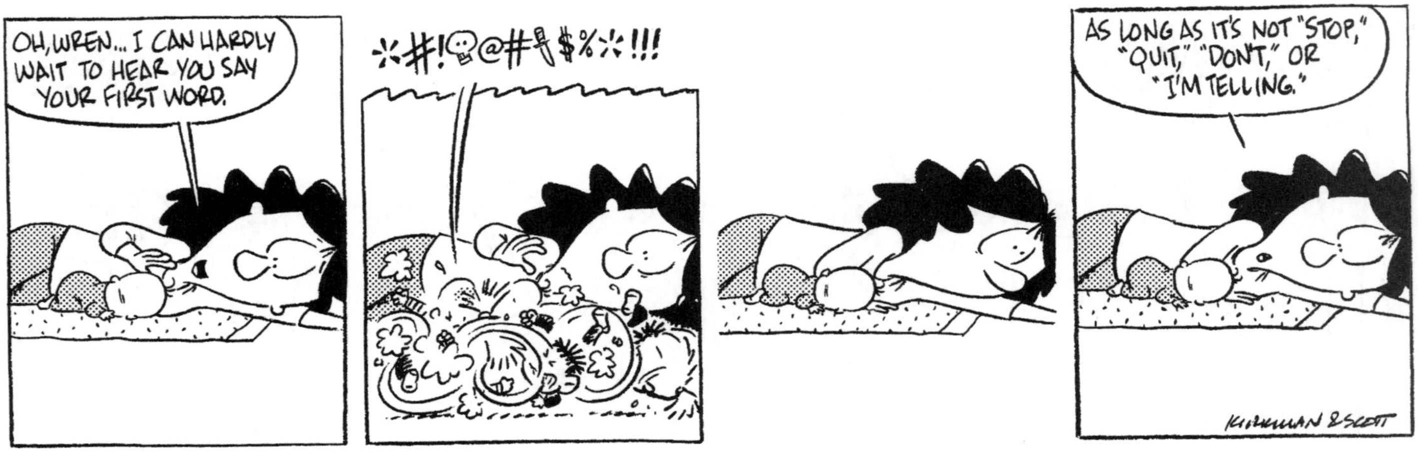
OH, WREN... I CAN HARDLY WAIT TO HEAR YOU SAY YOUR FIRST WORD.
#!@#$%!!!
AS LONG AS IT'S NOT "STOP," "QUIT," "DON'T," OR "I'M TELLING."
KIRKMAN & SCOTT

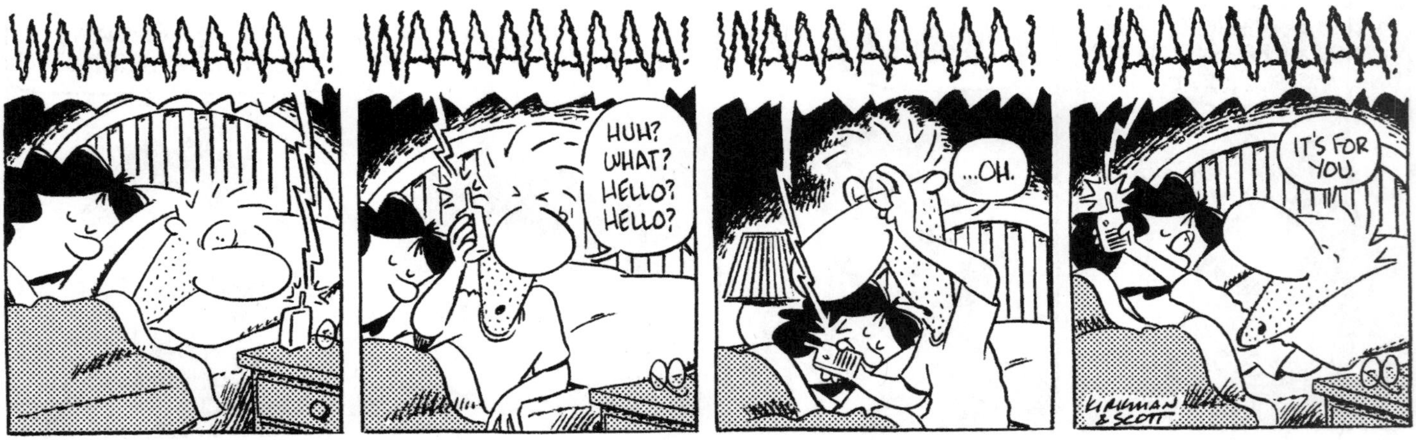
WAAAAAAAAA!
WAAAAAAAAAA!
HUH? WHAT? HELLO? HELLO?
WAAAAAAAAA!
...OH.
WAAAAAAAA!
IT'S FOR YOU.
KIRKMAN & SCOTT

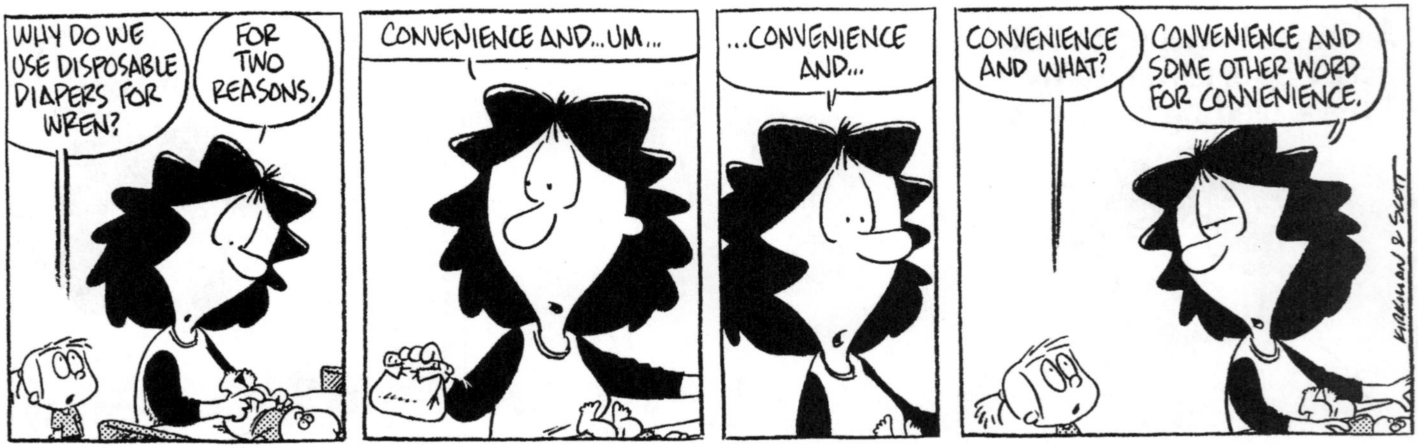
WHY DO WE USE DISPOSABLE DIAPERS FOR WREN?
FOR TWO REASONS.
CONVENIENCE AND...UM...
...CONVENIENCE AND...
CONVENIENCE AND WHAT?
CONVENIENCE AND SOME OTHER WORD FOR CONVENIENCE.
KIRKMAN & SCOTT

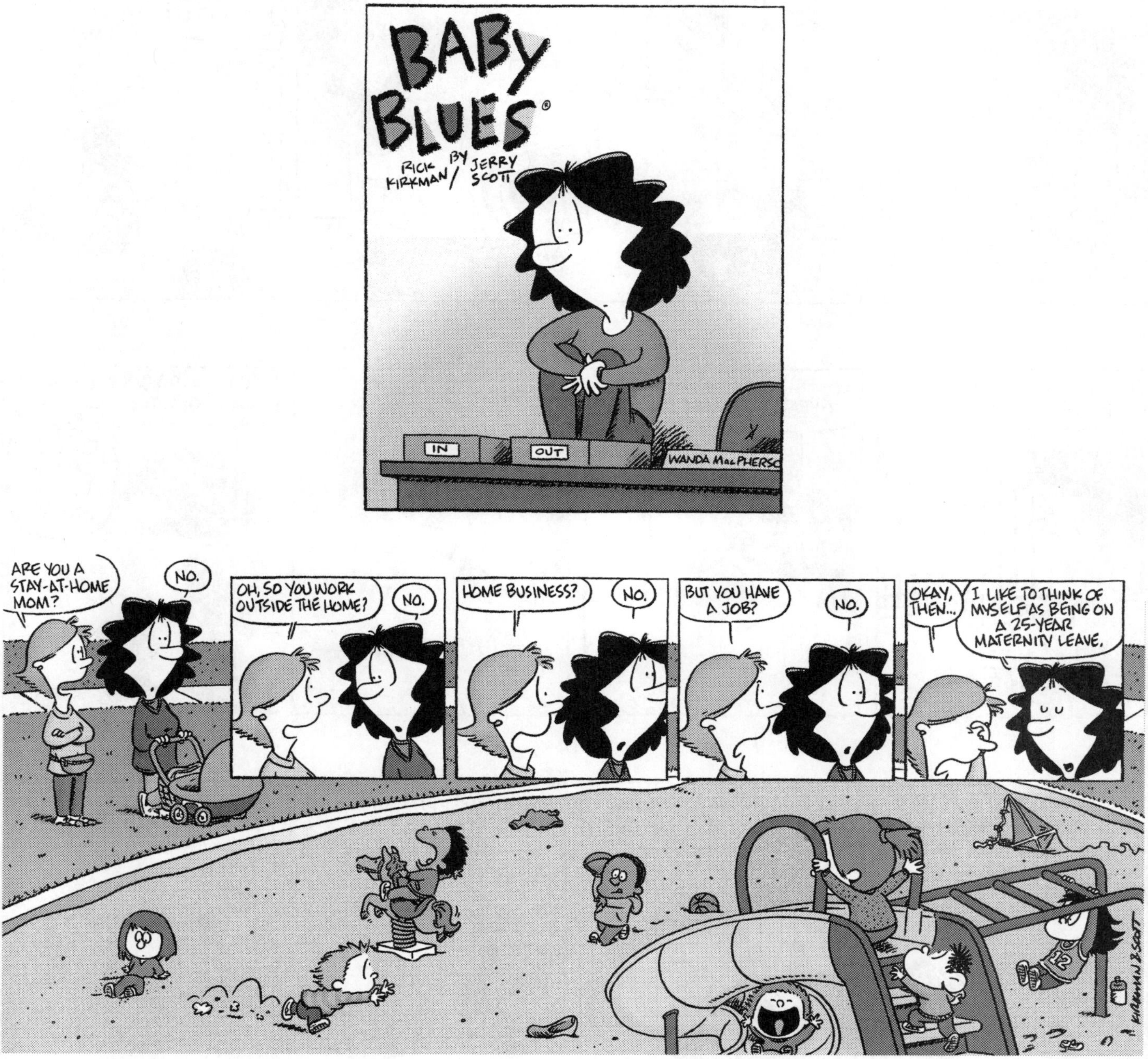
BABY BLUES®
BY RICK KIRKMAN / JERRY SCOTT
IN
OUT
WANDA MacPHERSO
ARE YOU A STAY-AT-HOME MOM?
NO.
OH, SO YOU WORK OUTSIDE THE HOME?
NO.
HOME BUSINESS?
NO.
BUT YOU HAVE A JOB?
NO.
OKAY, THEN...
I LIKE TO THINK OF MYSELF AS BEING ON A 25-YEAR MATERNITY LEAVE.
12
KIRKMAN & SCOTT

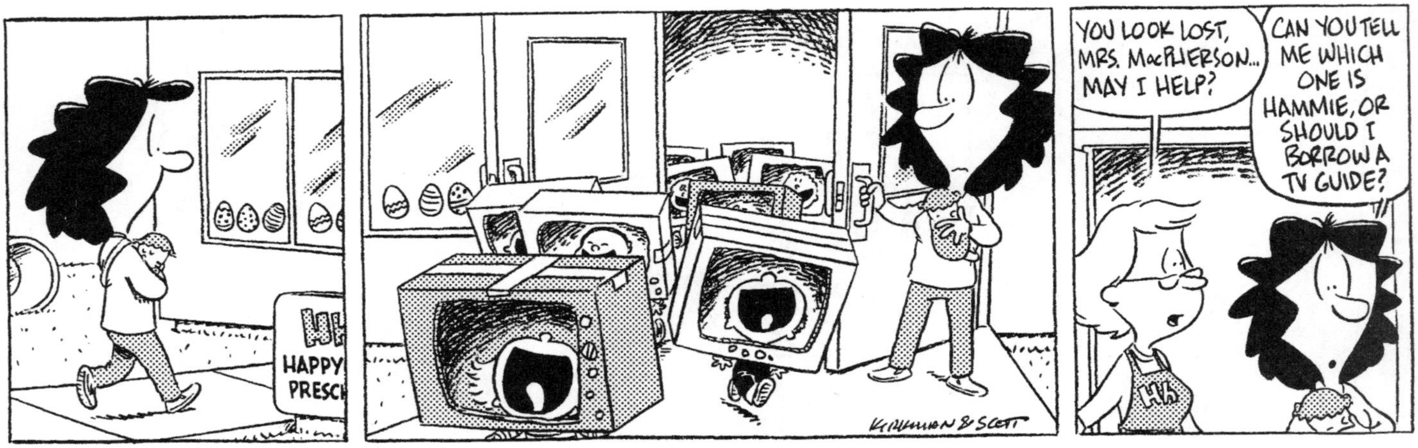
HAPPY
YOU LOOK LOST, MRS. MacPHERSON... MAY I HELP?
CAN YOU TELL ME WHICH ONE IS HAMMIE, OR SHOULD I BORROW A TV GUIDE?

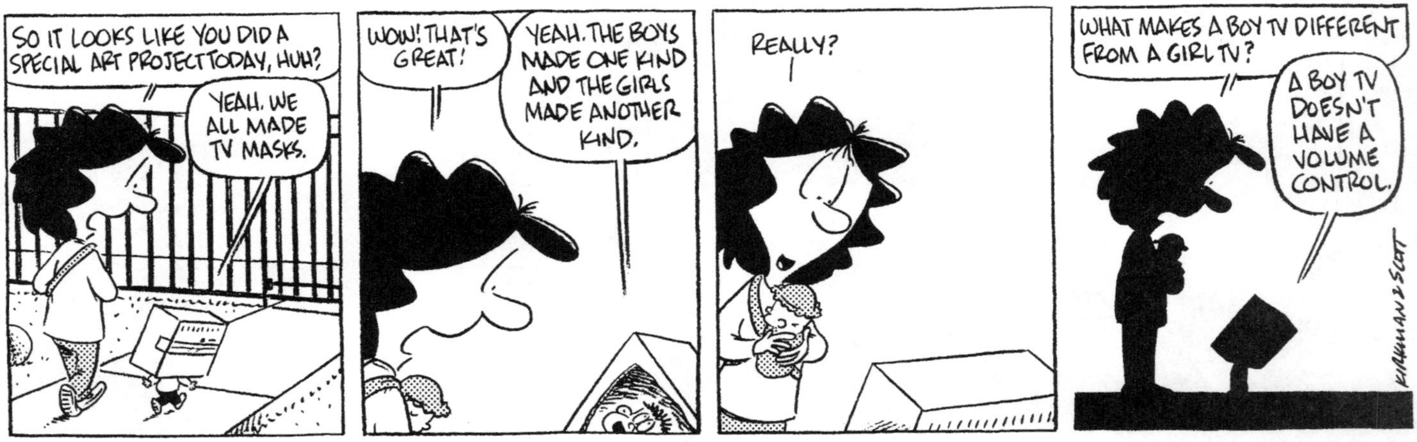
SO IT LOOKS LIKE YOU DID A SPECIAL ART PROJECT TODAY, HUH?
YEAH. WE ALL MADE TV MASKS.
WOW! THAT'S GREAT!
YEAH. THE BOYS MADE ONE KIND AND THE GIRLS MADE ANOTHER KIND.
REALLY?
WHAT MAKES A BOY TV DIFFERENT FROM A GIRL TV?
A BOY TV DOESN'T HAVE A VOLUME CONTROL.

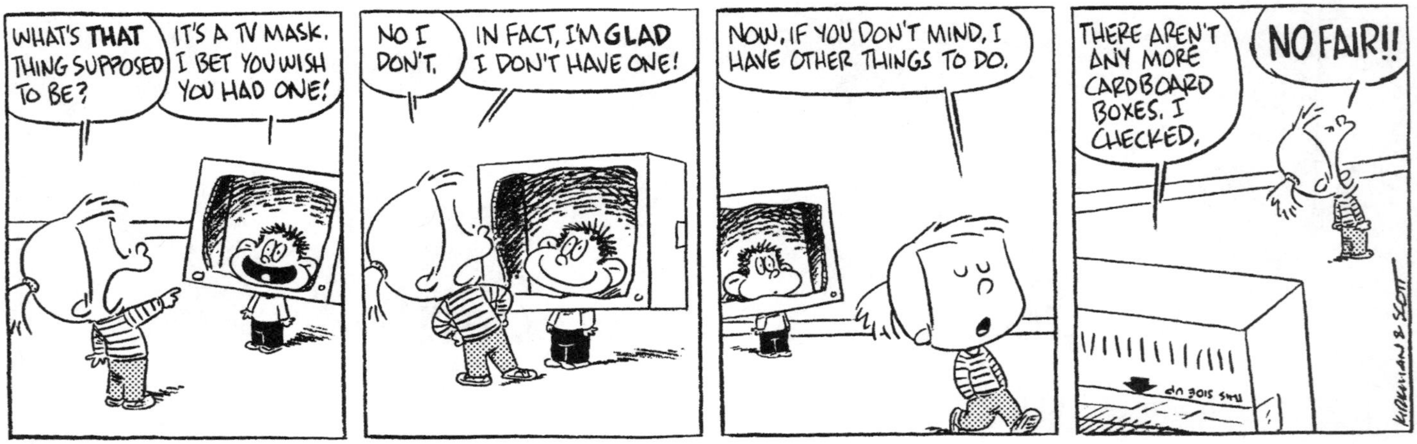
WHAT'S THAT THING SUPPOSED TO BE?
IT'S A TV MASK. I BET YOU WISH YOU HAD ONE!
NO I DON'T.
IN FACT, I'M GLAD I DON'T HAVE ONE!
NOW, IF YOU DON'T MIND, I HAVE OTHER THINGS TO DO.
THERE AREN'T ANY MORE CARDBOARD BOXES. I CHECKED.
NO FAIR!!

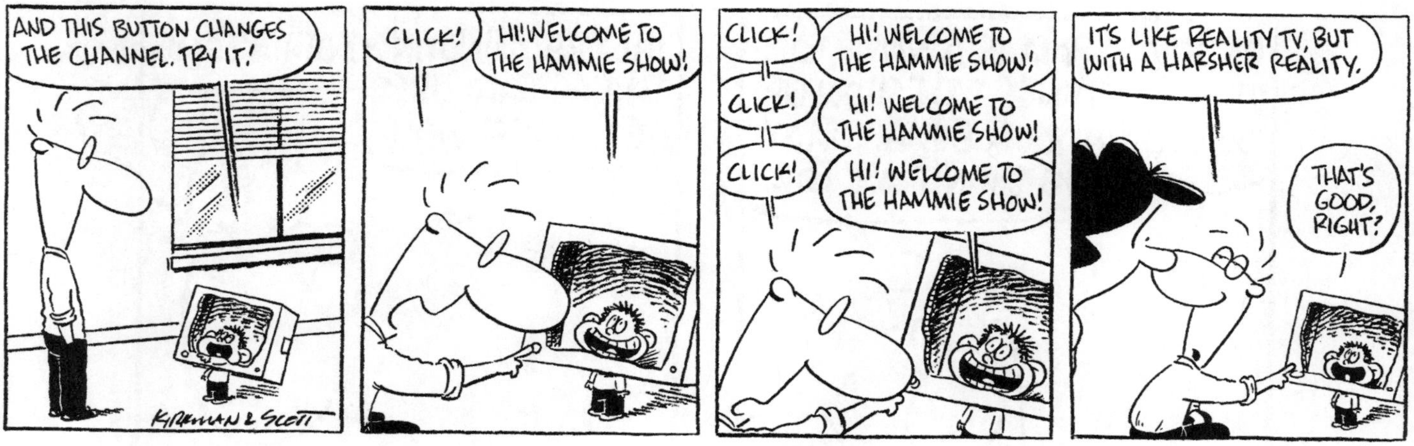
AND THIS BUTTON CHANGES THE CHANNEL. TRY IT!
KIRKMAN & SCOTT
CLICK!
HI! WELCOME TO THE HAMMIE SHOW!
CLICK!
HI! WELCOME TO THE HAMMIE SHOW!
CLICK!
HI! WELCOME TO THE HAMMIE SHOW!
CLICK!
HI! WELCOME TO THE HAMMIE SHOW!
IT'S LIKE REALITY TV, BUT WITH A HARSHER REALITY.
THAT'S GOOD, RIGHT?

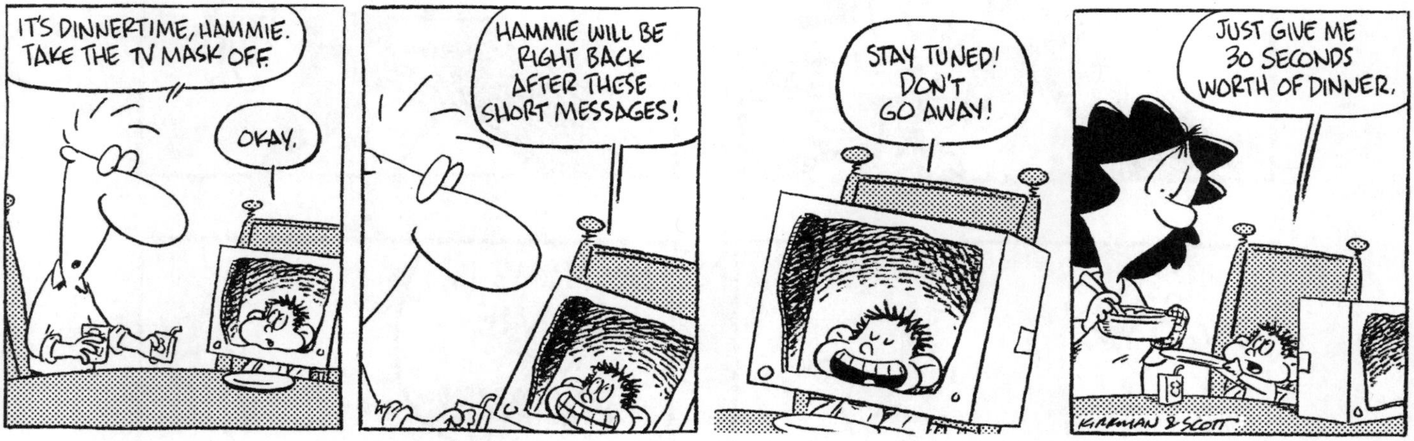
IT'S DINNERTIME, HAMMIE. TAKE THE TV MASK OFF.
OKAY.
HAMMIE WILL BE RIGHT BACK AFTER THESE SHORT MESSAGES!
STAY TUNED! DON'T GO AWAY!
JUST GIVE ME 30 SECONDS WORTH OF DINNER.
KIRKMAN & SCOTT

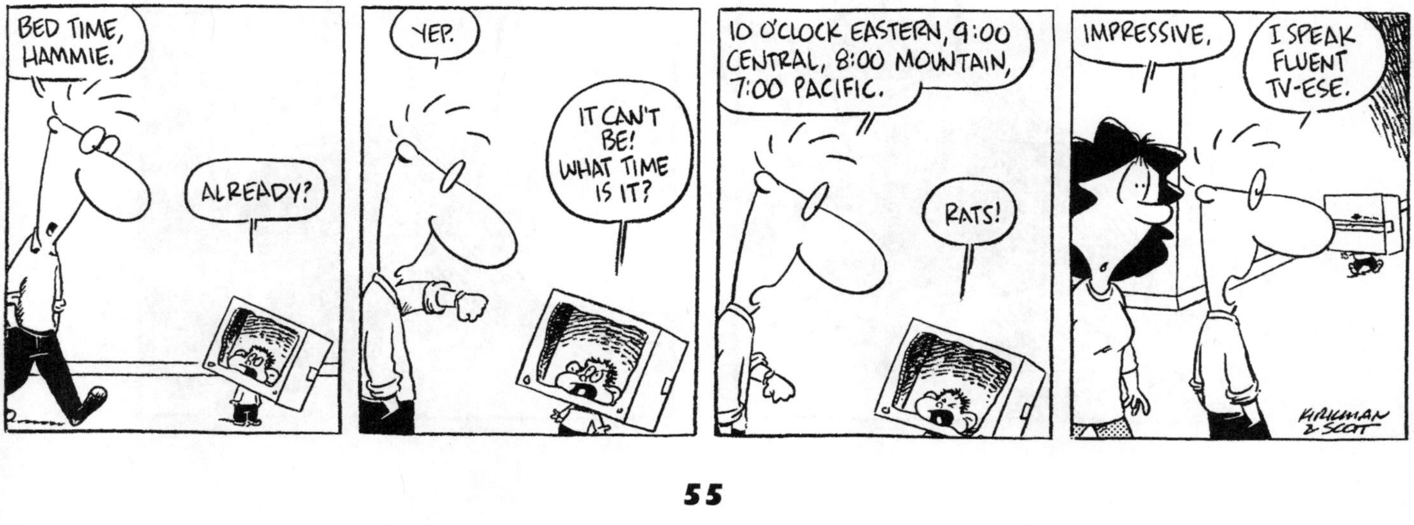
BED TIME, HAMMIE.
ALREADY?
YEP.
IT CAN'T BE! WHAT TIME IS IT?
10 O'CLOCK EASTERN, 9:00 CENTRAL, 8:00 MOUNTAIN, 7:00 PACIFIC.
RATS!
IMPRESSIVE.
I SPEAK FLUENT TV-ESE.
KIRKMAN & SCOTT

DADDY, WHAT'S SPAM?
SPAM IS A NAME FOR THINGS THAT SHOW UP IN YOUR E-MAIL THAT YOU DIDN'T ASK FOR.
THEY'RE ANNOYING, BOTHERSOME THINGS THAT JUST GET IN THE WAY.
SEE? I TOLD YOU. IT FITS PERFECTLY.
MY NAME IS HAMMIE, NOT SPAMMIE!
KIRKMAN & SCOTT

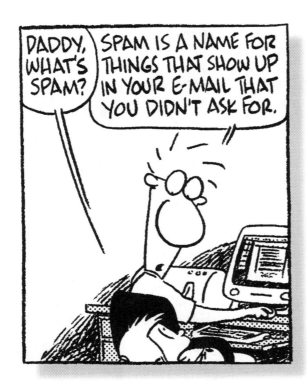

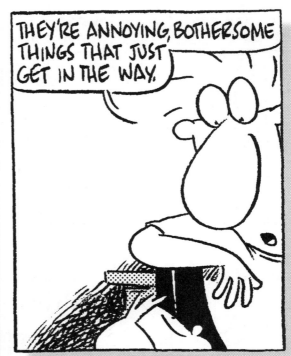

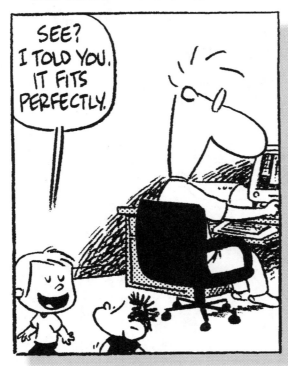

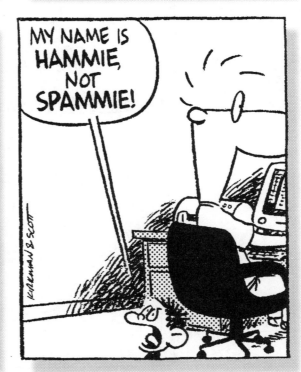

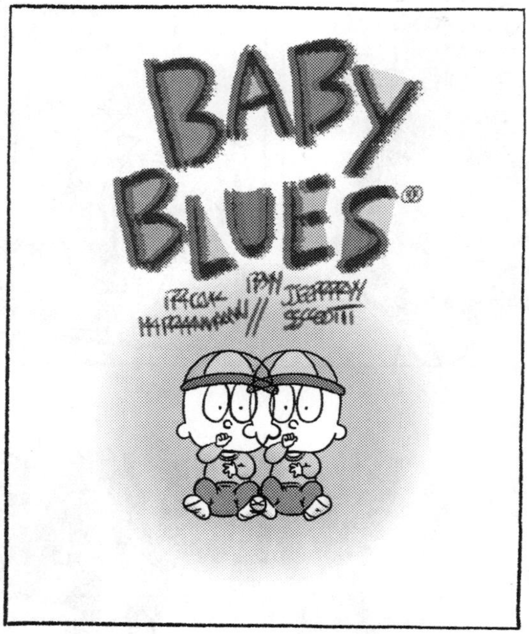
BABY BLUES

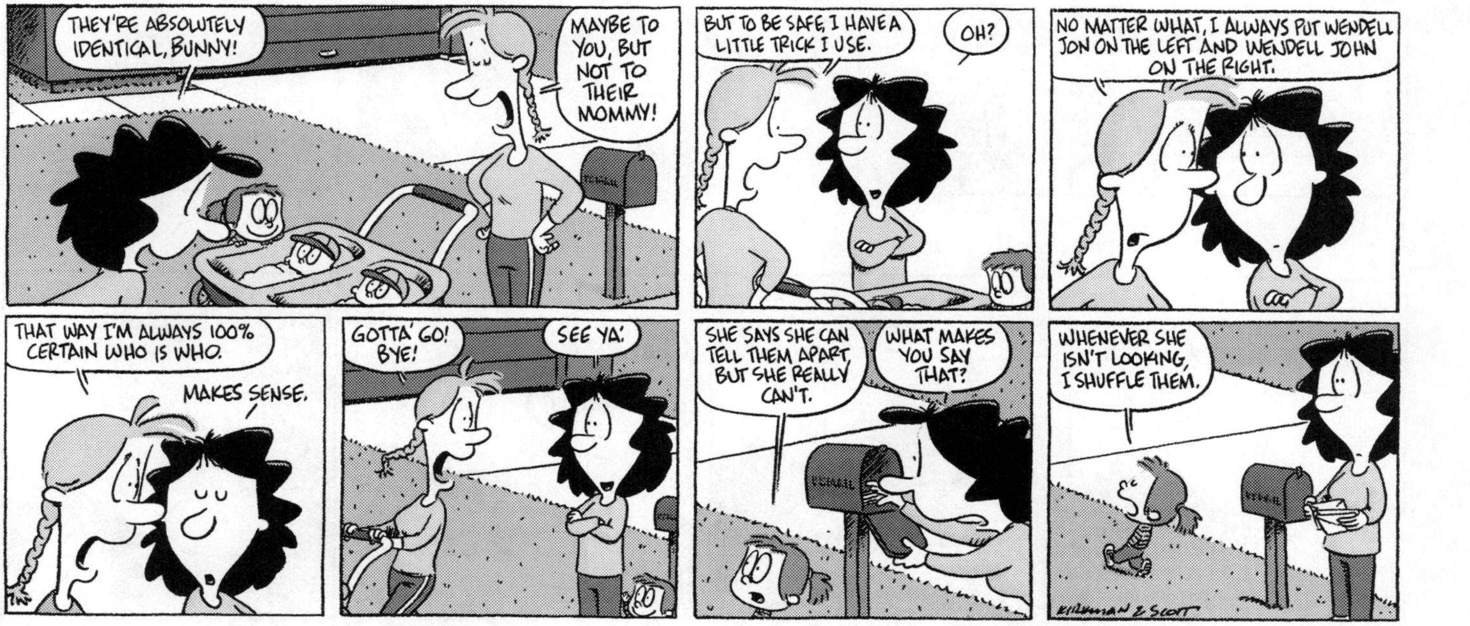
THEY'RE ABSOLUTELY IDENTICAL, BUNNY!
MAYBE TO YOU, BUT NOT TO THEIR MOMMY!
BUT TO BE SAFE, I HAVE A LITTLE TRICK I USE.
OH?
NO MATTER WHAT, I ALWAYS PUT WENDELL JON ON THE LEFT AND WENDELL JOHN ON THE RIGHT.
THAT WAY I'M ALWAYS 100% CERTAIN WHO IS WHO.
MAKES SENSE.
GOTTA' GO! BYE!
SEE YA'.
SHE SAYS SHE CAN TELL THEM APART, BUT SHE REALLY CAN'T.
WHAT MAKES YOU SAY THAT?
WHENEVER SHE ISN'T LOOKING, I SHUFFLE THEM.
KIRKMAN & SCOTT

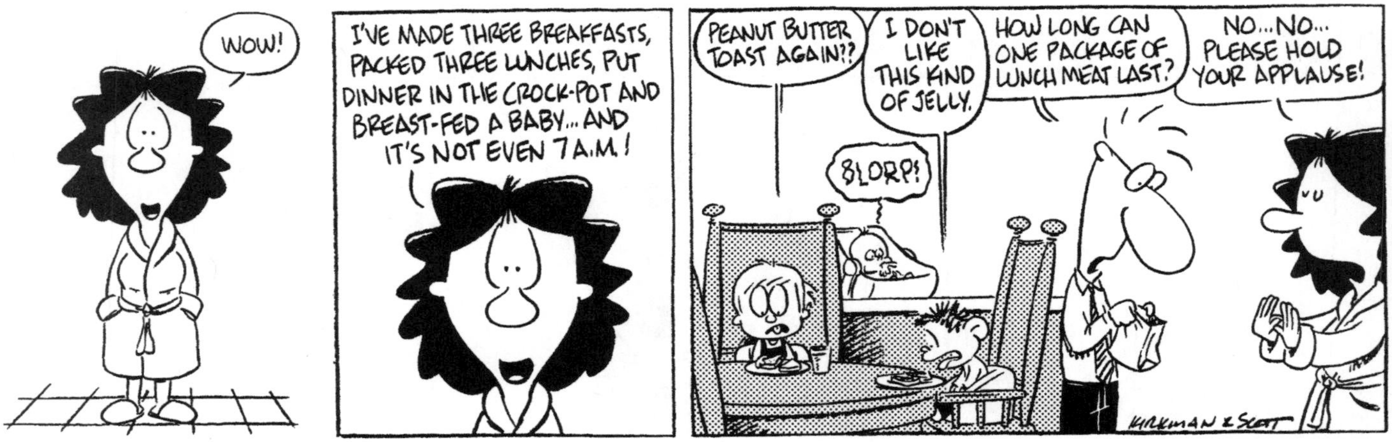
WOW!
I'VE MADE THREE BREAKFASTS, PACKED THREE LUNCHES, PUT DINNER IN THE CROCK-POT AND BREAST-FED A BABY... AND IT'S NOT EVEN 7 A.M.!
PEANUT BUTTER TOAST AGAIN??
I DON'T LIKE THIS KIND OF JELLY.
SLORP!
HOW LONG CAN ONE PACKAGE OF LUNCH MEAT LAST?
NO...NO... PLEASE HOLD YOUR APPLAUSE!
KIRKMAN & SCOTT

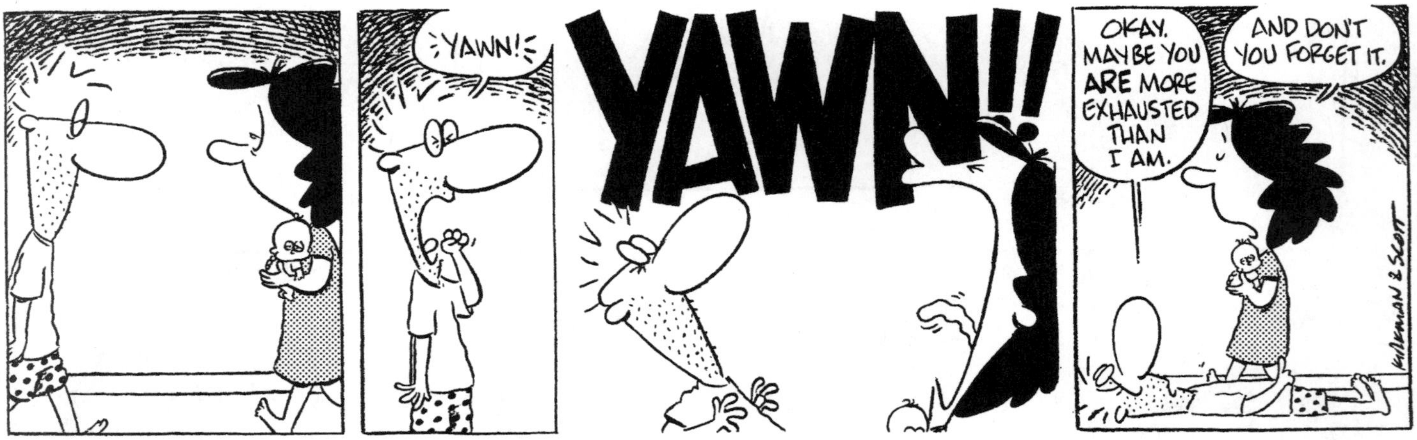
YAWN!
YAWN!!
OKAY. MAYBE YOU ARE MORE EXHAUSTED THAN I AM.
AND DON'T YOU FORGET IT.
KIRKMAN & SCOTT

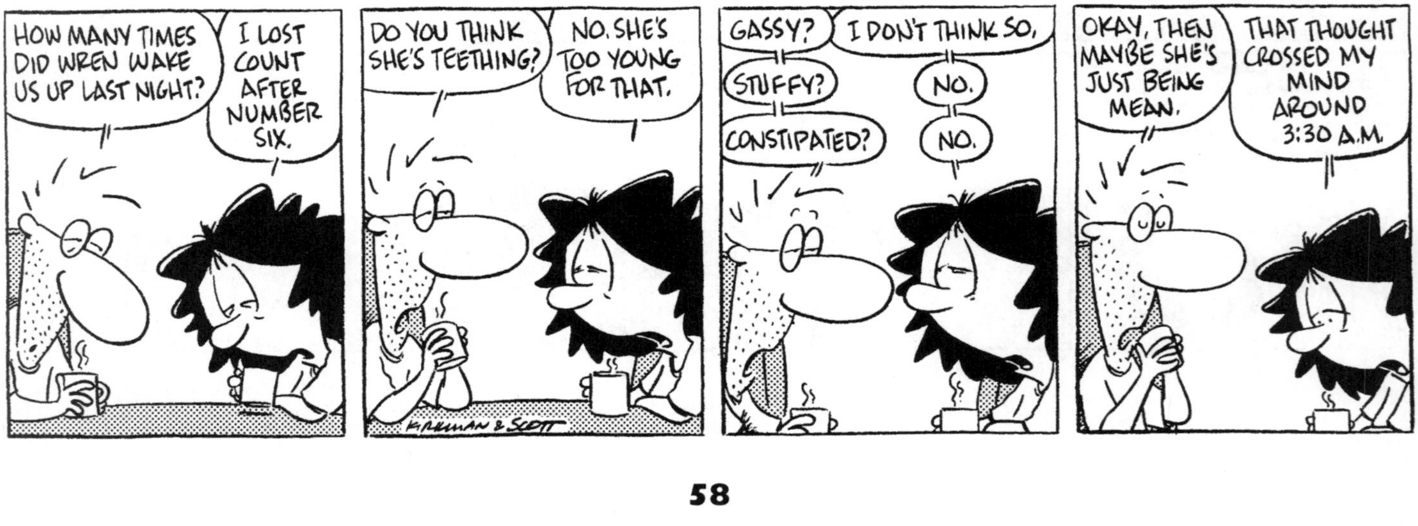
HOW MANY TIMES DID WREN WAKE US UP LAST NIGHT?
I LOST COUNT AFTER NUMBER SIX.
DO YOU THINK SHE'S TEETHING?
NO. SHE'S TOO YOUNG FOR THAT.
KIRKMAN & SCOTT
GASSY?
I DON'T THINK SO.
STUFFY?
NO.
CONSTIPATED?
NO.
OKAY, THEN MAYBE SHE'S JUST BEING MEAN.
THAT THOUGHT CROSSED MY MIND AROUND 3:30 A.M.

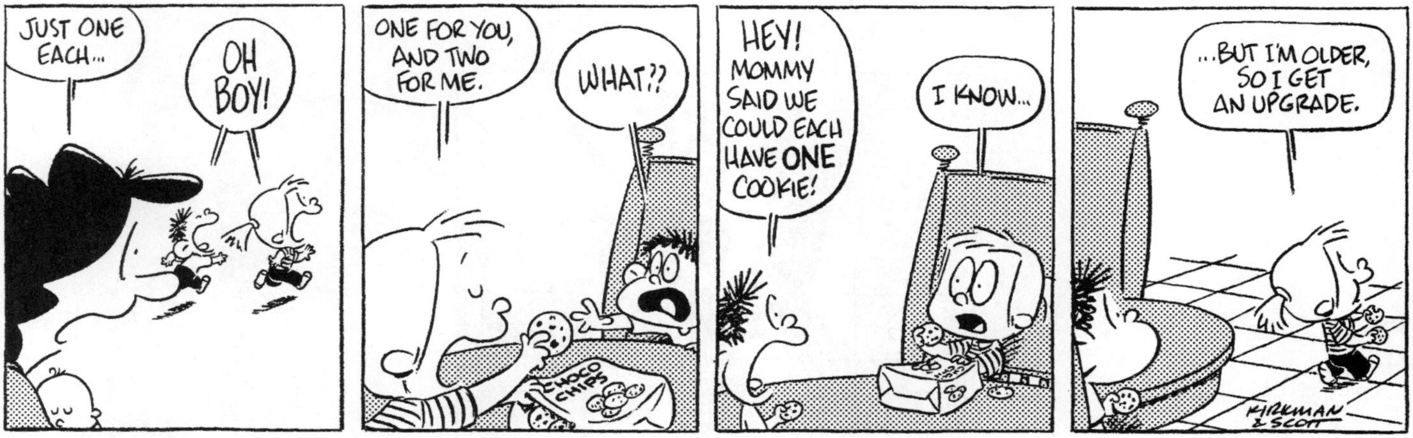
JUST ONE EACH...
OH BOY!
ONE FOR YOU, AND TWO FOR ME.
WHAT??
CHOCO CHIPS
HEY! MOMMY SAID WE COULD EACH HAVE **ONE** COOKIE!
I KNOW...
...BUT I'M OLDER, SO I GET AN UPGRADE.
KIRKMAN & SCOTT

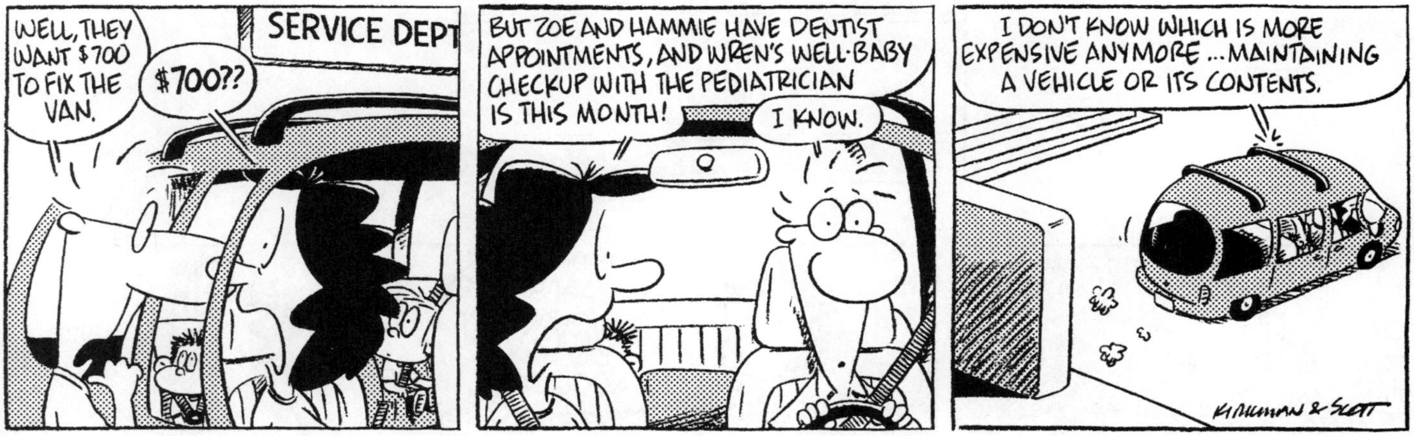
WELL, THEY WANT $700 TO FIX THE VAN.
SERVICE DEPT
$700??
BUT ZOE AND HAMMIE HAVE DENTIST APPOINTMENTS, AND WREN'S WELL-BABY CHECKUP WITH THE PEDIATRICIAN IS THIS MONTH!
I KNOW.
I DON'T KNOW WHICH IS MORE EXPENSIVE ANYMORE ...MAINTAINING A VEHICLE OR ITS CONTENTS.
KIRKMAN & SCOTT

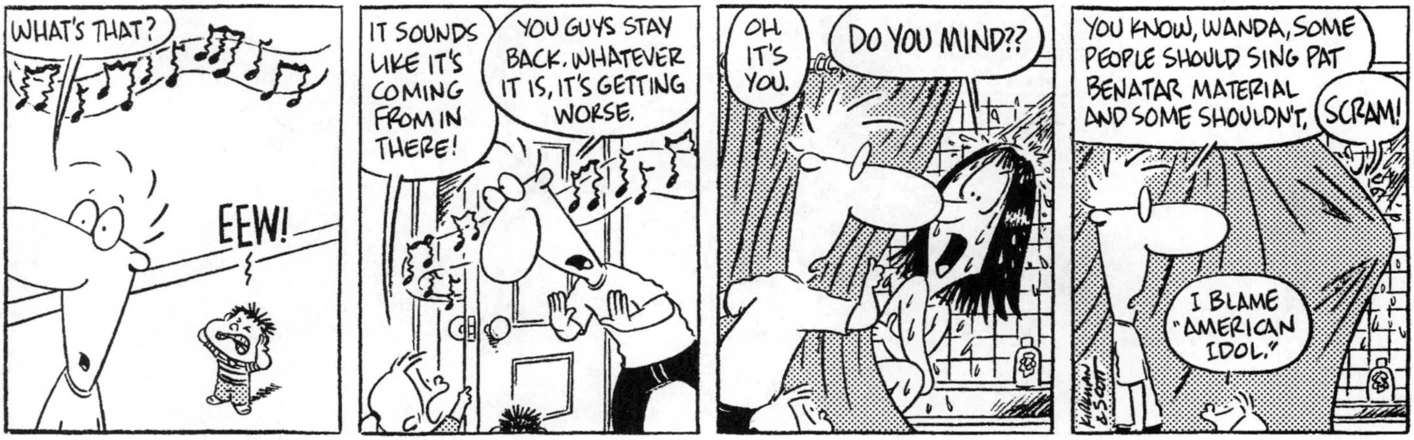
WHAT'S THAT?
EEW!
IT SOUNDS LIKE IT'S COMING FROM IN THERE!
YOU GUYS STAY BACK. WHATEVER IT IS, IT'S GETTING WORSE.
OH. IT'S YOU.
DO YOU MIND??
KIRKMAN & SCOTT
YOU KNOW, WANDA, SOME PEOPLE SHOULD SING PAT BENATAR MATERIAL AND SOME SHOULDN'T.
SCRAM!
I BLAME "AMERICAN IDOL."

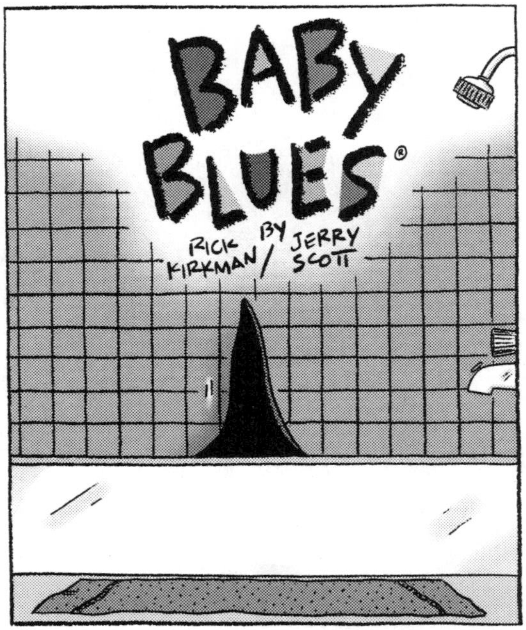
BABY BLUES®
BY RICK KIRKMAN / JERRY SCOTT

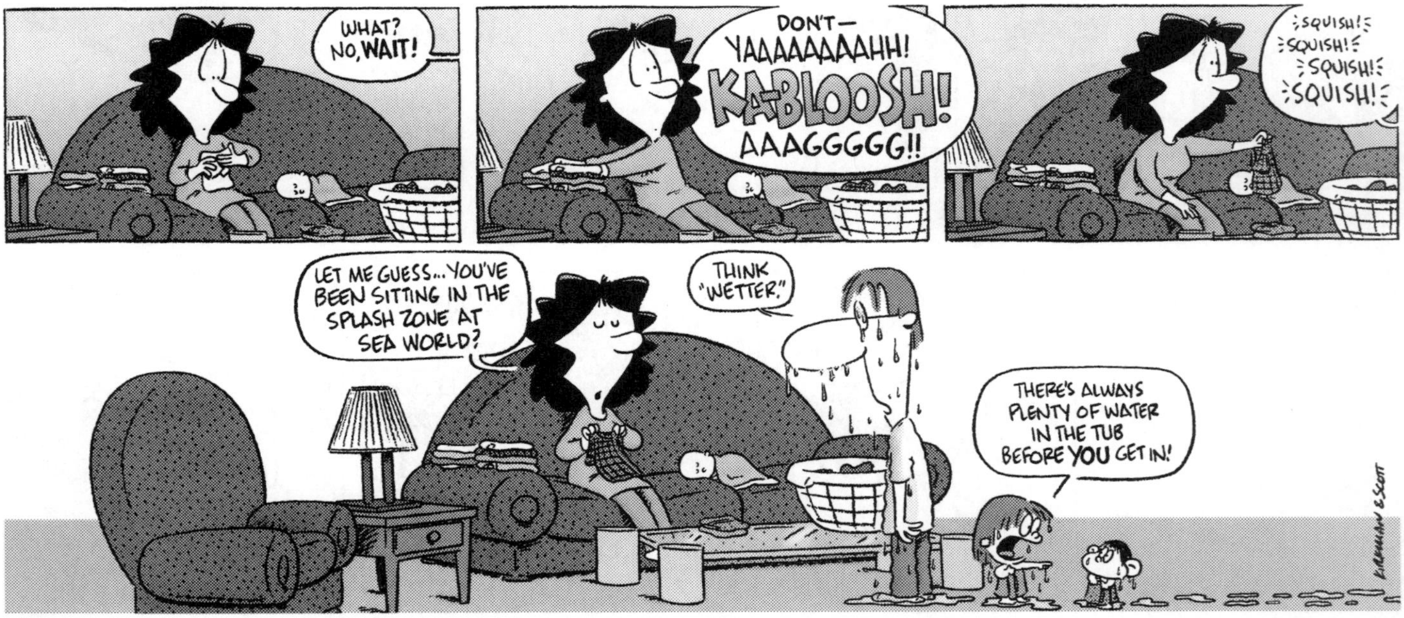
WHAT? NO, WAIT!
DON'T—
YAAAAAAAAHH!
KA-BLOOSH!
AAAGGGGG!!
SQUISH! SQUISH! SQUISH! SQUISH!
LET ME GUESS... YOU'VE BEEN SITTING IN THE SPLASH ZONE AT SEA WORLD?
THINK "WETTER."
THERE'S ALWAYS PLENTY OF WATER IN THE TUB BEFORE YOU GET IN!

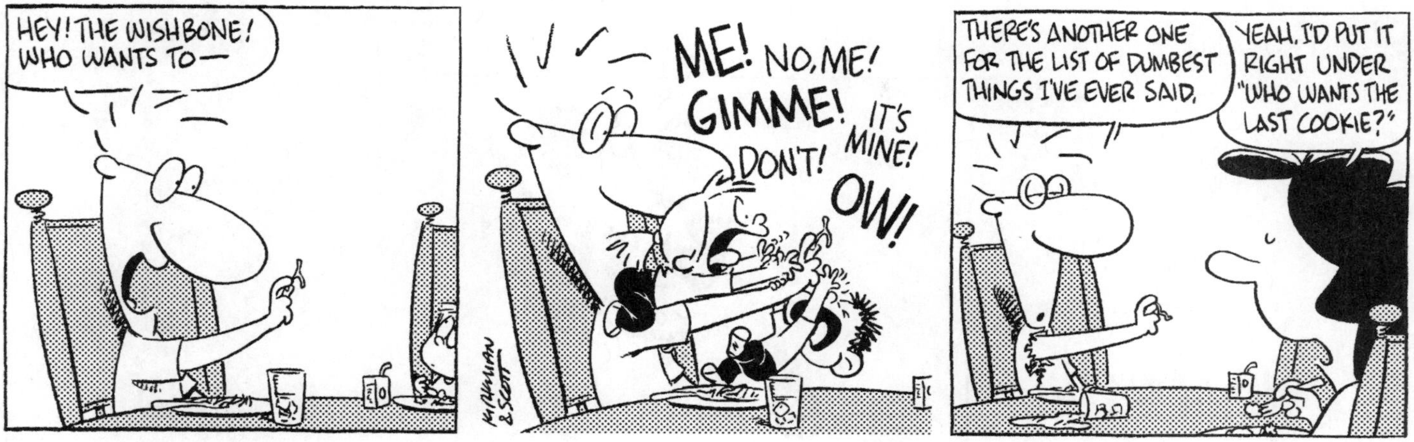
HEY! THE WISHBONE! WHO WANTS TO—
ME!
NO, ME!
GIMME!
IT'S MINE!
DON'T!
OW!
THERE'S ANOTHER ONE FOR THE LIST OF DUMBEST THINGS I'VE EVER SAID.
YEAH, I'D PUT IT RIGHT UNDER "WHO WANTS THE LAST COOKIE?"

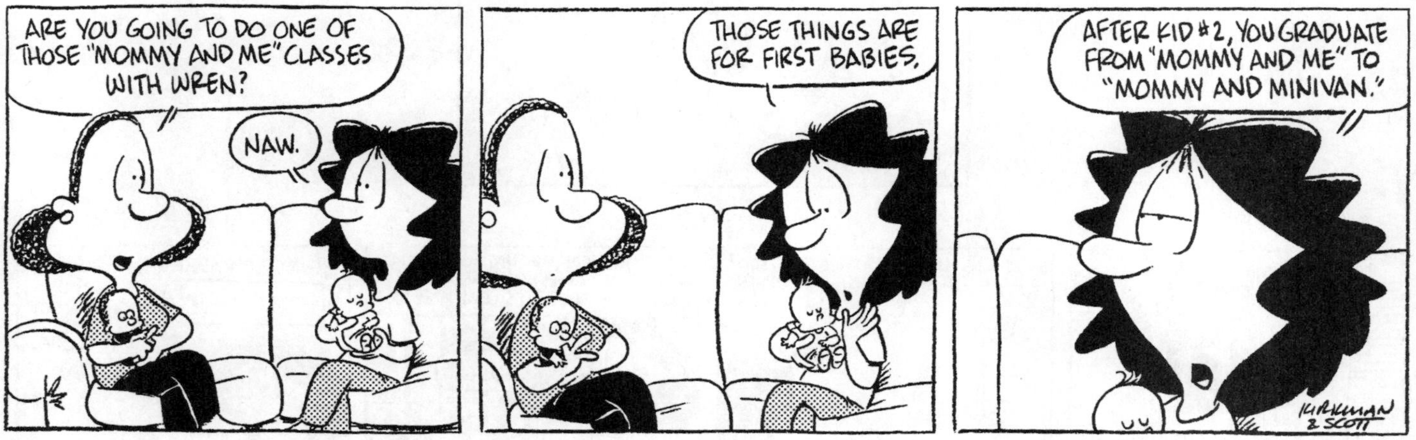
ARE YOU GOING TO DO ONE OF THOSE "MOMMY AND ME" CLASSES WITH WREN?
NAW.
THOSE THINGS ARE FOR FIRST BABIES.
AFTER KID #2, YOU GRADUATE FROM "MOMMY AND ME" TO "MOMMY AND MINIVAN."
KIRKMAN & SCOTT

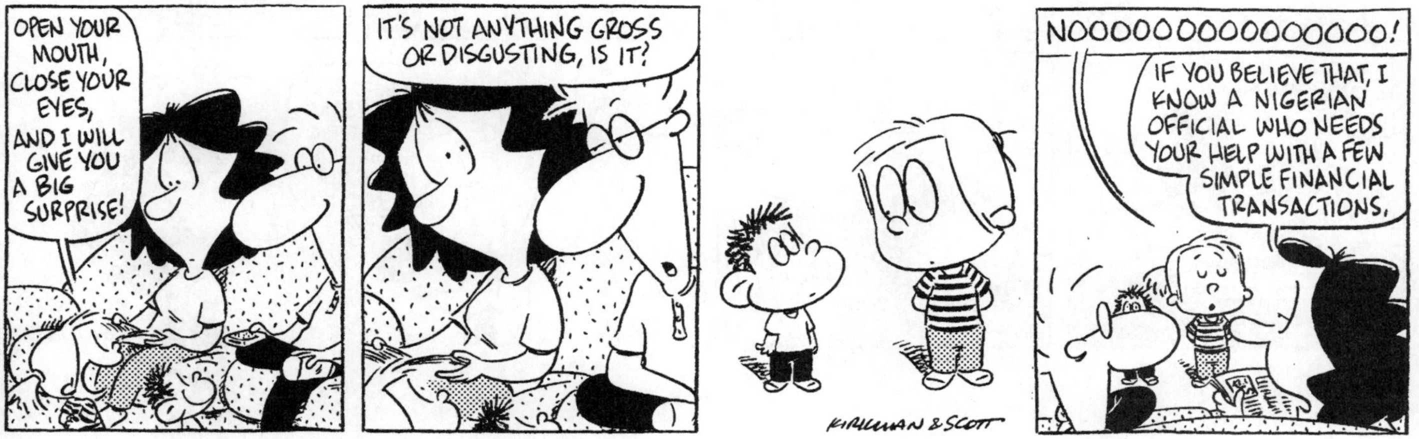
OPEN YOUR MOUTH, CLOSE YOUR EYES, AND I WILL GIVE YOU A BIG SURPRISE!
IT'S NOT ANYTHING GROSS OR DISGUSTING, IS IT?
KIRKMAN & SCOTT
NOOOOOOOOOOOOOOO!
IF YOU BELIEVE THAT, I KNOW A NIGERIAN OFFICIAL WHO NEEDS YOUR HELP WITH A FEW SIMPLE FINANCIAL TRANSACTIONS.

BABY BLUES®
BY RICK KIRKMAN / JERRY SCOTT

DWEEDLE! DWEEDLE! DWEEDLE!
WHAT WAS THAT?
YOU HEARD IT, TOO? OH, THANK GOODNESS! I THOUGHT I WAS GOING NUTS!
I'VE BEEN HEARING THAT SOUND ON AND OFF ALL AFTERNOON, AND I CAN'T FIGURE OUT WHERE IT'S COMING FROM!
STRANGE...
DWEEDLE! DWEEDLE! DWEEDLE!
THERE IT IS AGAIN!
IT'S NOT THE PHONE...
DWEEDLE! DWEEDLE! DWEEDLE!
IT'S NOT THE OVEN TIMER...
MAYBE THE SMOKE DETECTOR NEEDS NEW BATTERIES.
OR COULD IT BE THE FRIDGE?
DWEEDLE! DWEEDLE! DWEEDLE!
NO, IT'S MORE LIKE A NOISE THAT WOULD COME FROM A TIMER, OR AN ALARM CLOCK, OR—
DWEEDLE! DWEEDLE! DWEEDLE!
—A PAIR OF MUSICAL SNEAKERS.
TRENT'S MOM SAID I COULD HAVE THEM BECAUSE THEY DRIVE HER NUTS!
KIRKMAN & SCOTT

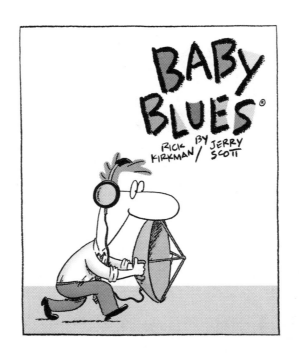

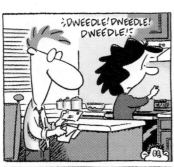

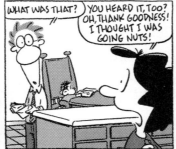

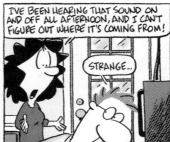

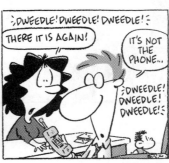

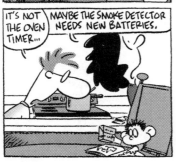

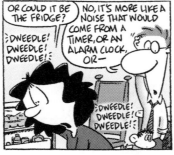

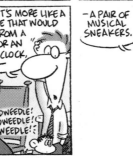

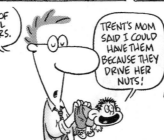

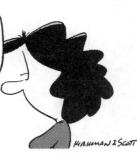

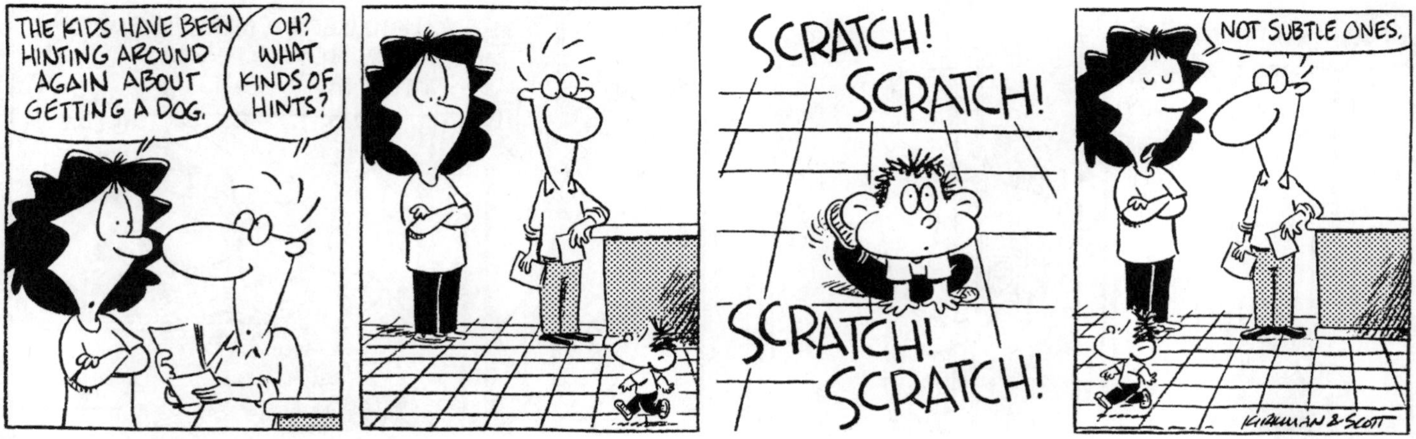
THE KIDS HAVE BEEN HINTING AROUND AGAIN ABOUT GETTING A DOG.
OH? WHAT KINDS OF HINTS?
SCRATCH! SCRATCH!
SCRATCH! SCRATCH!
NOT SUBTLE ONES.
KIRKMAN & SCOTT

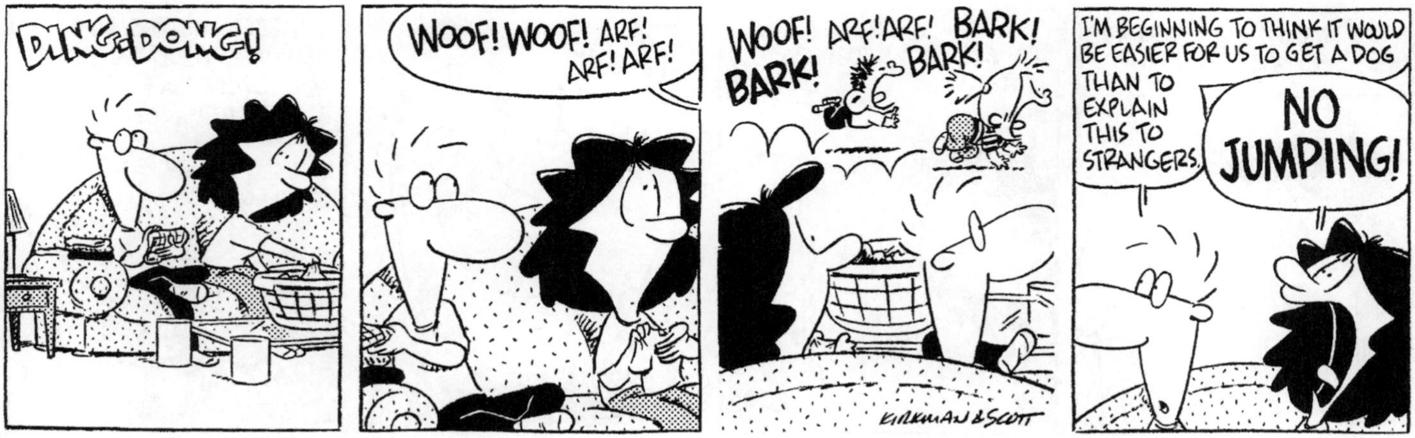
DING-DONG!
WOOF! WOOF! ARF! ARF! ARF!
WOOF! ARF! ARF! BARK! BARK! BARK!
KIRKMAN & SCOTT
I'M BEGINNING TO THINK IT WOULD BE EASIER FOR US TO GET A DOG THAN TO EXPLAIN THIS TO STRANGERS.
NO JUMPING!

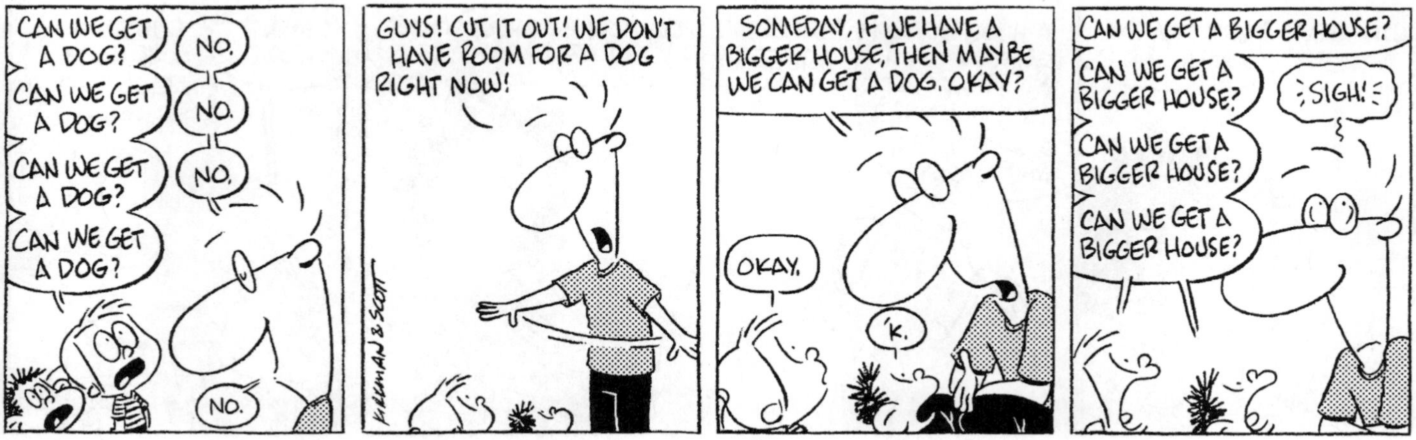
CAN WE GET A DOG?
NO.
CAN WE GET A DOG?
NO.
CAN WE GET A DOG?
NO.
CAN WE GET A DOG?
NO.
GUYS! CUT IT OUT! WE DON'T HAVE ROOM FOR A DOG RIGHT NOW!
KIRKMAN & SCOTT
SOMEDAY, IF WE HAVE A BIGGER HOUSE, THEN MAYBE WE CAN GET A DOG. OKAY?
OKAY.
K.
CAN WE GET A BIGGER HOUSE?
CAN WE GET A BIGGER HOUSE?
SIGH!
CAN WE GET A BIGGER HOUSE?
CAN WE GET A BIGGER HOUSE?

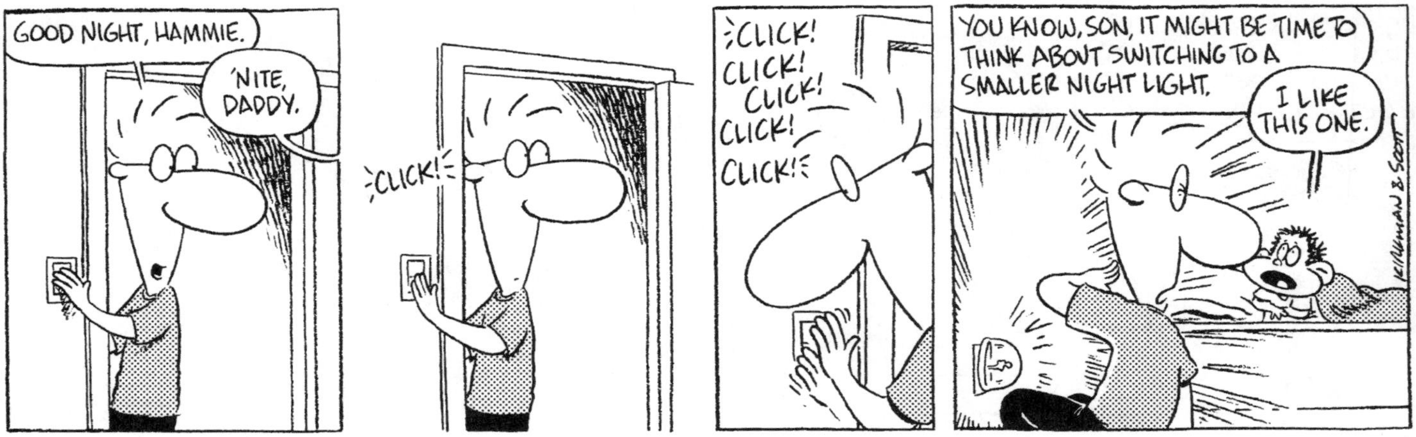
GOOD NIGHT, HAMMIE.
'NITE, DADDY.
CLICK!
CLICK! CLICK! CLICK! CLICK! CLICK!
YOU KNOW, SON, IT MIGHT BE TIME TO THINK ABOUT SWITCHING TO A SMALLER NIGHT LIGHT.
I LIKE THIS ONE.
KIRKMAN & SCOTT

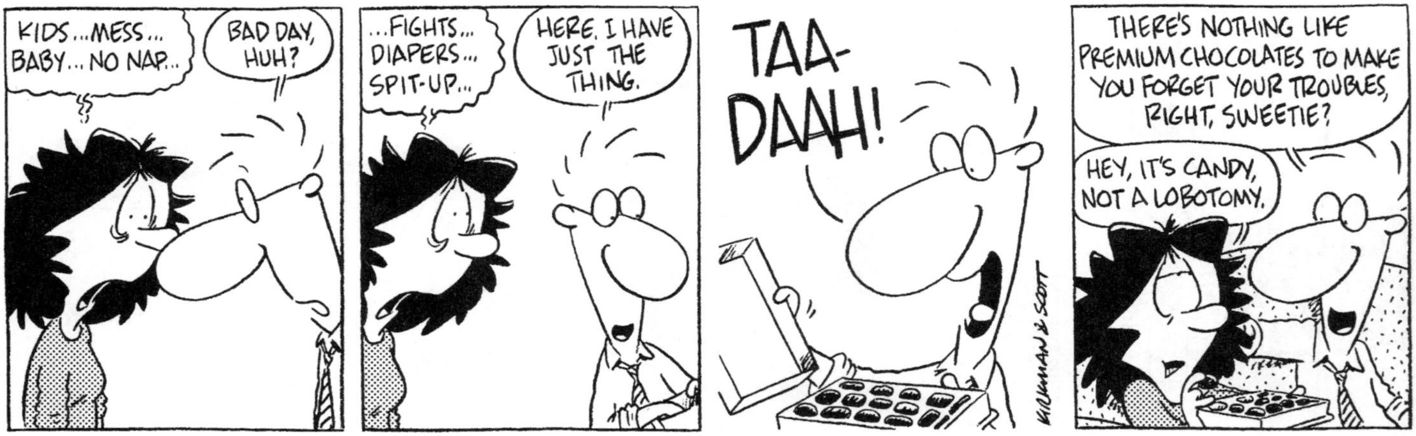
KIDS...MESS... BABY... NO NAP...
BAD DAY, HUH?
...FIGHTS... DIAPERS... SPIT-UP...
HERE. I HAVE JUST THE THING.
TAA-DAAH!
KIRKMAN & SCOTT
THERE'S NOTHING LIKE PREMIUM CHOCOLATES TO MAKE YOU FORGET YOUR TROUBLES, RIGHT, SWEETIE?
HEY, IT'S CANDY, NOT A LOBOTOMY.

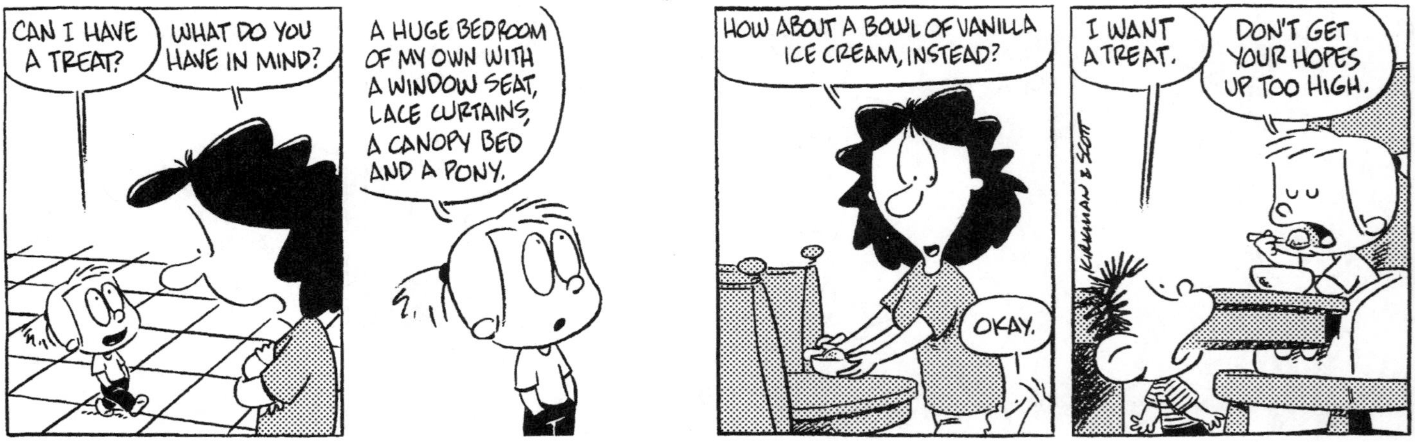
CAN I HAVE A TREAT?
WHAT DO YOU HAVE IN MIND?
A HUGE BEDROOM OF MY OWN WITH A WINDOW SEAT, LACE CURTAINS, A CANOPY BED AND A PONY.
HOW ABOUT A BOWL OF VANILLA ICE CREAM, INSTEAD?
OKAY.
I WANT A TREAT.
DON'T GET YOUR HOPES UP TOO HIGH.
KIRKMAN & SCOTT

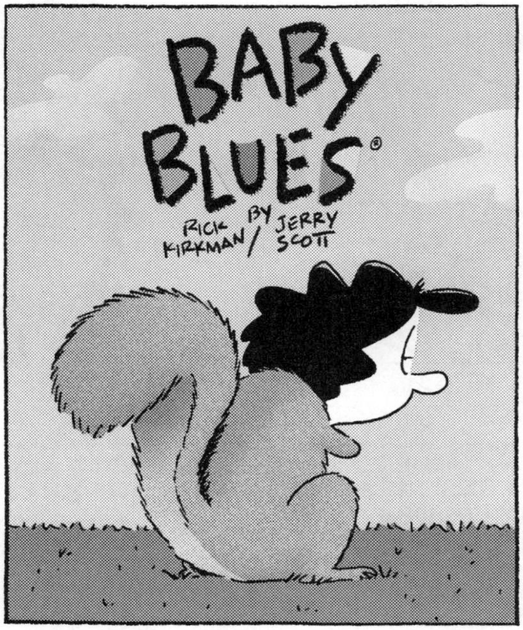
BABY BLUES®
BY RICK KIRKMAN / JERRY SCOTT

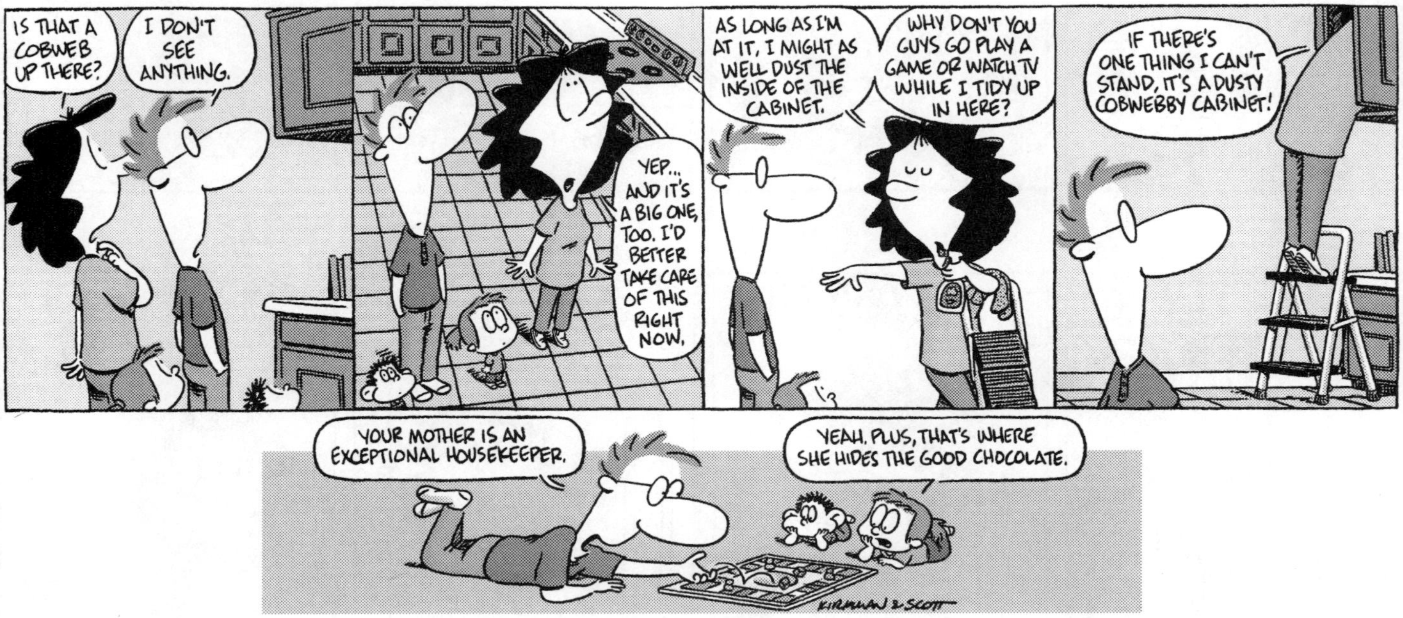
IS THAT A COBWEB UP THERE?
I DON'T SEE ANYTHING.
YEP... AND IT'S A BIG ONE, TOO. I'D BETTER TAKE CARE OF THIS RIGHT NOW.
AS LONG AS I'M AT IT, I MIGHT AS WELL DUST THE INSIDE OF THE CABINET.
WHY DON'T YOU GUYS GO PLAY A GAME OR WATCH TV WHILE I TIDY UP IN HERE?
IF THERE'S ONE THING I CAN'T STAND, IT'S A DUSTY COBWEBBY CABINET!
YOUR MOTHER IS AN EXCEPTIONAL HOUSEKEEPER.
YEAH. PLUS, THAT'S WHERE SHE HIDES THE GOOD CHOCOLATE.
KIRKMAN & SCOTT

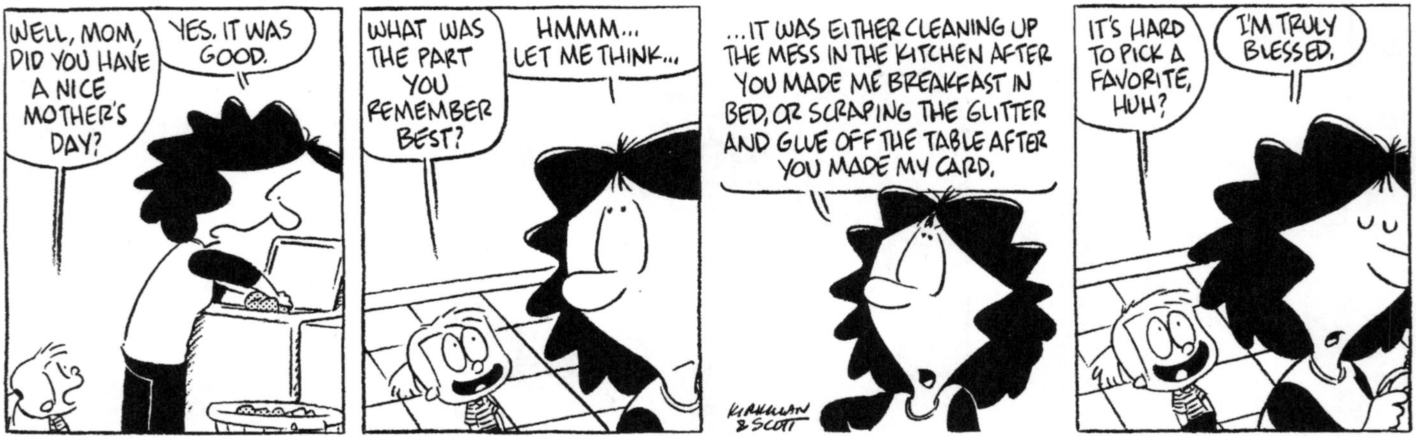
WELL, MOM, DID YOU HAVE A NICE MOTHER'S DAY?
YES. IT WAS GOOD.
WHAT WAS THE PART YOU REMEMBER BEST?
HMMM... LET ME THINK...
...IT WAS EITHER CLEANING UP THE MESS IN THE KITCHEN AFTER YOU MADE ME BREAKFAST IN BED, OR SCRAPING THE GLITTER AND GLUE OFF THE TABLE AFTER YOU MADE MY CARD.
KIRKMAN & SCOTT
IT'S HARD TO PICK A FAVORITE, HUH?
I'M TRULY BLESSED.

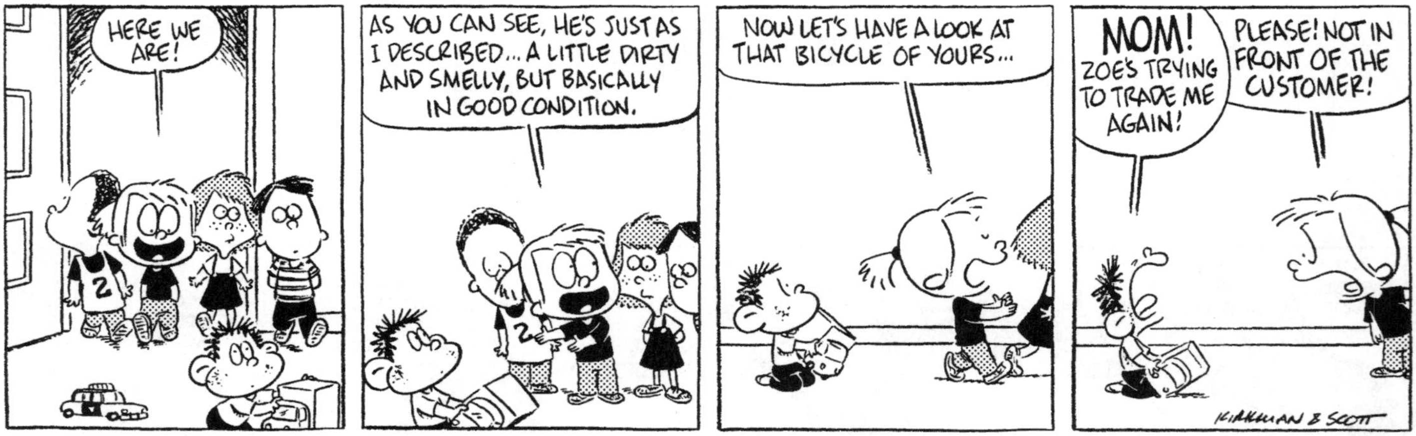
HERE WE ARE!
AS YOU CAN SEE, HE'S JUST AS I DESCRIBED... A LITTLE DIRTY AND SMELLY, BUT BASICALLY IN GOOD CONDITION.
NOW LET'S HAVE A LOOK AT THAT BICYCLE OF YOURS...
MOM! ZOE'S TRYING TO TRADE ME AGAIN!
PLEASE! NOT IN FRONT OF THE CUSTOMER!
KIRKMAN & SCOTT

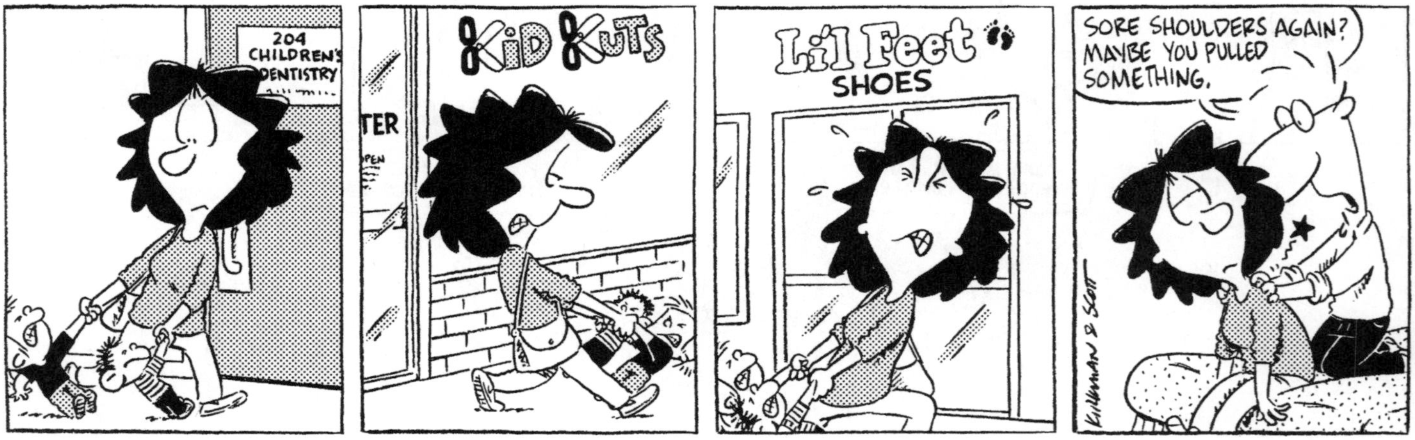
204 CHILDREN'S DENTISTRY
KID KUTS
LI'L FEET
SHOES
KIRKMAN & SCOTT
SORE SHOULDERS AGAIN? MAYBE YOU PULLED SOMETHING.

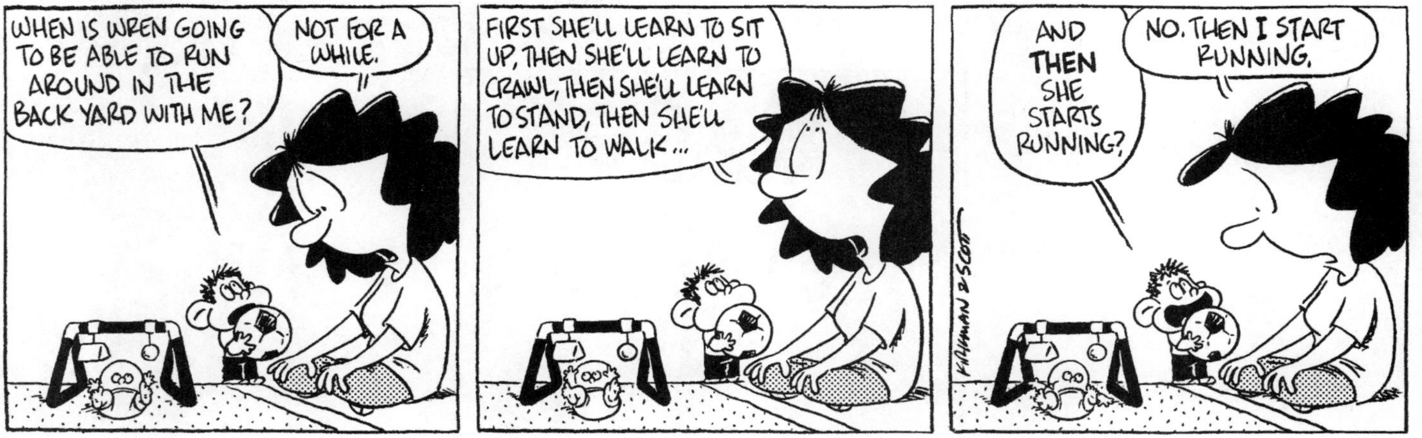
WHEN IS WREN GOING TO BE ABLE TO RUN AROUND IN THE BACK YARD WITH ME?
NOT FOR A WHILE.
FIRST SHE'LL LEARN TO SIT UP, THEN SHE'LL LEARN TO CRAWL, THEN SHE'LL LEARN TO STAND, THEN SHE'LL LEARN TO WALK...
AND **THEN** SHE STARTS RUNNING?
NO. THEN **I** START RUNNING.
KIRKMAN & SCOTT

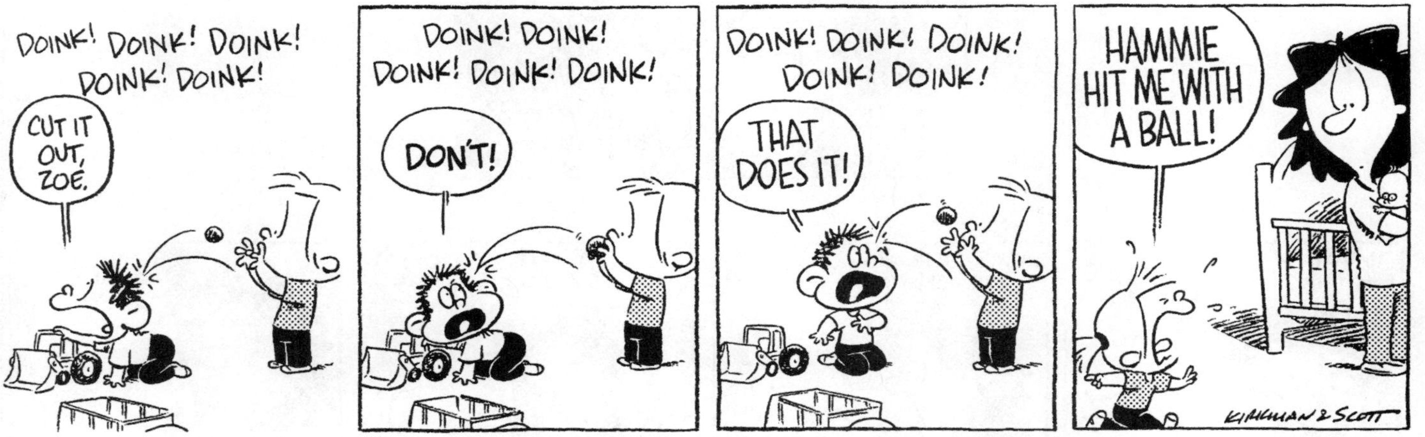
DOINK! DOINK! DOINK! DOINK! DOINK!
CUT IT OUT, ZOE.
DOINK! DOINK! DOINK! DOINK! DOINK!
DON'T!
DOINK! DOINK! DOINK! DOINK! DOINK!
THAT DOES IT!
HAMMIE HIT ME WITH A BALL!
KIRKMAN & SCOTT

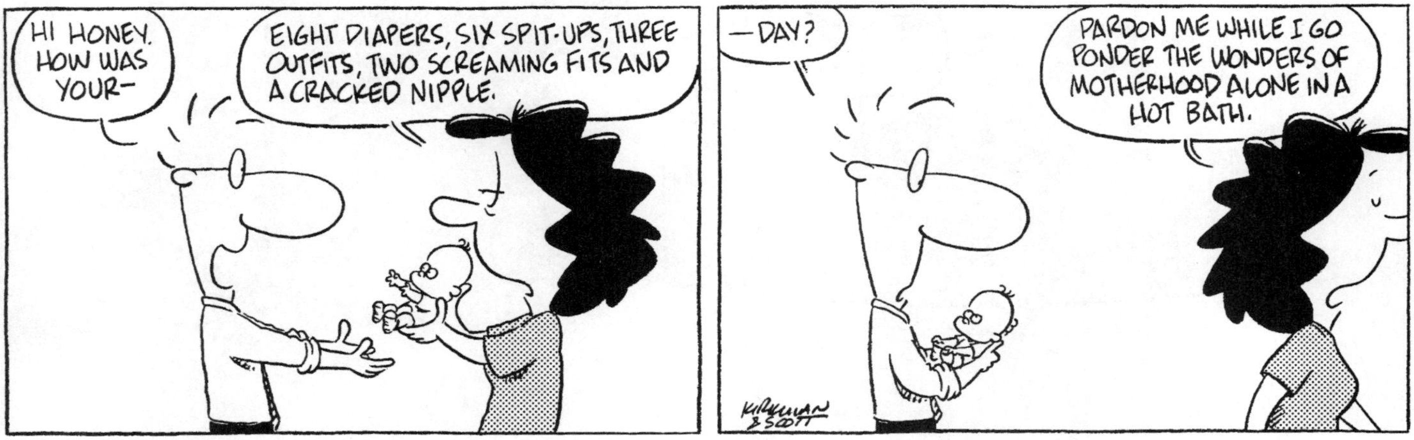
HI HONEY. HOW WAS YOUR–
EIGHT DIAPERS, SIX SPIT-UPS, THREE OUTFITS, TWO SCREAMING FITS AND A CRACKED NIPPLE.
–DAY?
PARDON ME WHILE I GO PONDER THE WONDERS OF MOTHERHOOD ALONE IN A HOT BATH.
KIRKMAN & SCOTT

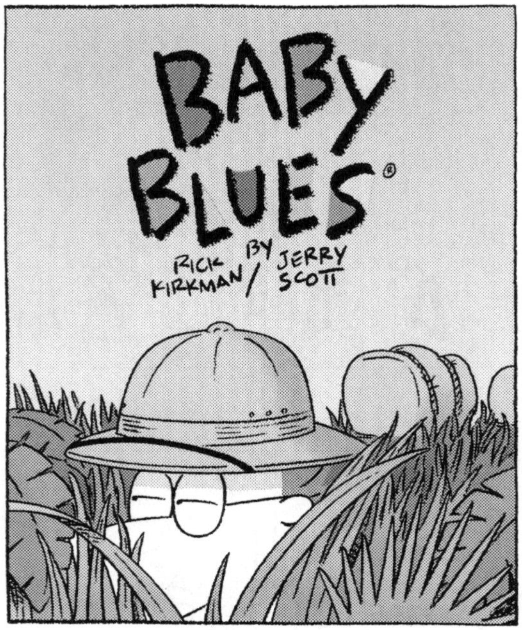
BABY BLUES®
BY RICK KIRKMAN / JERRY SCOTT

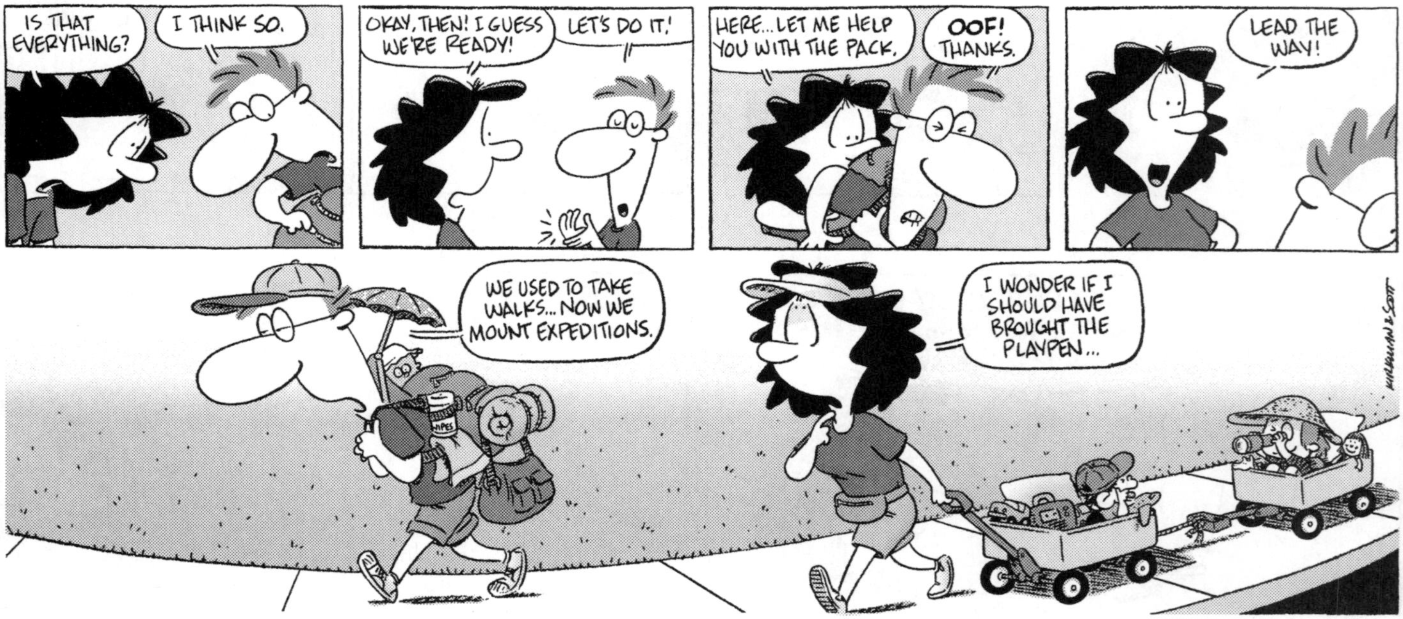
IS THAT EVERYTHING?
I THINK SO.
OKAY, THEN! I GUESS WE'RE READY!
LET'S DO IT!
HERE... LET ME HELP YOU WITH THE PACK.
OOF! THANKS.
LEAD THE WAY!
WE USED TO TAKE WALKS... NOW WE MOUNT EXPEDITIONS.
I WONDER IF I SHOULD HAVE BROUGHT THE PLAYPEN...
WIPES

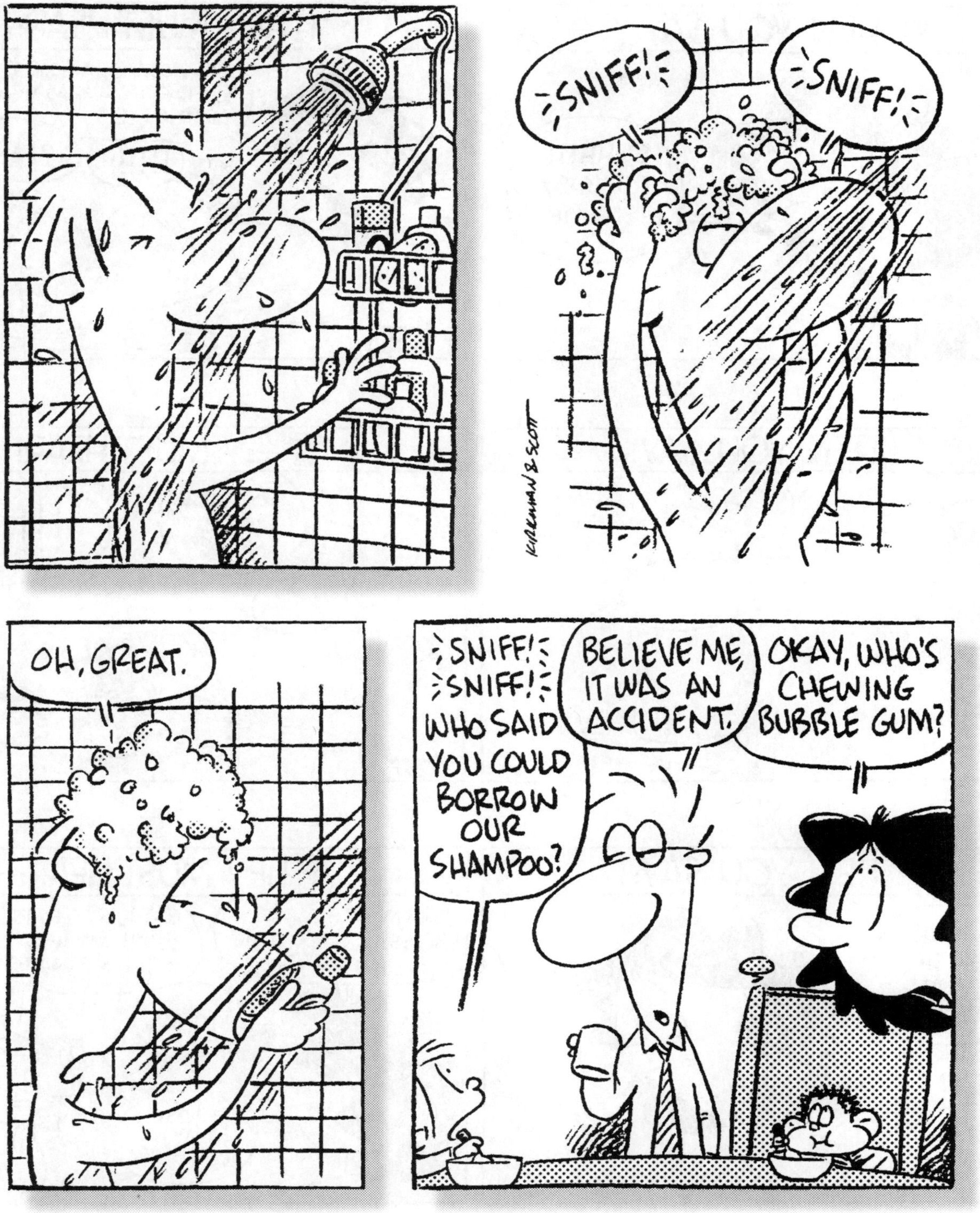
SNIFF!
SNIFF!
KIRKMAN & SCOTT
OH, GREAT.
SNIFF! SNIFF! WHO SAID YOU COULD BORROW OUR SHAMPOO?
BELIEVE ME, IT WAS AN ACCIDENT.
OKAY, WHO'S CHEWING BUBBLE GUM?

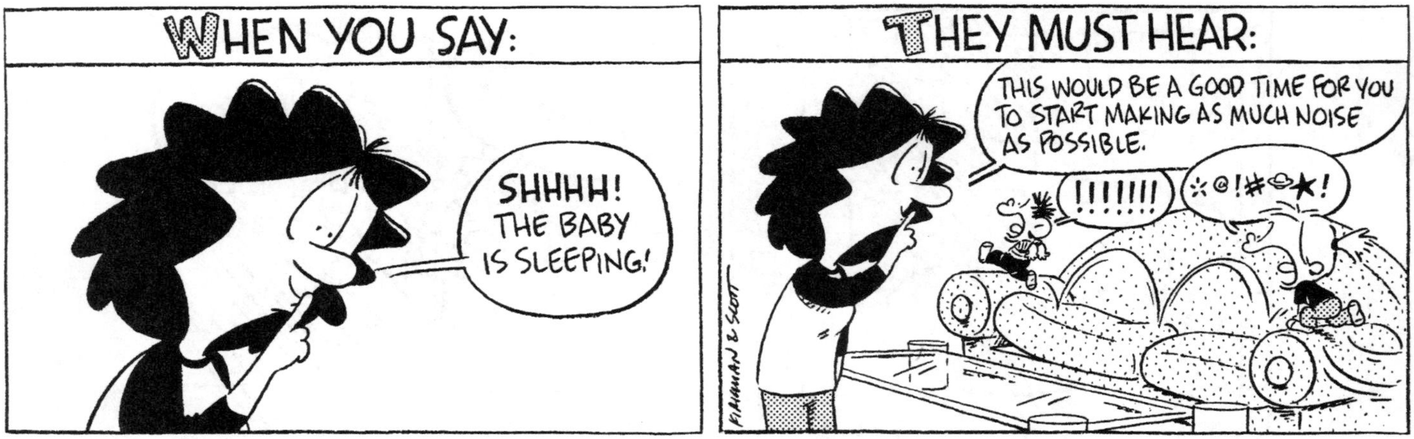
WHEN YOU SAY:
SHHHH! THE BABY IS SLEEPING!
THEY MUST HEAR:
THIS WOULD BE A GOOD TIME FOR YOU TO START MAKING AS MUCH NOISE AS POSSIBLE.
!!!!!!!
KIRKMAN & SCOTT

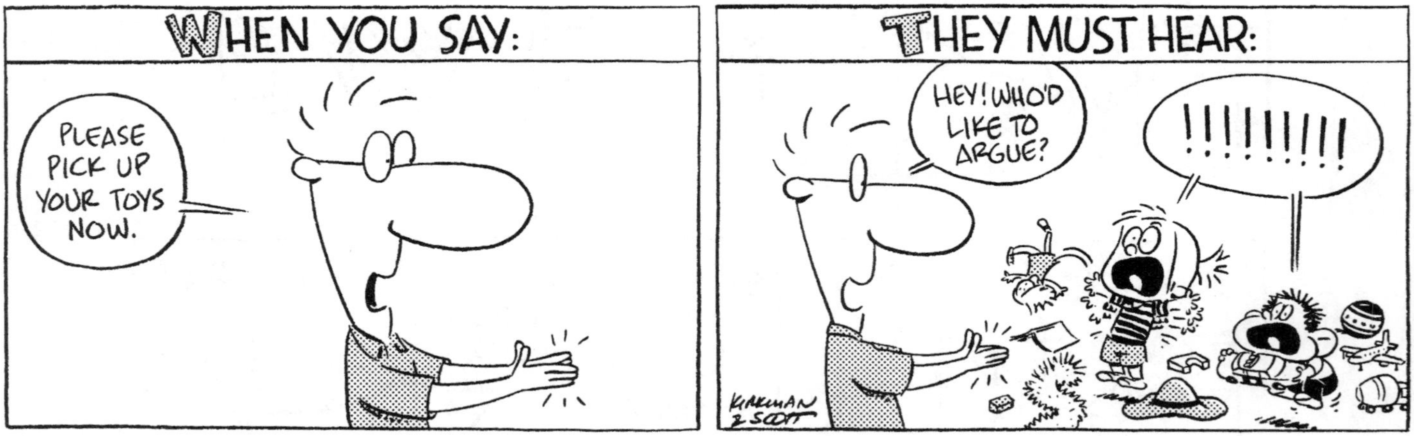
WHEN YOU SAY:
PLEASE PICK UP YOUR TOYS NOW.
THEY MUST HEAR:
HEY! WHO'D LIKE TO ARGUE?
!!!!!!!!!
KIRKMAN & SCOTT

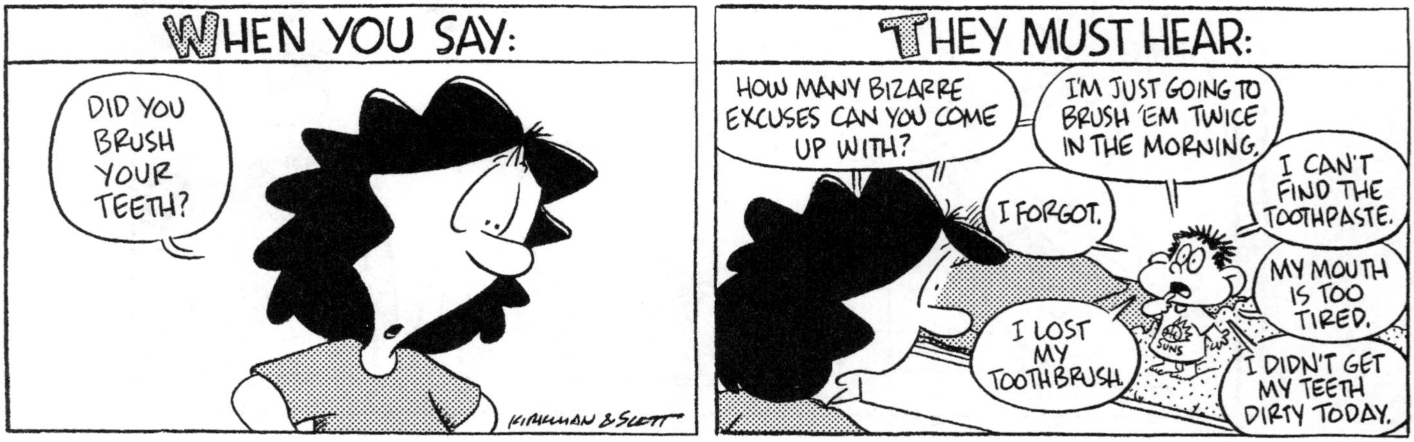
WHEN YOU SAY:
DID YOU BRUSH YOUR TEETH?
KIRKMAN & SCOTT
THEY MUST HEAR:
HOW MANY BIZARRE EXCUSES CAN YOU COME UP WITH?
I'M JUST GOING TO BRUSH 'EM TWICE IN THE MORNING.
I FORGOT.
I CAN'T FIND THE TOOTHPASTE.
MY MOUTH IS TOO TIRED.
I LOST MY TOOTHBRUSH.
I DIDN'T GET MY TEETH DIRTY TODAY.
SUNS

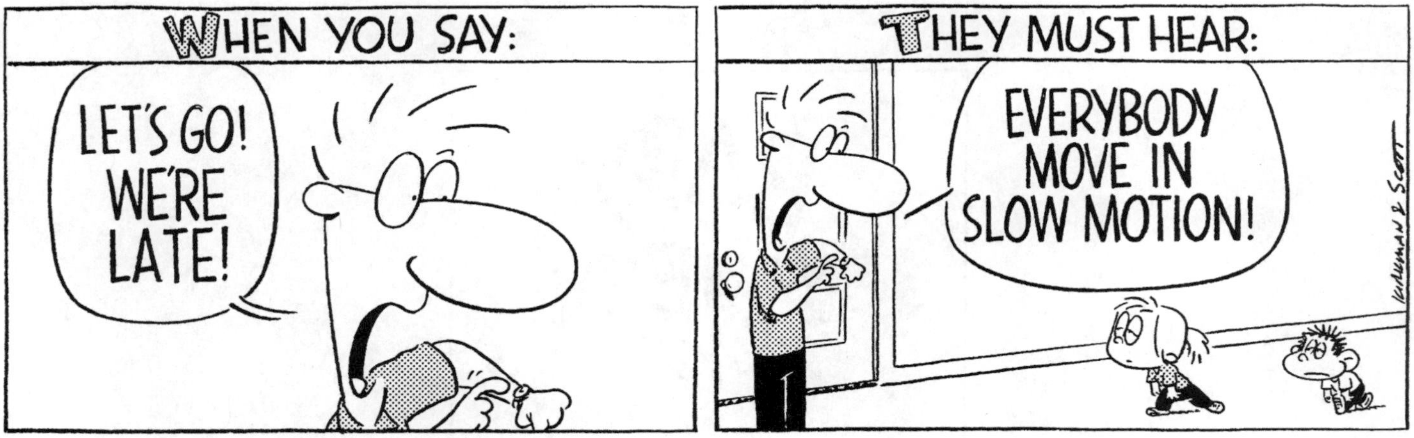
WHEN YOU SAY:
LET'S GO! WE'RE LATE!
THEY MUST HEAR:
EVERYBODY MOVE IN SLOW MOTION!
KIRKMAN & SCOTT

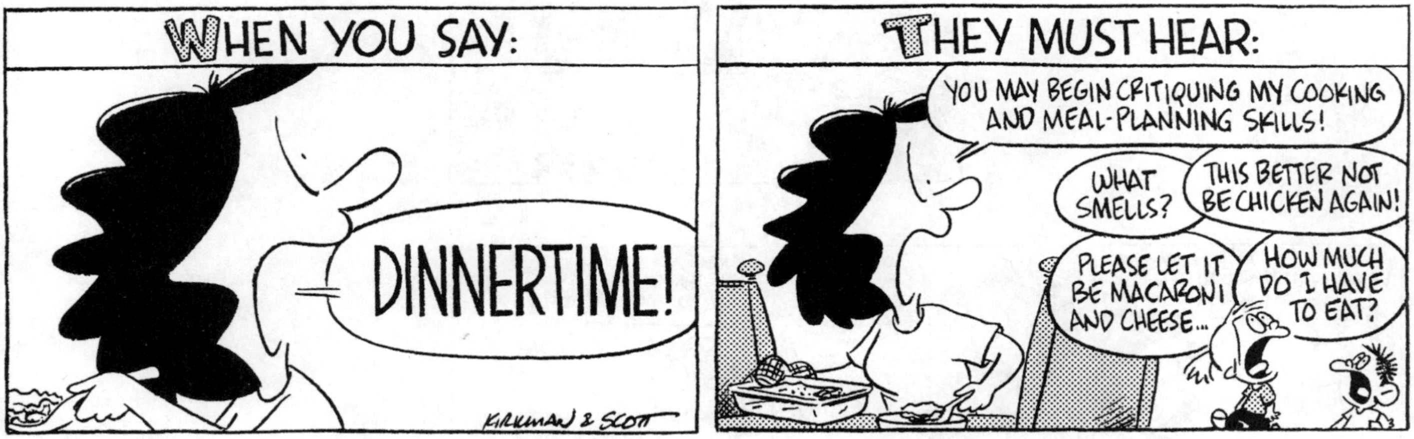
WHEN YOU SAY:
DINNERTIME!
KIRKMAN & SCOTT
THEY MUST HEAR:
YOU MAY BEGIN CRITIQUING MY COOKING AND MEAL-PLANNING SKILLS!
WHAT SMELLS?
THIS BETTER NOT BE CHICKEN AGAIN!
PLEASE LET IT BE MACARONI AND CHEESE...
HOW MUCH DO I HAVE TO EAT?

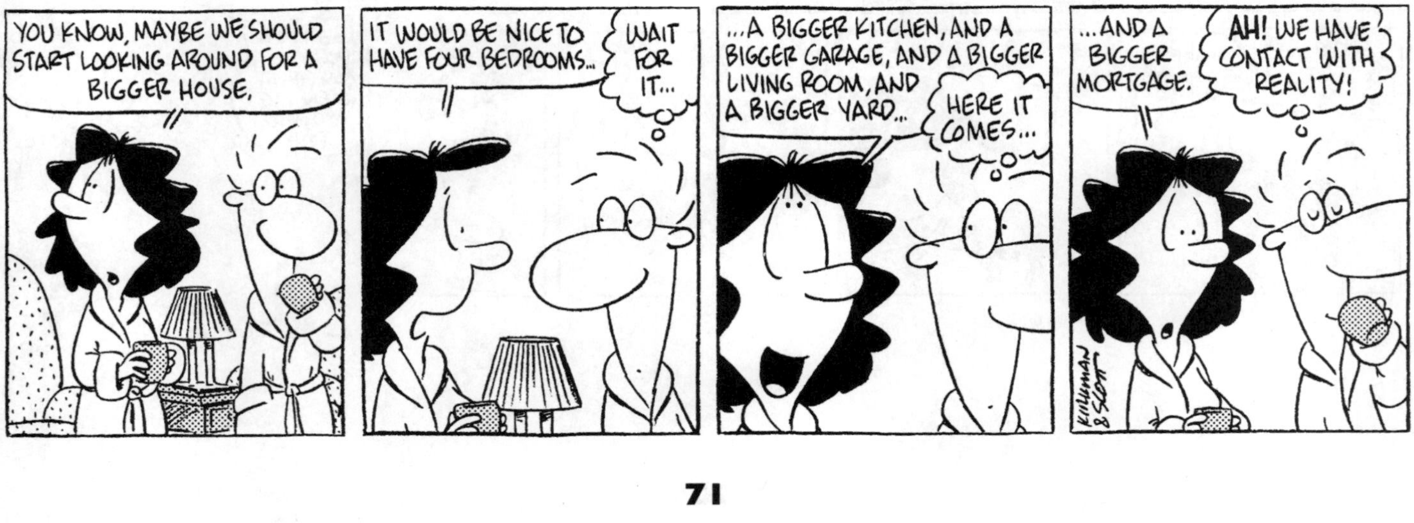
YOU KNOW, MAYBE WE SHOULD START LOOKING AROUND FOR A BIGGER HOUSE.
IT WOULD BE NICE TO HAVE FOUR BEDROOMS...
WAIT FOR IT...
...A BIGGER KITCHEN, AND A BIGGER GARAGE, AND A BIGGER LIVING ROOM, AND A BIGGER YARD...
HERE IT COMES...
...AND A BIGGER MORTGAGE.
AH! WE HAVE CONTACT WITH REALITY!
KIRKMAN & SCOTT

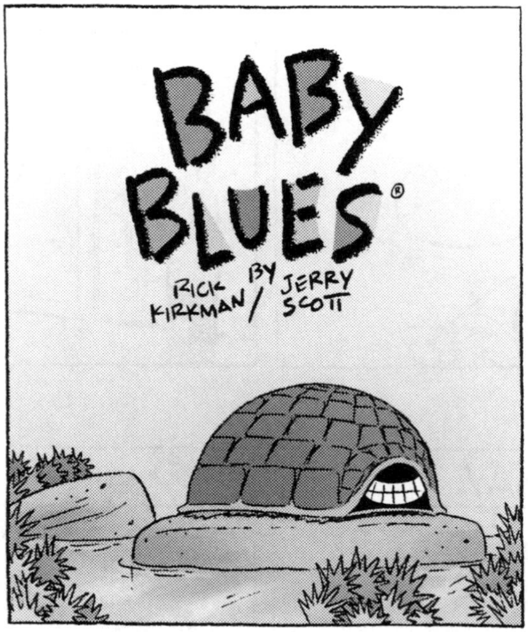
BABY BLUES®
BY
RICK KIRKMAN / JERRY SCOTT

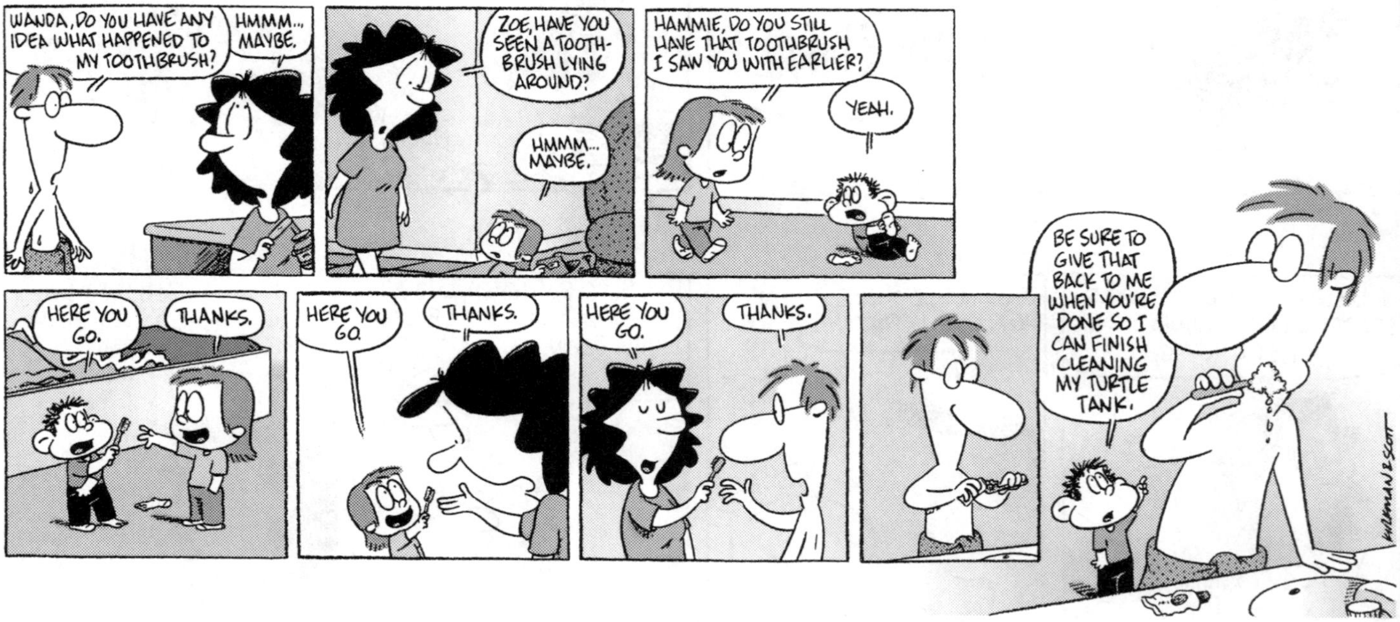
WANDA, DO YOU HAVE ANY IDEA WHAT HAPPENED TO MY TOOTHBRUSH?
HMMM... MAYBE.
ZOE, HAVE YOU SEEN A TOOTHBRUSH LYING AROUND?
HMMM... MAYBE.
HAMMIE, DO YOU STILL HAVE THAT TOOTHBRUSH I SAW YOU WITH EARLIER?
YEAH.
HERE YOU GO.
THANKS.
HERE YOU GO.
THANKS.
HERE YOU GO.
THANKS.
BE SURE TO GIVE THAT BACK TO ME WHEN YOU'RE DONE SO I CAN FINISH CLEANING MY TURTLE TANK.
KIRKMAN & SCOTT

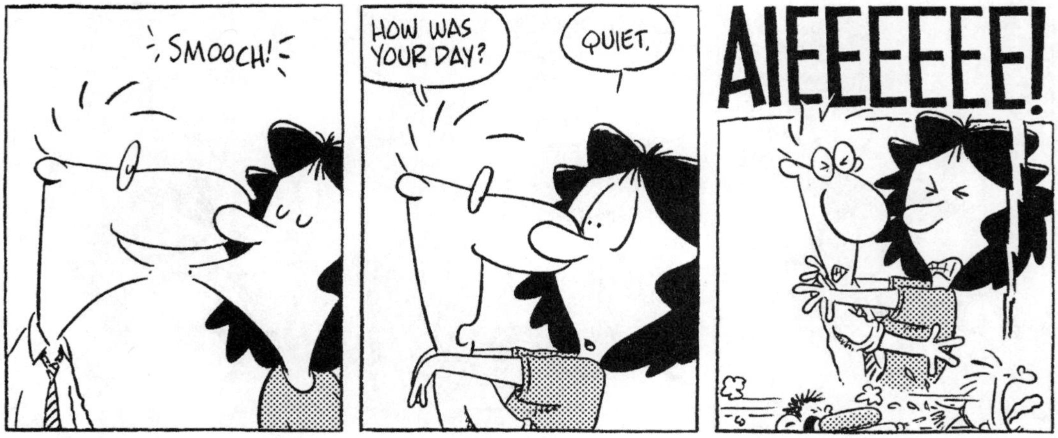
SMOOCH!
HOW WAS YOUR DAY?
QUIET.
AIEEEEEEE!
RELATIVE TO WHAT?
I DUNNO'... SAY, AN ARTILLERY RANGE.
KIRKMAN & SCOTT

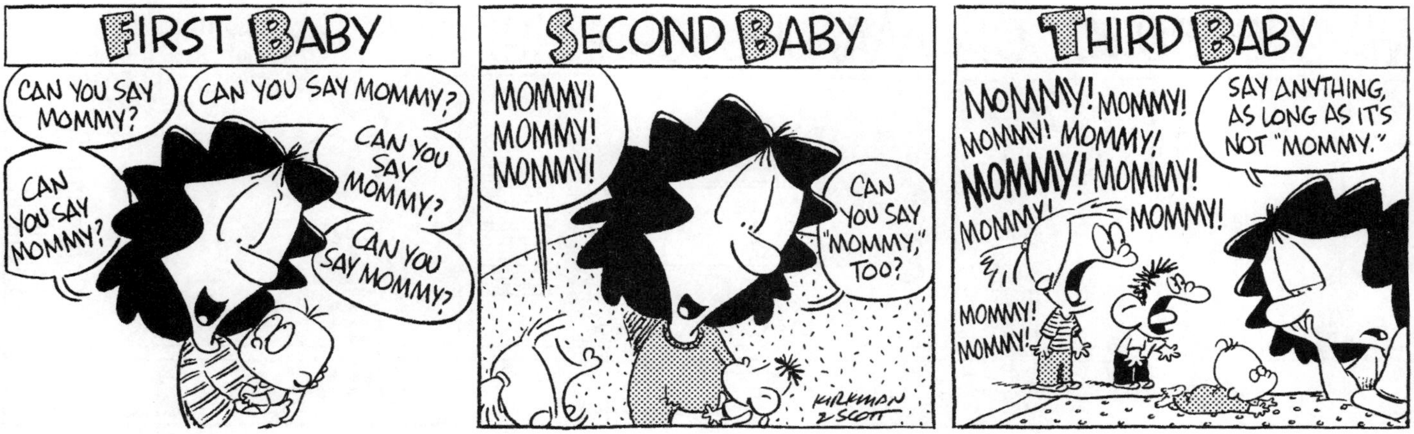
FIRST BABY
CAN YOU SAY MOMMY?
CAN YOU SAY MOMMY?
CAN YOU SAY MOMMY?
CAN YOU SAY MOMMY?
CAN YOU SAY MOMMY?
SECOND BABY
MOMMY! MOMMY! MOMMY!
CAN YOU SAY "MOMMY," TOO?
KIRKMAN & SCOTT
THIRD BABY
MOMMY! MOMMY! MOMMY! MOMMY! MOMMY! MOMMY! MOMMY! MOMMY! MOMMY! MOMMY!
SAY ANYTHING, AS LONG AS IT'S NOT "MOMMY."

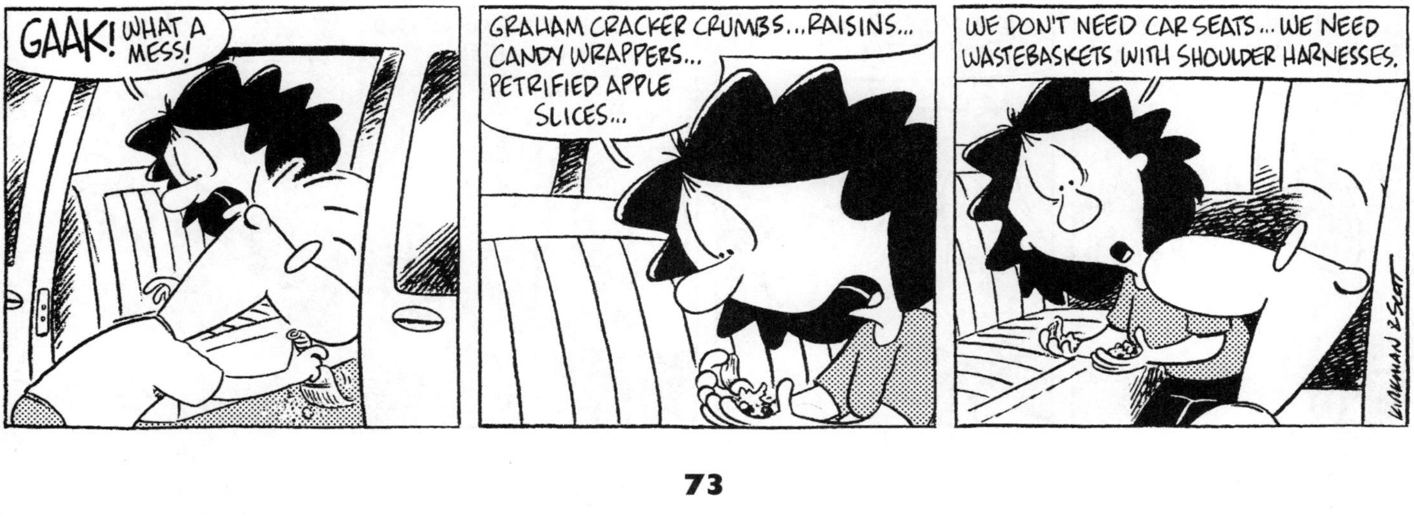
GAAK! WHAT A MESS!
GRAHAM CRACKER CRUMBS... RAISINS... CANDY WRAPPERS... PETRIFIED APPLE SLICES...
WE DON'T NEED CAR SEATS... WE NEED WASTEBASKETS WITH SHOULDER HARNESSES.
KIRKMAN & SCOTT

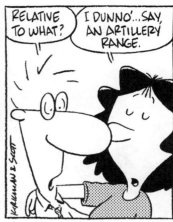

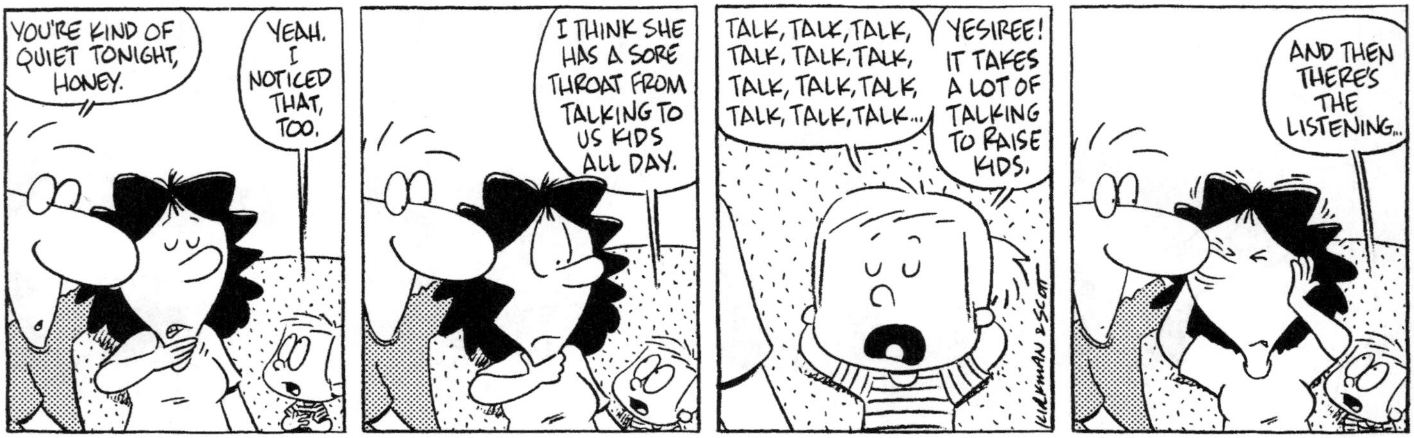
YOU'RE KIND OF QUIET TONIGHT, HONEY.
YEAH. I NOTICED THAT, TOO.
I THINK SHE HAS A SORE THROAT FROM TALKING TO US KIDS ALL DAY.
TALK, TALK, TALK, TALK, TALK, TALK, TALK, TALK, TALK, TALK, TALK, TALK...
YESIREE! IT TAKES A LOT OF TALKING TO RAISE KIDS.
AND THEN THERE'S THE LISTENING...
KIRKMAN & SCOTT

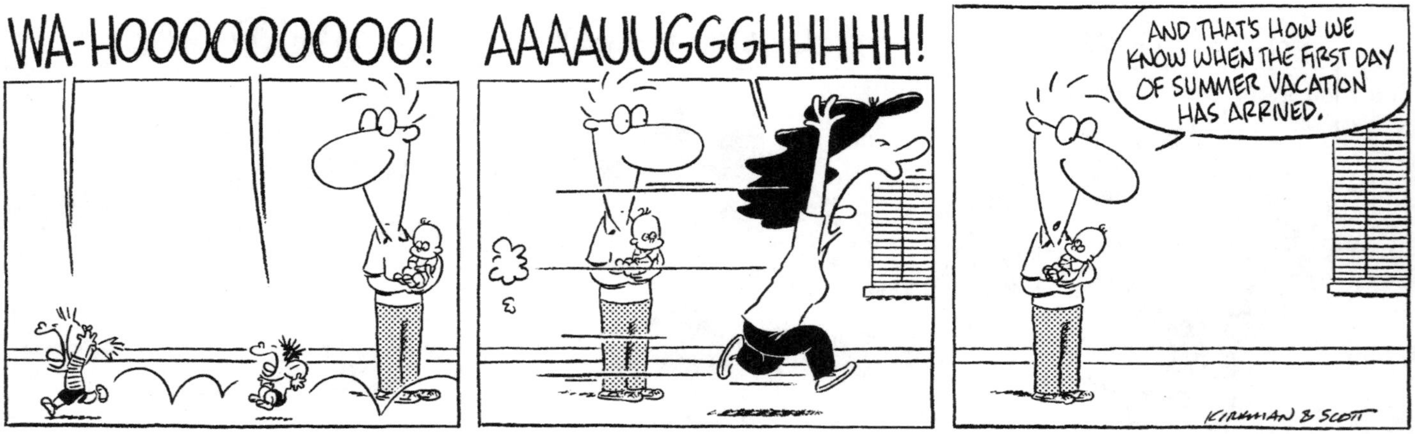
WA-HOOOOOOOOOO!
AAAAUUGGGHHHHH!
AND THAT'S HOW WE KNOW WHEN THE FIRST DAY OF SUMMER VACATION HAS ARRIVED.
KIRKMAN & SCOTT

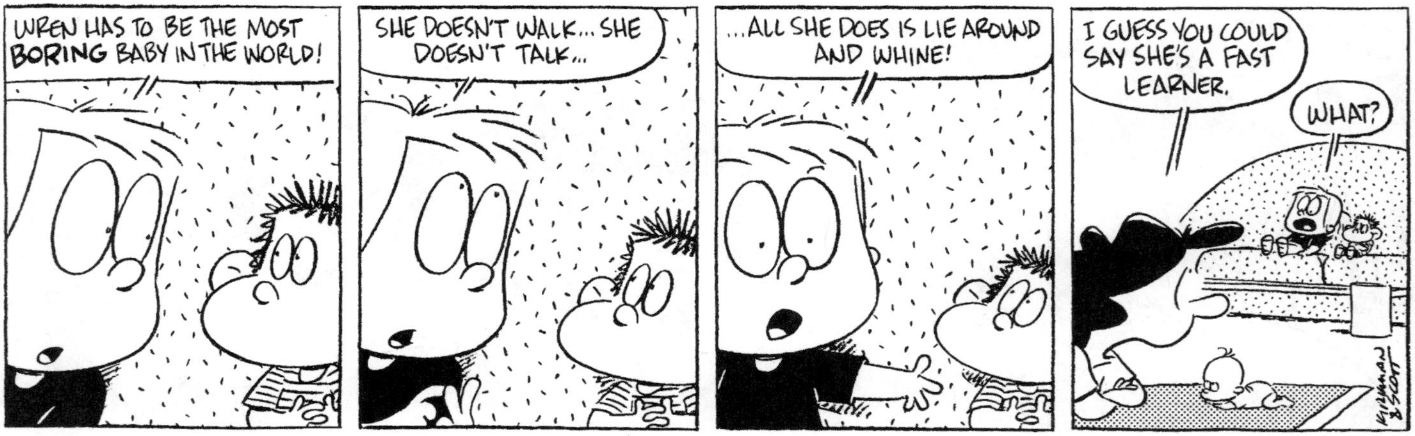
WREN HAS TO BE THE MOST BORING BABY IN THE WORLD!
SHE DOESN'T WALK... SHE DOESN'T TALK...
...ALL SHE DOES IS LIE AROUND AND WHINE!
I GUESS YOU COULD SAY SHE'S A FAST LEARNER.
WHAT?
KIRKMAN & SCOTT

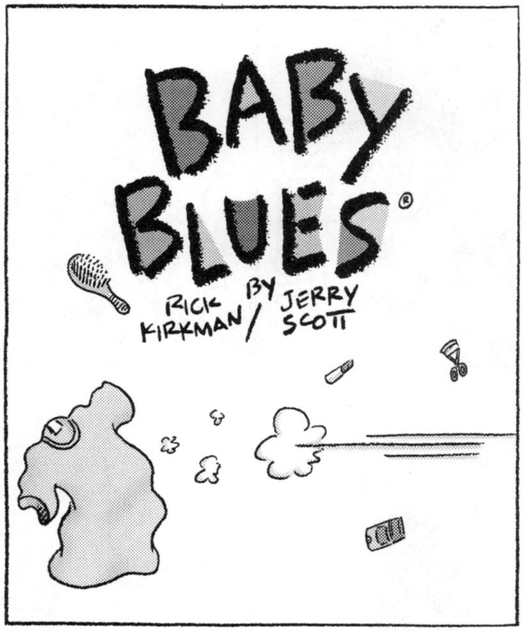
BABY BLUES®
BY RICK KIRKMAN / JERRY SCOTT

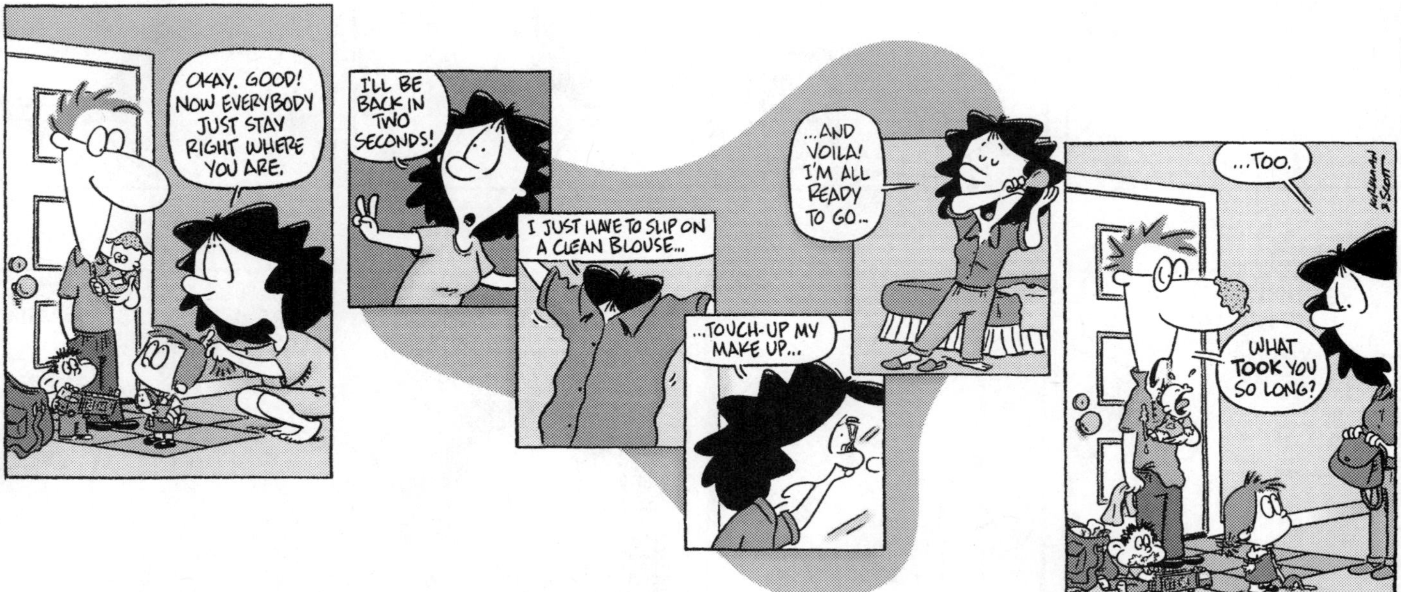
OKAY. GOOD! NOW EVERYBODY JUST STAY RIGHT WHERE YOU ARE.
I'LL BE BACK IN TWO SECONDS!
I JUST HAVE TO SLIP ON A CLEAN BLOUSE...
...TOUCH-UP MY MAKE UP...
...AND VOILA! I'M ALL READY TO GO..
...TOO.
WHAT TOOK YOU SO LONG?

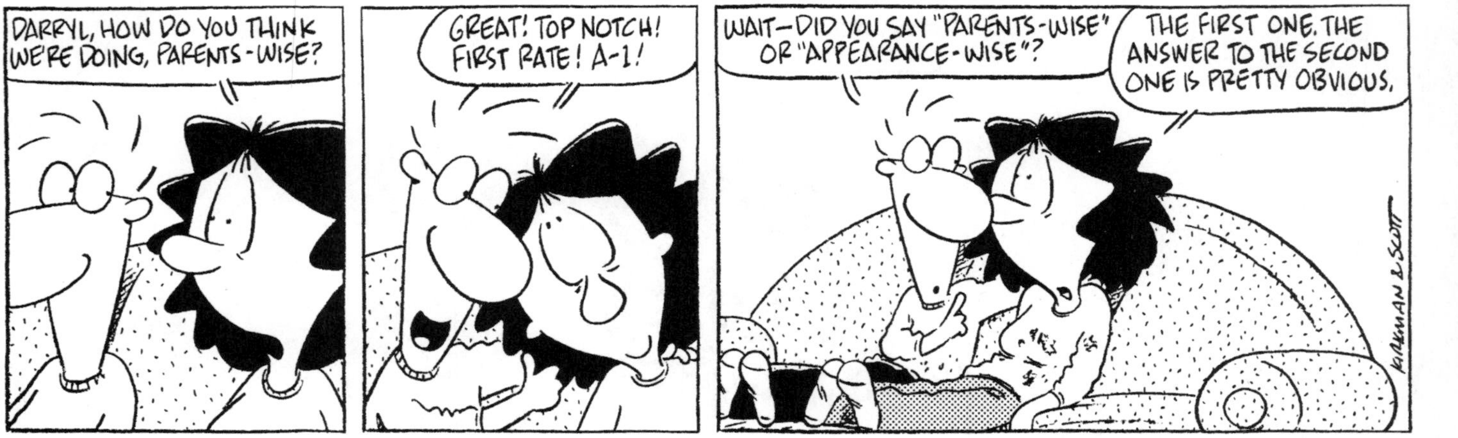
DARRYL, HOW DO YOU THINK WE'RE DOING, PARENTS-WISE?
GREAT! TOP NOTCH! FIRST RATE! A-1!
WAIT—DID YOU SAY "PARENTS-WISE" OR "APPEARANCE-WISE"?
THE FIRST ONE. THE ANSWER TO THE SECOND ONE IS PRETTY OBVIOUS.
KIRKMAN & SCOTT

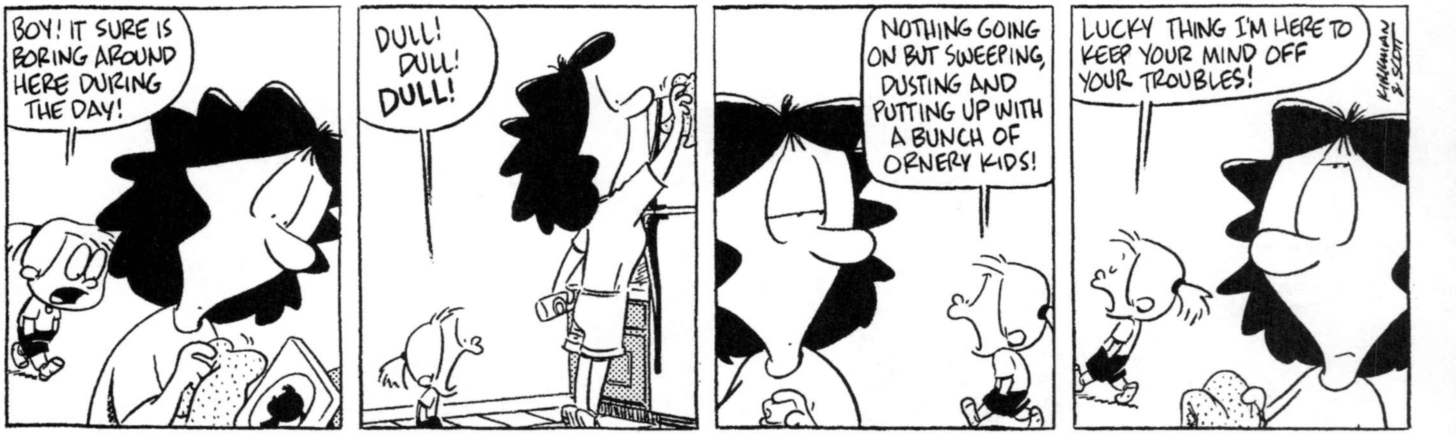
BOY! IT SURE IS BORING AROUND HERE DURING THE DAY!
DULL! DULL! **DULL!**
NOTHING GOING ON BUT SWEEPING, DUSTING AND PUTTING UP WITH A BUNCH OF ORNERY KIDS!
LUCKY THING I'M HERE TO KEEP YOUR MIND OFF YOUR TROUBLES!
KIRKMAN & SCOTT

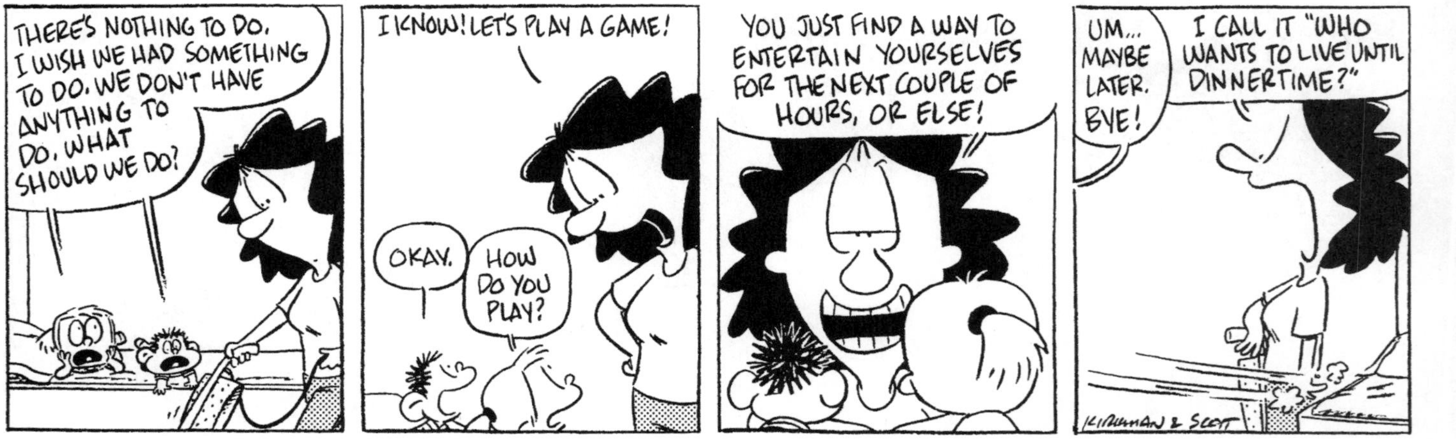
THERE'S NOTHING TO DO. I WISH WE HAD SOMETHING TO DO. WE DON'T HAVE ANYTHING TO DO. WHAT SHOULD WE DO?
I KNOW! LET'S PLAY A GAME!
OKAY.
HOW DO YOU PLAY?
YOU JUST FIND A WAY TO ENTERTAIN YOURSELVES FOR THE NEXT COUPLE OF HOURS, OR ELSE!
UM... MAYBE LATER. BYE!
I CALL IT "WHO WANTS TO LIVE UNTIL DINNERTIME?"
KIRKMAN & SCOTT

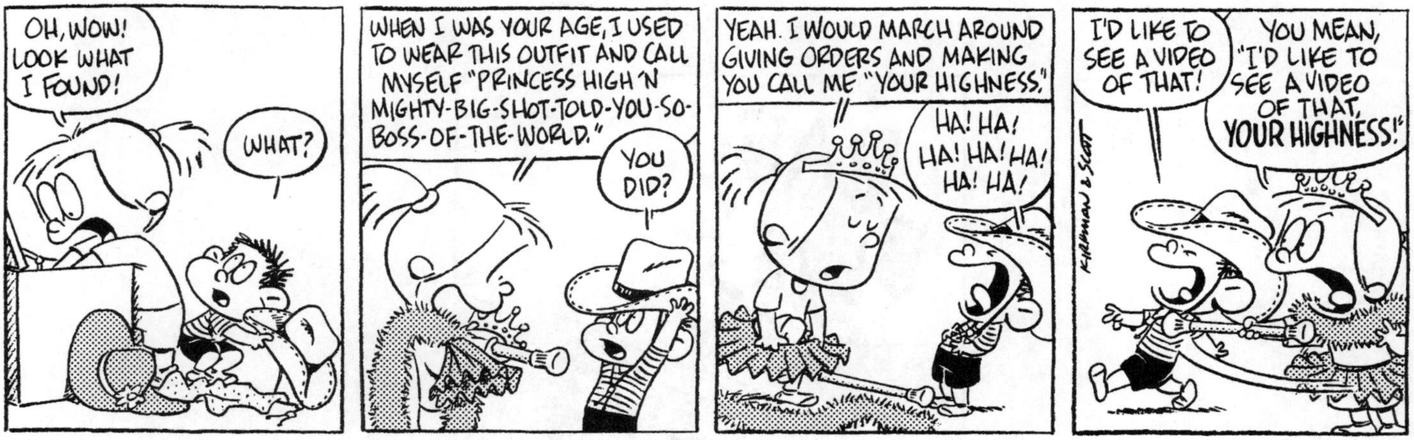
OH, WOW! LOOK WHAT I FOUND!
WHAT?
WHEN I WAS YOUR AGE, I USED TO WEAR THIS OUTFIT AND CALL MYSELF "PRINCESS HIGH 'N MIGHTY-BIG-SHOT-TOLD-YOU-SO-BOSS-OF-THE-WORLD."
YOU DID?
YEAH. I WOULD MARCH AROUND GIVING ORDERS AND MAKING YOU CALL ME "YOUR HIGHNESS."
HA! HA! HA! HA! HA! HA! HA!
I'D LIKE TO SEE A VIDEO OF THAT!
YOU MEAN, "I'D LIKE TO SEE A VIDEO OF THAT, YOUR HIGHNESS!"

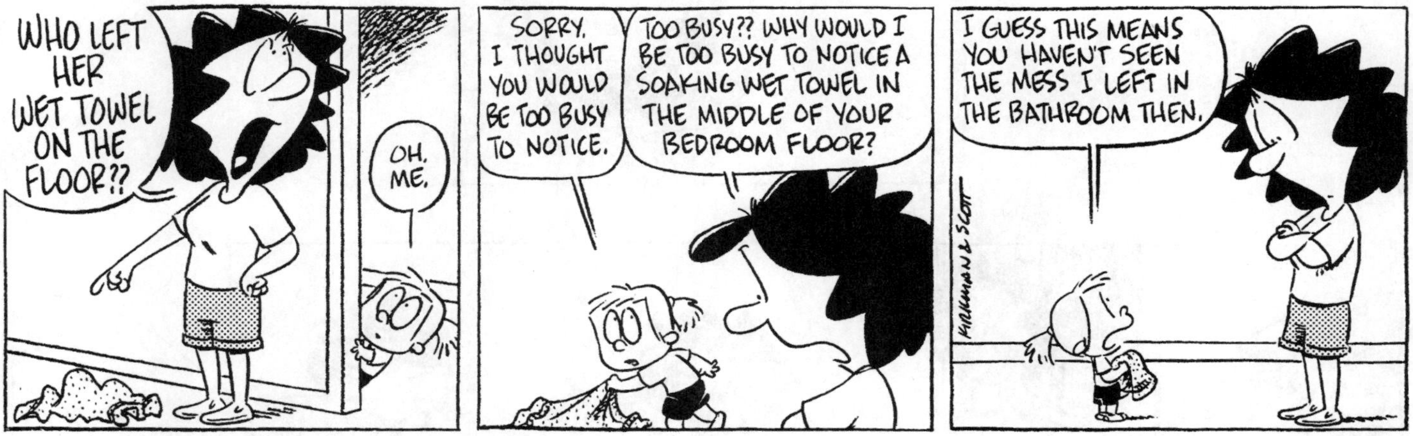
WHO LEFT HER WET TOWEL ON THE FLOOR??
OH. ME.
SORRY. I THOUGHT YOU WOULD BE TOO BUSY TO NOTICE.
TOO BUSY?? WHY WOULD I BE TOO BUSY TO NOTICE A SOAKING WET TOWEL IN THE MIDDLE OF YOUR BEDROOM FLOOR?
I GUESS THIS MEANS YOU HAVEN'T SEEN THE MESS I LEFT IN THE BATHROOM THEN.

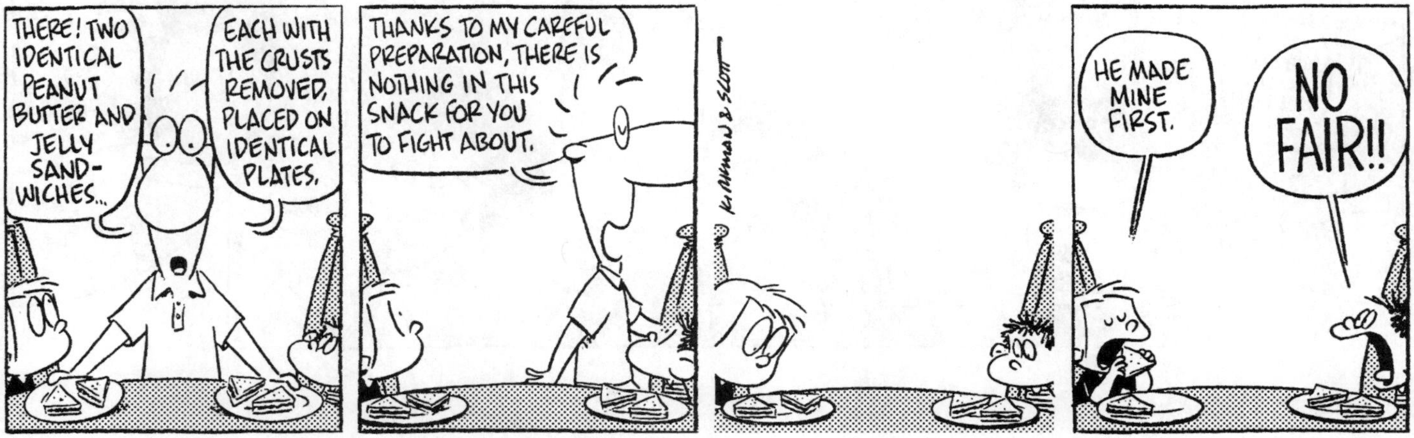
THERE! TWO IDENTICAL PEANUT BUTTER AND JELLY SAND-WICHES...
EACH WITH THE CRUSTS REMOVED, PLACED ON IDENTICAL PLATES.
THANKS TO MY CAREFUL PREPARATION, THERE IS NOTHING IN THIS SNACK FOR YOU TO FIGHT ABOUT.
HE MADE MINE FIRST.
NO FAIR!!

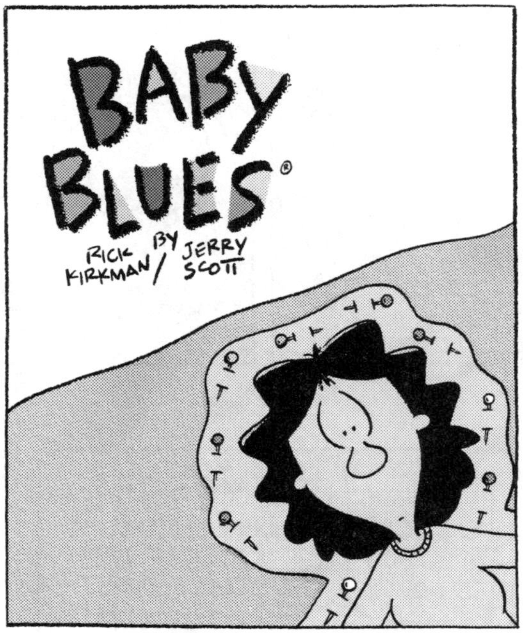
BABY BLUES®
BY
RICK KIRKMAN / JERRY SCOTT

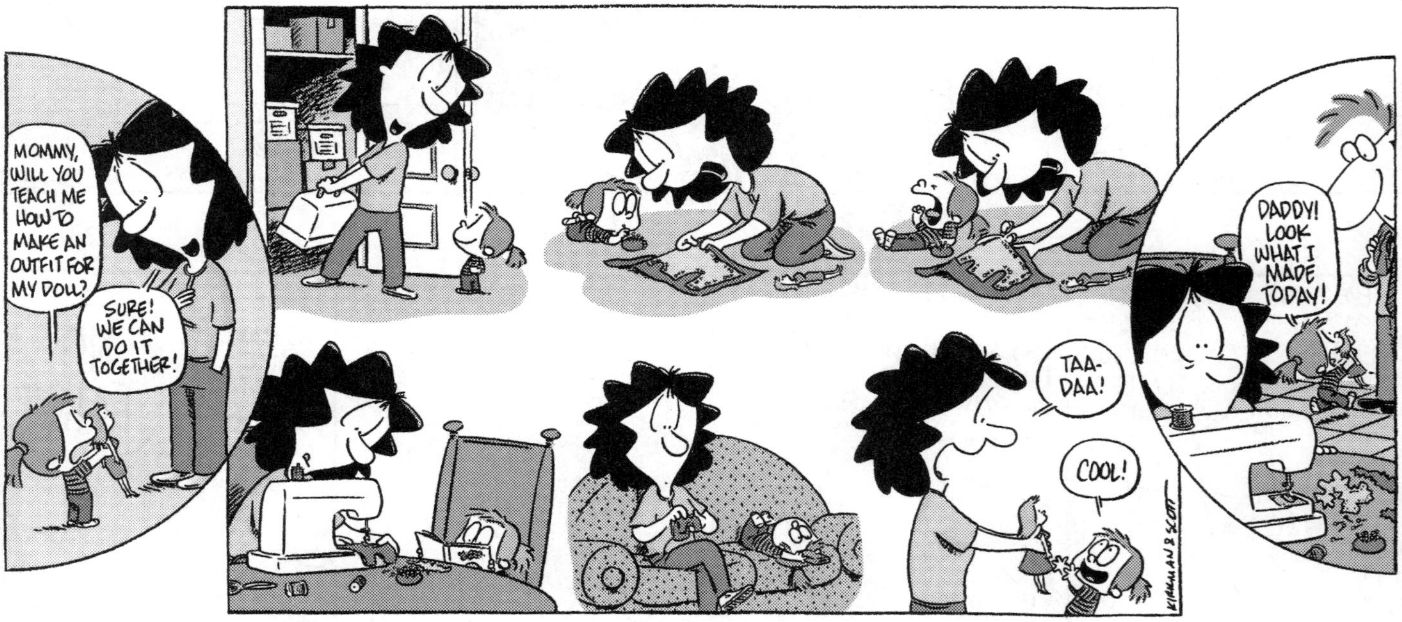
MOMMY, WILL YOU TEACH ME HOW TO MAKE AN OUTFIT FOR MY DOLL?
SURE! WE CAN DO IT TOGETHER!
TAA-DAA!
COOL!
DADDY! LOOK WHAT I MADE TODAY!
KIRKMAN & SCOTT

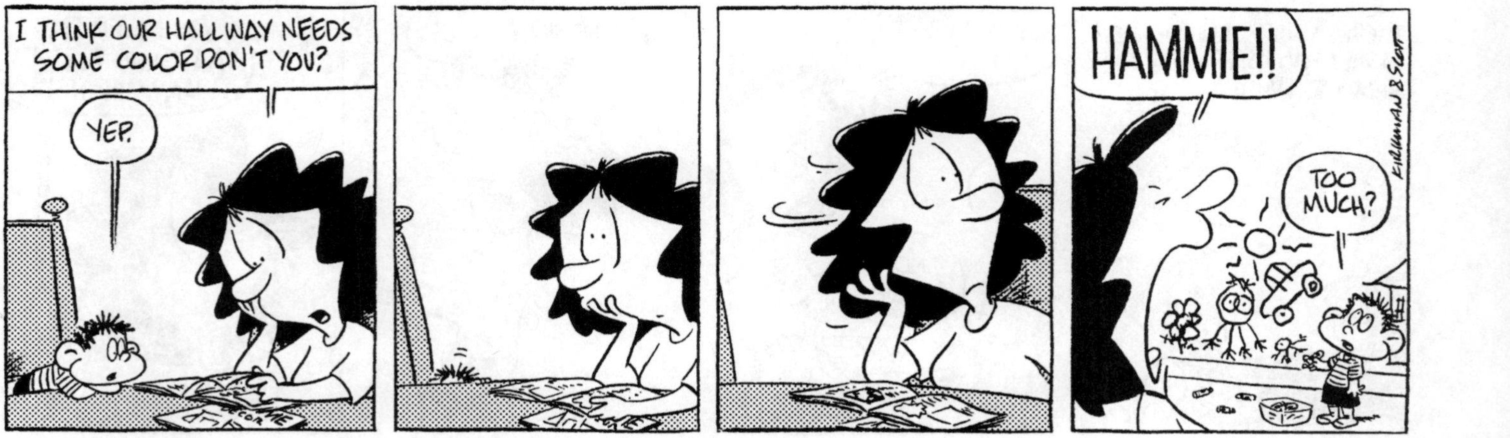
I THINK OUR HALLWAY NEEDS SOME COLOR DON'T YOU?
YEP.
HAMMIE!!
TOO MUCH?
KIRKMAN & SCOTT

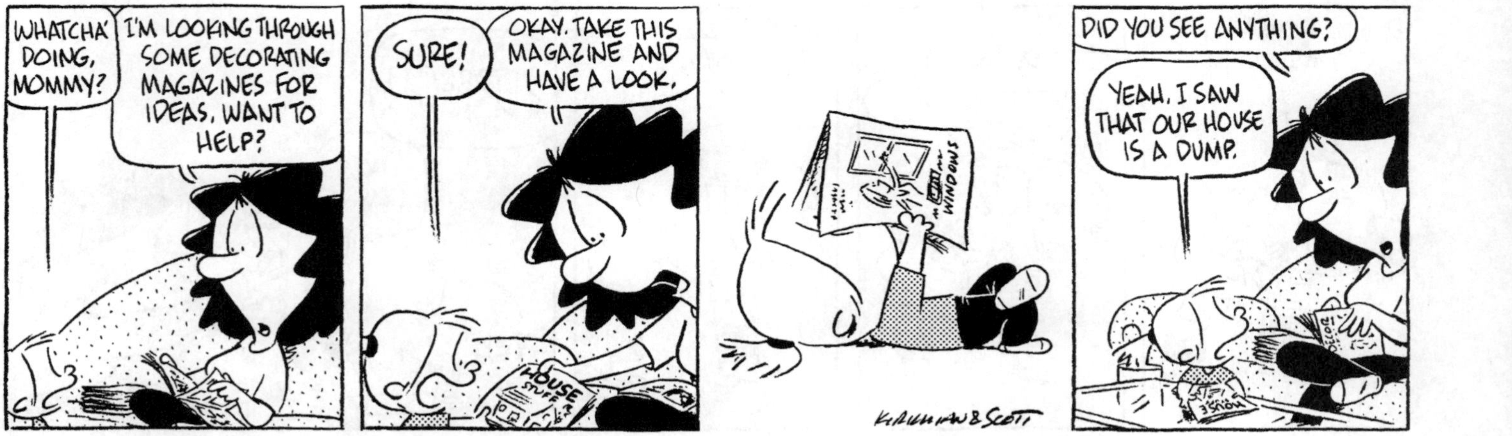
WHATCHA' DOING, MOMMY?
I'M LOOKING THROUGH SOME DECORATING MAGAZINES FOR IDEAS. WANT TO HELP?
SURE!
OKAY. TAKE THIS MAGAZINE AND HAVE A LOOK.
HOUSE STUFF
WINDOWS
KIRKMAN & SCOTT
DID YOU SEE ANYTHING?
YEAH. I SAW THAT OUR HOUSE IS A DUMP.

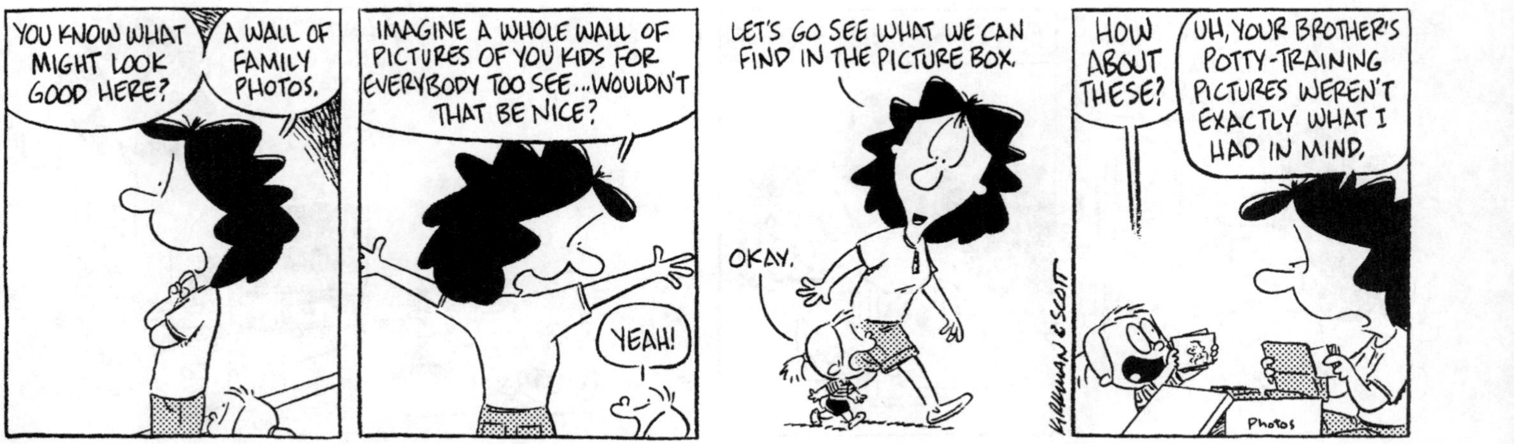
YOU KNOW WHAT MIGHT LOOK GOOD HERE?
A WALL OF FAMILY PHOTOS.
IMAGINE A WHOLE WALL OF PICTURES OF YOU KIDS FOR EVERYBODY TOO SEE...WOULDN'T THAT BE NICE?
YEAH!
LET'S GO SEE WHAT WE CAN FIND IN THE PICTURE BOX.
OKAY.
KIRKMAN & SCOTT
HOW ABOUT THESE?
UH, YOUR BROTHER'S POTTY-TRAINING PICTURES WEREN'T EXACTLY WHAT I HAD IN MIND.
PHOTOS

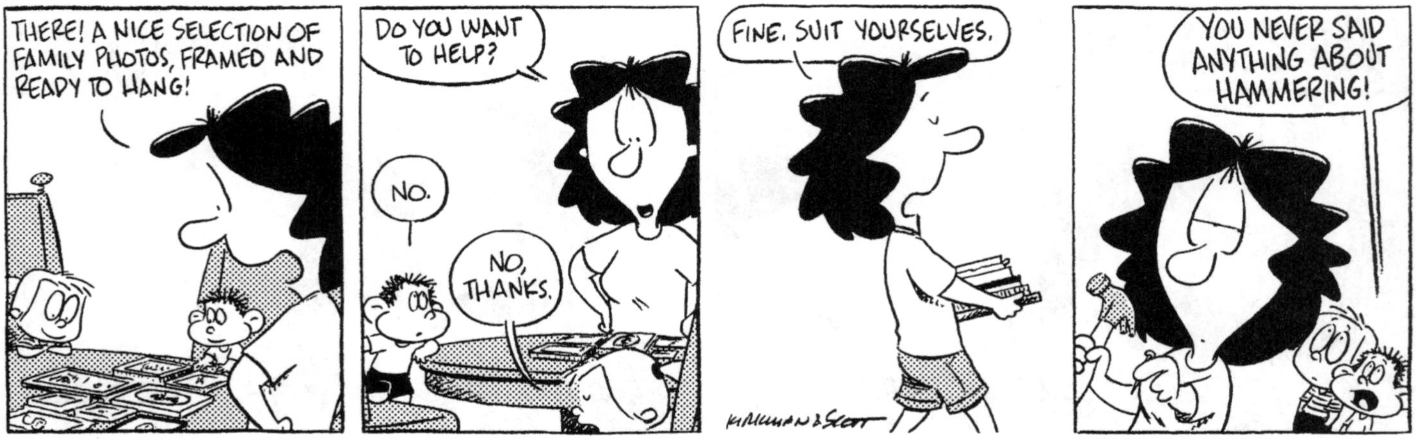
THERE! A NICE SELECTION OF FAMILY PHOTOS, FRAMED AND READY TO HANG!
DO YOU WANT TO HELP?
NO.
NO, THANKS.
FINE. SUIT YOURSELVES.
KIRKMAN & SCOTT
YOU NEVER SAID ANYTHING ABOUT HAMMERING!

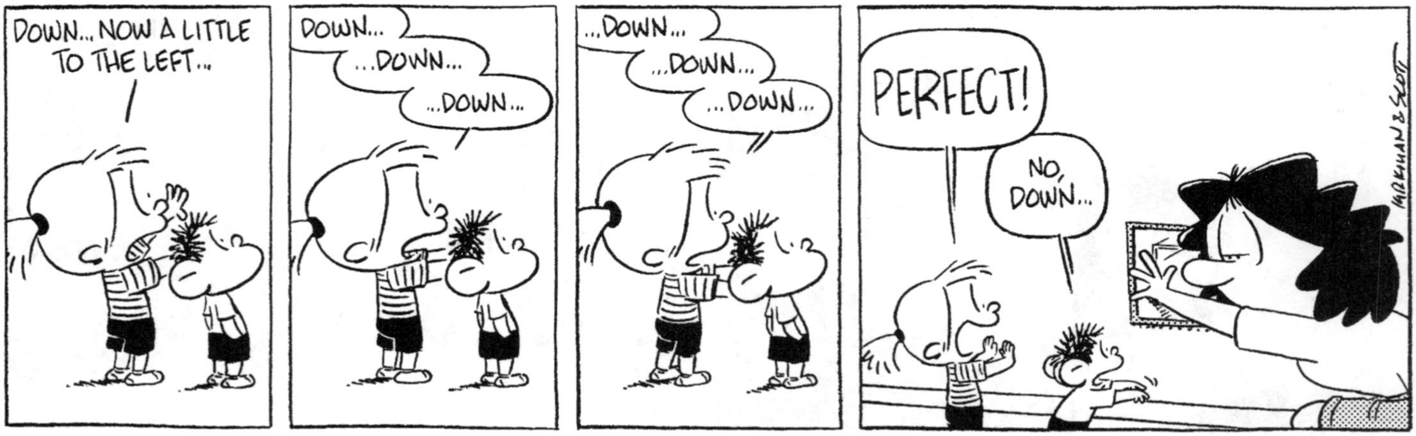
DOWN... NOW A LITTLE TO THE LEFT...
DOWN...
...DOWN...
...DOWN...
...DOWN...
...DOWN...
...DOWN...
PERFECT!
NO, DOWN...
KIRKMAN & SCOTT

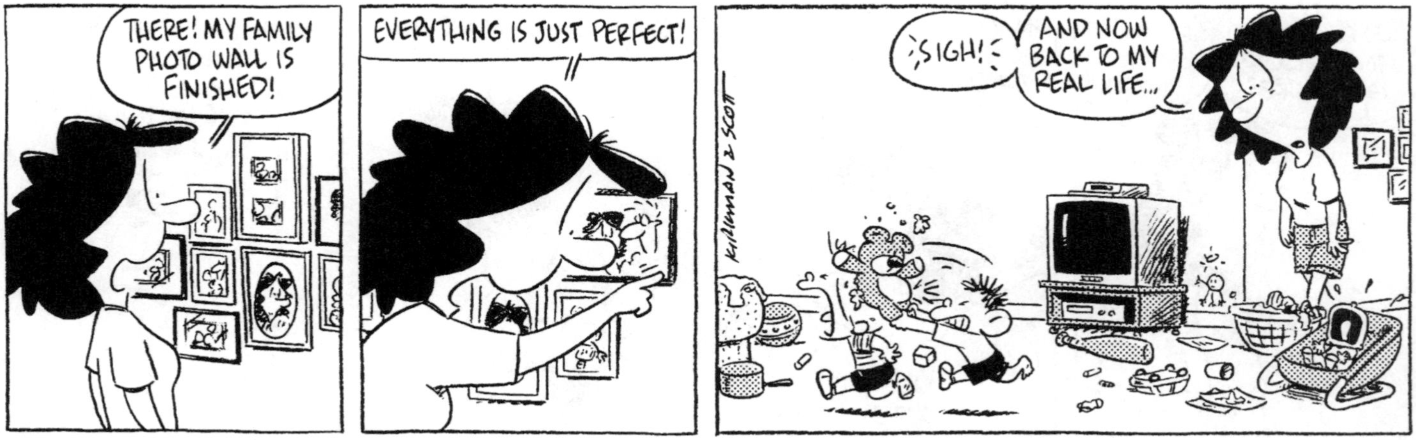
THERE! MY FAMILY PHOTO WALL IS FINISHED!
EVERYTHING IS JUST PERFECT!
KIRKMAN & SCOTT
SIGH!
AND NOW BACK TO MY REAL LIFE...

HOW GOES THE BILL-PAYING?

I AM...

...FINISHED!

I GUESS I CAN TOSS THESE OLD STATEMENTS...

...BUT TO BE ON THE SAFE SIDE, I'LL RUN THEM THROUGH THE SHREDDER FIRST.

WE HAVE A SHREDDER?

WE DO SINCE HAMMIE MASTERED SCISSORS.

CUT!

CUT! CLIP!

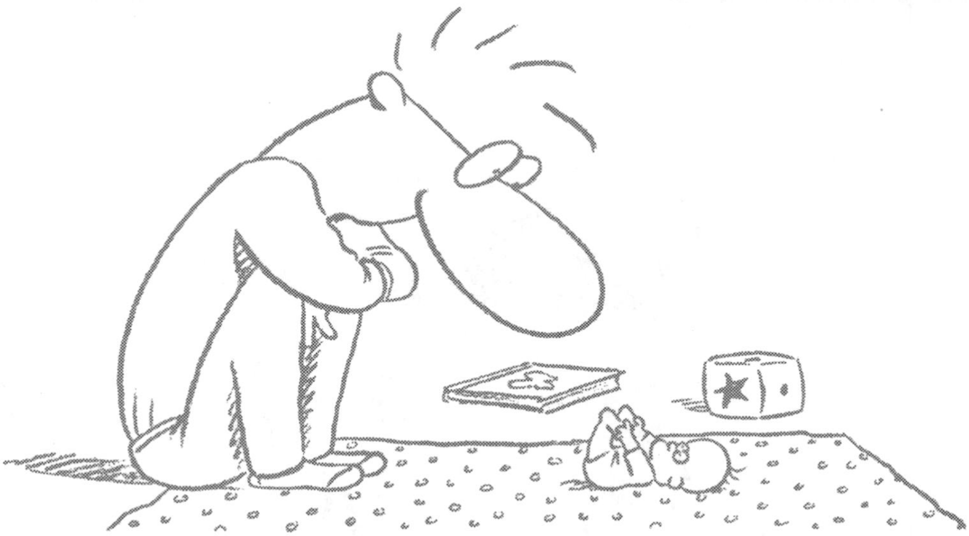

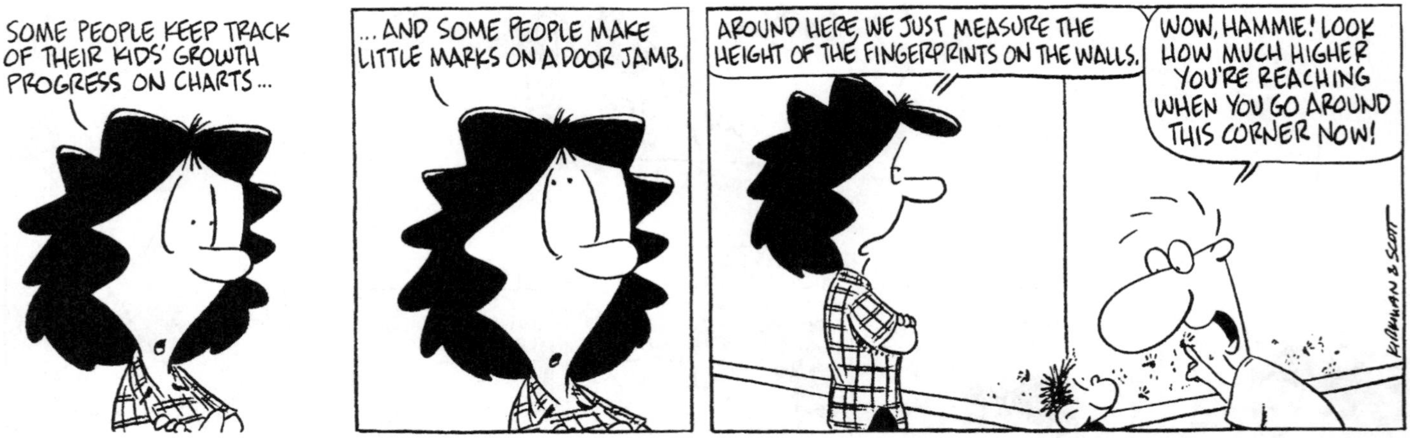
SOME PEOPLE KEEP TRACK OF THEIR KIDS' GROWTH PROGRESS ON CHARTS...
...AND SOME PEOPLE MAKE LITTLE MARKS ON A DOOR JAMB.
AROUND HERE, WE JUST MEASURE THE HEIGHT OF THE FINGERPRINTS ON THE WALLS.
WOW, HAMMIE! LOOK HOW MUCH HIGHER YOU'RE REACHING WHEN YOU GO AROUND THIS CORNER NOW!
KIRKMAN & SCOTT

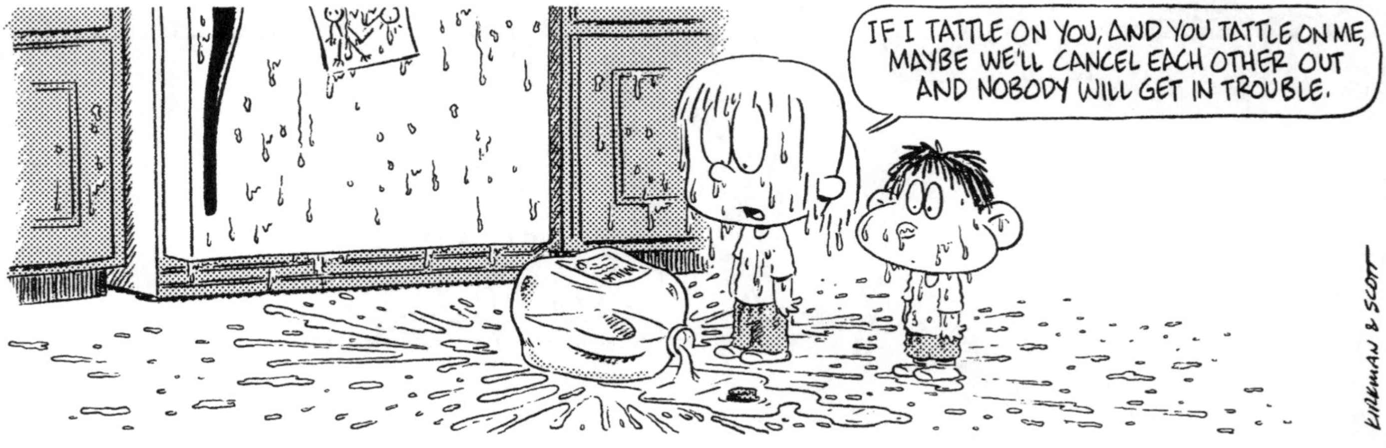
IF I TATTLE ON YOU, AND YOU TATTLE ON ME, MAYBE WE'LL CANCEL EACH OTHER OUT AND NOBODY WILL GET IN TROUBLE.
KIRKMAN & SCOTT

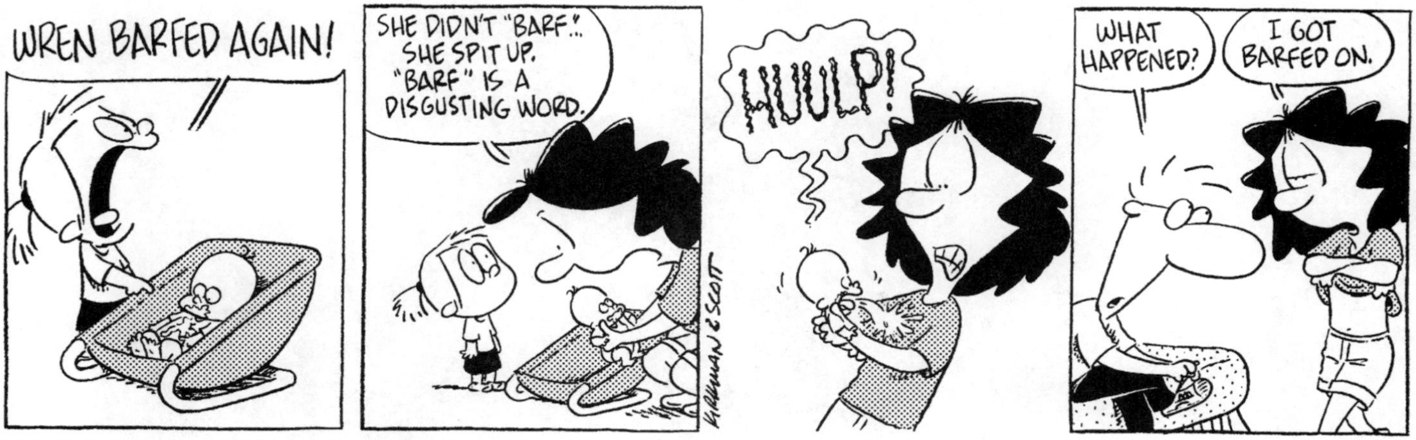
WREN BARFED AGAIN!
SHE DIDN'T "BARF."... SHE SPIT UP. "BARF" IS A DISGUSTING WORD.
KIRKMAN & SCOTT
HUULP!
WHAT HAPPENED?
I GOT BARFED ON.

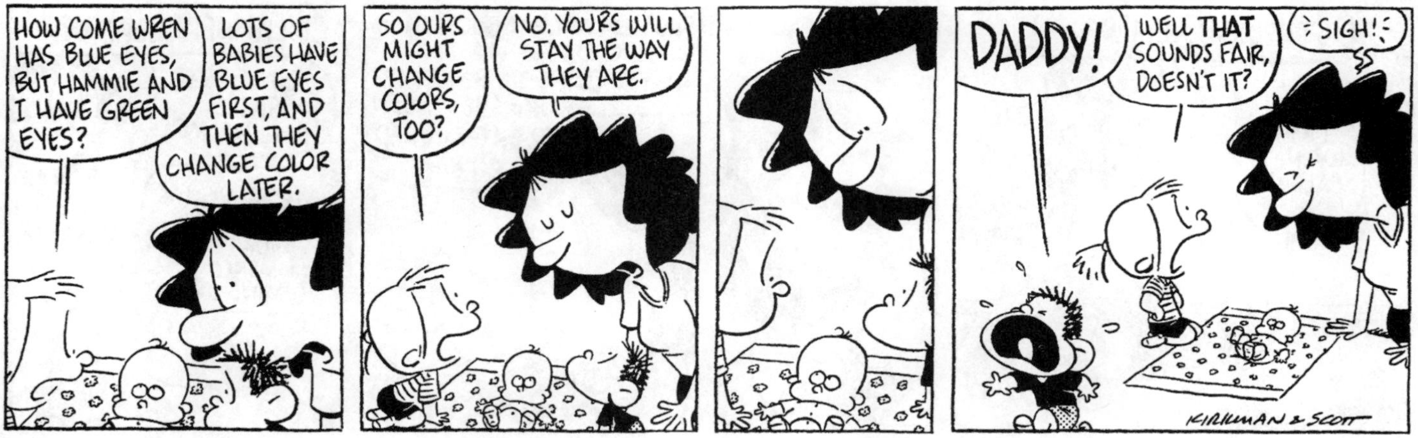
HOW COME WREN HAS BLUE EYES, BUT HAMMIE AND I HAVE GREEN EYES?
LOTS OF BABIES HAVE BLUE EYES FIRST, AND THEN THEY CHANGE COLOR LATER.
SO OURS MIGHT CHANGE COLORS, TOO?
NO. YOURS WILL STAY THE WAY THEY ARE.
DADDY!
WELL THAT SOUNDS FAIR, DOESN'T IT?
SIGH!
KIRKMAN & SCOTT

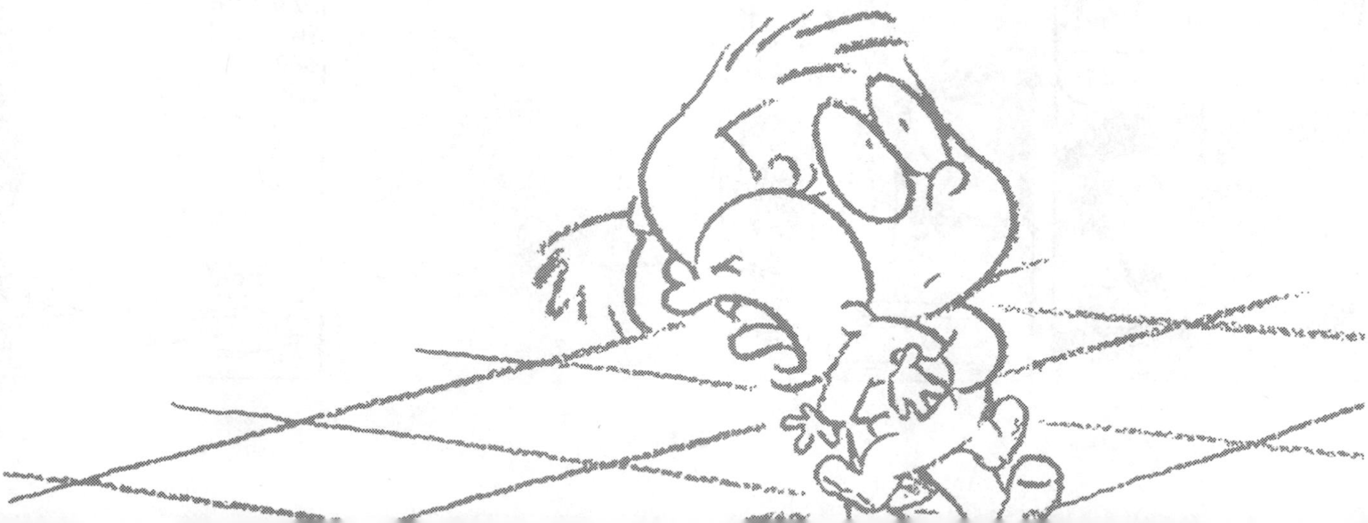

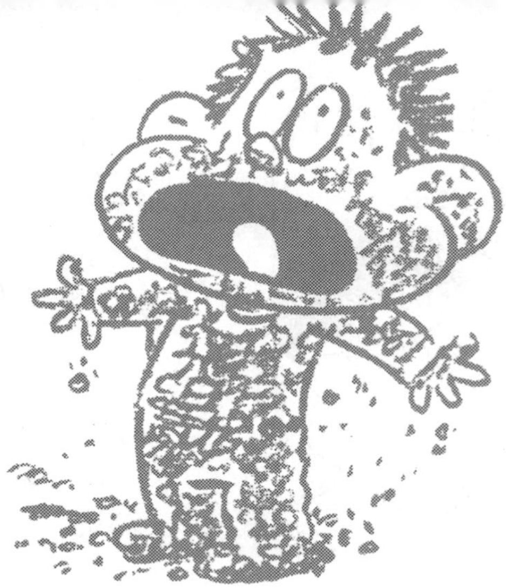

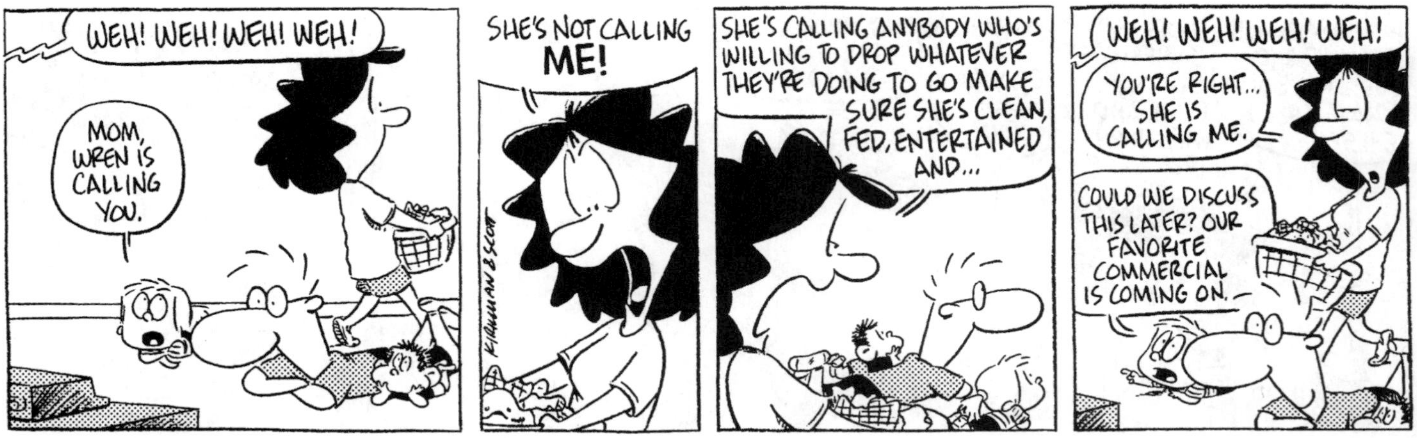
WEH! WEH! WEH! WEH!
MOM, WREN IS CALLING YOU.
KIRKMAN & SCOTT
SHE'S NOT CALLING ME!
SHE'S CALLING ANYBODY WHO'S WILLING TO DROP WHATEVER THEY'RE DOING TO GO MAKE SURE SHE'S CLEAN, FED, ENTERTAINED AND...
WEH! WEH! WEH! WEH!
YOU'RE RIGHT... SHE IS CALLING ME.
COULD WE DISCUSS THIS LATER? OUR FAVORITE COMMERCIAL IS COMING ON.

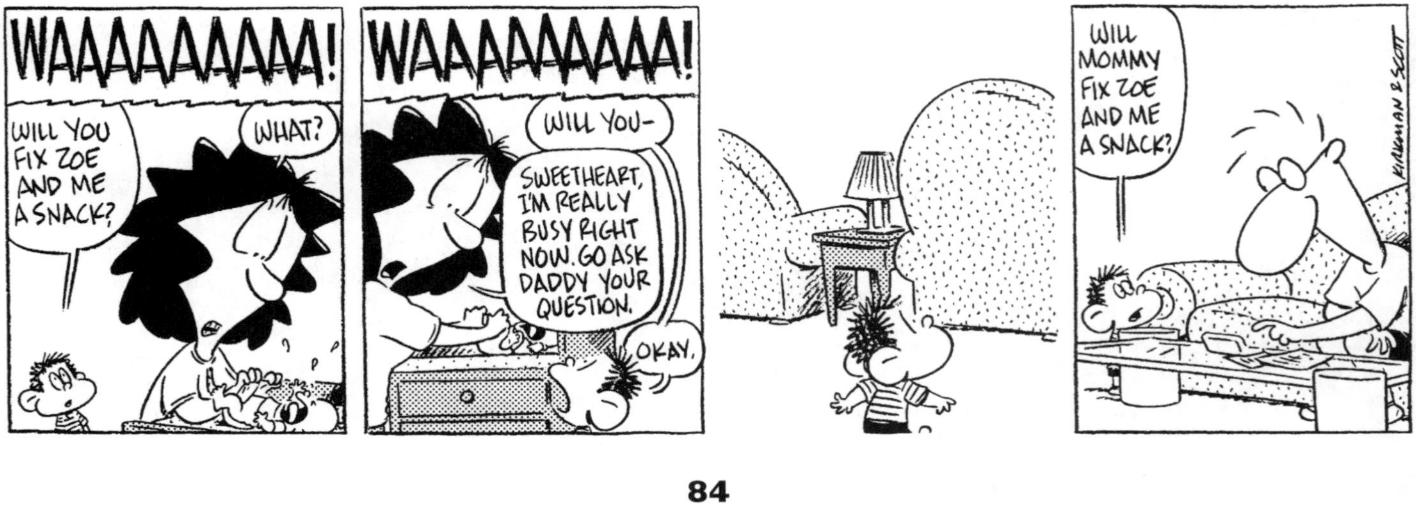
WAAAAAAAAA!
WILL YOU FIX ZOE AND ME A SNACK?
WHAT?
WAAAAAAAAA!
WILL YOU-
SWEETHEART, I'M REALLY BUSY RIGHT NOW. GO ASK DADDY YOUR QUESTION.
OKAY.
WILL MOMMY FIX ZOE AND ME A SNACK?
KIRKMAN & SCOTT

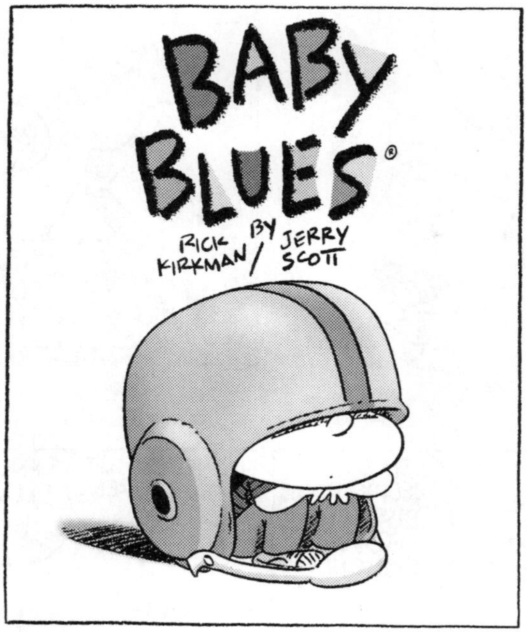
BABY BLUES®
RICK KIRKMAN / BY JERRY SCOTT

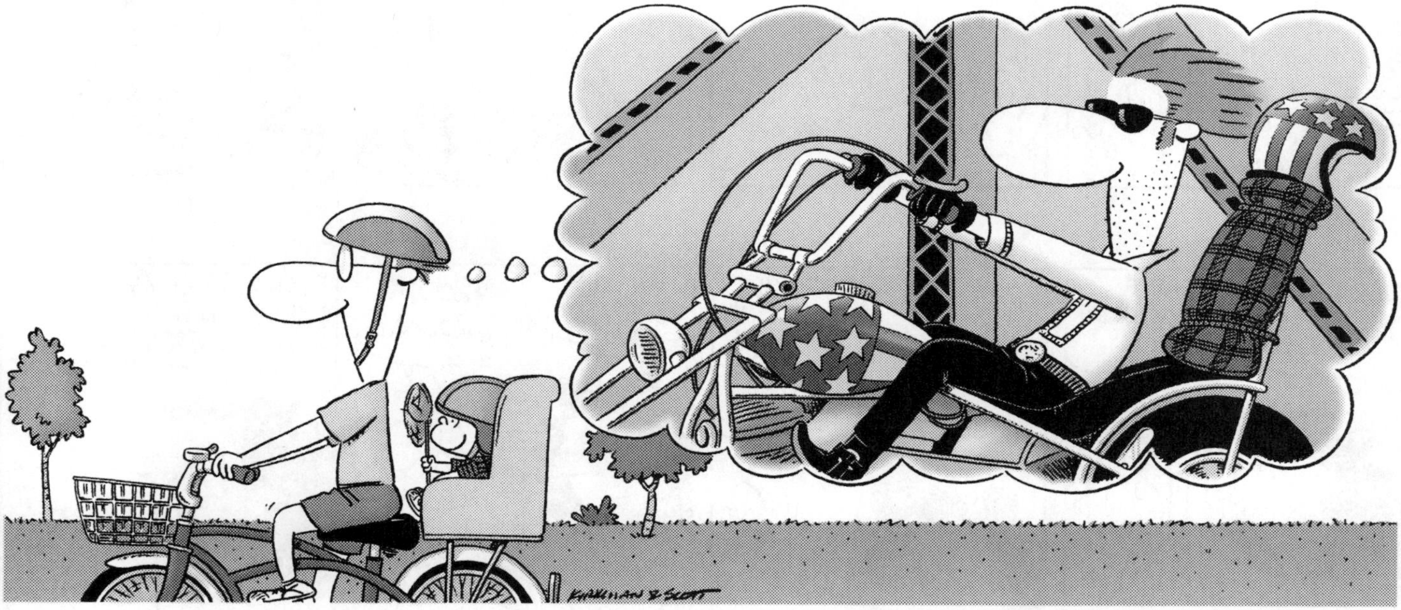
KIRKMAN & SCOTT

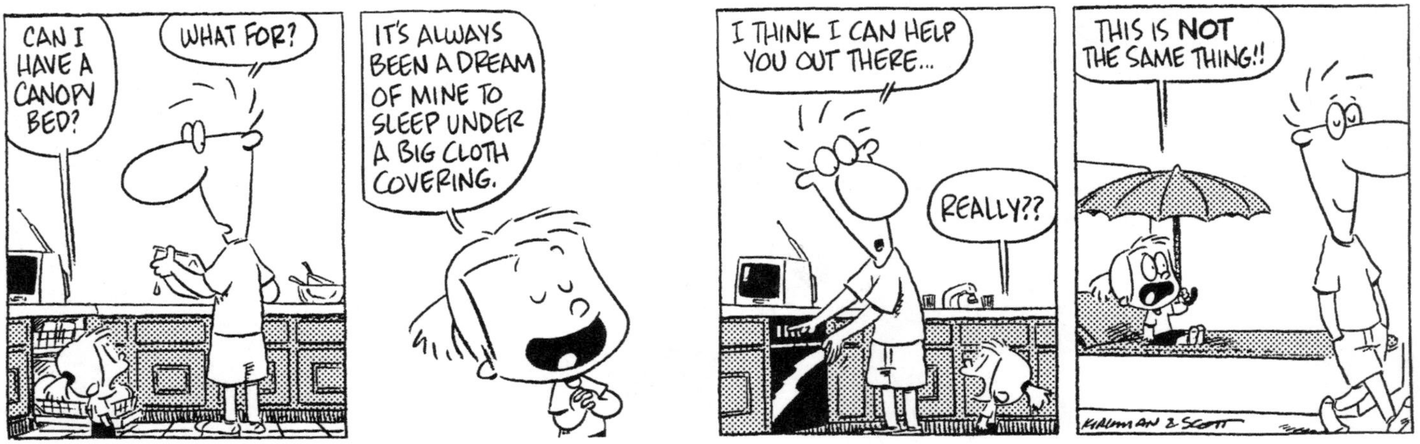
CAN I HAVE A CANOPY BED?
WHAT FOR?
IT'S ALWAYS BEEN A DREAM OF MINE TO SLEEP UNDER A BIG CLOTH COVERING.
I THINK I CAN HELP YOU OUT THERE...
REALLY??
THIS IS **NOT** THE SAME THING!!
KIRKMAN & SCOTT

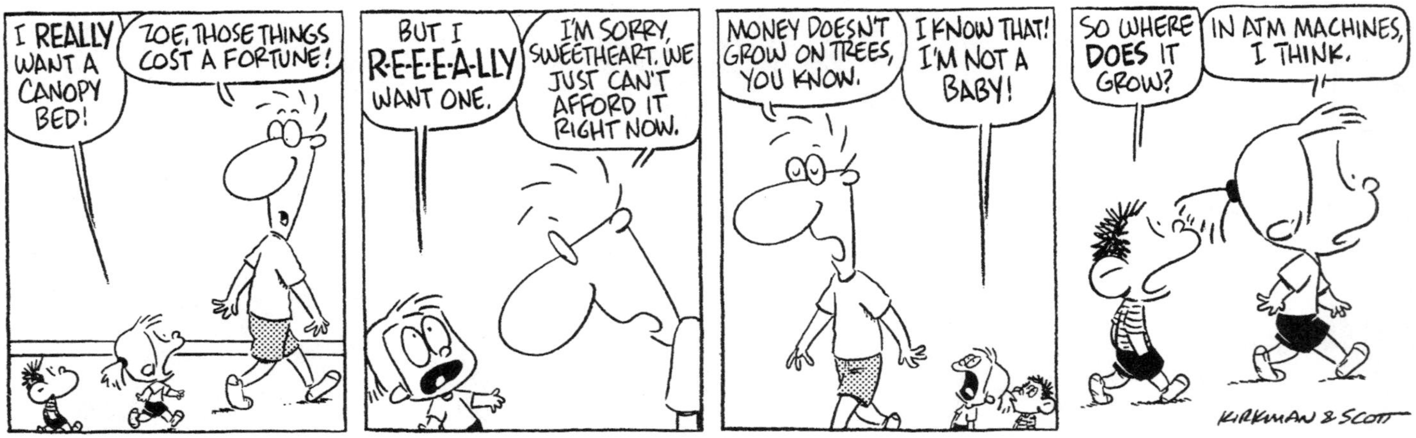
I **REALLY** WANT A CANOPY BED!
ZOE, THOSE THINGS COST A FORTUNE!
BUT I **R-E-E-E-A-LLY** WANT ONE.
I'M SORRY, SWEETHEART. WE JUST CAN'T AFFORD IT RIGHT NOW.
MONEY DOESN'T GROW ON TREES, YOU KNOW.
I KNOW THAT! I'M NOT A BABY!
SO WHERE **DOES** IT GROW?
IN ATM MACHINES, I THINK.
KIRKMAN & SCOTT

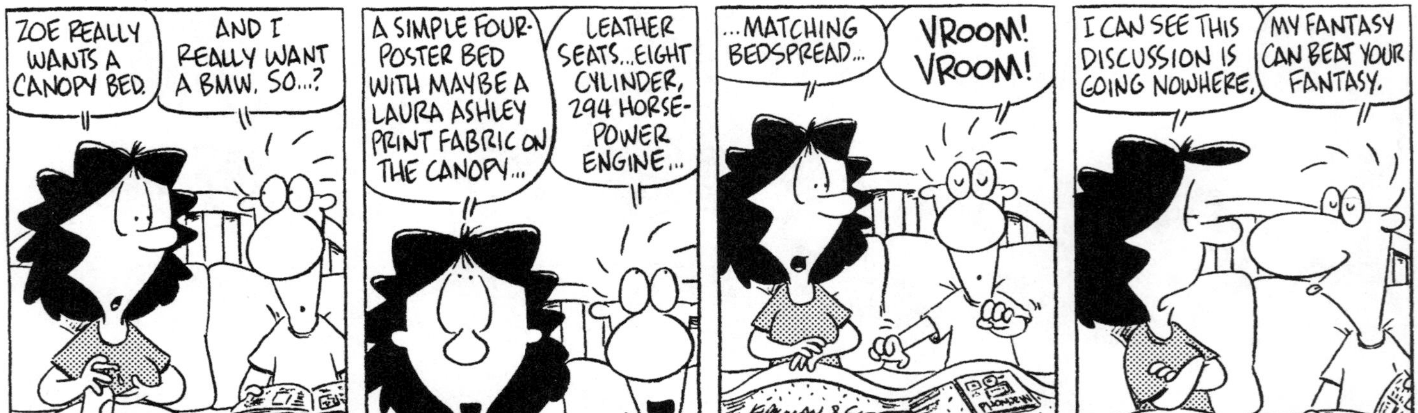
ZOE REALLY WANTS A CANOPY BED.
AND I REALLY WANT A BMW. SO...?
A SIMPLE FOUR-POSTER BED WITH MAYBE A LAURA ASHLEY PRINT FABRIC ON THE CANOPY...
LEATHER SEATS...EIGHT CYLINDER, 294 HORSE-POWER ENGINE...
...MATCHING BEDSPREAD...
VROOM! VROOM!
KIRKMAN & SCOTT
I CAN SEE THIS DISCUSSION IS GOING NOWHERE.
MY FANTASY CAN BEAT YOUR FANTASY.

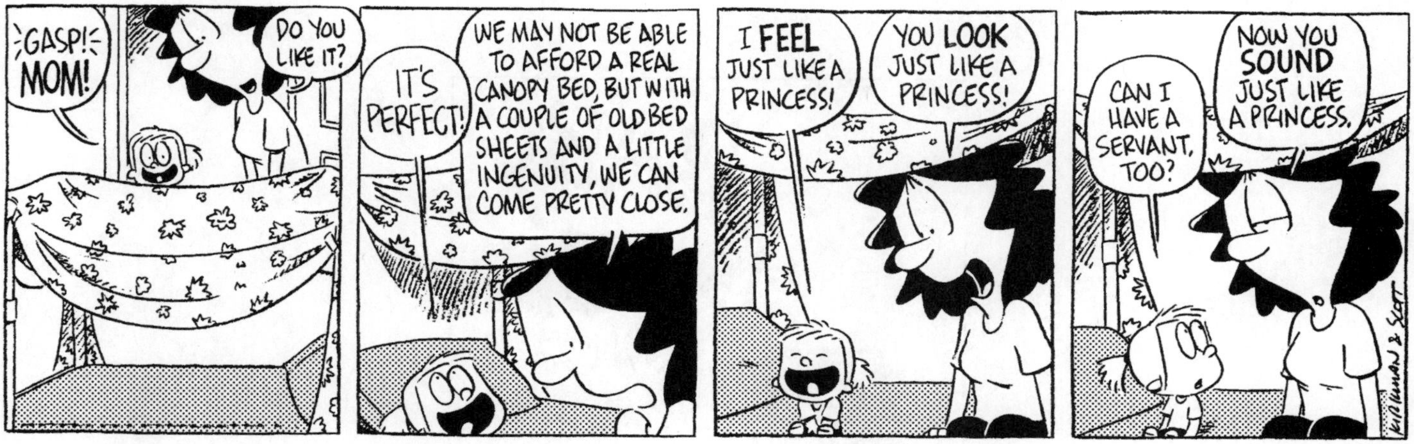
GASP! MOM!
DO YOU LIKE IT?
IT'S PERFECT!
WE MAY NOT BE ABLE TO AFFORD A REAL CANOPY BED, BUT WITH A COUPLE OF OLD BED SHEETS AND A LITTLE INGENUITY, WE CAN COME PRETTY CLOSE.
I **FEEL** JUST LIKE A PRINCESS!
YOU **LOOK** JUST LIKE A PRINCESS!
CAN I HAVE A SERVANT, TOO?
NOW YOU **SOUND** JUST LIKE A PRINCESS.
KIRKMAN & SCOTT

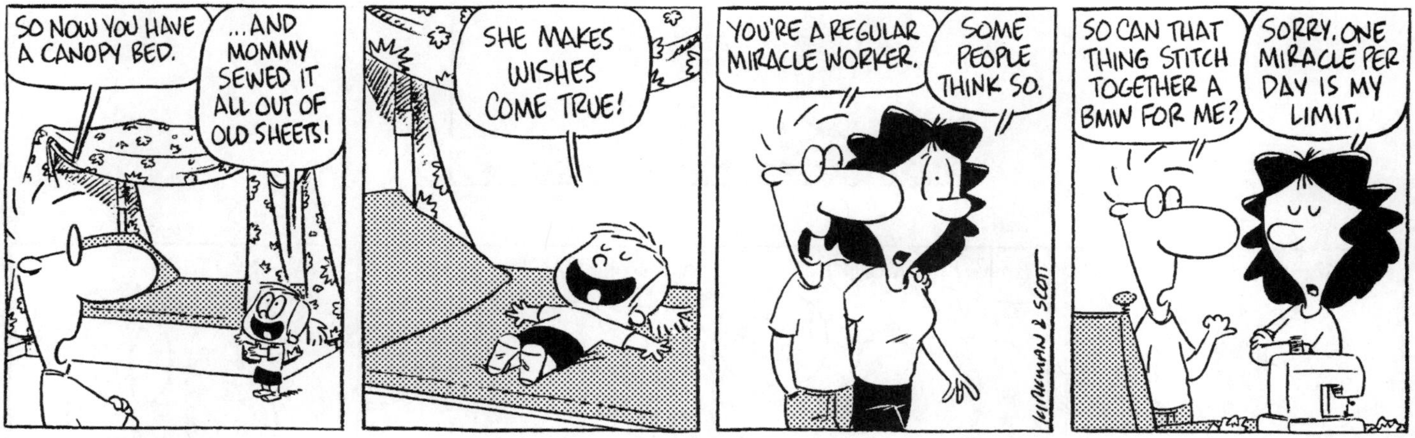
SO NOW YOU HAVE A CANOPY BED.
...AND MOMMY SEWED IT ALL OUT OF OLD SHEETS!
SHE MAKES WISHES COME TRUE!
YOU'RE A REGULAR MIRACLE WORKER.
SOME PEOPLE THINK SO.
KIRKMAN & SCOTT
SO CAN THAT THING STITCH TOGETHER A BMW FOR ME?
SORRY. ONE MIRACLE PER DAY IS MY LIMIT.

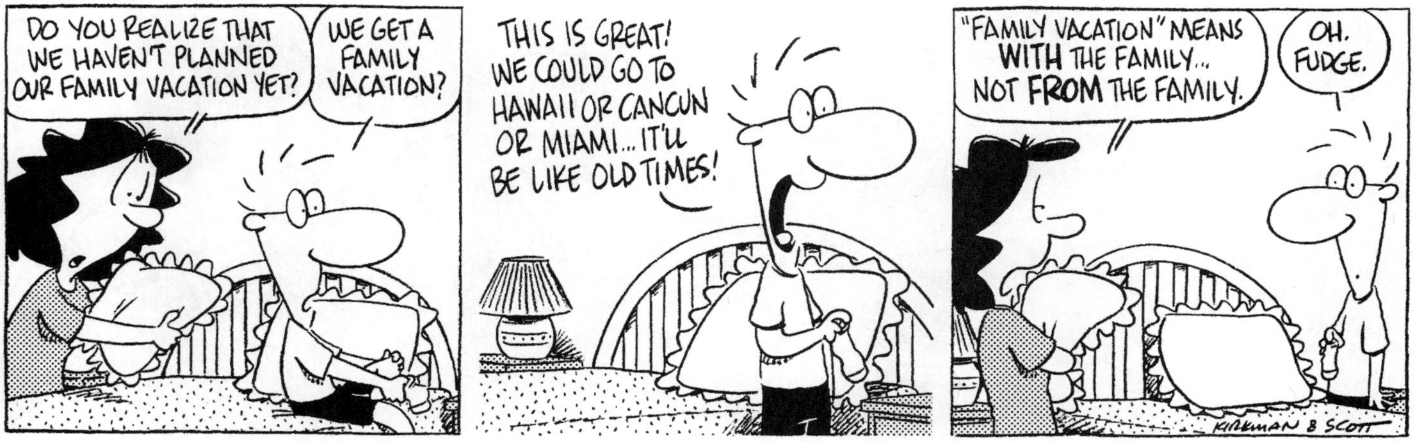
DO YOU REALIZE THAT WE HAVEN'T PLANNED OUR FAMILY VACATION YET?
WE GET A FAMILY VACATION?
THIS IS GREAT! WE COULD GO TO HAWAII OR CANCUN OR MIAMI... IT'LL BE LIKE OLD TIMES!
"FAMILY VACATION" MEANS **WITH** THE FAMILY... NOT **FROM** THE FAMILY.
OH. FUDGE.
KIRKMAN & SCOTT

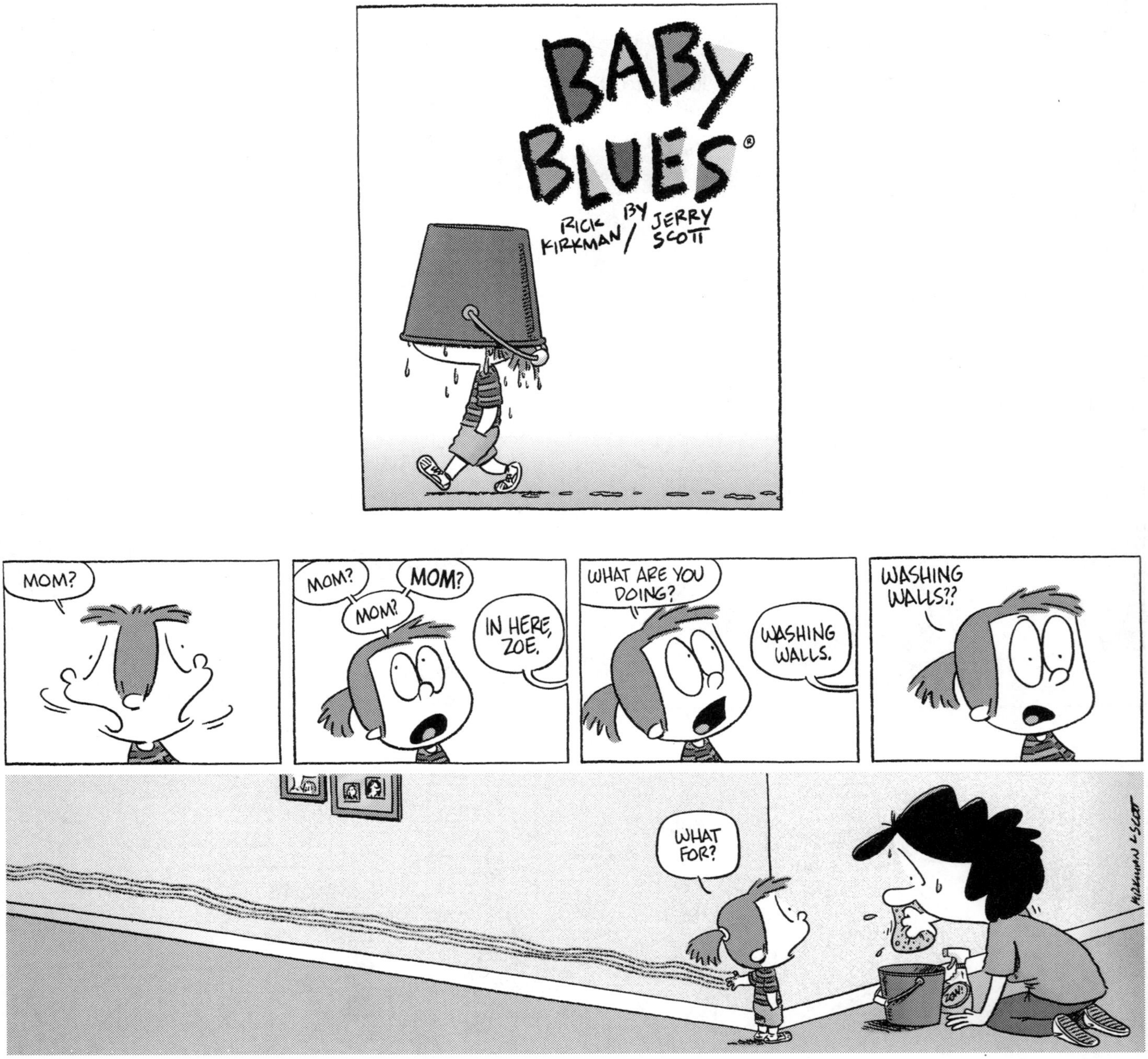
BABY BLUES®
BY RICK KIRKMAN / JERRY SCOTT
MOM?
MOM?
MOM?
MOM?
IN HERE, ZOE.
WHAT ARE YOU DOING?
WASHING WALLS.
WASHING WALLS??
WHAT FOR?
KIRKMAN & SCOTT

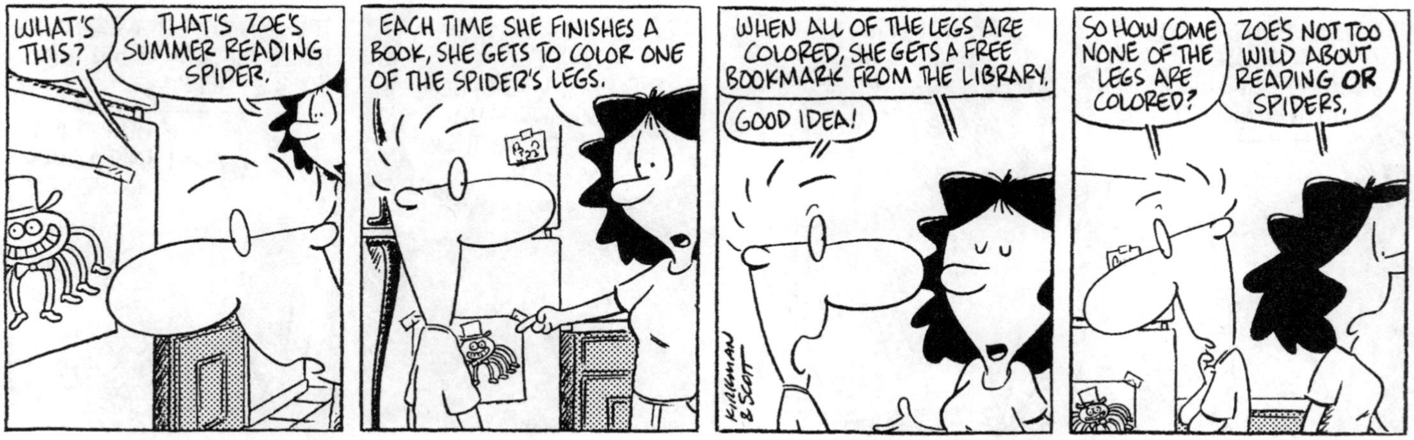
WHAT'S THIS?
THAT'S ZOE'S SUMMER READING SPIDER.
EACH TIME SHE FINISHES A BOOK, SHE GETS TO COLOR ONE OF THE SPIDER'S LEGS.
WHEN ALL OF THE LEGS ARE COLORED, SHE GETS A FREE BOOKMARK FROM THE LIBRARY.
GOOD IDEA!
KIRKMAN & SCOTT
SO HOW COME NONE OF THE LEGS ARE COLORED?
ZOE'S NOT TOO WILD ABOUT READING **OR** SPIDERS.

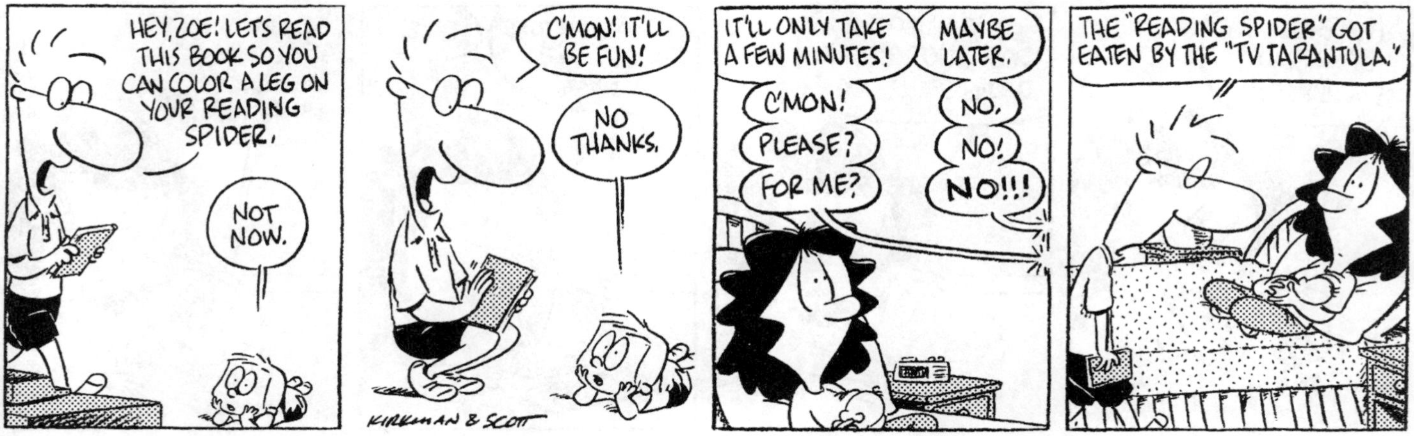
HEY, ZOE! LET'S READ THIS BOOK SO YOU CAN COLOR A LEG ON YOUR READING SPIDER.
NOT NOW.
C'MON! IT'LL BE FUN!
NO THANKS.
KIRKMAN & SCOTT
IT'LL ONLY TAKE A FEW MINUTES!
MAYBE LATER.
C'MON!
NO.
PLEASE?
NO!
FOR ME?
NO!!!
THE "READING SPIDER" GOT EATEN BY THE "TV TARANTULA."

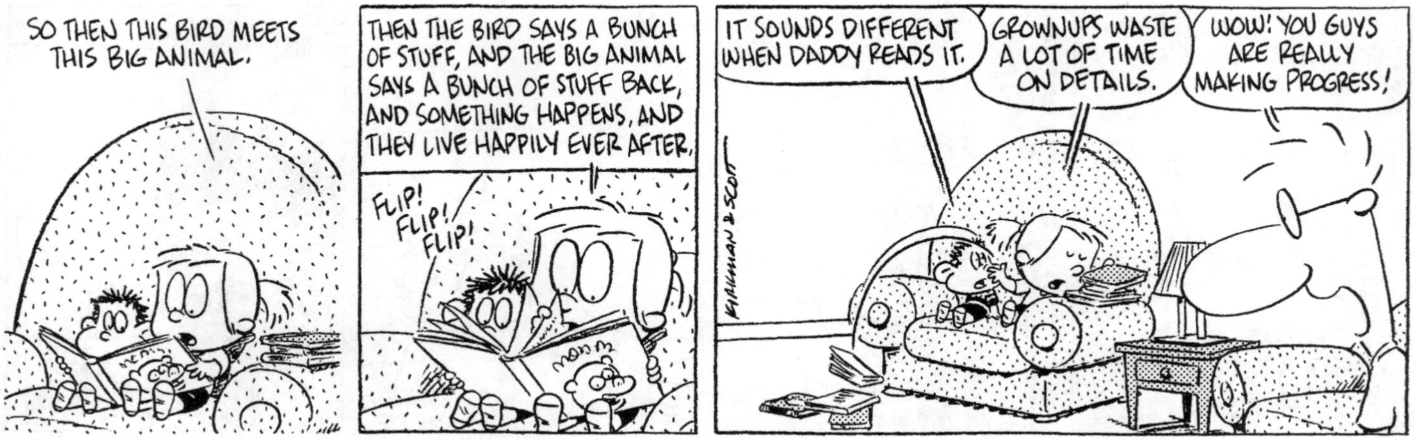
SO THEN THIS BIRD MEETS THIS BIG ANIMAL.
THEN THE BIRD SAYS A BUNCH OF STUFF, AND THE BIG ANIMAL SAYS A BUNCH OF STUFF BACK, AND SOMETHING HAPPENS, AND THEY LIVE HAPPILY EVER AFTER.
FLIP! FLIP! FLIP!
KIRKMAN & SCOTT
IT SOUNDS DIFFERENT WHEN DADDY READS IT.
GROWNUPS WASTE A LOT OF TIME ON DETAILS.
WOW! YOU GUYS ARE REALLY MAKING PROGRESS!

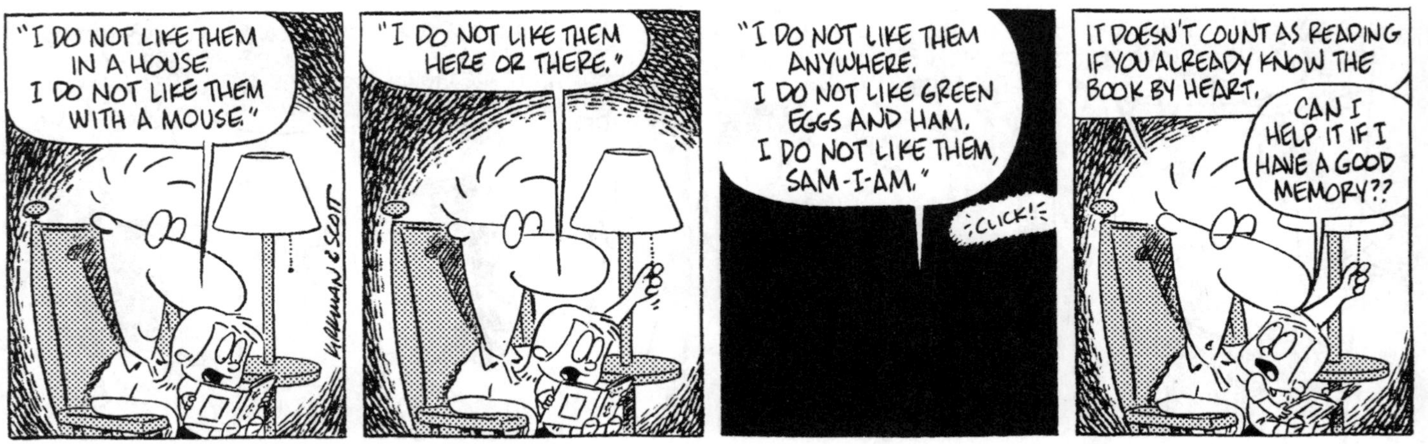
"I DO NOT LIKE THEM IN A HOUSE. I DO NOT LIKE THEM WITH A MOUSE."
KIRKMAN & SCOTT
"I DO NOT LIKE THEM HERE OR THERE."
"I DO NOT LIKE THEM ANYWHERE. I DO NOT LIKE GREEN EGGS AND HAM. I DO NOT LIKE THEM, SAM-I-AM."
CLICK!
IT DOESN'T COUNT AS READING IF YOU ALREADY KNOW THE BOOK BY HEART.
CAN I HELP IT IF I HAVE A GOOD MEMORY??

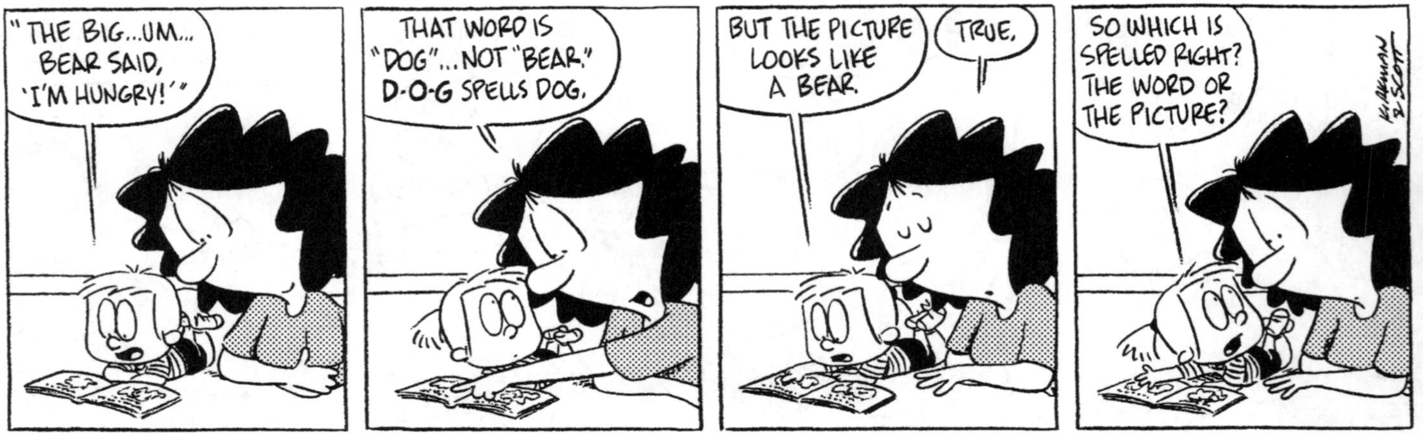
"THE BIG...UM... BEAR SAID, 'I'M HUNGRY!'"
THAT WORD IS "DOG"... NOT "BEAR." D-O-G SPELLS DOG.
BUT THE PICTURE LOOKS LIKE A BEAR.
TRUE.
SO WHICH IS SPELLED RIGHT? THE WORD OR THE PICTURE?
KIRKMAN & SCOTT

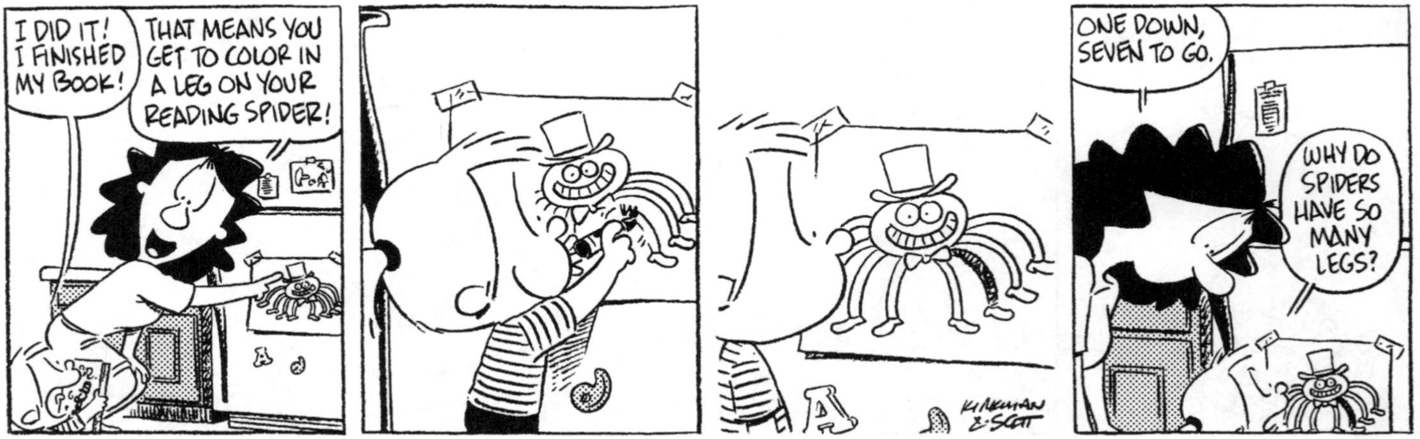
I DID IT! I FINISHED MY BOOK!
THAT MEANS YOU GET TO COLOR IN A LEG ON YOUR READING SPIDER!
KIRKMAN & SCOTT
ONE DOWN, SEVEN TO GO.
WHY DO SPIDERS HAVE SO MANY LEGS?

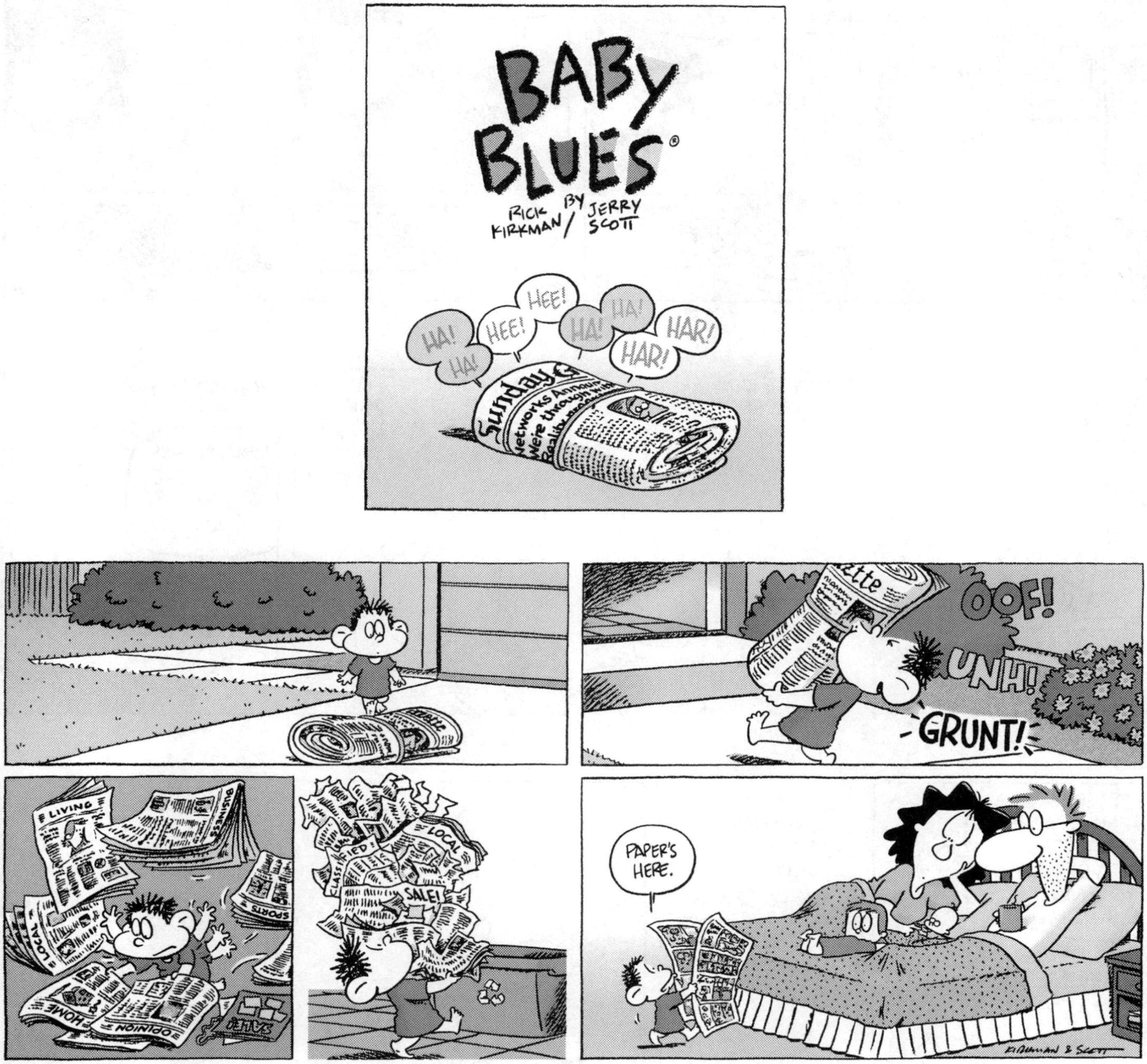
BABY BLUES®
BY RICK KIRKMAN / JERRY SCOTT
HA! HA!
HEE! HEE!
HA! HA!
HAR! HAR!
Sunday
OOF!
UNH!
GRUNT!
LIVING
BUSINESS
SPORTS
LOCAL
HOME
OPINION
CLASSIFIED
LOCAL
SALE!
PAPER'S HERE.
KIRKMAN & SCOTT

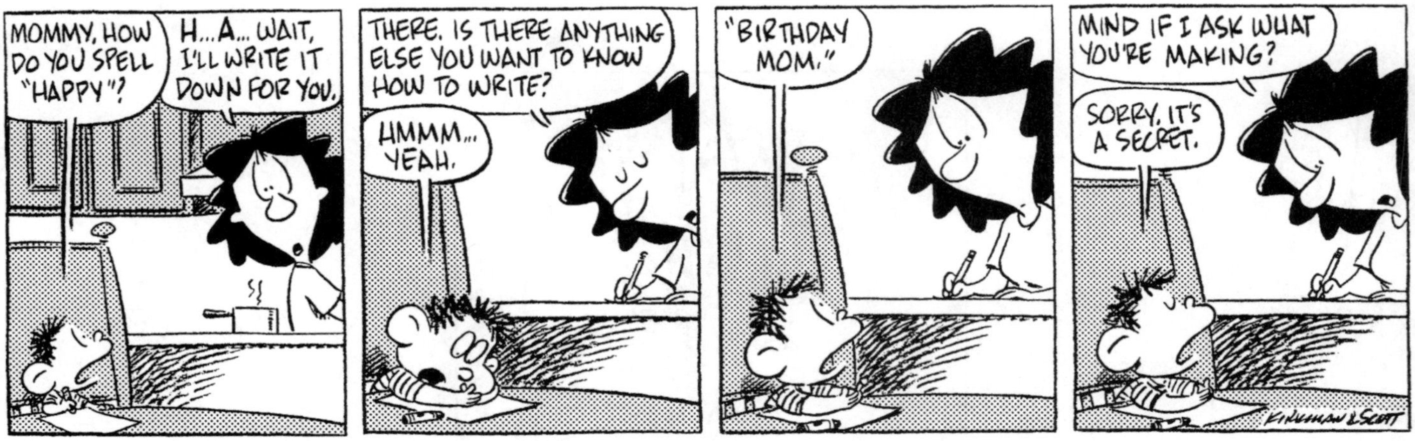
MOMMY, HOW DO YOU SPELL "HAPPY"?
H...A... WAIT, I'LL WRITE IT DOWN FOR YOU.
THERE. IS THERE ANYTHING ELSE YOU WANT TO KNOW HOW TO WRITE?
HMMM... YEAH.
"BIRTHDAY MOM."
MIND IF I ASK WHAT YOU'RE MAKING?
SORRY. IT'S A SECRET.
KIRKMAN & SCOTT

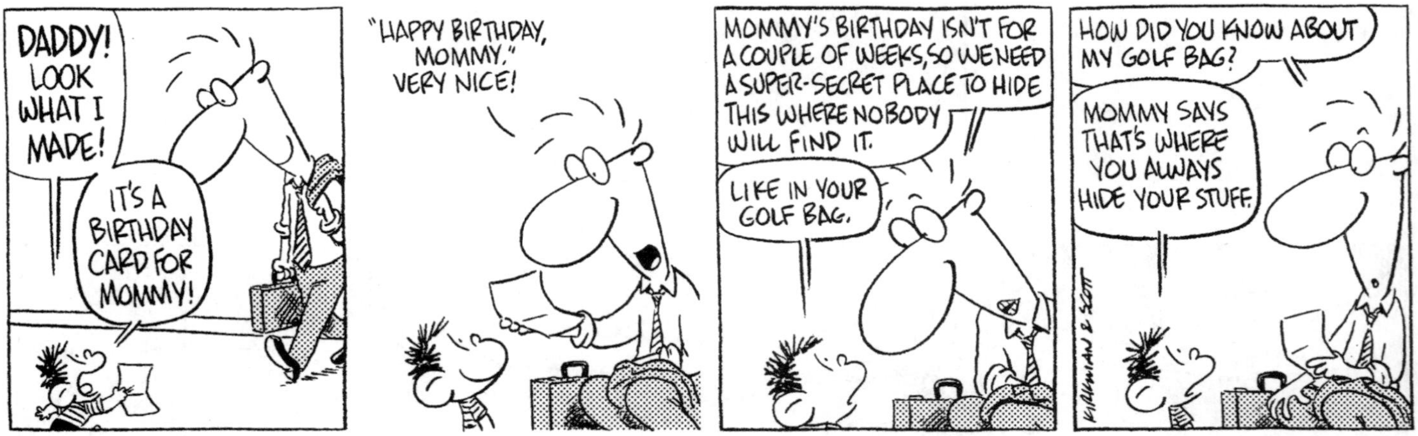
DADDY! LOOK WHAT I MADE!
IT'S A BIRTHDAY CARD FOR MOMMY!
"HAPPY BIRTHDAY, MOMMY." VERY NICE!
MOMMY'S BIRTHDAY ISN'T FOR A COUPLE OF WEEKS, SO WE NEED A SUPER-SECRET PLACE TO HIDE THIS WHERE NOBODY WILL FIND IT.
LIKE IN YOUR GOLF BAG.
KIRKMAN & SCOTT
HOW DID YOU KNOW ABOUT MY GOLF BAG?
MOMMY SAYS THAT'S WHERE YOU ALWAYS HIDE YOUR STUFF.

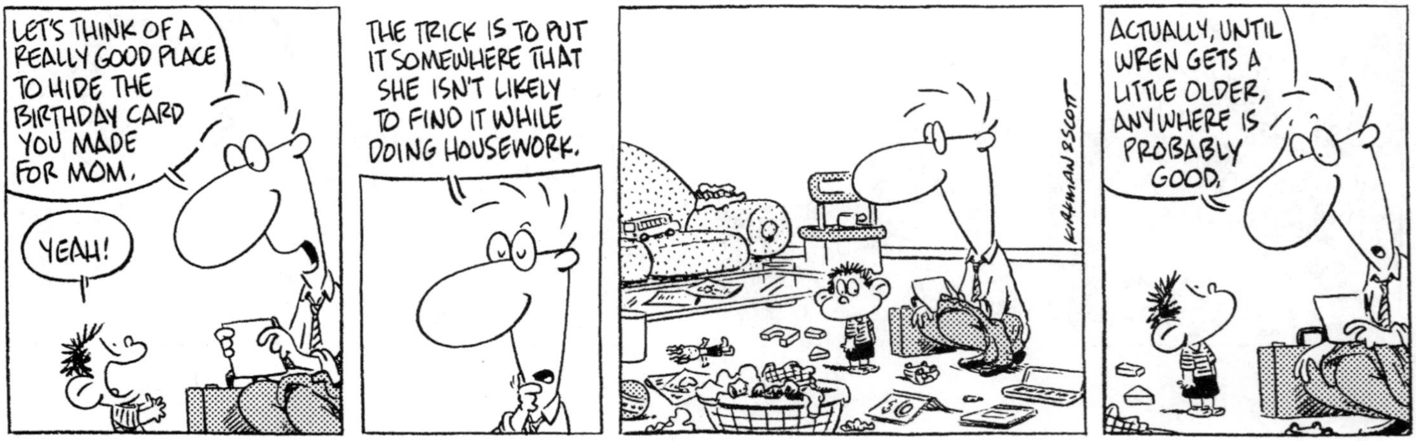
LET'S THINK OF A REALLY GOOD PLACE TO HIDE THE BIRTHDAY CARD YOU MADE FOR MOM.
YEAH!
THE TRICK IS TO PUT IT SOMEWHERE THAT SHE ISN'T LIKELY TO FIND IT WHILE DOING HOUSEWORK.
KIRKMAN & SCOTT
ACTUALLY, UNTIL WREN GETS A LITTLE OLDER, ANYWHERE IS PROBABLY GOOD.

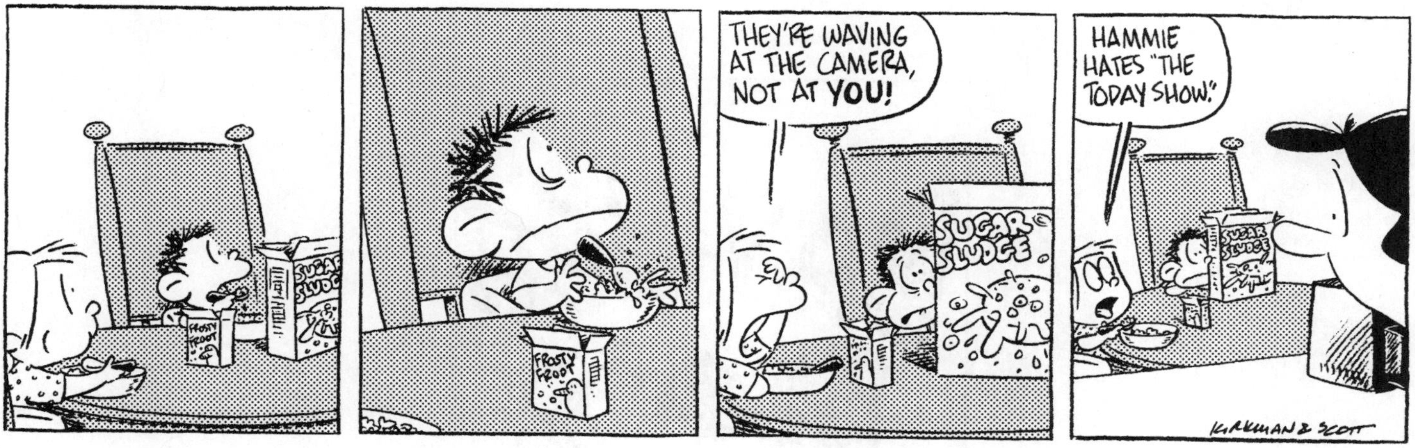
SUGAR SLUDGE
FROSTY FROOT
THEY'RE WAVING AT THE CAMERA, NOT AT YOU!
HAMMIE HATES "THE TODAY SHOW."
KIRKMAN & SCOTT

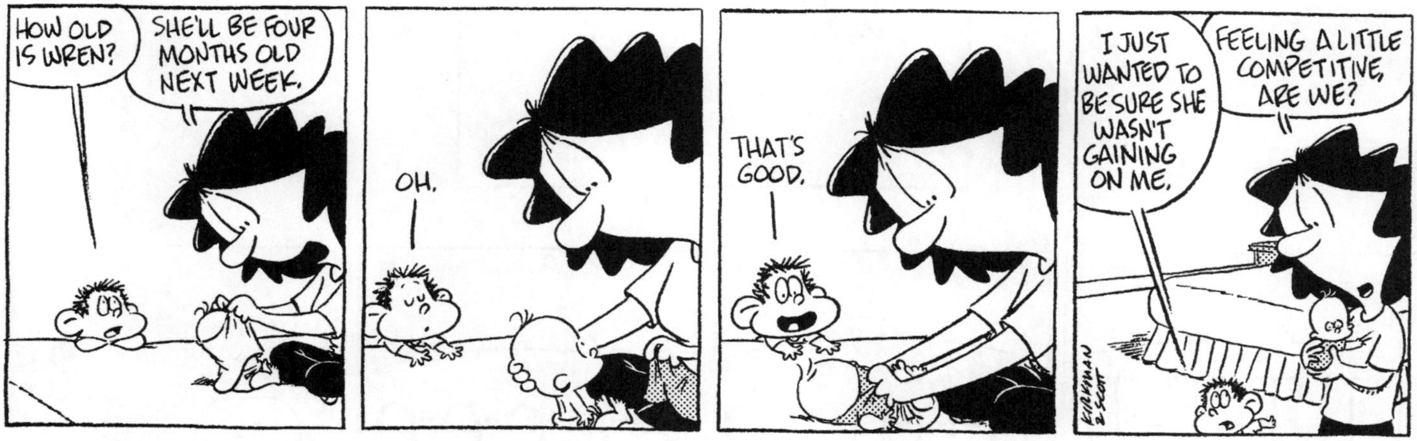
HOW OLD IS WREN?
SHE'LL BE FOUR MONTHS OLD NEXT WEEK.
OH.
THAT'S GOOD.
I JUST WANTED TO BE SURE SHE WASN'T GAINING ON ME.
FEELING A LITTLE COMPETITIVE, ARE WE?
KIRKMAN & SCOTT

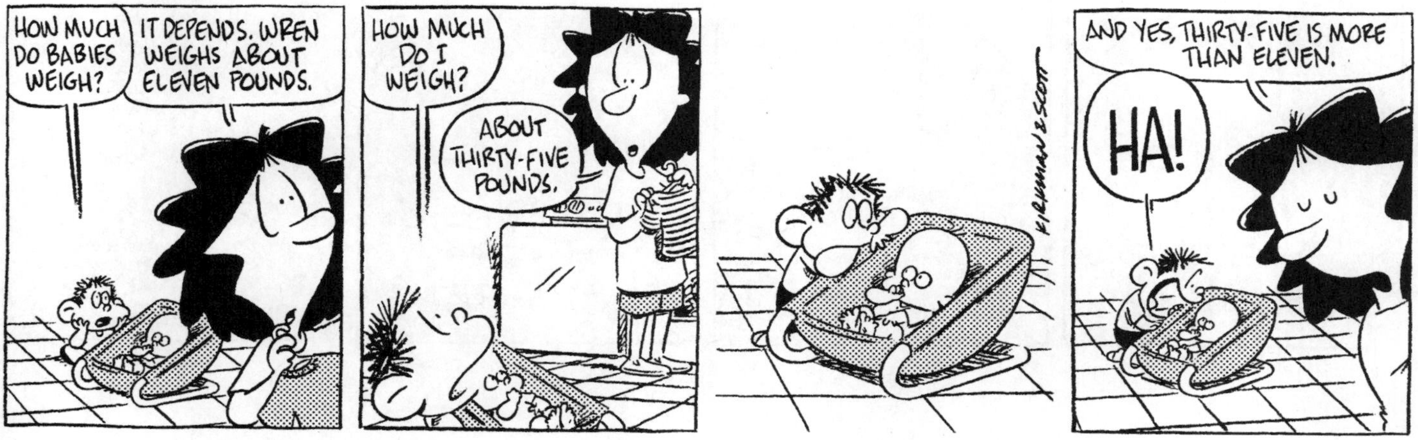
HOW MUCH DO BABIES WEIGH?
IT DEPENDS. WREN WEIGHS ABOUT ELEVEN POUNDS.
HOW MUCH DO I WEIGH?
ABOUT THIRTY-FIVE POUNDS.
KIRKMAN & SCOTT
AND YES, THIRTY-FIVE IS MORE THAN ELEVEN.
HA!

BAY-BEE BLOOZ
BY
RIK KURK-MAN / JER-EE SKOT

T-T-T-T
h-u-u-h-h
e-e-e-e-e
KIRKMAN & SCOTT
IT'S "THE."
OH.
HOW'S THE READING LESSON GOING?

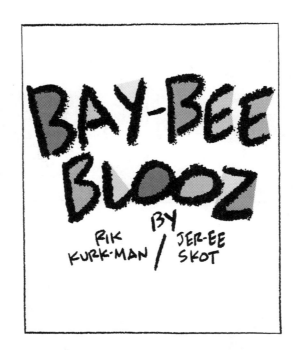

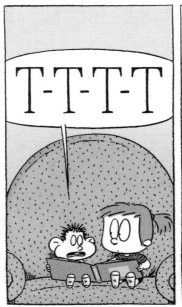

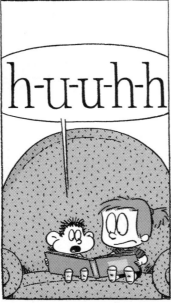

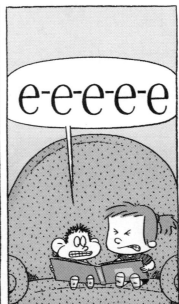

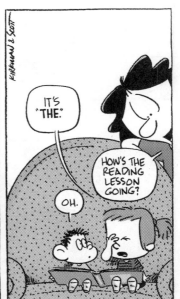

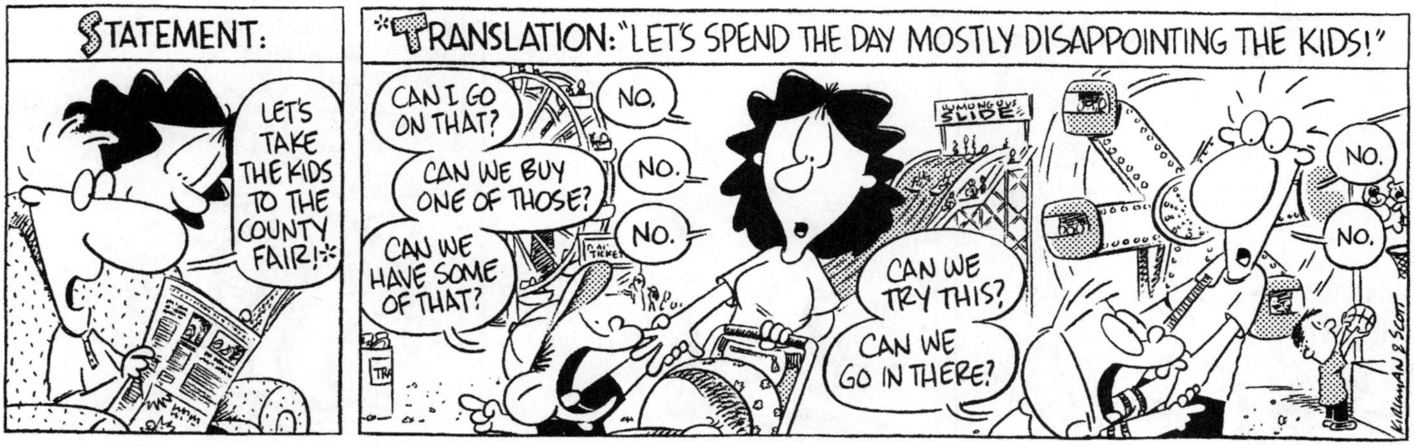
STATEMENT:
LET'S TAKE THE KIDS TO THE COUNTY FAIR!*
*TRANSLATION: "LET'S SPEND THE DAY MOSTLY DISAPPOINTING THE KIDS!"
CAN I GO ON THAT?
NO.
CAN WE BUY ONE OF THOSE?
NO.
CAN WE HAVE SOME OF THAT?
NO.
HUMONGOUS SLIDE
CAN WE TRY THIS?
CAN WE GO IN THERE?
NO.
NO.
KIRKMAN & SCOTT

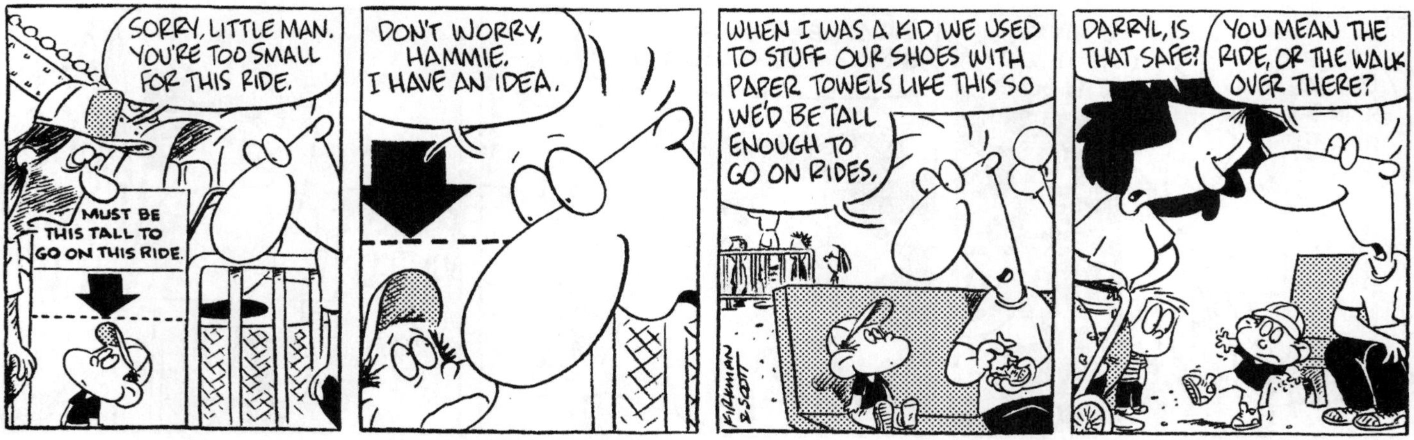
SORRY, LITTLE MAN. YOU'RE TOO SMALL FOR THIS RIDE.
MUST BE THIS TALL TO GO ON THIS RIDE.
DON'T WORRY, HAMMIE. I HAVE AN IDEA.
KIRKMAN & SCOTT
WHEN I WAS A KID WE USED TO STUFF OUR SHOES WITH PAPER TOWELS LIKE THIS SO WE'D BE TALL ENOUGH TO GO ON RIDES.
DARRYL, IS THAT SAFE?
YOU MEAN THE RIDE, OR THE WALK OVER THERE?

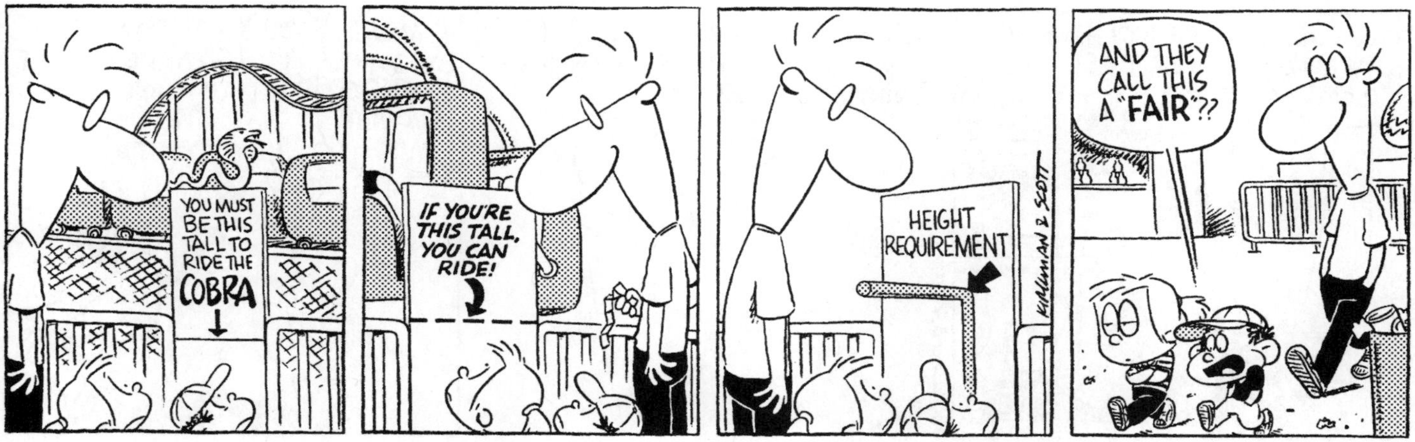
YOU MUST BE THIS TALL TO RIDE THE COBRA
IF YOU'RE THIS TALL, YOU CAN RIDE!
HEIGHT REQUIREMENT
KIRKMAN & SCOTT
AND THEY CALL THIS A "FAIR"??

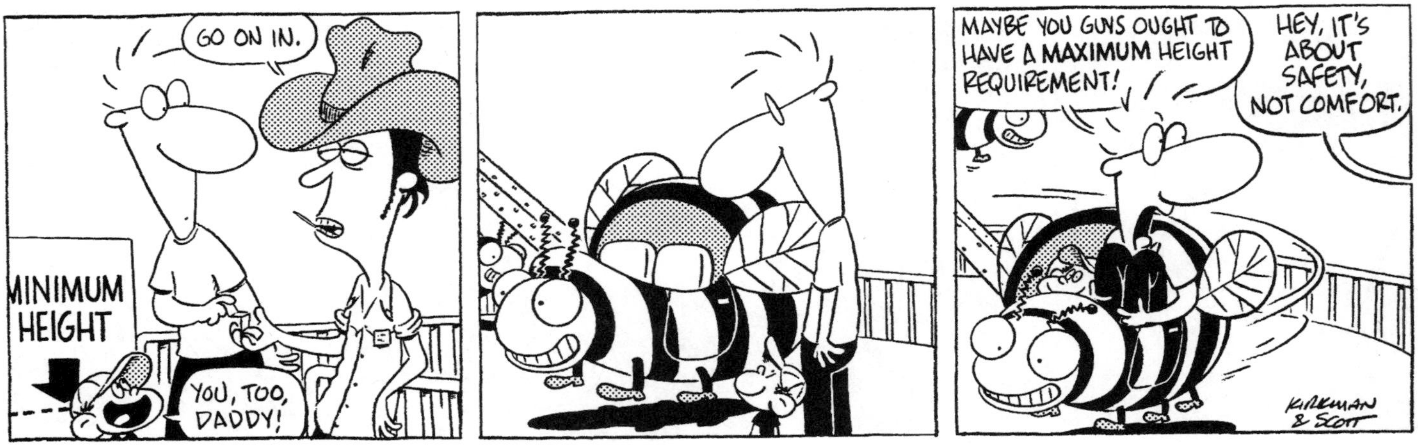
GO ON IN.
MINIMUM HEIGHT
YOU, TOO, DADDY!
MAYBE YOU GUYS OUGHT TO HAVE A **MAXIMUM** HEIGHT REQUIREMENT!
HEY, IT'S ABOUT SAFETY, NOT COMFORT.
KIRKMAN & SCOTT

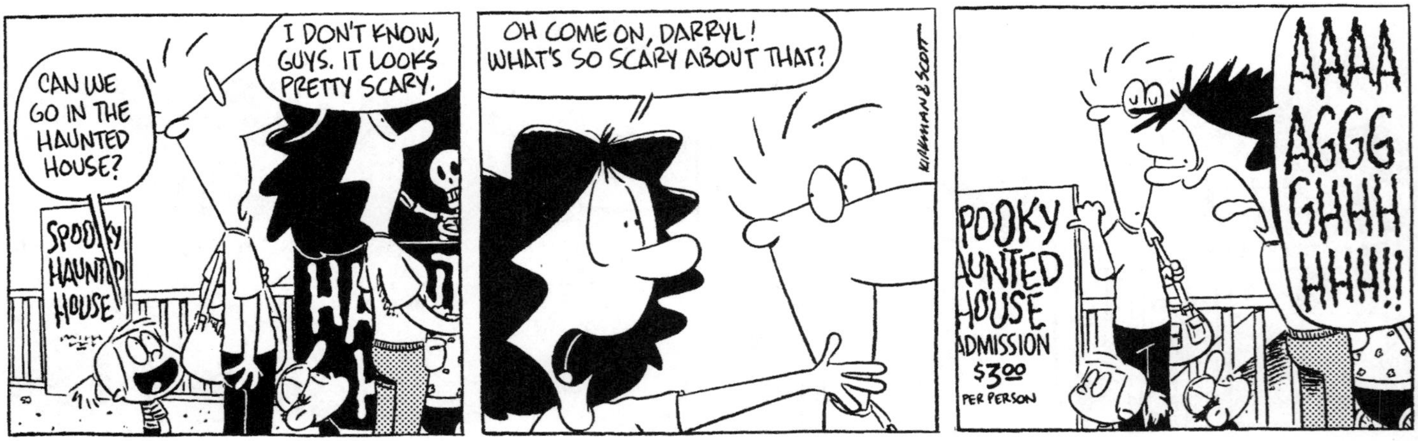
CAN WE GO IN THE HAUNTED HOUSE?
I DON'T KNOW, GUYS. IT LOOKS PRETTY SCARY.
OH COME ON, DARRYL! WHAT'S SO SCARY ABOUT THAT?
KIRKMAN & SCOTT
POOKY
AUNTED
HOUSE
ADMISSION
$3.00
PER PERSON
AAAA AGGG GHHH HHH!!

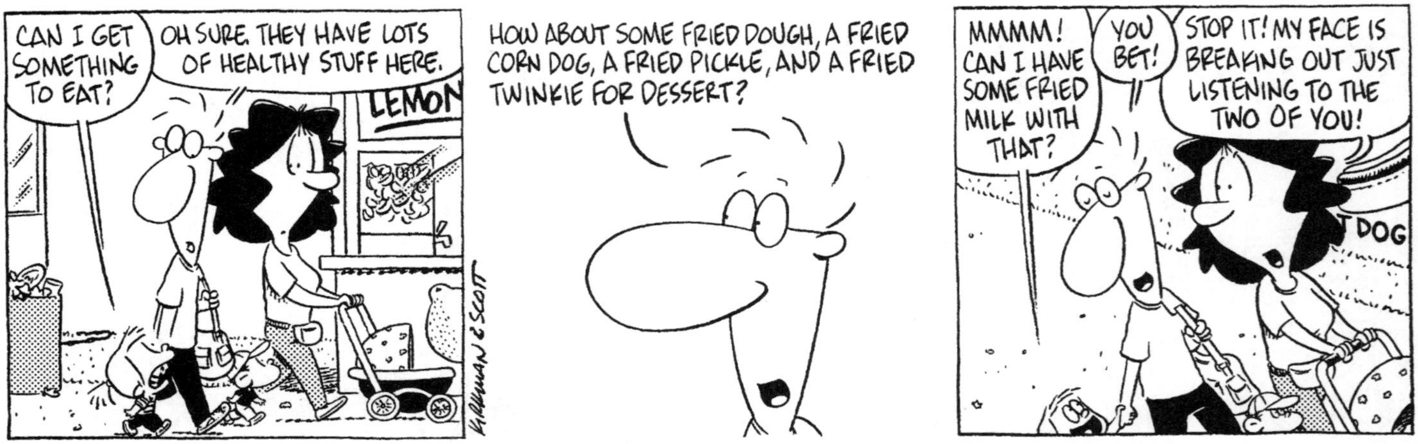
CAN I GET SOMETHING TO EAT?
OH SURE. THEY HAVE LOTS OF HEALTHY STUFF HERE.
LEMON
KIRKMAN & SCOTT
HOW ABOUT SOME FRIED DOUGH, A FRIED CORN DOG, A FRIED PICKLE, AND A FRIED TWINKIE FOR DESSERT?
MMMM! CAN I HAVE SOME FRIED MILK WITH THAT?
YOU BET!
STOP IT! MY FACE IS BREAKING OUT JUST LISTENING TO THE TWO OF YOU!
DOG

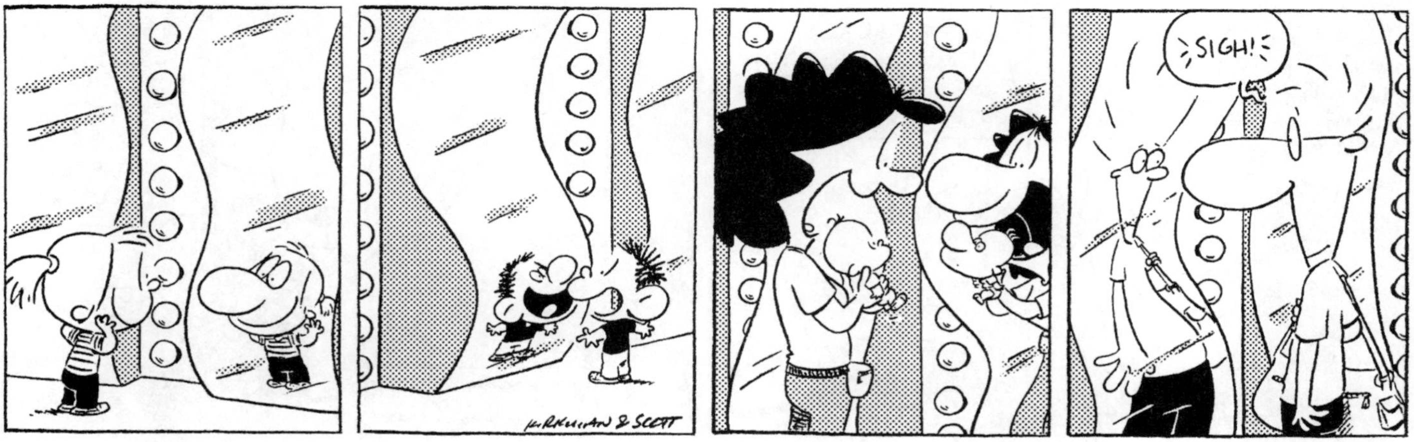
KIRKMAN & SCOTT
SIGH!

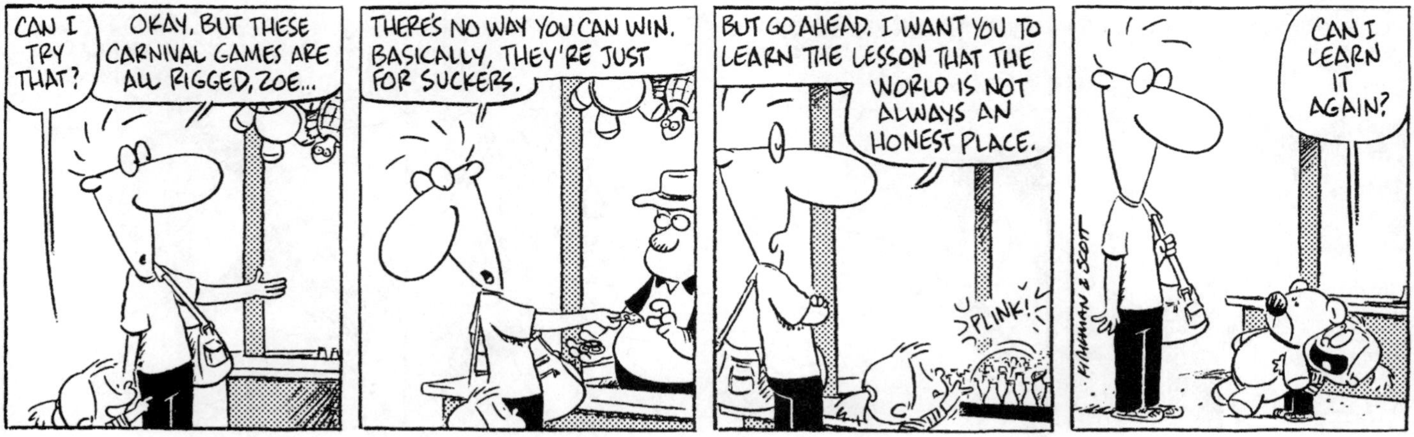
CAN I TRY THAT?
OKAY, BUT THESE CARNIVAL GAMES ARE ALL RIGGED, ZOE...
THERE'S NO WAY YOU CAN WIN. BASICALLY, THEY'RE JUST FOR SUCKERS.
BUT GO AHEAD. I WANT YOU TO LEARN THE LESSON THAT THE WORLD IS NOT ALWAYS AN HONEST PLACE.
PLINK!
KIRKMAN & SCOTT
CAN I LEARN IT AGAIN?

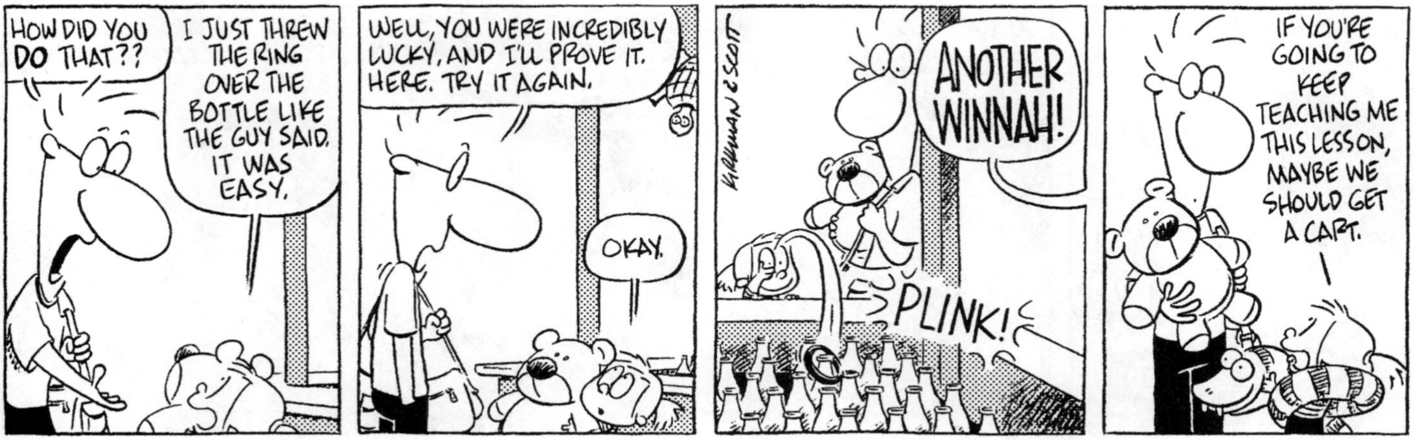
HOW DID YOU DO THAT??
I JUST THREW THE RING OVER THE BOTTLE LIKE THE GUY SAID. IT WAS EASY.
WELL, YOU WERE INCREDIBLY LUCKY, AND I'LL PROVE IT. HERE. TRY IT AGAIN.
OKAY.
KIRKMAN & SCOTT
ANOTHER WINNAH!
PLINK!
IF YOU'RE GOING TO KEEP TEACHING ME THIS LESSON, MAYBE WE SHOULD GET A CART.

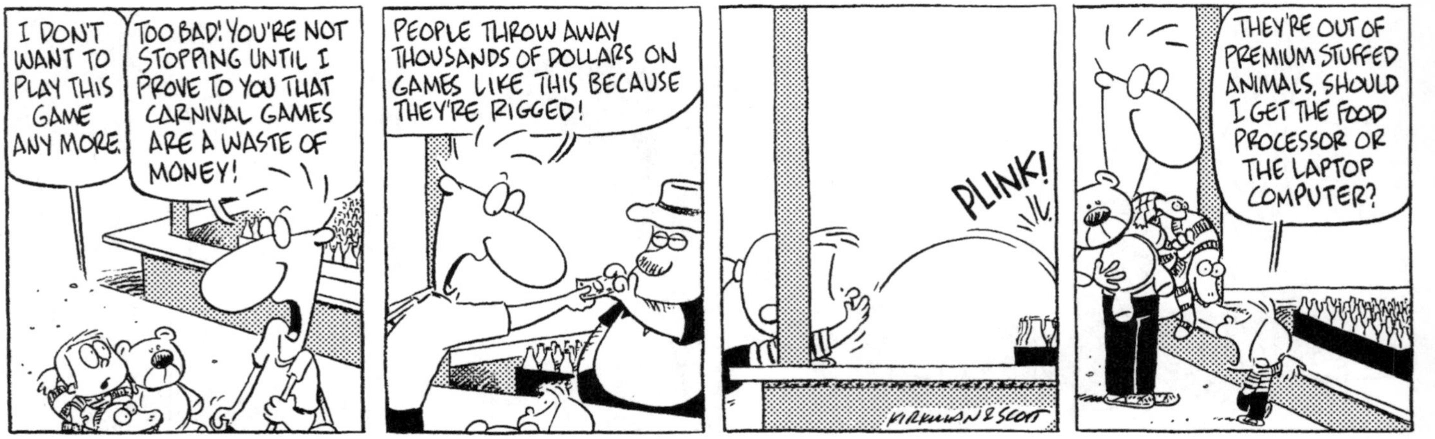
I DON'T WANT TO PLAY THIS GAME ANY MORE.
TOO BAD! YOU'RE NOT STOPPING UNTIL I PROVE TO YOU THAT CARNIVAL GAMES ARE A WASTE OF MONEY!
PEOPLE THROW AWAY THOUSANDS OF DOLLARS ON GAMES LIKE THIS BECAUSE THEY'RE RIGGED!
PLINK!
THEY'RE OUT OF PREMIUM STUFFED ANIMALS. SHOULD I GET THE FOOD PROCESSOR OR THE LAPTOP COMPUTER?

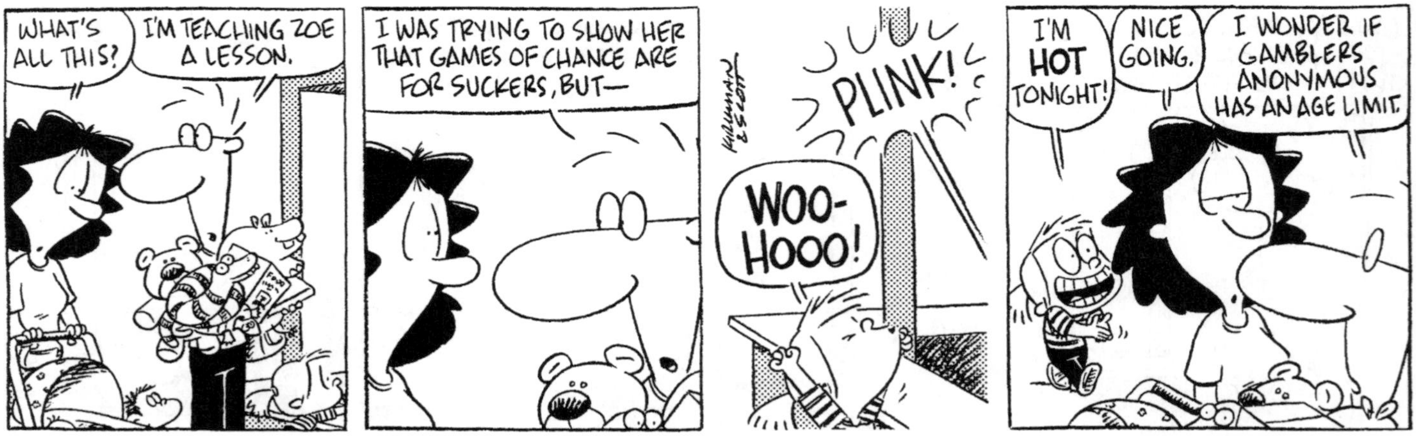
WHAT'S ALL THIS?
I'M TEACHING ZOE A LESSON.
I WAS TRYING TO SHOW HER THAT GAMES OF CHANCE ARE FOR SUCKERS, BUT—
PLINK!
WOO-HOOO!
I'M HOT TONIGHT!
NICE GOING.
I WONDER IF GAMBLERS ANONYMOUS HAS AN AGE LIMIT.

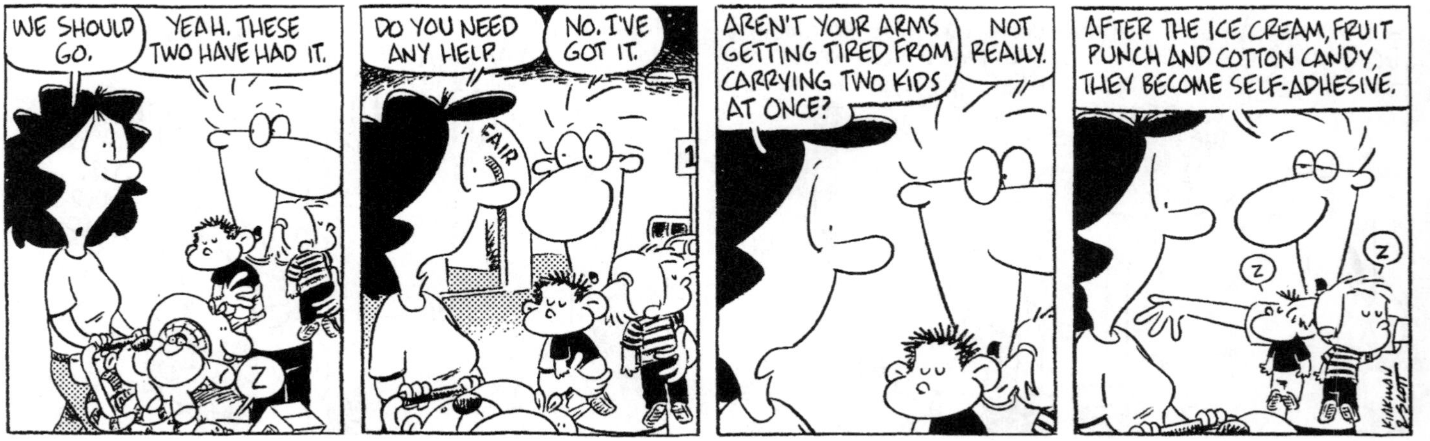
WE SHOULD GO.
YEAH. THESE TWO HAVE HAD IT.
DO YOU NEED ANY HELP?
NO. I'VE GOT IT.
AREN'T YOUR ARMS GETTING TIRED FROM CARRYING TWO KIDS AT ONCE?
NOT REALLY.
AFTER THE ICE CREAM, FRUIT PUNCH AND COTTON CANDY, THEY BECOME SELF-ADHESIVE.

BABY BLUES®
RICK KIRKMAN / BY JERRY SCOTT

SHAKE!
SHAKE!
SHAKE!
AAAAGH!
KIRKMAN & SCOTT
SOMETHING WRONG?
SIGH! NOT REALLY. JUST FEELING A LITTLE OLD.
WHY? SORE MUSCLES? ACHY JOINTS?
WORSE.
WREN WAS JUST USING MY PILL MINDER AS A RATTLE.

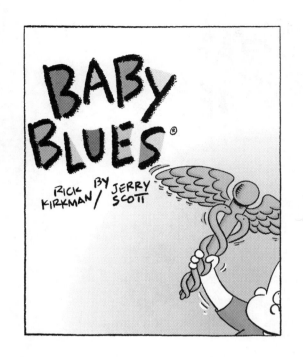

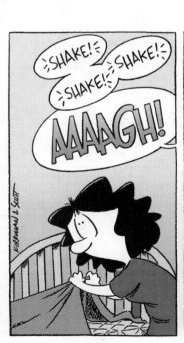

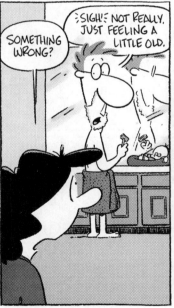

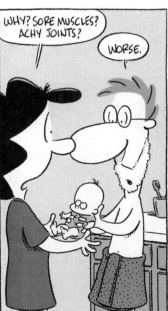

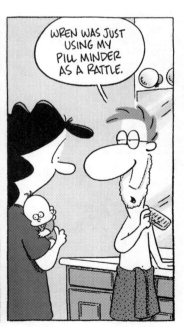

BABY BLUES®
By Rick Kirkman / Jerry Scott

HUH. I NEVER HEARD THAT BEFORE.

WHAT?

THUP! THUP! THUP!

THIS COMPANY SAYS THAT THEIR NEW BABY FORMULA WILL MAKE YOUR BABY SMARTER AND IMPROVE HER EYESIGHT, TOO.

REALLY?

THEY SAY THEIR FORMULA PROVIDES THE BRAIN WITH SPECIAL FATTY ACIDS THAT WILL GIVE A CHILD THE MIND OF A ROCKET SCIENTIST.

INTERESTING.

OH, LOOK! THERE'S A COUPON, TOO.

RIP!

STOMP! STOMP! STOMP!

STOMP! STOMP! STOMP!

ONCE A BREAST-FEEDER, ALWAYS A BREAST-FEEDER, HUH?

YOU COULD SAY THAT.

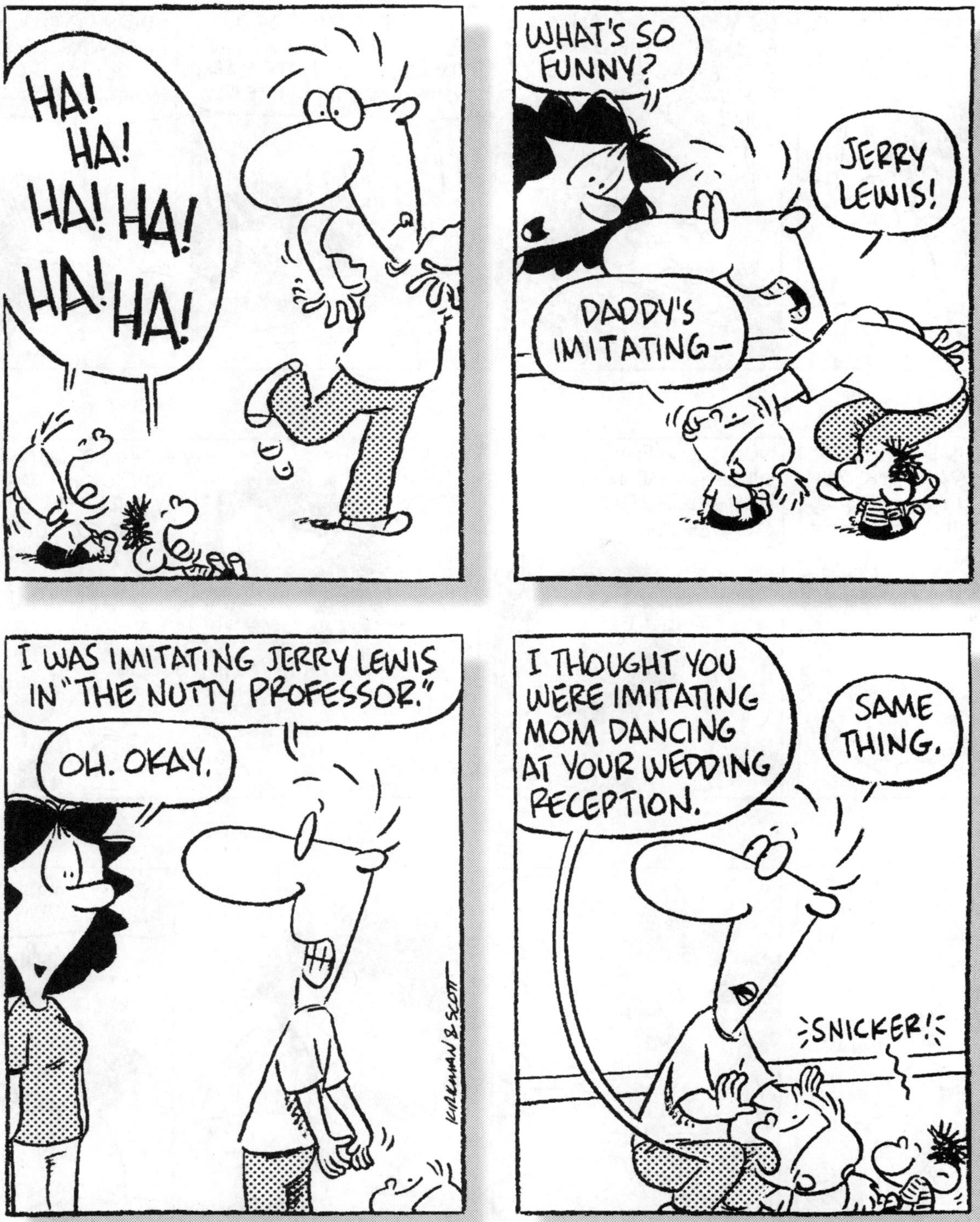
HA! HA! HA! HA! HA! HA!
WHAT'S SO FUNNY?
JERRY LEWIS!
DADDY'S IMITATING—
I WAS IMITATING JERRY LEWIS IN "THE NUTTY PROFESSOR."
OH. OKAY.
KIRKMAN & SCOTT
I THOUGHT YOU WERE IMITATING MOM DANCING AT YOUR WEDDING RECEPTION.
SAME THING.
SNICKER!

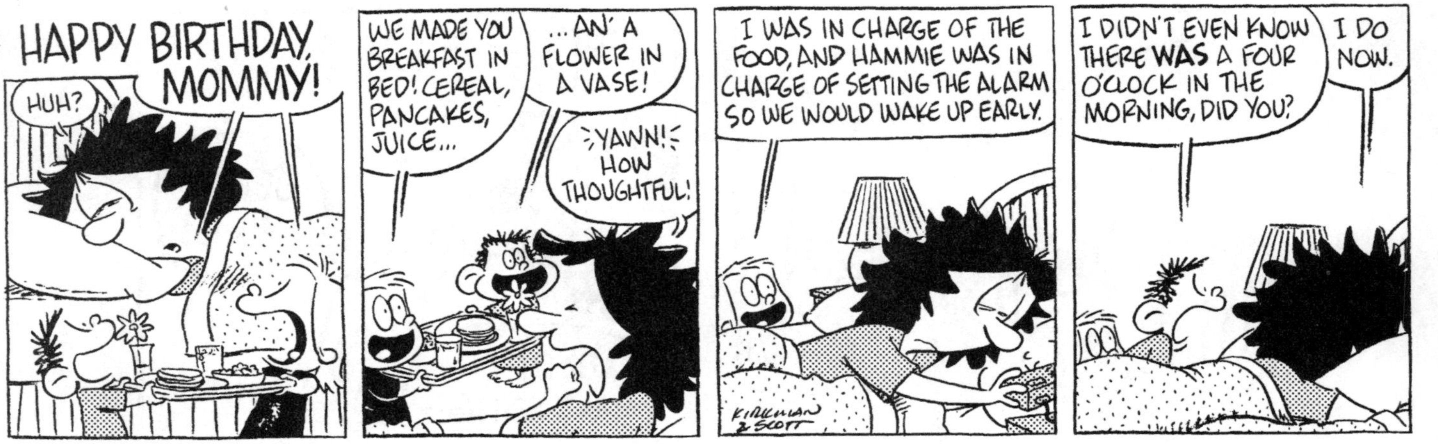
HAPPY BIRTHDAY, MOMMY!
HUH?
WE MADE YOU BREAKFAST IN BED! CEREAL, PANCAKES, JUICE...
... AN' A FLOWER IN A VASE!
YAWN! HOW THOUGHTFUL!
I WAS IN CHARGE OF THE FOOD, AND HAMMIE WAS IN CHARGE OF SETTING THE ALARM SO WE WOULD WAKE UP EARLY.
KIRKMAN & SCOTT
I DIDN'T EVEN KNOW THERE **WAS** A FOUR O'CLOCK IN THE MORNING, DID YOU?
I DO NOW.

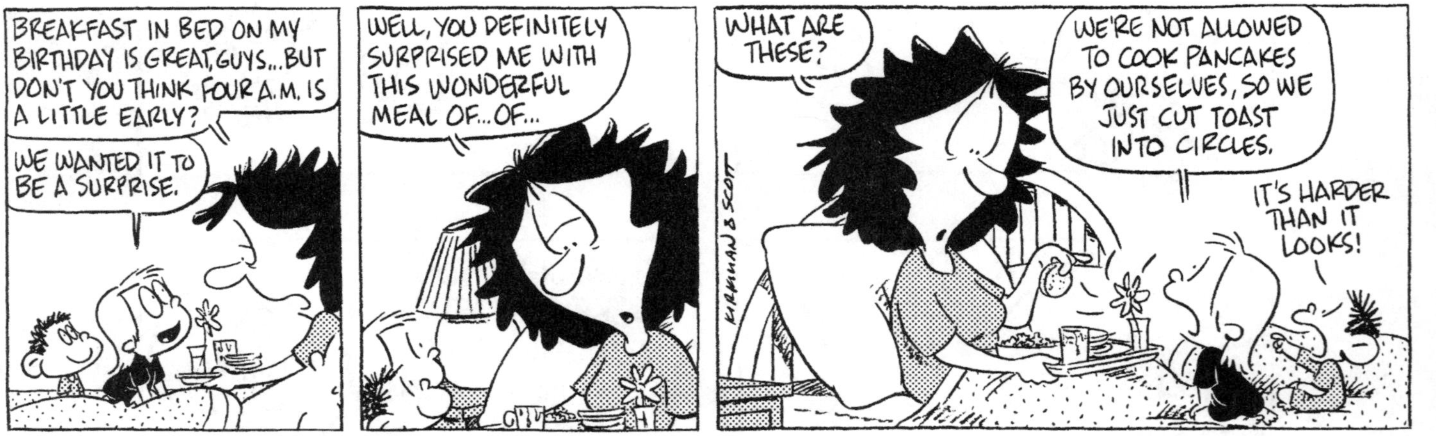
BREAKFAST IN BED ON MY BIRTHDAY IS GREAT, GUYS... BUT DON'T YOU THINK FOUR A.M. IS A LITTLE EARLY?
WE WANTED IT TO BE A SURPRISE.
WELL, YOU DEFINITELY SURPRISED ME WITH THIS WONDERFUL MEAL OF... OF...
KIRKMAN & SCOTT
WHAT ARE THESE?
WE'RE NOT ALLOWED TO COOK PANCAKES BY OURSELVES, SO WE JUST CUT TOAST INTO CIRCLES.
IT'S HARDER THAN IT LOOKS!

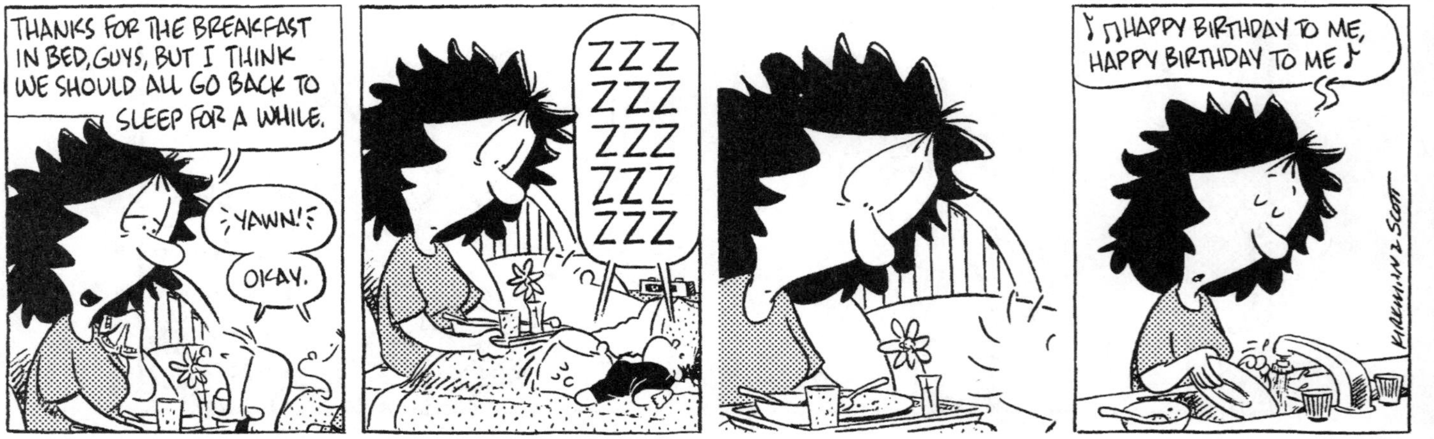
THANKS FOR THE BREAKFAST IN BED, GUYS, BUT I THINK WE SHOULD ALL GO BACK TO SLEEP FOR A WHILE.
YAWN!
OKAY.
ZZZ ZZZ ZZZ ZZZ ZZZ
HAPPY BIRTHDAY TO ME, HAPPY BIRTHDAY TO ME
KIRKMAN & SCOTT

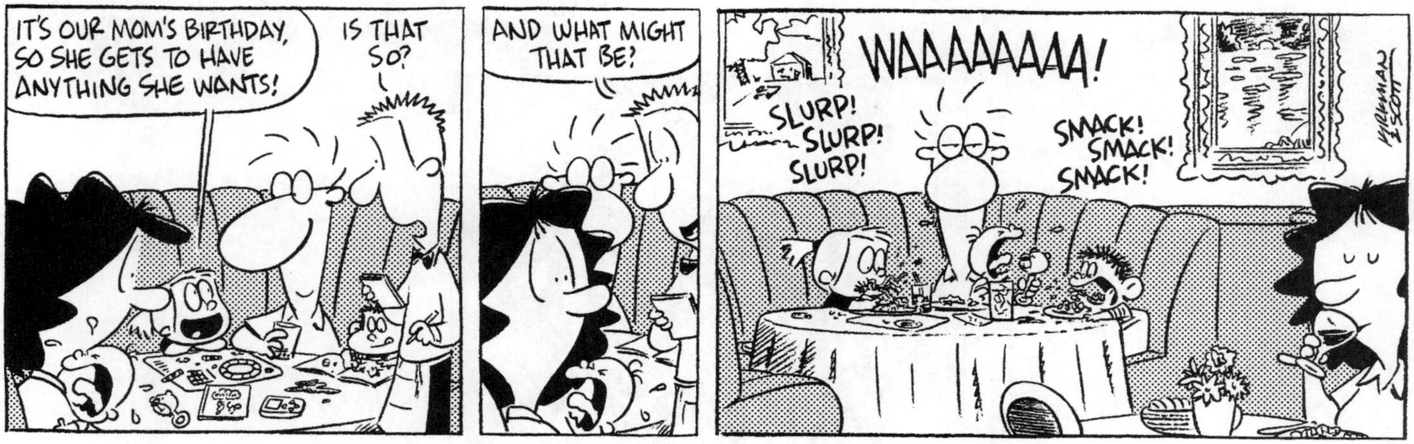
IT'S OUR MOM'S BIRTHDAY, SO SHE GETS TO HAVE ANYTHING SHE WANTS!
IS THAT SO?
AND WHAT MIGHT THAT BE?
WAAAAAAAA!
SLURP! SLURP! SLURP!
SMACK! SMACK! SMACK!
KIRKMAN & SCOTT

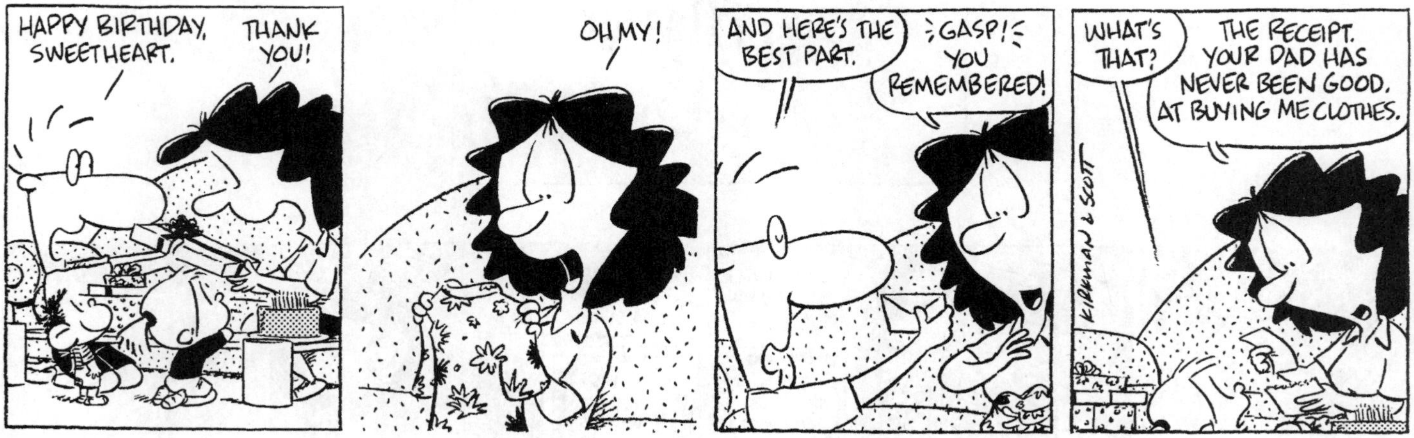
HAPPY BIRTHDAY, SWEETHEART.
THANK YOU!
OH MY!
AND HERE'S THE BEST PART.
GASP! YOU REMEMBERED!
WHAT'S THAT?
THE RECEIPT. YOUR DAD HAS NEVER BEEN GOOD AT BUYING ME CLOTHES.
KIRKMAN & SCOTT

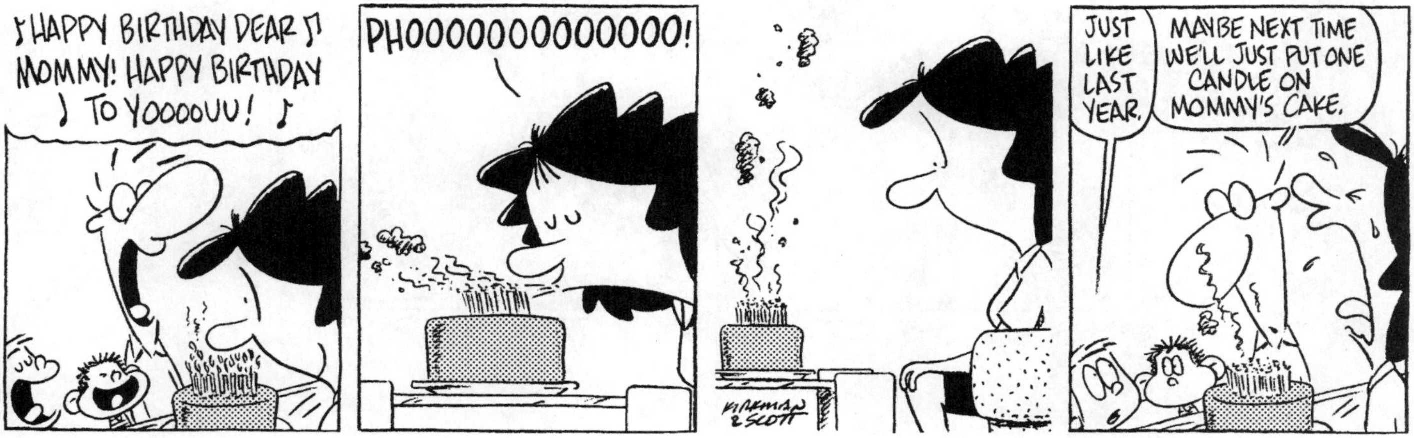
♪ HAPPY BIRTHDAY DEAR ♫ MOMMY! HAPPY BIRTHDAY ♪ TO YOOOOUU! ♪
PHOOOOOOOOOOOOO!
KIRKMAN & SCOTT
JUST LIKE LAST YEAR.
MAYBE NEXT TIME WE'LL JUST PUT ONE CANDLE ON MOMMY'S CAKE.

BABY BLUES®
BY
RICK KIRKMAN / JERRY SCOTT

WOW! THE WIND IS REALLY BLOWING OUT THERE!
IT LOOKS LIKE WE'LL BE STUCK IN HERE THE REST OF THE DAY.
IS IT A TORNADO, MOMMY?
NO, IT'S NOT A TORNADO.
...NOT OUT THERE, AT LEAST.

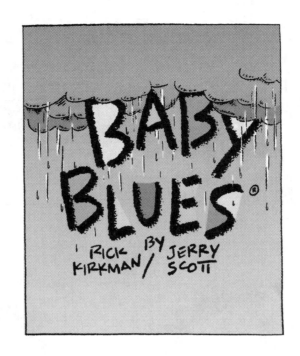

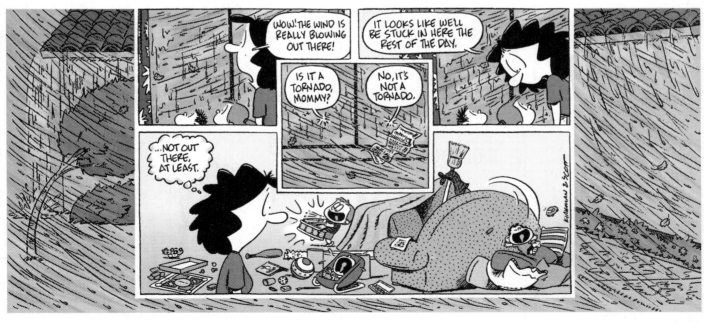

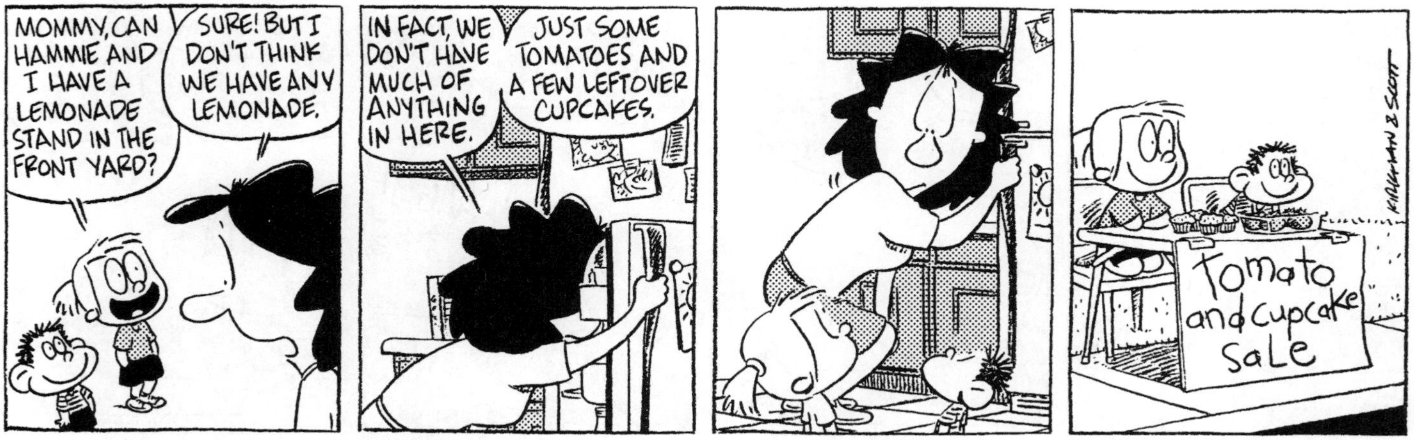
MOMMY, CAN HAMMIE AND I HAVE A LEMONADE STAND IN THE FRONT YARD?
SURE! BUT I DON'T THINK WE HAVE ANY LEMONADE.
IN FACT, WE DON'T HAVE MUCH OF ANYTHING IN HERE.
JUST SOME TOMATOES AND A FEW LEFTOVER CUPCAKES.
Tomato and Cupcake SaLe
KIRKMAN & SCOTT

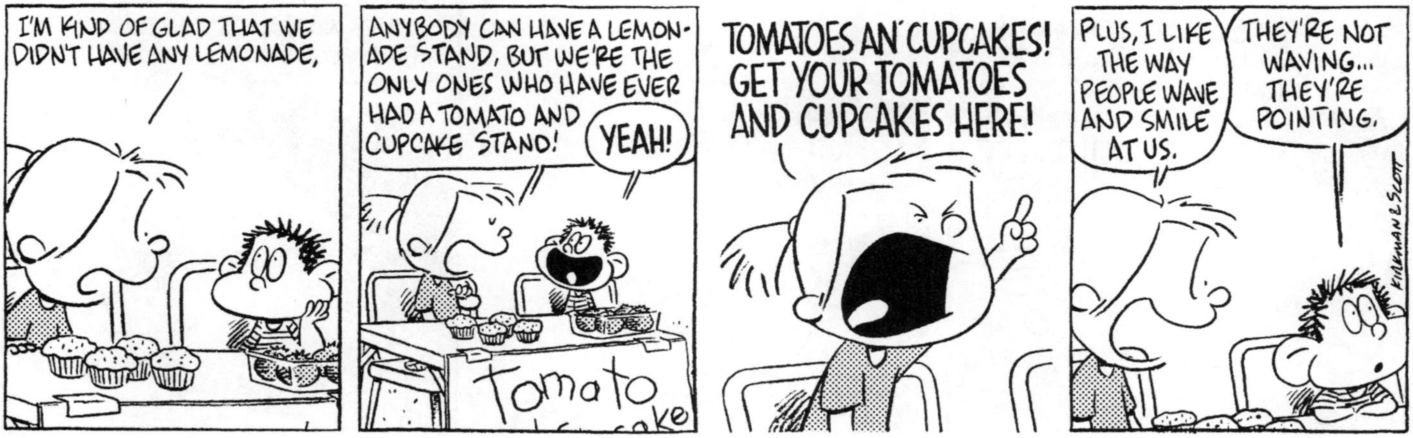
I'M KIND OF GLAD THAT WE DIDN'T HAVE ANY LEMONADE,
ANYBODY CAN HAVE A LEMONADE STAND, BUT WE'RE THE ONLY ONES WHO HAVE EVER HAD A TOMATO AND CUPCAKE STAND!
YEAH!
TOMATOES AN' CUPCAKES! GET YOUR TOMATOES AND CUPCAKES HERE!
PLUS, I LIKE THE WAY PEOPLE WAVE AND SMILE AT US.
THEY'RE NOT WAVING... THEY'RE POINTING.
KIRKMAN & SCOTT

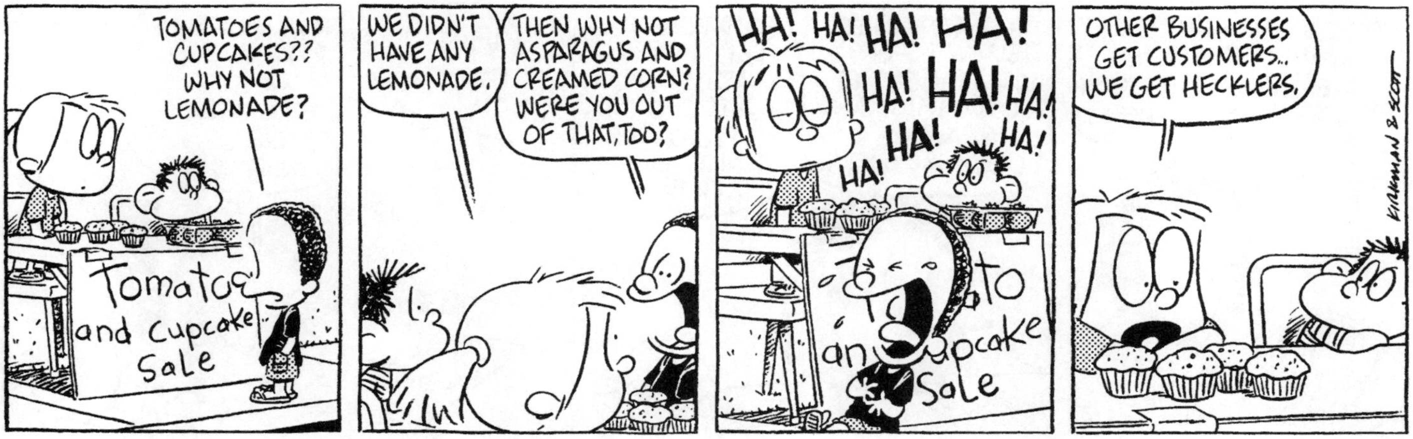
TOMATOES AND CUPCAKES?? WHY NOT LEMONADE?
Tomatoe and Cupcake SaLe
WE DIDN'T HAVE ANY LEMONADE.
THEN WHY NOT ASPARAGUS AND CREAMED CORN? WERE YOU OUT OF THAT, TOO?
HA! HA! HA! HA! HA! HA! HA! HA! HA! HA!
OTHER BUSINESSES GET CUSTOMERS... WE GET HECKLERS.
KIRKMAN & SCOTT

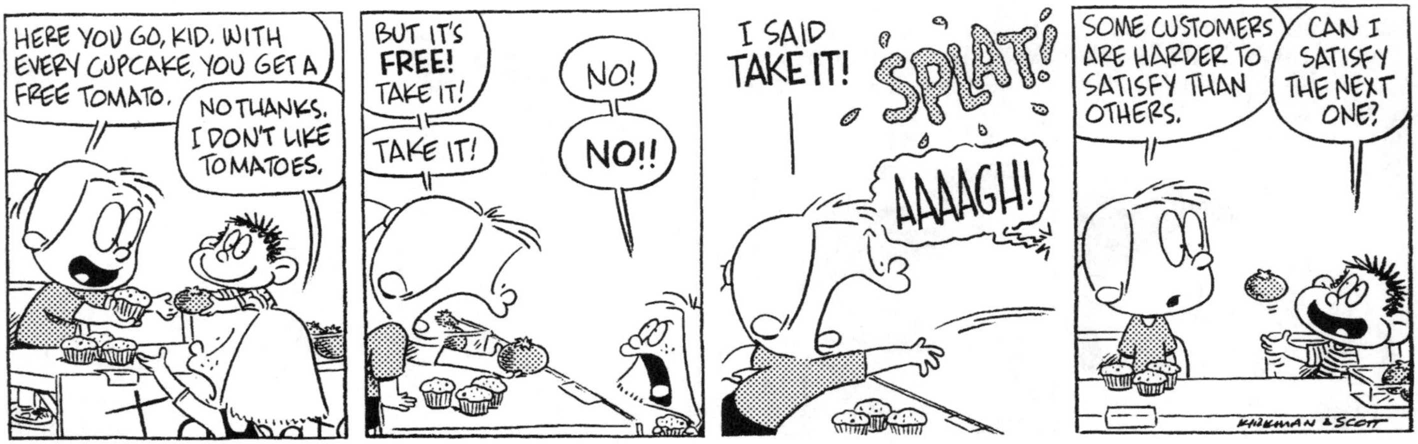
HERE YOU GO, KID. WITH EVERY CUPCAKE, YOU GET A FREE TOMATO.
NO THANKS. I DON'T LIKE TOMATOES.
BUT IT'S **FREE!** TAKE IT!
TAKE IT!
NO!
NO!!
I SAID **TAKE IT!**
SPLAT!
AAAAGH!
SOME CUSTOMERS ARE HARDER TO SATISFY THAN OTHERS.
CAN I SATISFY THE NEXT ONE?
KIRKMAN & SCOTT

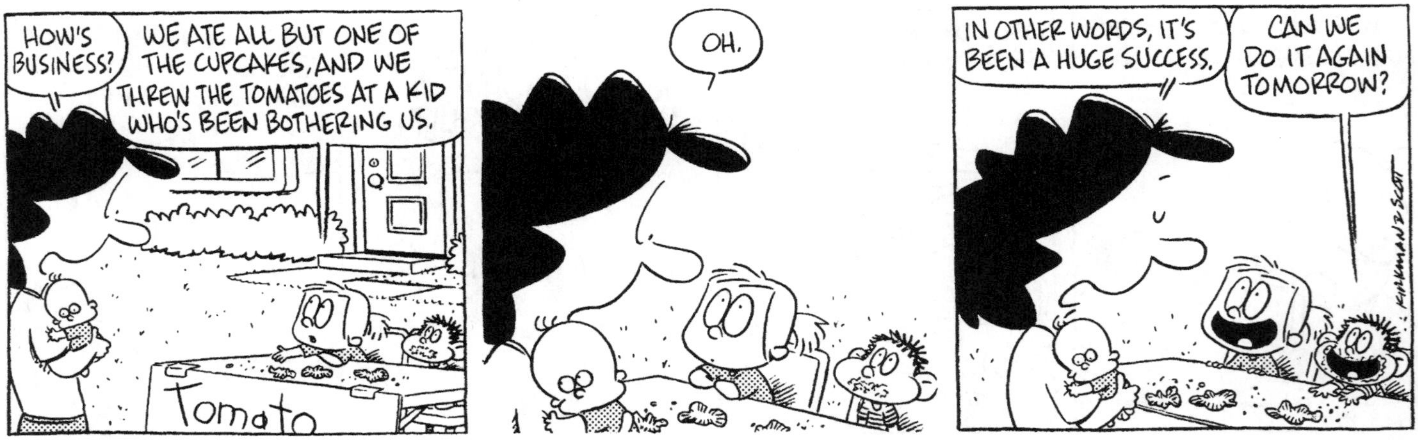
HOW'S BUSINESS?
WE ATE ALL BUT ONE OF THE CUPCAKES, AND WE THREW THE TOMATOES AT A KID WHO'S BEEN BOTHERING US.
Tomato
OH.
IN OTHER WORDS, IT'S BEEN A HUGE SUCCESS.
CAN WE DO IT AGAIN TOMORROW?
KIRKMAN & SCOTT

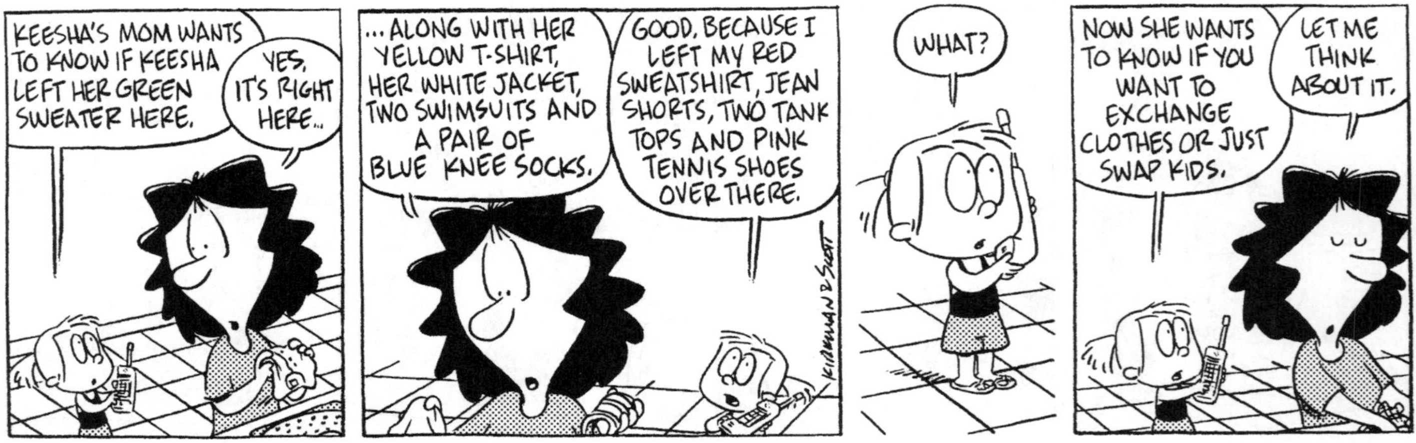
KEESHA'S MOM WANTS TO KNOW IF KEESHA LEFT HER GREEN SWEATER HERE.
YES, IT'S RIGHT HERE...
...ALONG WITH HER YELLOW T-SHIRT, HER WHITE JACKET, TWO SWIMSUITS AND A PAIR OF BLUE KNEE SOCKS.
GOOD, BECAUSE I LEFT MY RED SWEATSHIRT, JEAN SHORTS, TWO TANK TOPS AND PINK TENNIS SHOES OVER THERE.
KIRKMAN & SCOTT
WHAT?
NOW SHE WANTS TO KNOW IF YOU WANT TO EXCHANGE CLOTHES OR JUST SWAP KIDS.
LET ME THINK ABOUT IT.

BABY BLUES®
RICK KIRKMAN / BY JERRY SCOTT

OKAY, SO WE'LL EACH NEED CLOTHES FOR SEVEN DAYS.
WE'LL BE GONE SEVEN DAYS. I THINK WE SHOULD PLAN ON THE KIDS GOING THROUGH TWO OUTFITS A DAY EACH.
GOOD POINT. AND WE SHOULD BRING RAINGEAR.
WREN IS STILL USING ABOUT FIVE DIAPERS A DAY, SO PUT DOWN "35 DIAPERS."
PLUS WIPES.
I'LL SAY SIXTY DIAPERS. THEN TOILETRIES... SNACKS... DRINKS...
I GUESS I COULD WEDGE THE COOLER BEHIND ONE OF THE SEATS.
...PLUS THE STROLLER, THE BACKPACK, AND ZOE AND HAMMIE'S BIKES, HELMETS, SKATES AND SCOOTERS.
KIRKMAN & SCOTT
IT'S A SEVEN-HOUR DRIVE, SO WE'LL NEED A BUNCH OF BOOKS AND GAMES TO KEEP THE KIDS OCCUPIED.
DON'T FORGET THE ASPIRIN.
HI, GUYS!
OOH! IT LOOKS LIKE SOMEBODY IS PLANNING A VACATION!
WE DON'T TAKE VACATIONS... WE JUST MOBILIZE OUR STRESS.

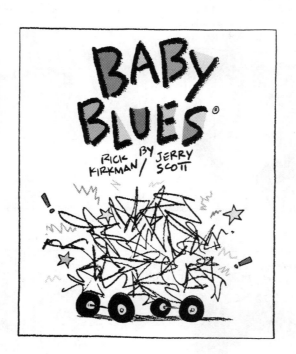

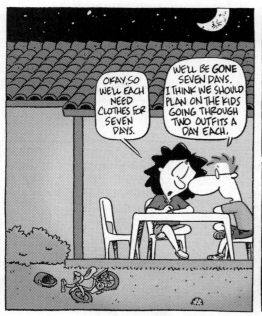

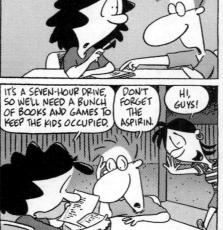

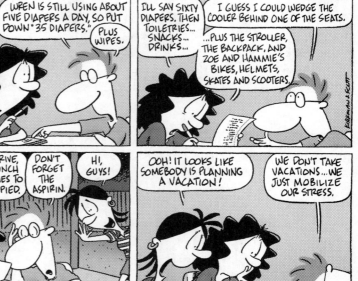

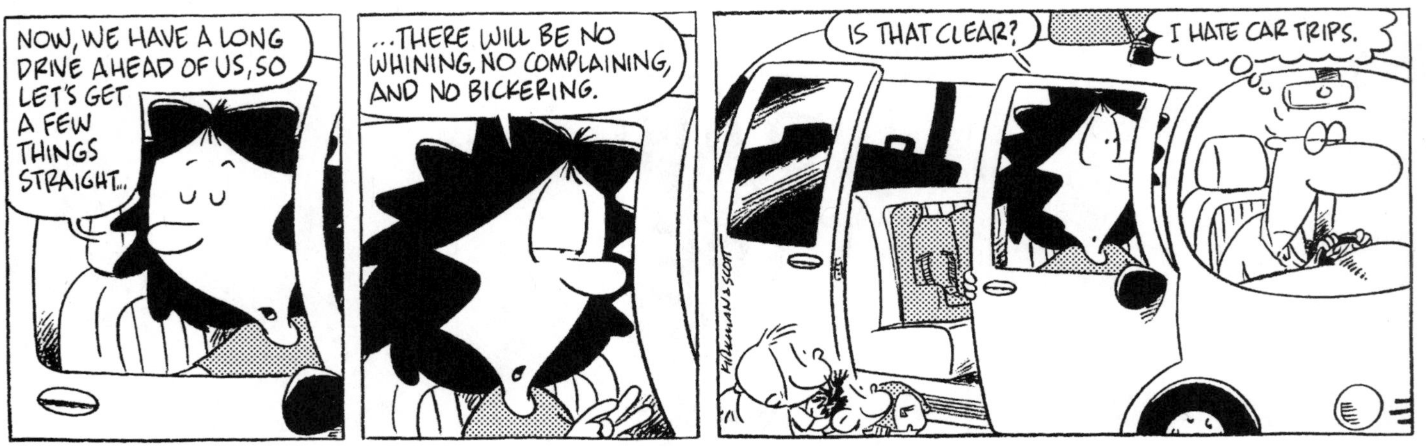
NOW, WE HAVE A LONG DRIVE AHEAD OF US, SO LET'S GET A FEW THINGS STRAIGHT...
...THERE WILL BE NO WHINING, NO COMPLAINING, AND NO BICKERING.
IS THAT CLEAR?
I HATE CAR TRIPS.
KIRKMAN & SCOTT

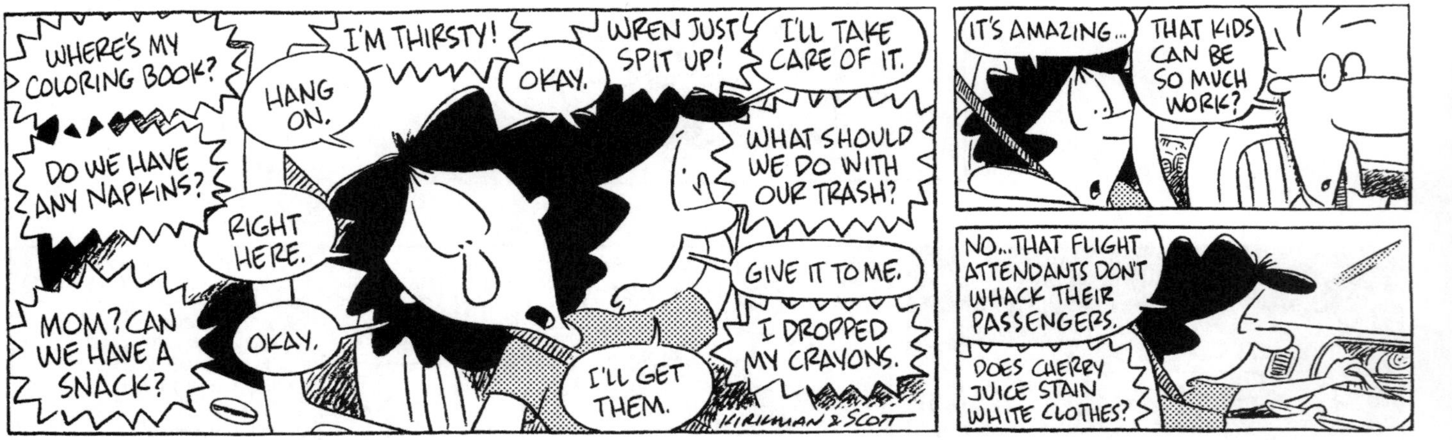
WHERE'S MY COLORING BOOK?
I'M THIRSTY!
HANG ON.
OKAY.
WREN JUST SPIT UP!
I'LL TAKE CARE OF IT.
DO WE HAVE ANY NAPKINS?
WHAT SHOULD WE DO WITH OUR TRASH?
RIGHT HERE.
GIVE IT TO ME.
MOM? CAN WE HAVE A SNACK?
OKAY.
I DROPPED MY CRAYONS.
I'LL GET THEM.
KIRKMAN & SCOTT
IT'S AMAZING...
THAT KIDS CAN BE SO MUCH WORK?
NO...THAT FLIGHT ATTENDANTS DON'T WHACK THEIR PASSENGERS.
DOES CHERRY JUICE STAIN WHITE CLOTHES?

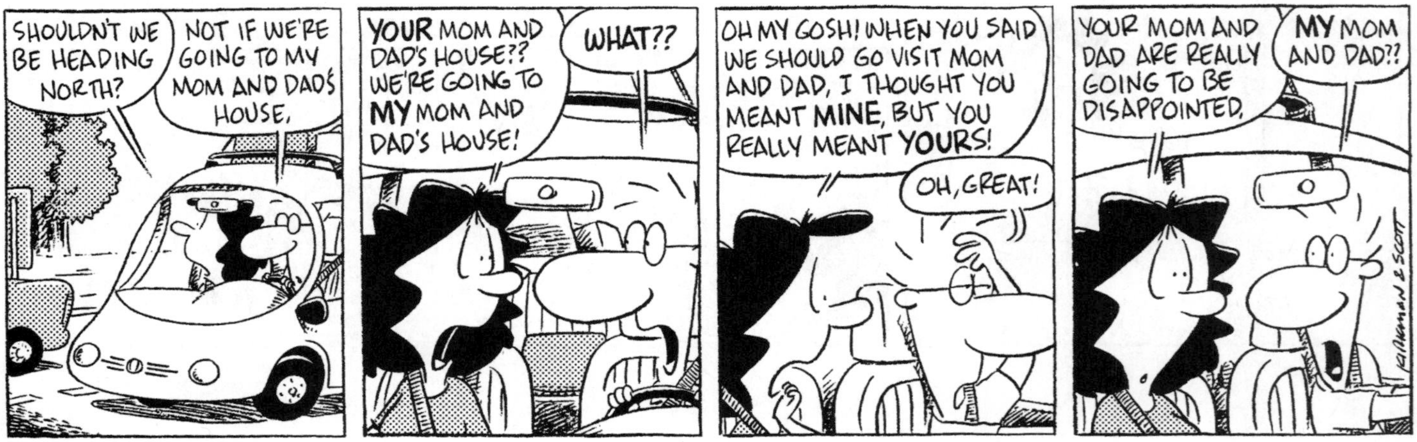
SHOULDN'T WE BE HEADING NORTH?
NOT IF WE'RE GOING TO MY MOM AND DAD'S HOUSE.
YOUR MOM AND DAD'S HOUSE?? WE'RE GOING TO MY MOM AND DAD'S HOUSE!
WHAT??
OH MY GOSH! WHEN YOU SAID WE SHOULD GO VISIT MOM AND DAD, I THOUGHT YOU MEANT MINE, BUT YOU REALLY MEANT YOURS!
OH, GREAT!
YOUR MOM AND DAD ARE REALLY GOING TO BE DISAPPOINTED.
MY MOM AND DAD??
KIRKMAN & SCOTT

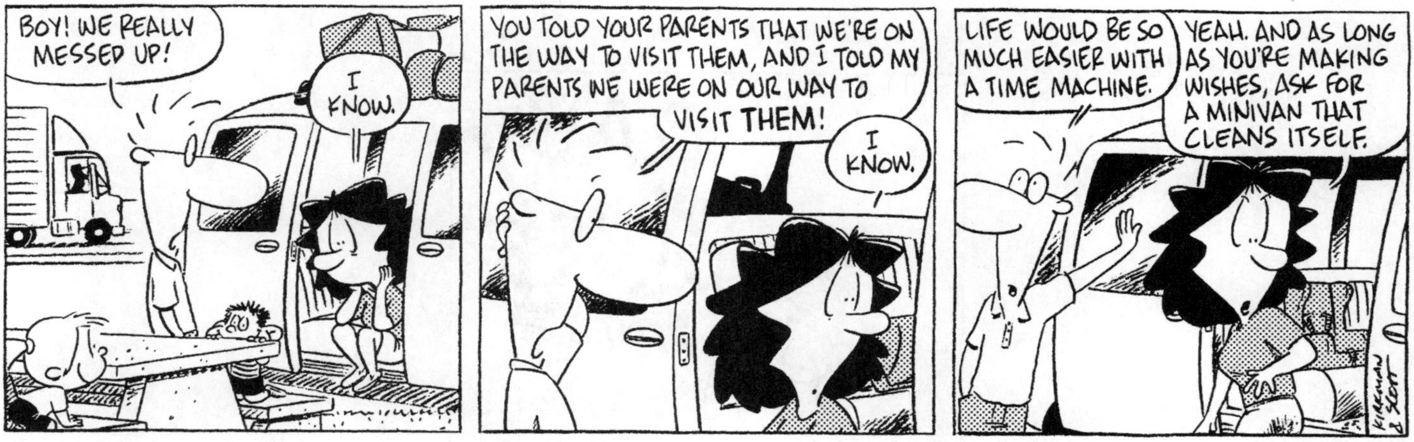
BOY! WE REALLY MESSED UP!
I KNOW.
YOU TOLD YOUR PARENTS THAT WE'RE ON THE WAY TO VISIT THEM, AND I TOLD MY PARENTS WE WERE ON OUR WAY TO VISIT **THEM**!
I KNOW.
LIFE WOULD BE SO MUCH EASIER WITH A TIME MACHINE.
YEAH. AND AS LONG AS YOU'RE MAKING WISHES, ASK FOR A MINIVAN THAT CLEANS ITSELF.
KIRKMAN & SCOTT

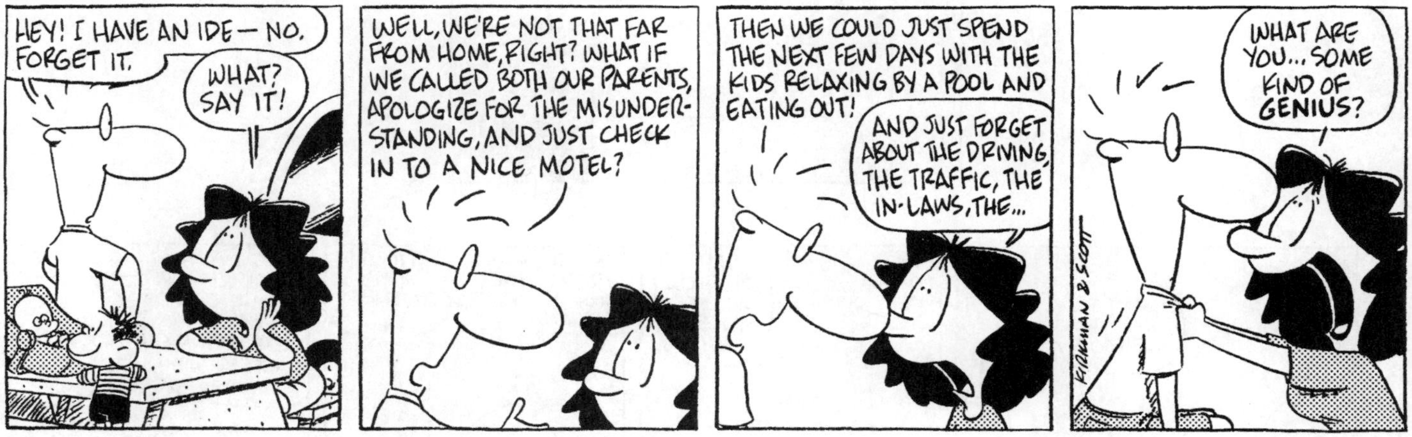
HEY! I HAVE AN IDE— NO. FORGET IT.
WHAT? SAY IT!
WELL, WE'RE NOT THAT FAR FROM HOME, RIGHT? WHAT IF WE CALLED BOTH OUR PARENTS, APOLOGIZE FOR THE MISUNDERSTANDING, AND JUST CHECK IN TO A NICE MOTEL?
THEN WE COULD JUST SPEND THE NEXT FEW DAYS WITH THE KIDS RELAXING BY A POOL AND EATING OUT!
AND JUST FORGET ABOUT THE DRIVING, THE TRAFFIC, THE IN-LAWS, THE...
KIRKMAN & SCOTT
WHAT ARE YOU... SOME KIND OF **GENIUS**?

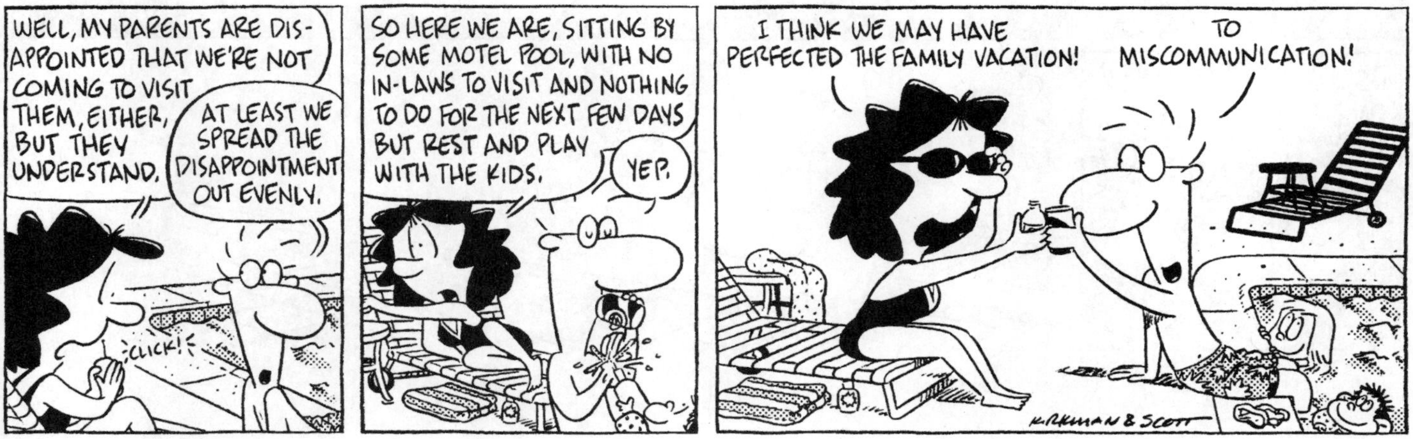
WELL, MY PARENTS ARE DISAPPOINTED THAT WE'RE NOT COMING TO VISIT THEM, EITHER, BUT THEY UNDERSTAND.
AT LEAST WE SPREAD THE DISAPPOINTMENT OUT EVENLY.
CLICK!
SO HERE WE ARE, SITTING BY SOME MOTEL POOL, WITH NO IN-LAWS TO VISIT AND NOTHING TO DO FOR THE NEXT FEW DAYS BUT REST AND PLAY WITH THE KIDS.
YEP.
I THINK WE MAY HAVE PERFECTED THE FAMILY VACATION!
TO MISCOMMUNICATION!
KIRKMAN & SCOTT

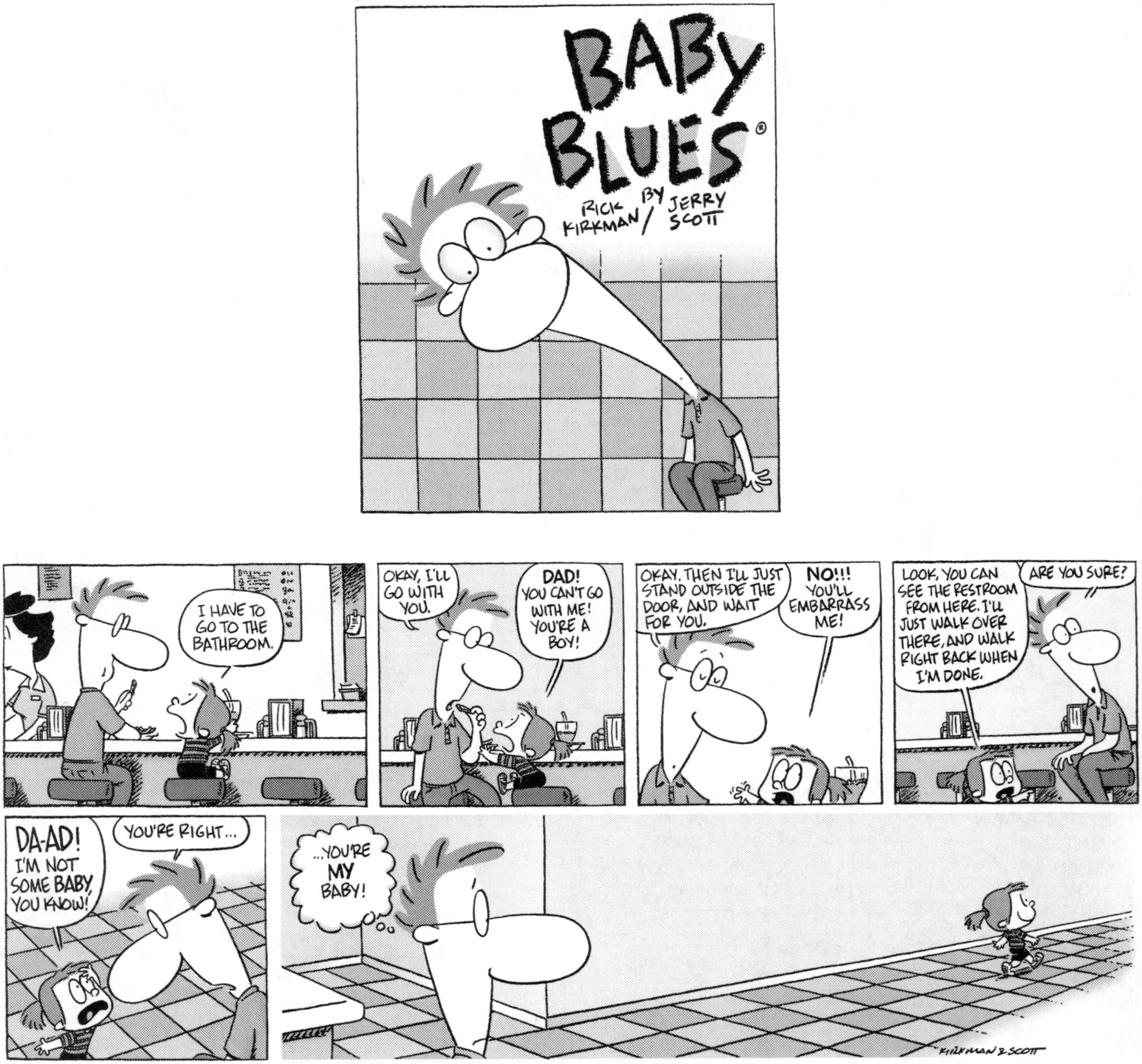
BABY BLUES®
BY RICK KIRKMAN / JERRY SCOTT
I HAVE TO GO TO THE BATHROOM.
OKAY, I'LL GO WITH YOU.
DAD! YOU CAN'T GO WITH ME! YOU'RE A BOY!
OKAY, THEN I'LL JUST STAND OUTSIDE THE DOOR, AND WAIT FOR YOU.
NO!!! YOU'LL EMBARRASS ME!
LOOK, YOU CAN SEE THE RESTROOM FROM HERE. I'LL JUST WALK OVER THERE, AND WALK RIGHT BACK WHEN I'M DONE.
ARE YOU SURE?
DA-AD! I'M NOT SOME BABY, YOU KNOW!
YOU'RE RIGHT...
...YOU'RE MY BABY!
KIRKMAN & SCOTT

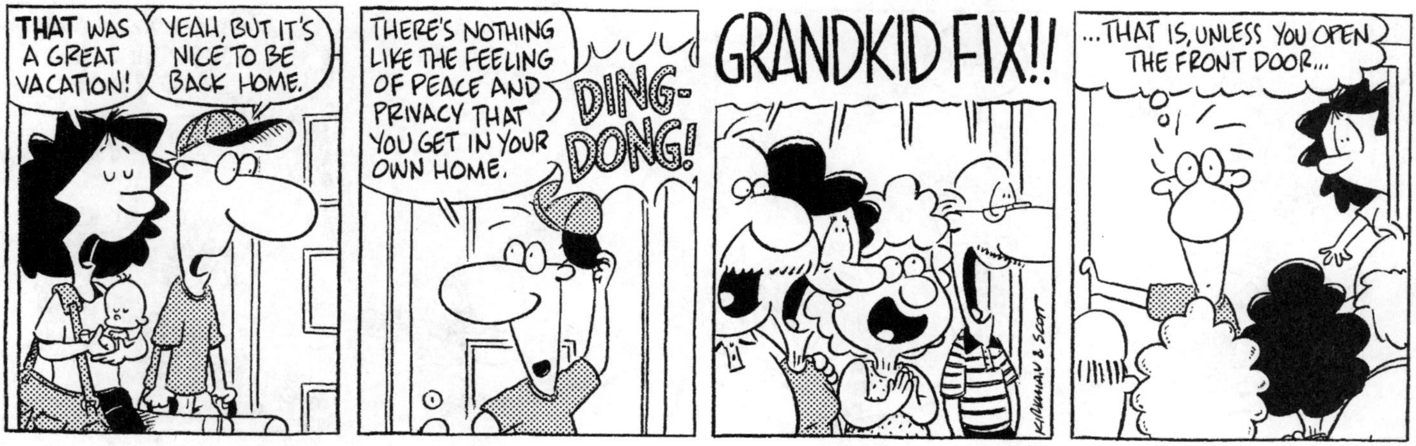
THAT WAS A GREAT VACATION!
YEAH, BUT IT'S NICE TO BE BACK HOME.
THERE'S NOTHING LIKE THE FEELING OF PEACE AND PRIVACY THAT YOU GET IN YOUR OWN HOME.
DING-DONG!
GRANDKID FIX!!
KIRKMAN & SCOTT
...THAT IS, UNLESS YOU OPEN THE FRONT DOOR...

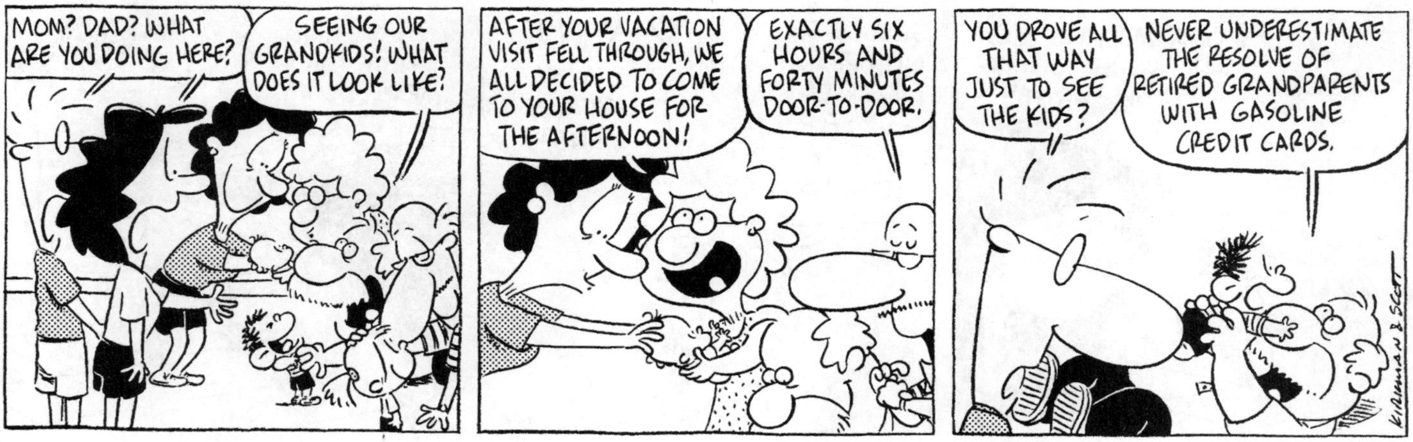
MOM? DAD? WHAT ARE YOU DOING HERE?
SEEING OUR GRANDKIDS! WHAT DOES IT LOOK LIKE?
AFTER YOUR VACATION VISIT FELL THROUGH, WE ALL DECIDED TO COME TO YOUR HOUSE FOR THE AFTERNOON!
EXACTLY SIX HOURS AND FORTY MINUTES DOOR-TO-DOOR.
YOU DROVE ALL THAT WAY JUST TO SEE THE KIDS?
NEVER UNDERESTIMATE THE RESOLVE OF RETIRED GRANDPARENTS WITH GASOLINE CREDIT CARDS.
KIRKMAN & SCOTT

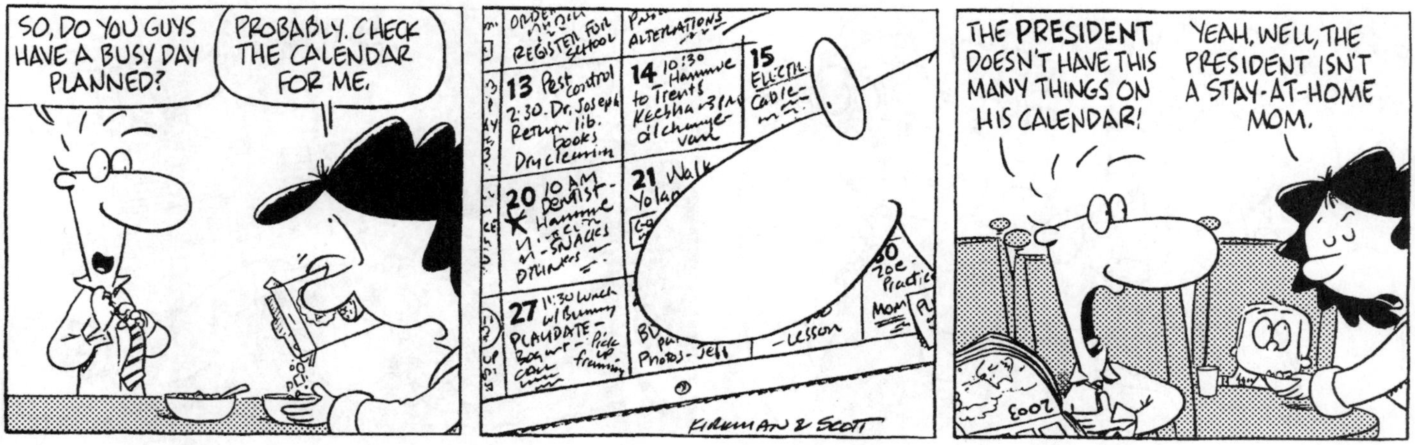
SO, DO YOU GUYS HAVE A BUSY DAY PLANNED?
PROBABLY. CHECK THE CALENDAR FOR ME.
REGISTER FOR SCHOOL
ALTERATIONS
13 Pest control
PLAYDATE
-LESSON
KIRKMAN & SCOTT
THE PRESIDENT DOESN'T HAVE THIS MANY THINGS ON HIS CALENDAR!
YEAH, WELL, THE PRESIDENT ISN'T A STAY-AT-HOME MOM.

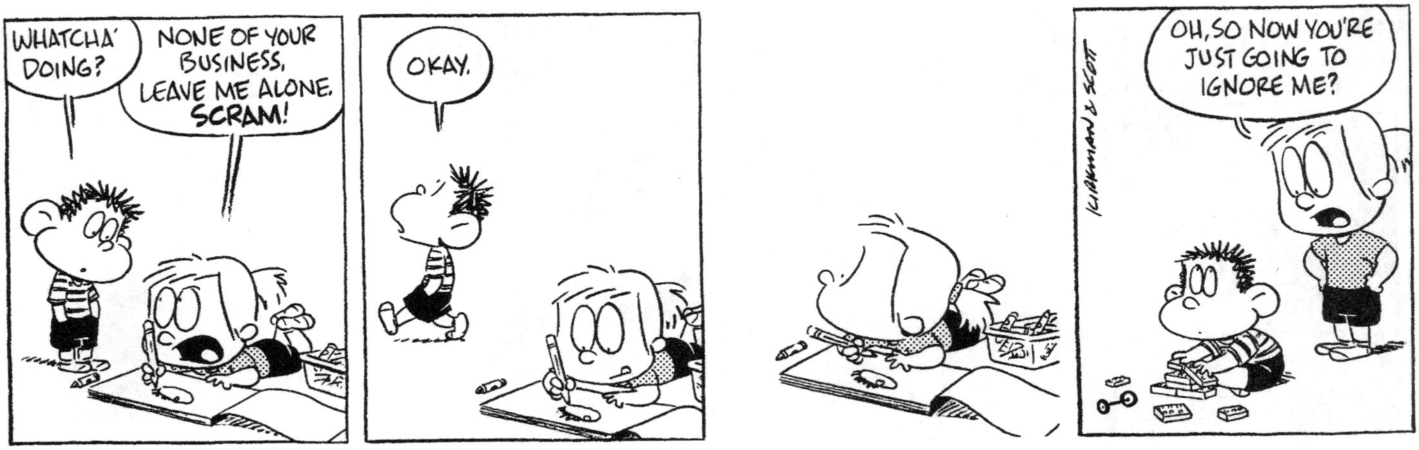
WHATCHA' DOING?
NONE OF YOUR BUSINESS, LEAVE ME ALONE. SCRAM!
OKAY.
OH, SO NOW YOU'RE JUST GOING TO IGNORE ME?
KIRKMAN & SCOTT

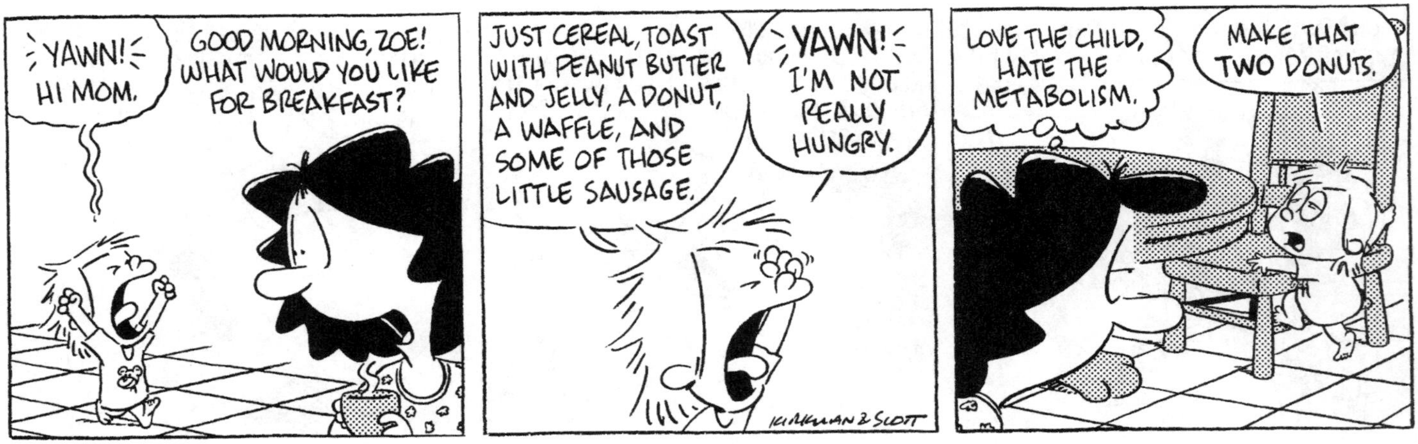
YAWN! HI MOM.
GOOD MORNING, ZOE! WHAT WOULD YOU LIKE FOR BREAKFAST?
JUST CEREAL, TOAST WITH PEANUT BUTTER AND JELLY, A DONUT, A WAFFLE, AND SOME OF THOSE LITTLE SAUSAGE.
YAWN! I'M NOT REALLY HUNGRY.
KIRKMAN & SCOTT
LOVE THE CHILD, HATE THE METABOLISM.
MAKE THAT TWO DONUTS.

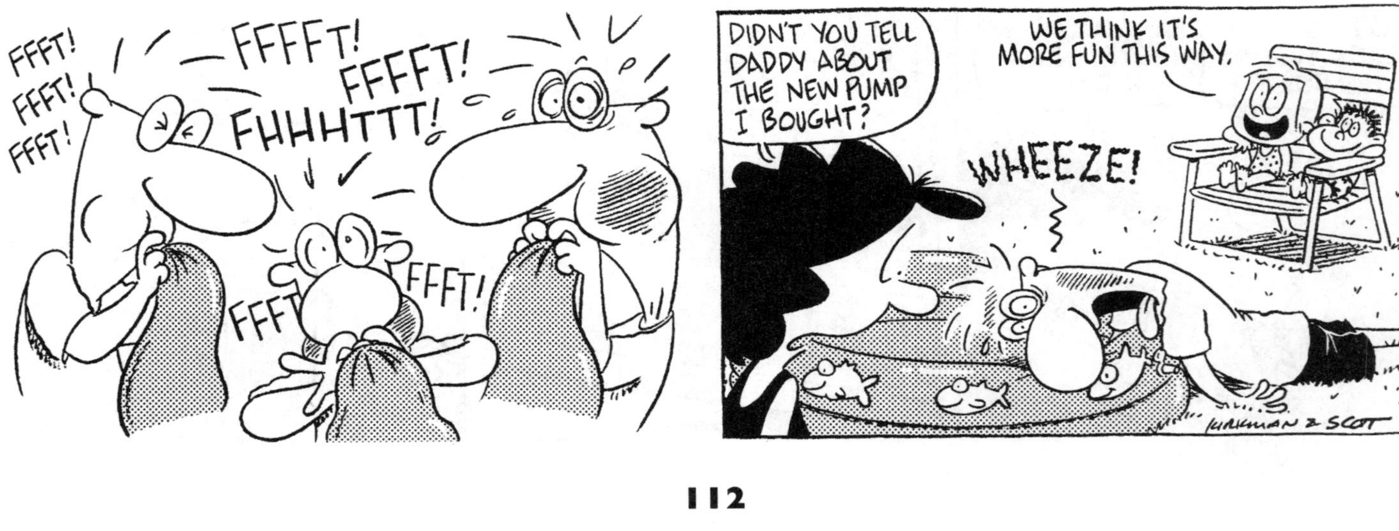
FFFT! FFFT! FFFT!
FFFFT!
FFFFT!
FHHHTTT!
FFFT
FFFT!
DIDN'T YOU TELL DADDY ABOUT THE NEW PUMP I BOUGHT?
WE THINK IT'S MORE FUN THIS WAY.
WHEEZE!
KIRKMAN & SCOTT

BABY BLUES®
RICK KIRKMAN / BY JERRY SCOTT
WEH! WEH! WEH!
SHHH! YOU'LL WAKE EVERYBODY UP! LET'S GO OUTSIDE!
WOW, WREN! LOOK AT ALL THE STARS! THERE'S THE BIG DIPPER.
SNIF!
AND OVER THERE IS THE MOON.
...AND THAT'S THE NORTH STAR.
SEE THAT REALLY BRIGHT THING? YAWN! I'M NOT SURE, BUT THAT COULD BE JUPITER, OR MAYBE SATURN, OR.... ZZZZZZZ...
YAWN!
HI WANDA.
HI YOLANDA.
WHAT'S THAT OVER THERE?
I'M NOT QUITE SURE...
...IT'S EITHER THE SWEETEST MOMENT, OR THE UGLIEST LAWN ORNAMENT I'VE EVER SEEN.
ZZZZZNXXX...
Z
KIRKMAN & SCOTT

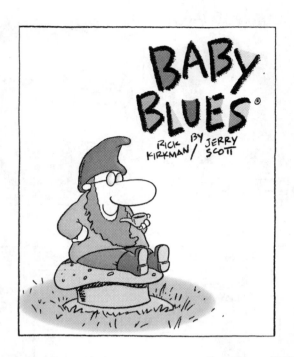

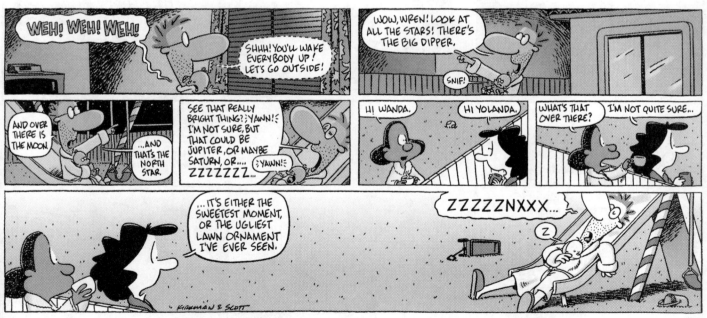

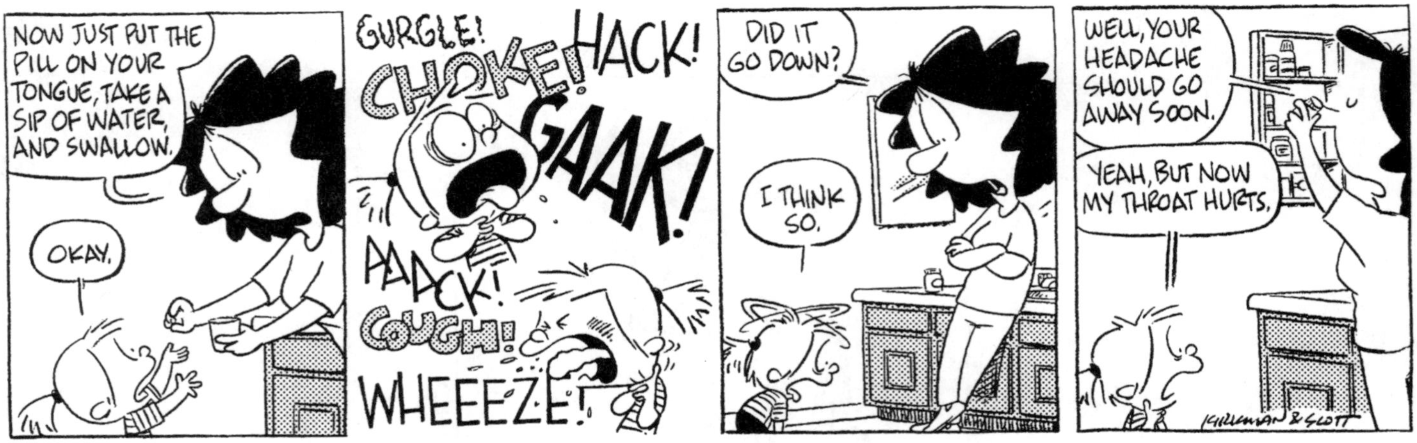
NOW JUST PUT THE PILL ON YOUR TONGUE, TAKE A SIP OF WATER, AND SWALLOW.
OKAY.
GURGLE!
CHOKE!
HACK!
GAAK!
PAACK!
COUGH!
WHEEEZE!
DID IT GO DOWN?
I THINK SO.
WELL, YOUR HEADACHE SHOULD GO AWAY SOON.
YEAH, BUT NOW MY THROAT HURTS.
KIRKMAN & SCOTT

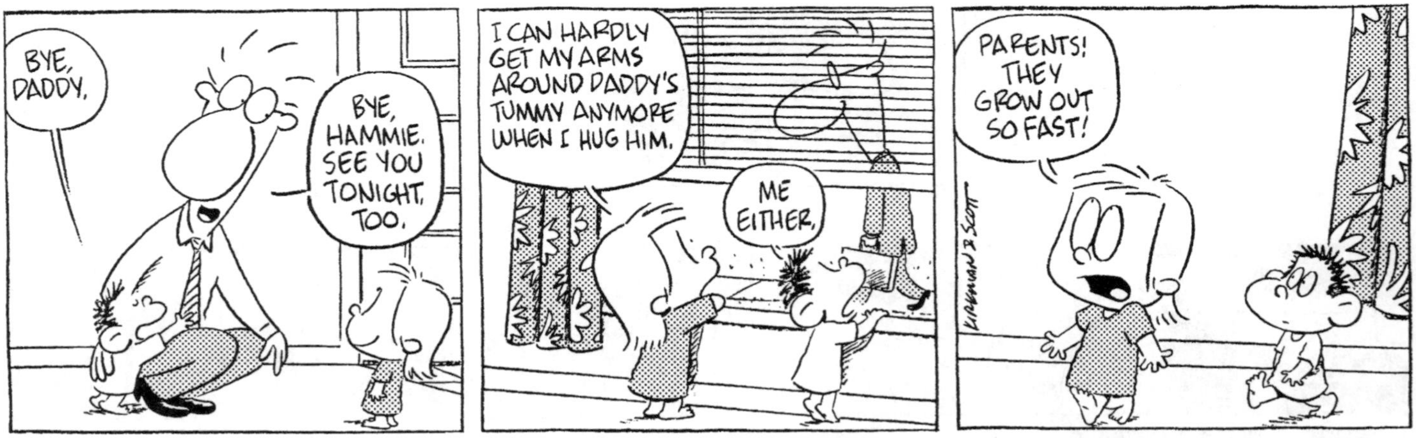
BYE, DADDY.
BYE, HAMMIE. SEE YOU TONIGHT, TOO.
I CAN HARDLY GET MY ARMS AROUND DADDY'S TUMMY ANYMORE WHEN I HUG HIM.
ME EITHER.
KIRKMAN & SCOTT
PARENTS! THEY GROW OUT SO FAST!

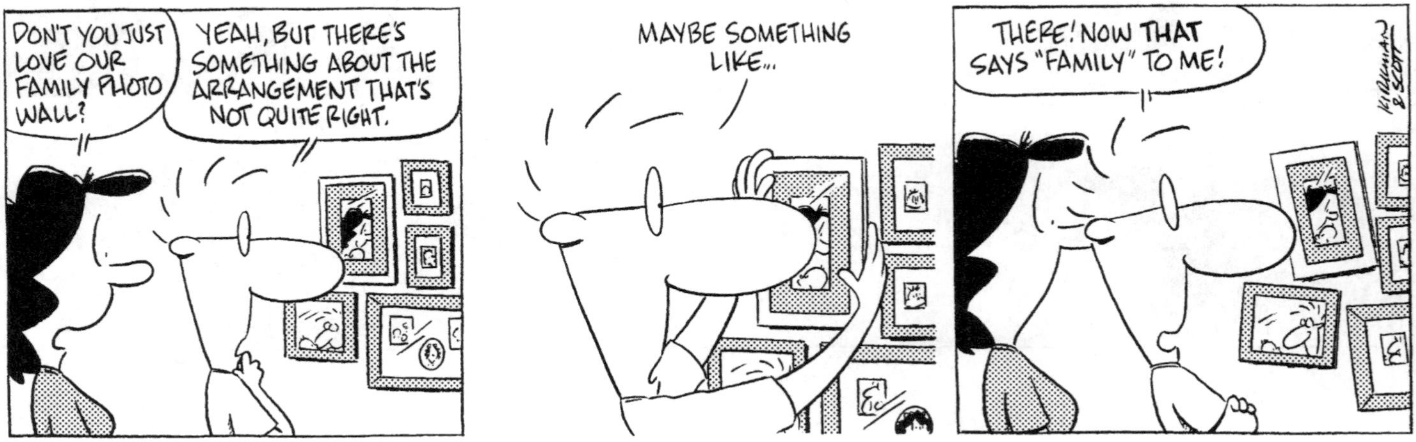
DON'T YOU JUST LOVE OUR FAMILY PHOTO WALL?
YEAH, BUT THERE'S SOMETHING ABOUT THE ARRANGEMENT THAT'S NOT QUITE RIGHT.
MAYBE SOMETHING LIKE...
THERE! NOW THAT SAYS "FAMILY" TO ME!
KIRKMAN & SCOTT

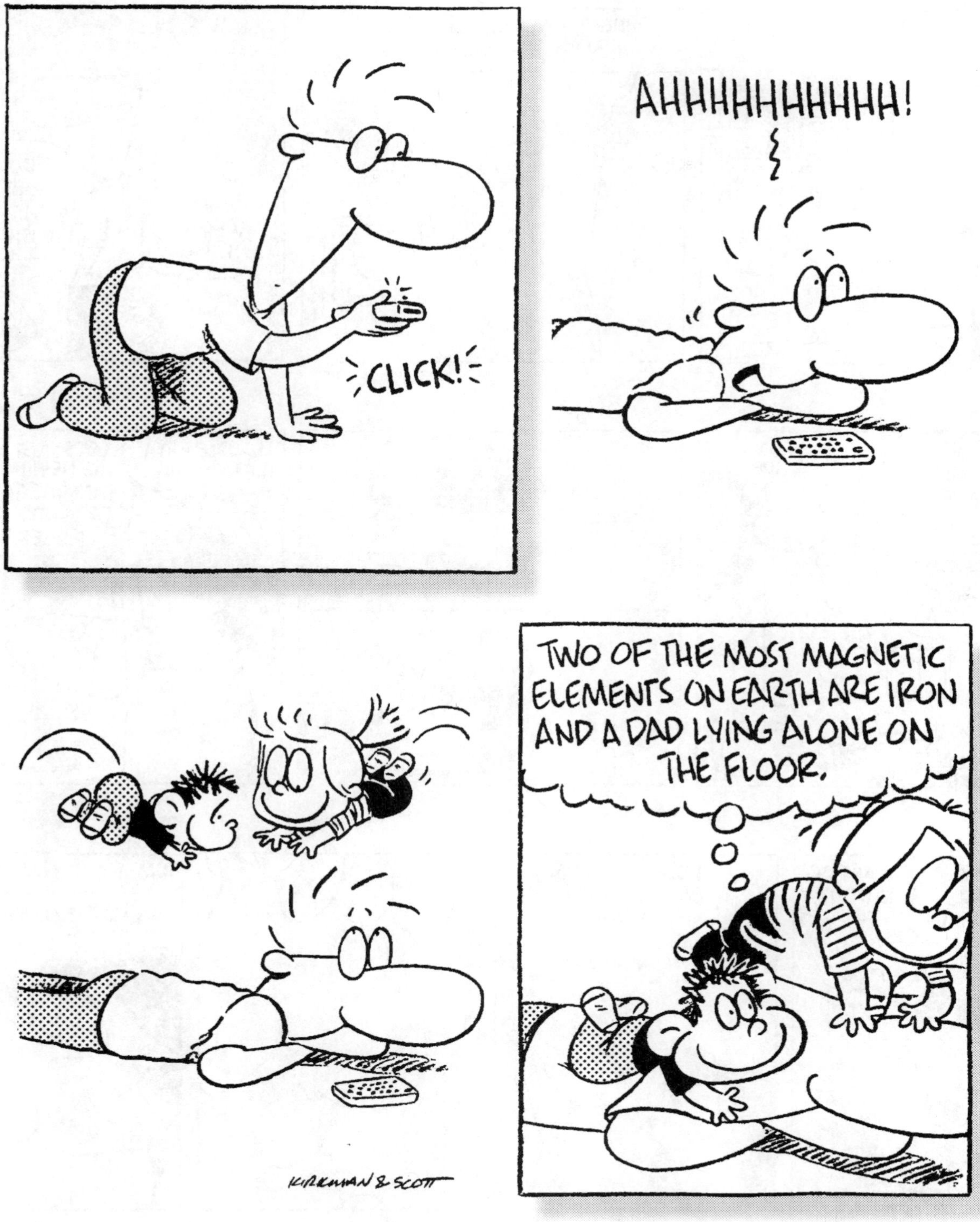
CLICK!
AHHHHHHHHHH!
KIRKMAN & SCOTT
TWO OF THE MOST MAGNETIC ELEMENTS ON EARTH ARE IRON AND A DAD LYING ALONE ON THE FLOOR.

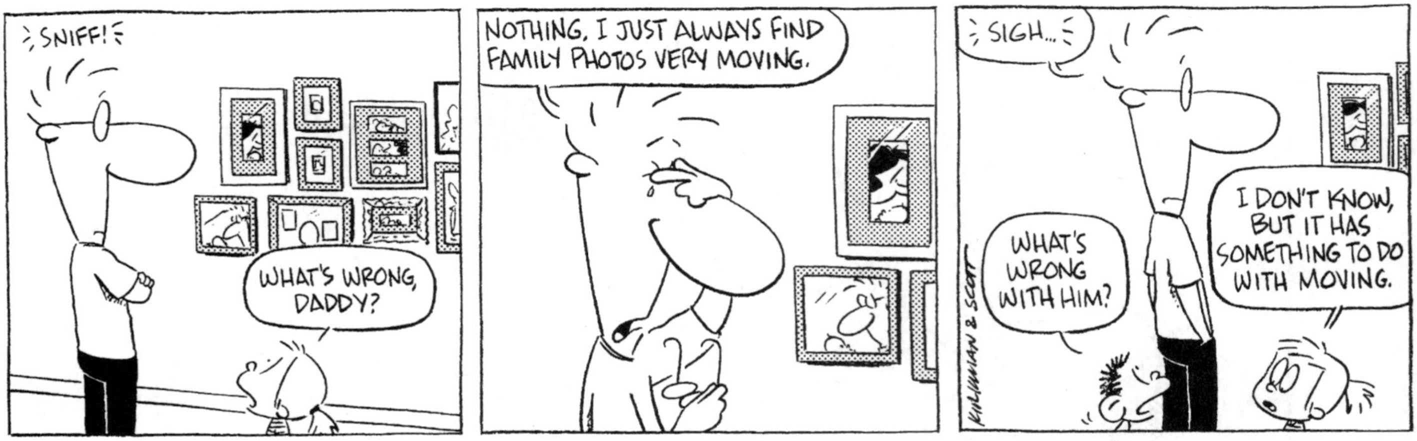
SNIFF!
WHAT'S WRONG, DADDY?
NOTHING. I JUST ALWAYS FIND FAMILY PHOTOS VERY MOVING.
SIGH...
KIRKMAN & SCOTT
WHAT'S WRONG WITH HIM?
I DON'T KNOW, BUT IT HAS SOMETHING TO DO WITH MOVING.

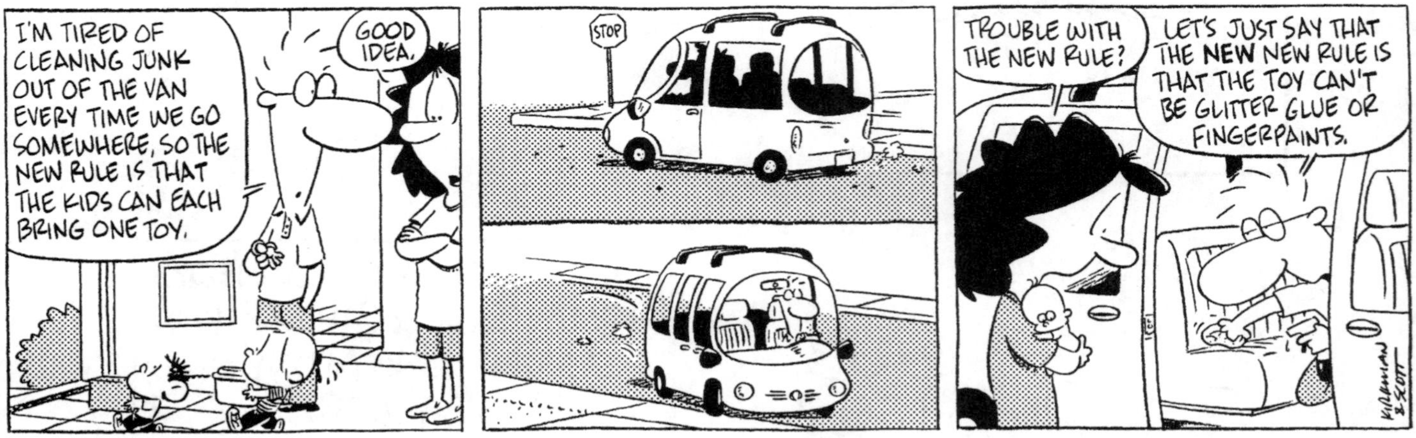
I'M TIRED OF CLEANING JUNK OUT OF THE VAN EVERY TIME WE GO SOMEWHERE, SO THE NEW RULE IS THAT THE KIDS CAN EACH BRING ONE TOY.
GOOD IDEA.
STOP
TROUBLE WITH THE NEW RULE?
LET'S JUST SAY THAT THE **NEW** NEW RULE IS THAT THE TOY CAN'T BE GLITTER GLUE OR FINGERPAINTS.
KIRKMAN & SCOTT

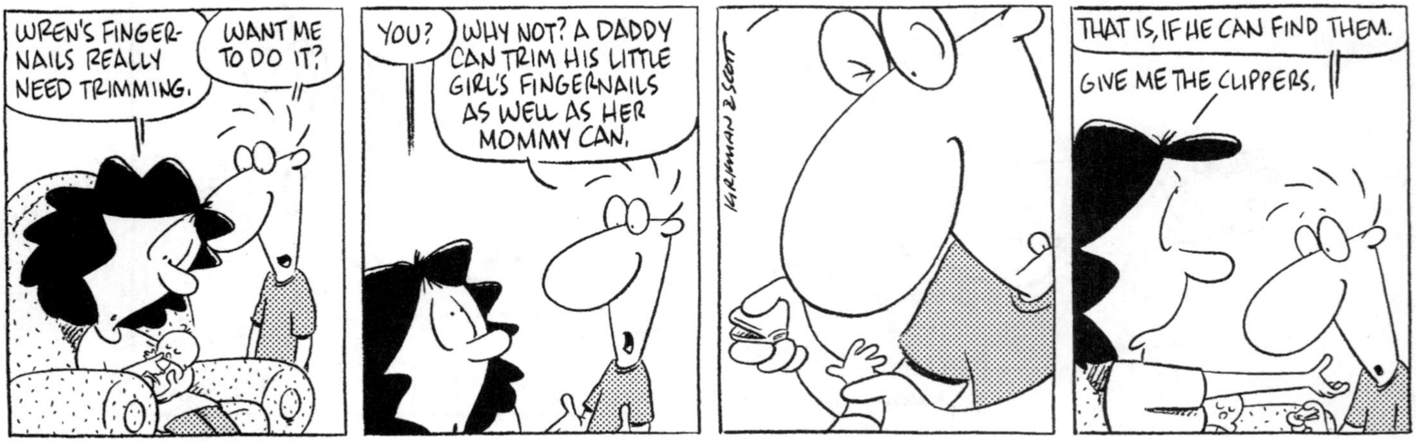
WREN'S FINGERNAILS REALLY NEED TRIMMING.
WANT ME TO DO IT?
YOU?
WHY NOT? A DADDY CAN TRIM HIS LITTLE GIRL'S FINGERNAILS AS WELL AS HER MOMMY CAN.
KIRKMAN & SCOTT
THAT IS, IF HE CAN FIND THEM.
GIVE ME THE CLIPPERS.

BABY BLUES®
BY RICK KIRKMAN / JERRY SCOTT

DADDY, WILL YOU BLOW UP OUR WAITING POOL?
SURE!
PUFFA PUFFA PUFFA PUFFA PUFFA PUFFA PUFFA PUFFA PUFFA PUFFA PUFFA PUFFA PUFFA PUFFA
BY THE WAY, IT'S A WADING POOL, NOT A WAITING POOL.
PUFFA PUFFA PUFFA PUFFA PUFFA PUFFA PUFFA
OH, REALLY? THEN HOW MUCH LONGER?
KIRKMAN & SCOTT

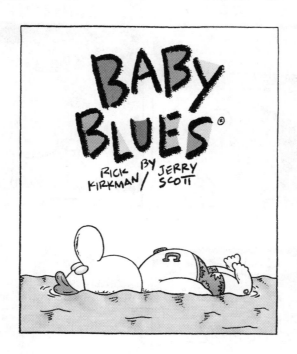

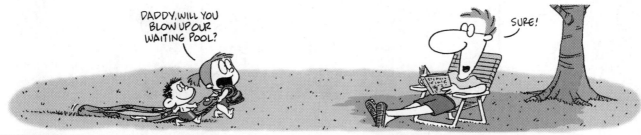

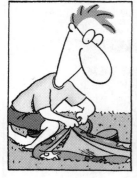

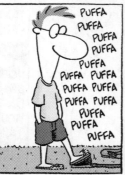

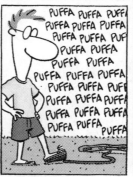

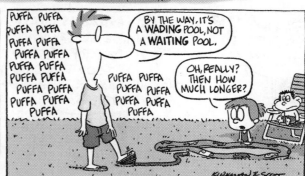

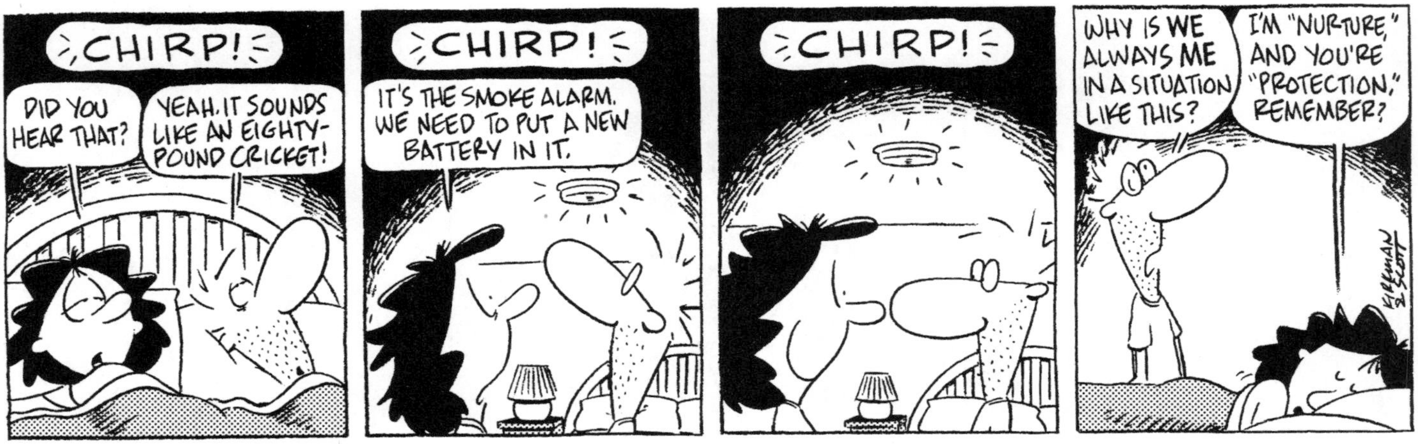
CHIRP!
DID YOU HEAR THAT?
YEAH. IT SOUNDS LIKE AN EIGHTY-POUND CRICKET!
CHIRP!
IT'S THE SMOKE ALARM. WE NEED TO PUT A NEW BATTERY IN IT.
CHIRP!
WHY IS **WE** ALWAYS **ME** IN A SITUATION LIKE THIS?
I'M "NURTURE," AND YOU'RE "PROTECTION," REMEMBER?
KIRKMAN & SCOTT

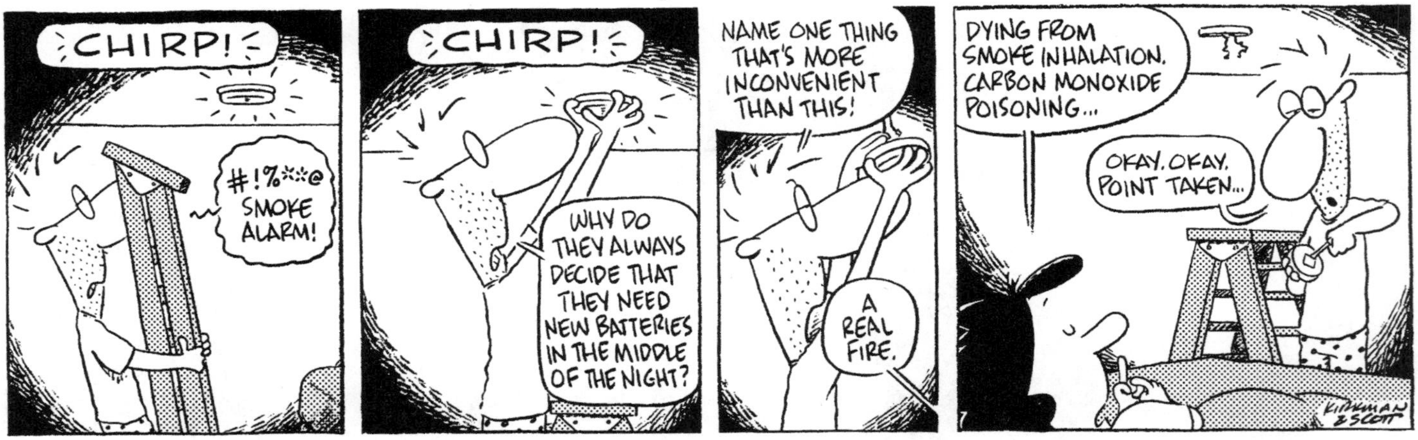
CHIRP!
#!%*:*@ SMOKE ALARM!
CHIRP!
WHY DO THEY ALWAYS DECIDE THAT THEY NEED NEW BATTERIES IN THE MIDDLE OF THE NIGHT?
NAME ONE THING THAT'S MORE INCONVENIENT THAN THIS!
A REAL FIRE.
DYING FROM SMOKE INHALATION. CARBON MONOXIDE POISONING...
OKAY. OKAY. POINT TAKEN...
KIRKMAN & SCOTT

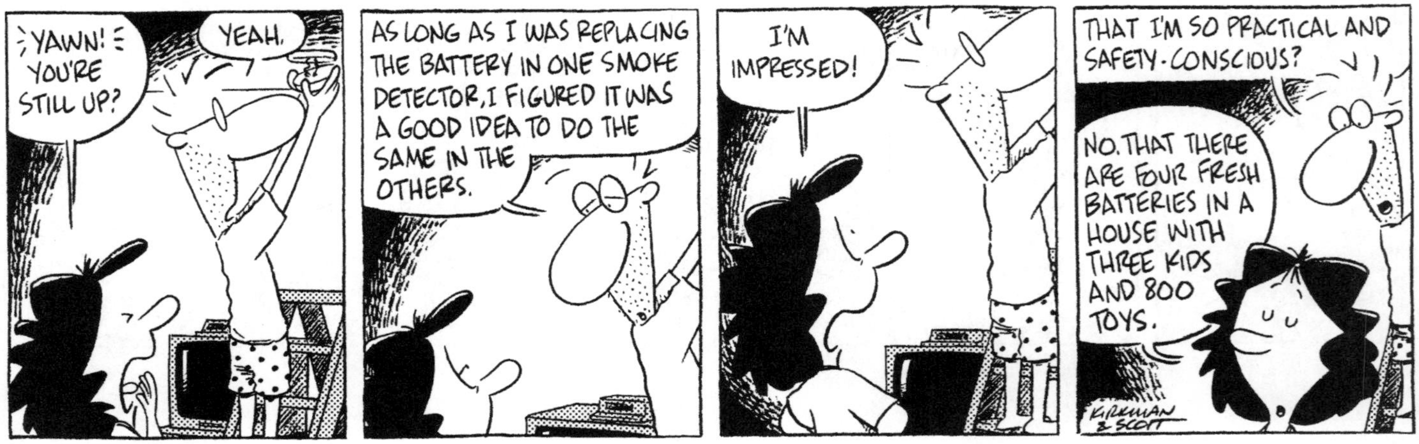
YAWN! YOU'RE STILL UP?
YEAH.
AS LONG AS I WAS REPLACING THE BATTERY IN ONE SMOKE DETECTOR, I FIGURED IT WAS A GOOD IDEA TO DO THE SAME IN THE OTHERS.
I'M IMPRESSED!
THAT I'M SO PRACTICAL AND SAFETY-CONSCIOUS?
NO. THAT THERE ARE FOUR FRESH BATTERIES IN A HOUSE WITH THREE KIDS AND 800 TOYS.
KIRKMAN & SCOTT

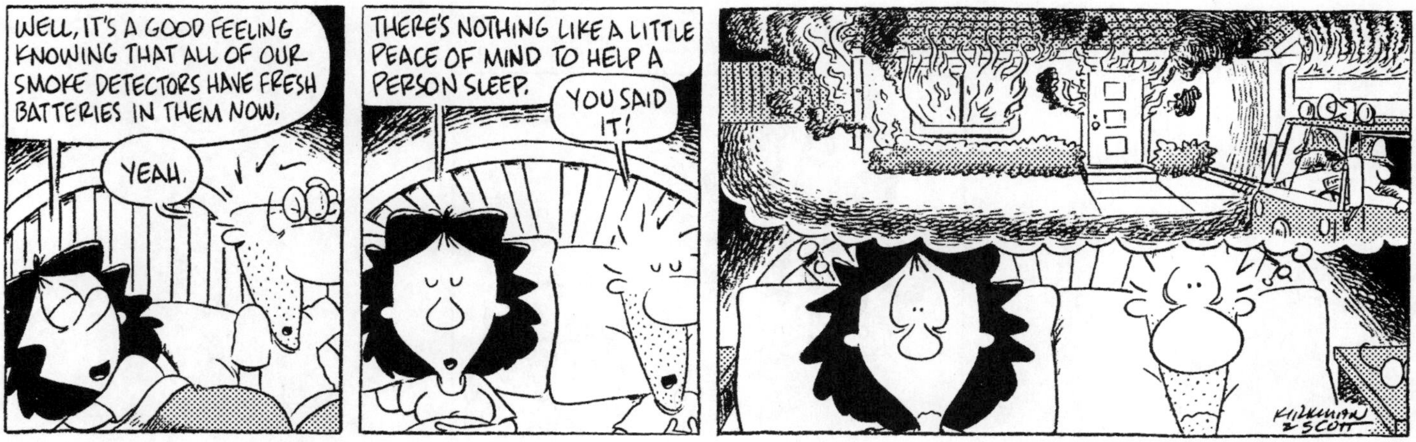

WELL, IT'S A GOOD FEELING KNOWING THAT ALL OF OUR SMOKE DETECTORS HAVE FRESH BATTERIES IN THEM NOW.
YEAH.
THERE'S NOTHING LIKE A LITTLE PEACE OF MIND TO HELP A PERSON SLEEP.
YOU SAID IT!
KIRKMAN & SCOTT

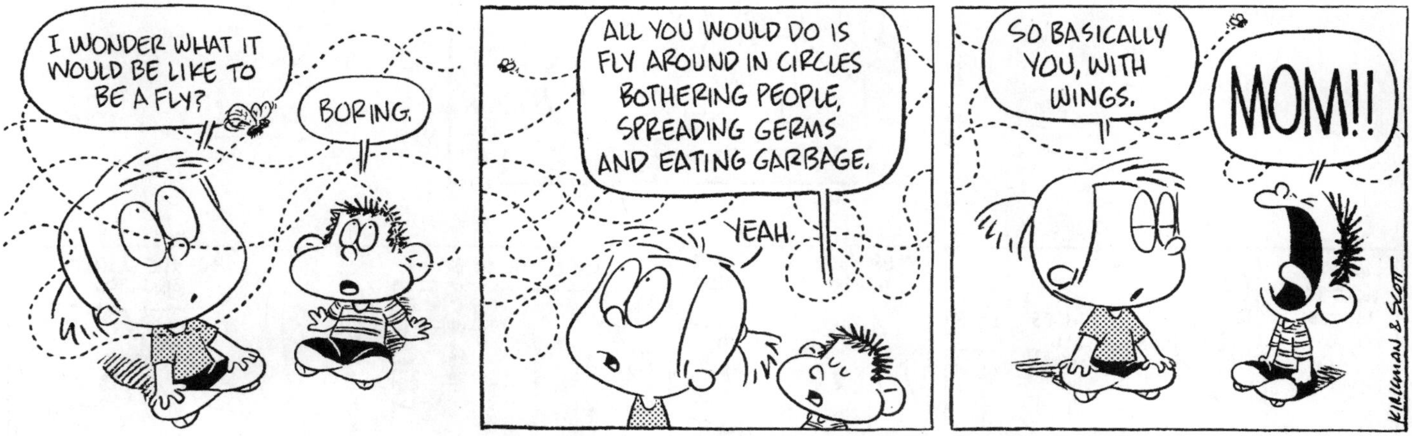

I WONDER WHAT IT WOULD BE LIKE TO BE A FLY?
BORING.
ALL YOU WOULD DO IS FLY AROUND IN CIRCLES BOTHERING PEOPLE, SPREADING GERMS AND EATING GARBAGE.
YEAH.
SO BASICALLY YOU, WITH WINGS.
MOM!!
KIRKMAN & SCOTT

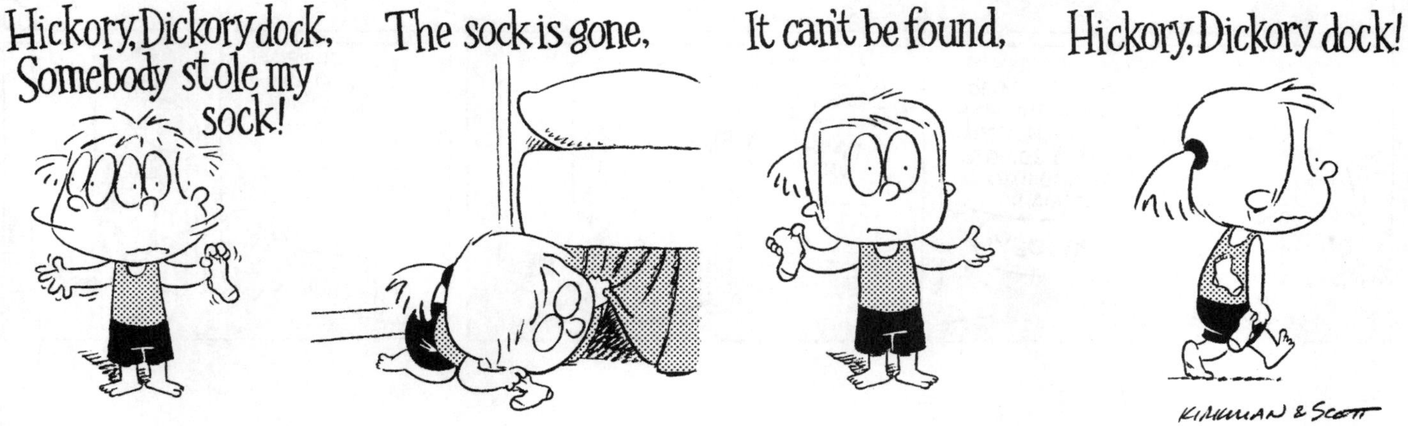

Hickory, Dickory dock, Somebody stole my sock!
The sock is gone,
It can't be found,
Hickory, Dickory dock!
KIRKMAN & SCOTT

BABY BLUES®
BY RICK KIRKMAN / JERRY SCOTT

HOLD IT... HOLD IT... WHAT'S ALL THIS?
WHAT'S ALL WHAT?
YOUR BUTT IS GREEN.
OH, YEAH. I'M NOT FINISHED.
I'M GOING TO BE THE HULK!
BUT THE MARKER RAN DRY.
SON, COLORING YOURSELF GREEN ISN'T GOING TO TURN YOU INTO THE HULK ANY MORE THAN PUTTING ON A CAPE IS GOING TO TURN YOU INTO BATMAN.
PHOOEY!
I DON'T KNOW WHERE YOU GET THESE CRAZY IDEAS!
TA-DAAH! MORE MARKERS!
OH YEAH... YOU HAVE A SISTER.
KIRKMAN & SCOTT

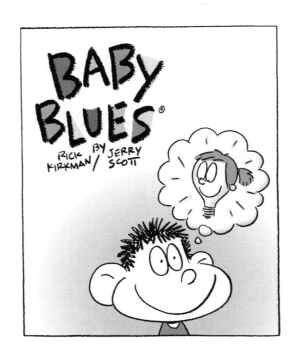

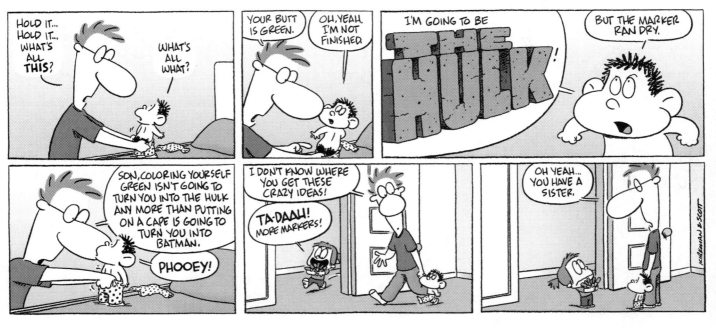

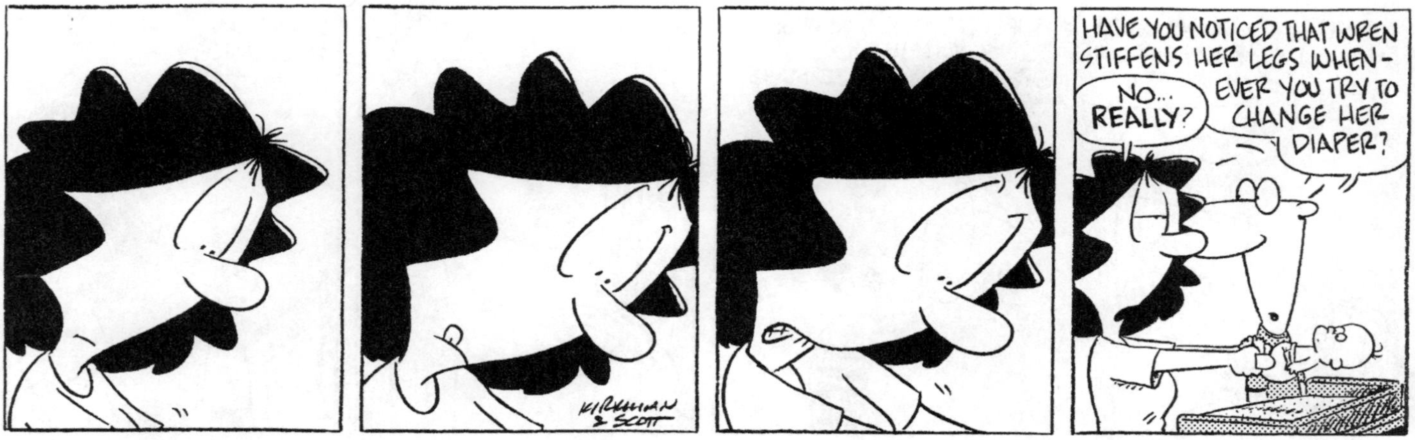
KIRKMAN & SCOTT
HAVE YOU NOTICED THAT WREN STIFFENS HER LEGS WHEN-EVER YOU TRY TO CHANGE HER DIAPER?
NO... REALLY?

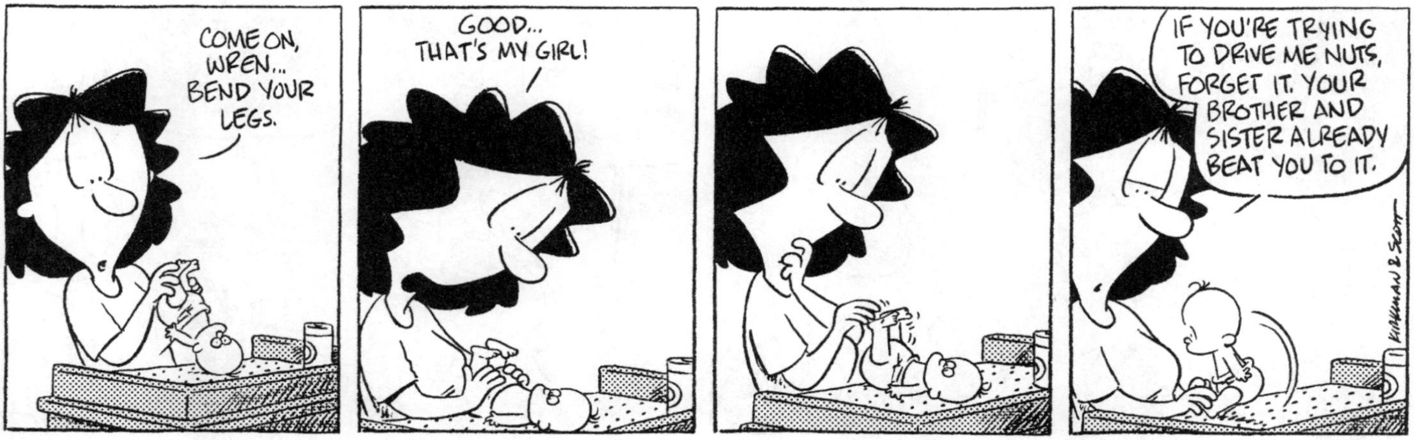
COME ON, WREN... BEND YOUR LEGS.
GOOD... THAT'S MY GIRL!
IF YOU'RE TRYING TO DRIVE ME NUTS, FORGET IT. YOUR BROTHER AND SISTER ALREADY BEAT YOU TO IT.
KIRKMAN & SCOTT

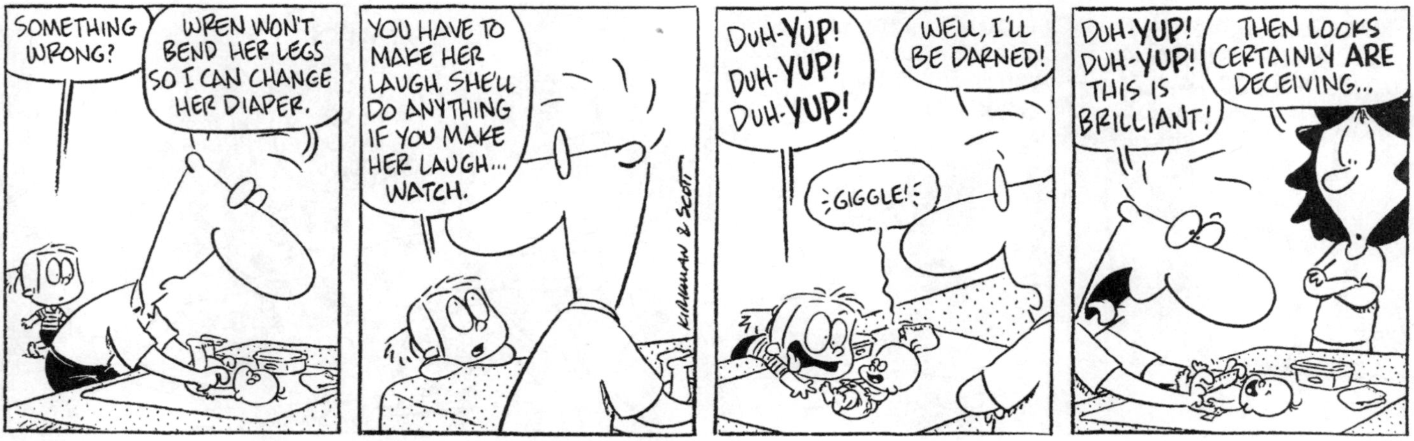
SOMETHING WRONG?
WREN WON'T BEND HER LEGS SO I CAN CHANGE HER DIAPER.
YOU HAVE TO MAKE HER LAUGH. SHE'LL DO ANYTHING IF YOU MAKE HER LAUGH... WATCH.
KIRKMAN & SCOTT
DUH-YUP! DUH-YUP! DUH-YUP!
WELL, I'LL BE DARNED!
GIGGLE!
DUH-YUP! DUH-YUP! THIS IS BRILLIANT!
THEN LOOKS CERTAINLY ARE DECEIVING...

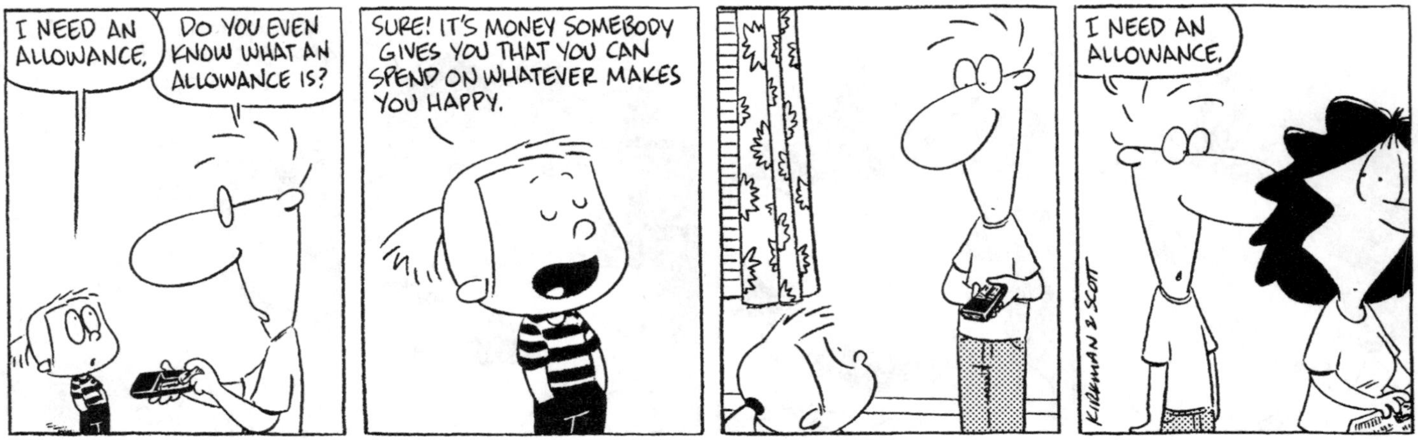
I NEED AN ALLOWANCE.
DO YOU EVEN KNOW WHAT AN ALLOWANCE IS?
SURE! IT'S MONEY SOMEBODY GIVES YOU THAT YOU CAN SPEND ON WHATEVER MAKES YOU HAPPY.
I NEED AN ALLOWANCE.
KIRKMAN & SCOTT

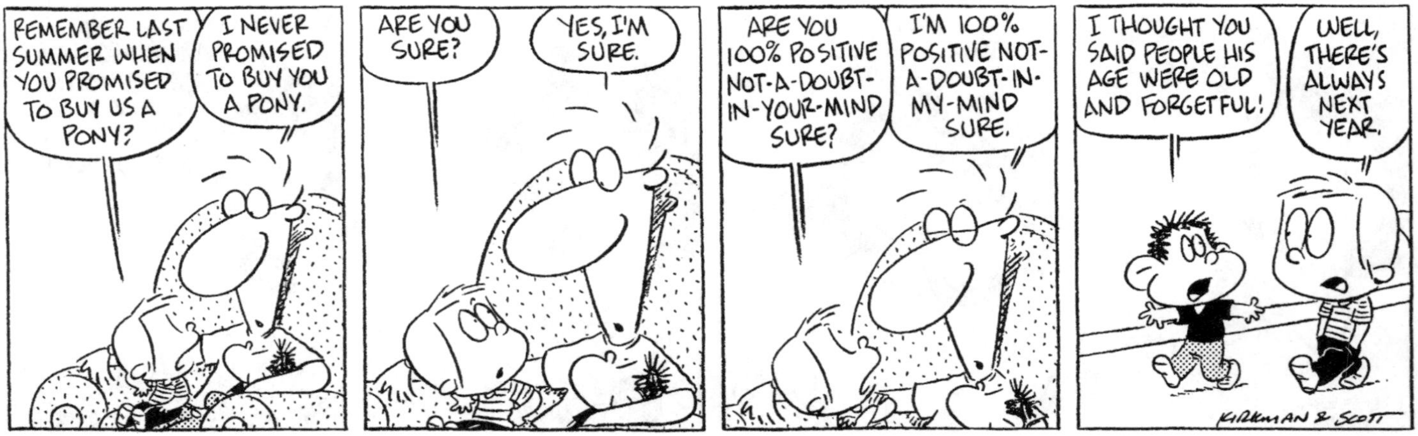
REMEMBER LAST SUMMER WHEN YOU PROMISED TO BUY US A PONY?
I NEVER PROMISED TO BUY YOU A PONY.
ARE YOU SURE?
YES, I'M SURE.
ARE YOU 100% POSITIVE NOT-A-DOUBT-IN-YOUR-MIND SURE?
I'M 100% POSITIVE NOT-A-DOUBT-IN-MY-MIND SURE.
I THOUGHT YOU SAID PEOPLE HIS AGE WERE OLD AND FORGETFUL!
WELL, THERE'S ALWAYS NEXT YEAR.
KIRKMAN & SCOTT

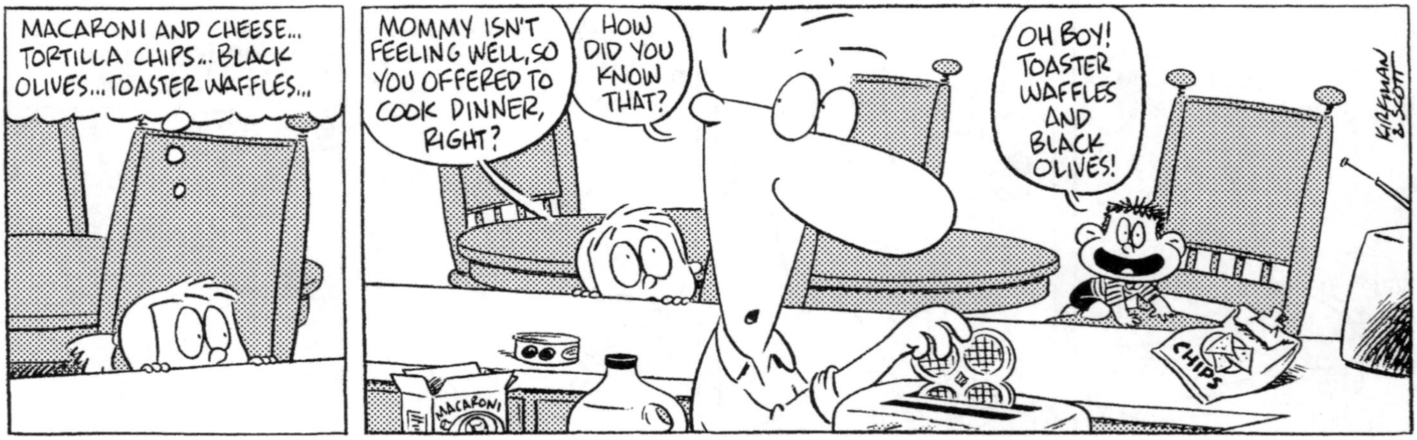
MACARONI AND CHEESE... TORTILLA CHIPS... BLACK OLIVES... TOASTER WAFFLES...
MOMMY ISN'T FEELING WELL, SO YOU OFFERED TO COOK DINNER, RIGHT?
HOW DID YOU KNOW THAT?
OH BOY! TOASTER WAFFLES AND BLACK OLIVES!
KIRKMAN & SCOTT
MACARONI
CHIPS

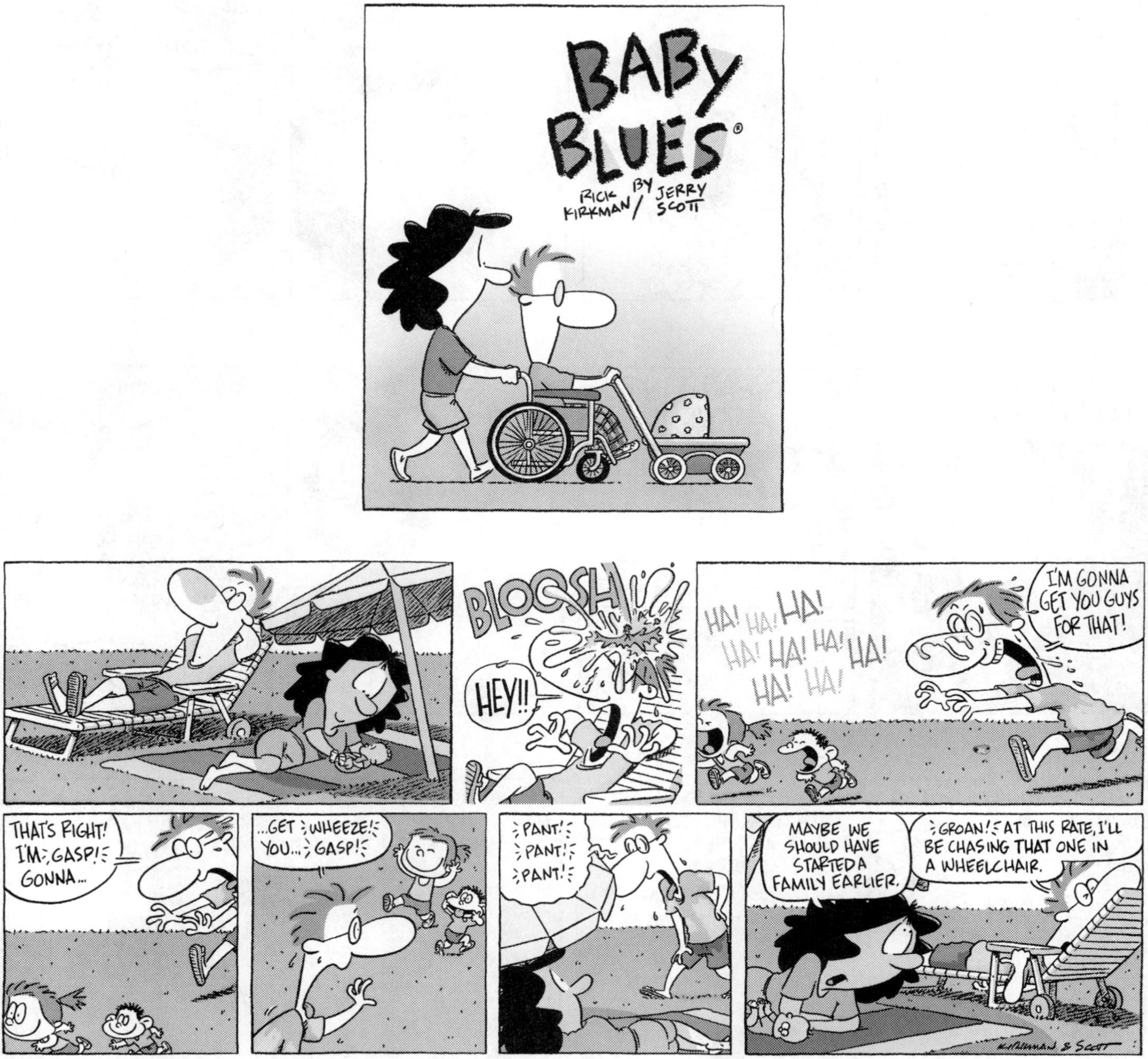
BABY BLUES®
BY RICK KIRKMAN / JERRY SCOTT
BLOOSH
HEY!!
HA! HA! HA! HA! HA! HA! HA! HA! HA!
I'M GONNA GET YOU GUYS FOR THAT!
THAT'S RIGHT! I'M GASP! GONNA...
...GET YOU... WHEEZE! GASP!
PANT! PANT! PANT!
MAYBE WE SHOULD HAVE STARTED A FAMILY EARLIER.
GROAN! AT THIS RATE, I'LL BE CHASING THAT ONE IN A WHEELCHAIR.
KIRKMAN & SCOTT

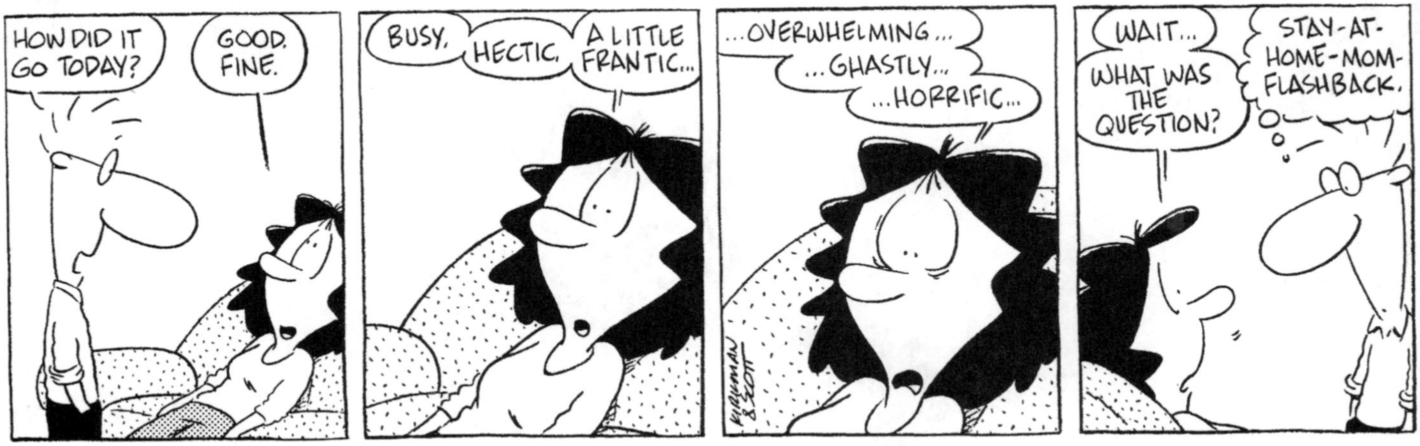
HOW DID IT GO TODAY?
GOOD. FINE.
BUSY,
HECTIC,
A LITTLE FRANTIC...
...OVERWHELMING...
...GHASTLY...
...HORRIFIC...
KIRKMAN & SCOTT
WAIT...
WHAT WAS THE QUESTION?
STAY-AT-HOME-MOM-FLASHBACK.

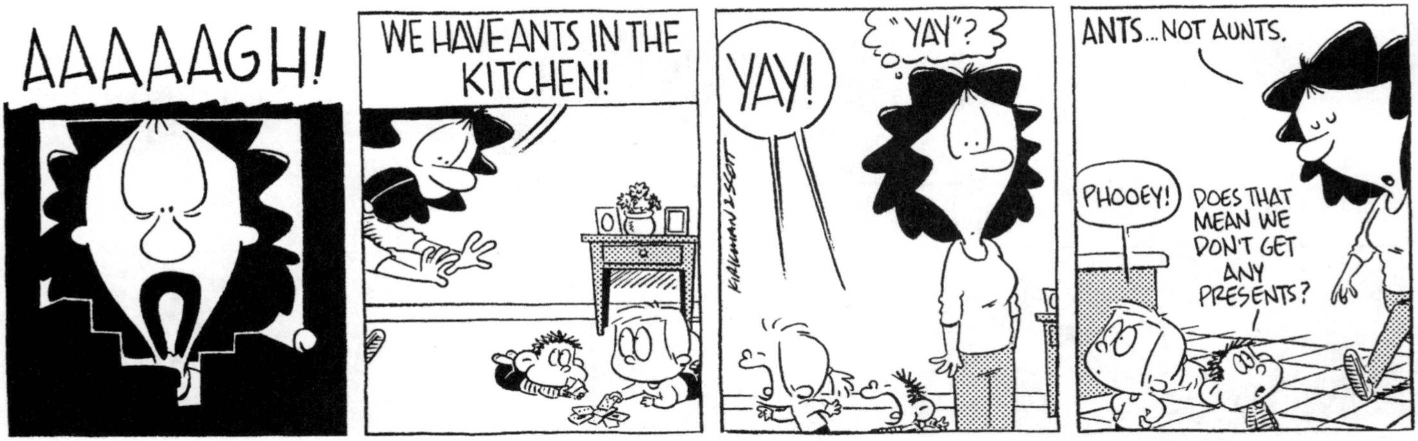
AAAAAGH!
WE HAVE ANTS IN THE KITCHEN!
YAY!
"YAY"?
KIRKMAN & SCOTT
ANTS...NOT AUNTS.
PHOOEY!
DOES THAT MEAN WE DON'T GET ANY PRESENTS?

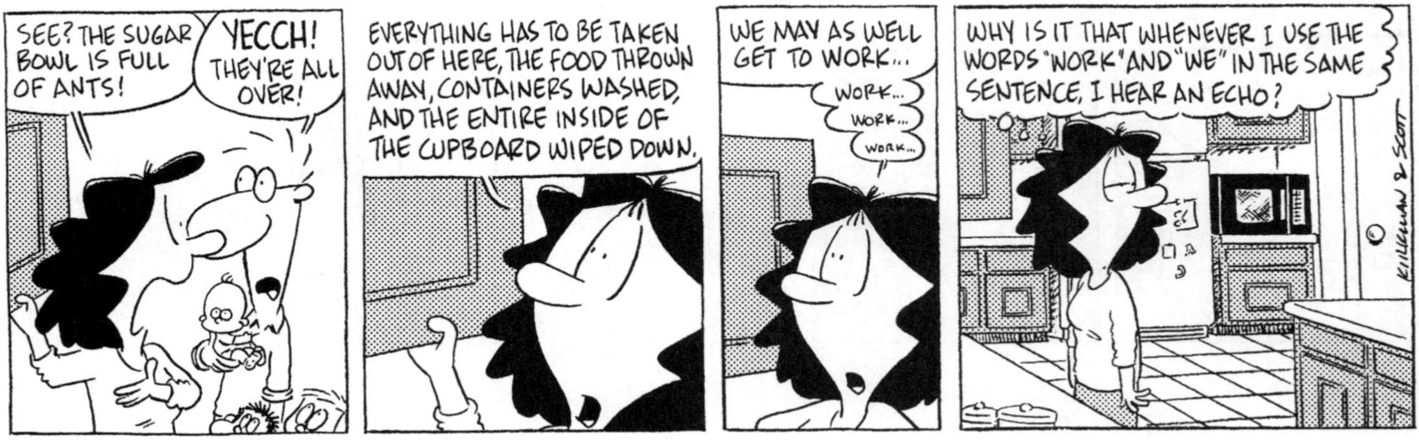
SEE? THE SUGAR BOWL IS FULL OF ANTS!
YECCH! THEY'RE ALL OVER!
EVERYTHING HAS TO BE TAKEN OUT OF HERE, THE FOOD THROWN AWAY, CONTAINERS WASHED, AND THE ENTIRE INSIDE OF THE CUPBOARD WIPED DOWN.
WE MAY AS WELL GET TO WORK...
WORK...
WORK...
WORK...
WHY IS IT THAT WHENEVER I USE THE WORDS "WORK" AND "WE" IN THE SAME SENTENCE, I HEAR AN ECHO?
KIRKMAN & SCOTT

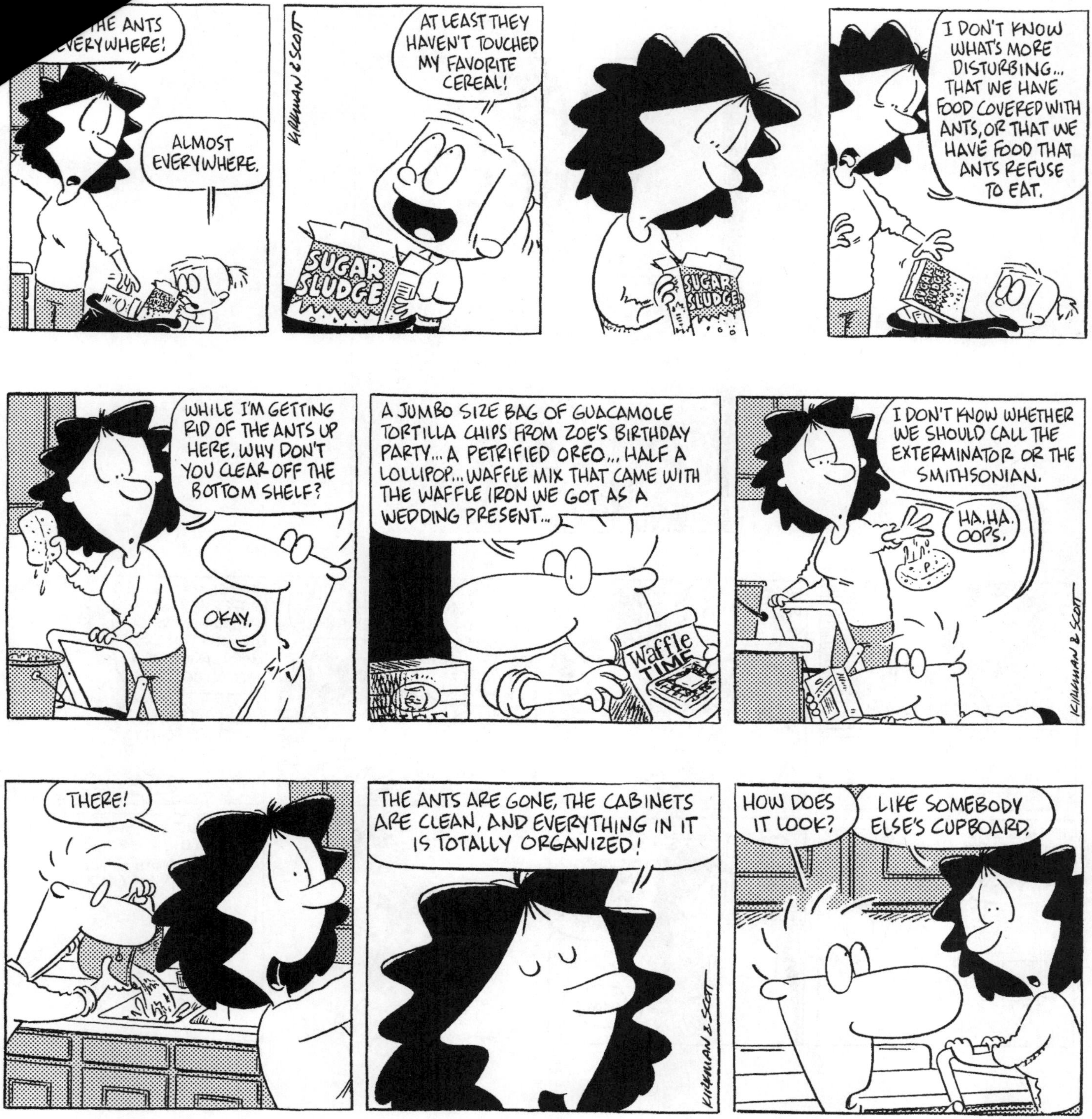
THE ANTS
EVERYWHERE!
ALMOST EVERYWHERE.
AT LEAST THEY HAVEN'T TOUCHED MY FAVORITE CEREAL!
SUGAR SLUDGE
SUGAR SLUDGE
I DON'T KNOW WHAT'S MORE DISTURBING... THAT WE HAVE FOOD COVERED WITH ANTS, OR THAT WE HAVE FOOD THAT ANTS REFUSE TO EAT.
WHILE I'M GETTING RID OF THE ANTS UP HERE, WHY DON'T YOU CLEAR OFF THE BOTTOM SHELF?
OKAY.
A JUMBO SIZE BAG OF GUACAMOLE TORTILLA CHIPS FROM ZOE'S BIRTHDAY PARTY... A PETRIFIED OREO... HALF A LOLLIPOP... WAFFLE MIX THAT CAME WITH THE WAFFLE IRON WE GOT AS A WEDDING PRESENT...
Waffle TIME
I DON'T KNOW WHETHER WE SHOULD CALL THE EXTERMINATOR OR THE SMITHSONIAN.
HA. HA. OOPS.
THERE!
THE ANTS ARE GONE, THE CABINETS ARE CLEAN, AND EVERYTHING IN IT IS TOTALLY ORGANIZED!
HOW DOES IT LOOK?
LIKE SOMEBODY ELSE'S CUPBOARD.

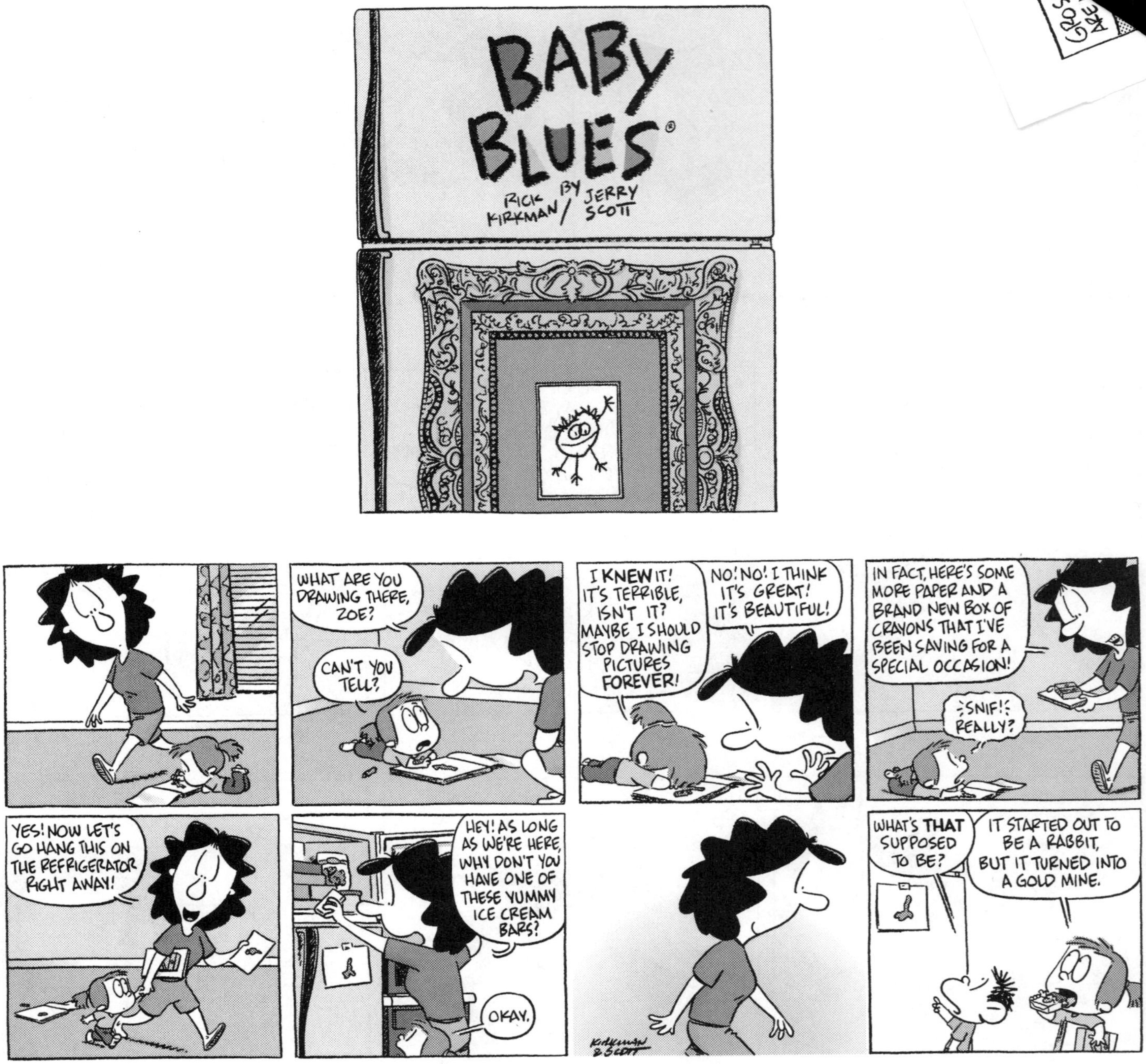
BABY BLUES®
BY RICK KIRKMAN / JERRY SCOTT
WHAT ARE YOU DRAWING THERE, ZOE?
CAN'T YOU TELL?
I KNEW IT! IT'S TERRIBLE, ISN'T IT? MAYBE I SHOULD STOP DRAWING PICTURES FOREVER!
NO! NO! I THINK IT'S GREAT! IT'S BEAUTIFUL!
IN FACT, HERE'S SOME MORE PAPER AND A BRAND NEW BOX OF CRAYONS THAT I'VE BEEN SAVING FOR A SPECIAL OCCASION!
SNIF! REALLY?
YES! NOW LET'S GO HANG THIS ON THE REFRIGERATOR RIGHT AWAY!
HEY! AS LONG AS WE'RE HERE, WHY DON'T YOU HAVE ONE OF THESE YUMMY ICE CREAM BARS?
OKAY.
KIRKMAN & SCOTT
WHAT'S THAT SUPPOSED TO BE?
IT STARTED OUT TO BE A RABBIT, BUT IT TURNED INTO A GOLD MINE.

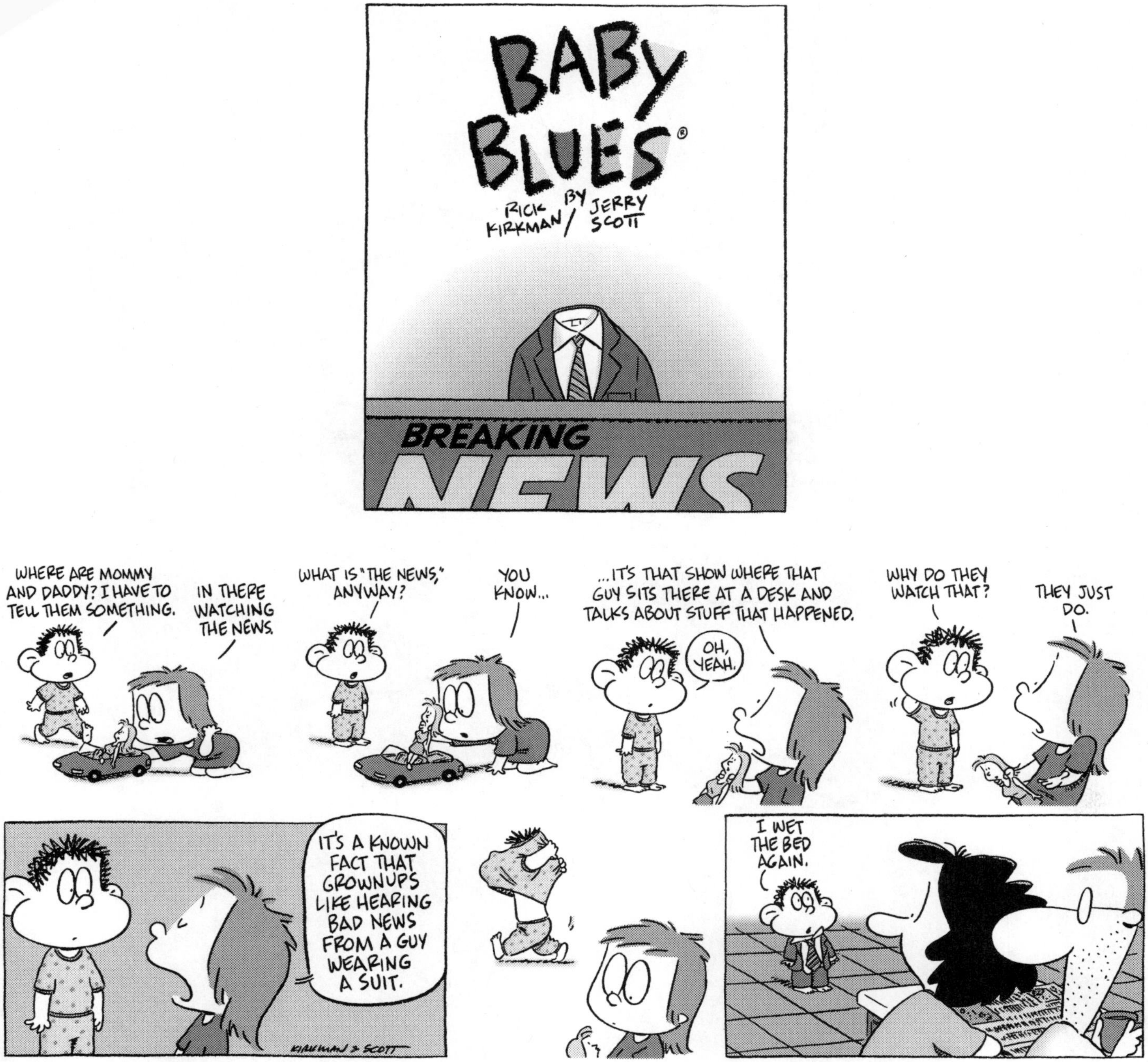
BABY BLUES®
BY RICK KIRKMAN / JERRY SCOTT
BREAKING NEWS
WHERE ARE MOMMY AND DADDY? I HAVE TO TELL THEM SOMETHING.
IN THERE WATCHING THE NEWS.
WHAT IS "THE NEWS," ANYWAY?
YOU KNOW...
...IT'S THAT SHOW WHERE THAT GUY SITS THERE AT A DESK AND TALKS ABOUT STUFF THAT HAPPENED.
OH, YEAH.
WHY DO THEY WATCH THAT?
THEY JUST DO.
IT'S A KNOWN FACT THAT GROWNUPS LIKE HEARING BAD NEWS FROM A GUY WEARING A SUIT.
KIRKMAN & SCOTT
I WET THE BED AGAIN.